# SPLIT BY SUN

## TOM FAUNCE

Illustrations by **Harriet Birks**

**World Scientific**

NEW JERSEY · LONDON · SINGAPORE · BEIJING · SHANGHAI · HONG KONG · TAIPEI · CHENNAI · TOKYO

*Published by*

World Scientific Publishing Europe Ltd.

57 Shelton Street, Covent Garden, London WC2H 9HE

*Head office:* 5 Toh Tuck Link, Singapore 596224

*USA office:* 27 Warren Street, Suite 401-402, Hackensack, NJ 07601

**Library of Congress Cataloging-in-Publication Data**
Names: Faunce, Thomas Alured, author.
Title: Split by sun : the tragic history of the sustainocene / by Tom Faunce
 (Australian National University, Australia).
Description: New Jersey : World Scientific, [2018] | Includes bibliographical references.
Identifiers: LCCN 2017052580 | ISBN 9781786345059 (hc : alk. paper)
Subjects: LCSH: Nanotechnology--Environmental aspects--Fiction. |
 Photosynthesis--Industrial applications--Fiction. |
 Sustainability--Fiction. | LCGFT: Utopian fiction. | Dystopian fiction.
Classification: LCC PR9619.4.F386 S65 2018 | DDC 823/.92--dc23
LC record available at https://lccn.loc.gov/2017052580

**British Library Cataloguing-in-Publication Data**
A catalogue record for this book is available from the British Library.

Cover design by Harriet Birks and World Scientific Publishing
Illustrations by Harriet Birks

Tom Faunce asserts the right to be recognised as the author of the work.

Copyright © 2019 by World Scientific Publishing Europe Ltd.

*All rights reserved. This book, or parts thereof, may not be reproduced in any form or by any means, electronic or mechanical, including photocopying, recording or any information storage and retrieval system now known or to be invented, without written permission from the Publisher.*

For photocopying of material in this volume, please pay a copying fee through the Copyright Clearance Center, Inc., 222 Rosewood Drive, Danvers, MA 01923, USA. In this case permission to photocopy is not required from the publisher.

**Disclaimer:** All characters and events in this publication, other than those clearly in the public domain, are fictitious and any resemblance to real persons, living or dead, is purely coincidental.

Desk Editors: Dr. Sree Meenakshi Sajani/Jennifer Brough/Koe Shi Ying

Typeset by Stallion Press
Email: enquiries@stallionpress.com

*To the friends of all life*

# PREFACE

In the world of this story, science has succeeded in shattering the notion that only plants can do photosynthesis, just as in the early 20th century (CE) science disproved the belief that only birds could fly. In the Sustainocene era (SE), the technology of global synthetic photosynthesis is engineered into every road and building to help them make clean fuel and food just from water, sun and air. This is revolutionising our relationships with each other and all forms of life on Earth.

But, as we shall see, not all humans think those are good ideas. Indeed, some are prepared to use violence and murder to overturn them. This is true even though the events in this tale occur after the war that ended the Corporatocene era (CE) and almost terminated life on Earth.

# ABBREVIATIONS

| | |
|---|---|
| AA | Alcoholics Anonymous |
| AI | Artificial Intelligence |
| AMDS | Acute Metabolic Distress Syndrome |
| AR | Augmented Reality |
| BECCSS | Bio-Energy Carbon Capture and Storage Scam |
| CA | Contemplative Absorption |
| CE | Corporatocene Era |
| CEO | Chief Executive Officer |
| CNT | Carbon Nanotubes |
| CSR | Corporate Social Responsibility |
| DEW | Directed Energy Weapon |
| EMP | Electromagnetic Pulse |
| GSPP | Global Synthetic Photosynthesis Project |
| IMPs | Intellectual Monopoly Privileges (i.e., patents) |
| Non-duality | Awareness not limited to sensory subject-object distinction |
| OTA | Organisation for Temporal Accommodation |
| PD | Privacy Dome |
| SE | Sustainocene Era |
| SGA | Set Genetic Age |
| They/Thay, Them, Their | Gender neutral pronouns |
| T-Net | Teleportation Net |
| TRIPS | Trade Related Intellectual Property Scam |
| TTD | Temporal Tremor Detector |
| UBI | Universal Basic Income |
| VHD | Verified Historical Data |
| VR | Virtual Reality |
| VX | Toxic nerve agent |
| WEC | Whole Earth Council |
| WTC | World Time Council |

# CONTENTS

| | | |
|---|---|---|
| *Preface* | | vii |
| *Abbreviations* | | ix |
| I | Light Harvesting Festival, Southwark | 1 |
| II | Sad Paradise, Hampstead | 37 |
| III | Earth Touch, Normandy | 95 |
| IV | Paradise White, Zebra River | 141 |
| V | Earth Stewardship, New York, Geneva & Alberta | 205 |
| VI | Transcendence Reach, Franklin River | 243 |
| VII | Kurlpurlunu, Tanamai Desert | 295 |
| VIII | Ecocide Truth & Reconciliation Court, The Hague | 319 |
| IX | Synthetic Photosynthesis Park, Normandy | 359 |
| X | Warrane, Near Kunanyi Mountain | 381 |
| *Postscript* | | 397 |
| *Acknowledgements* | | 401 |
| *About the Author* | | 403 |
| *About the Illustrator* | | 405 |
| *Bibliography* | | 407 |

The characters in this novel are fictional and
are not intended to represent any actual person, living or dead.

# I
# LIGHT HARVESTING FESTIVAL, SOUTHWARK

*Prophetic dream of murder of a scientist Buddha and a sacred tree — light harvesting festival — Gordon Lizzard Mayor of Southwark and Vice-President of the Whole Earth Council — death of Nancy Godel in Hampstead — connection of Nancy with assassination attempts on President Zula Calabiyau and with the Global Synthetic Photosynthesis Project — finding of the diaries — a doubtful witness — problems in Normandy —*

Sometimes the strangest dreams are the kindest. On a hill, one mid-winter night, alone; the Milky Way above and lights in a temple below. Inside, they're praying religion stay banned and corporations keep married to ecosystems. I walk down into a snow-covered valley towards that lonely, pale blue dot. I've been ordered to make a hit. The trunks of pines, pale blue-green in the pool of light cast by the temple, bear a pipe of snow and their branches slivers of ice. A snowflake falls before a tree and dissolves on a wilted rose. A little red fish swims beneath ice in a pond. Some half-forgotten fragment recalls I'm all that; prey for the bullies of outlawed faiths.

Fog rises in the distance, white against the mountains, and black before the clouds. It swirls out of the forest in wisps, silent, thick, engulfing. The wind gets up and a solitary pine begins to sway. The cold nobility of Earth seeps down to my bones.

Perfect is the half-full moon and the clouds about it with slight tinges of orange and brown. Sublime that block of pigmented ice and jaded my foot shattering it to tiny prisms. Beside my shoe is a dead bee. Poor character should be with her hive mates, shivering the Queen warm. I rest the bee in my palm; it revives and buzzes off.

*Like thin smoke*
*Waves of snow blown high;*
*Over the steep temple roof.*

PhDs and post-docs are inside the temple studying by candlelight an ancient commentary on the story of the monk Nagarjuna's gift of his head to the ambitious Shaktiman. The text holds that death is not annihilation, but germination of desires and that these can include compassion; for it's an error to cling to the indifference of space and time in all ten dimensions. I'm clinging to a long-lost shred of self-respect. I call it a hip-flask and it's only half-empty.

The scientist Buddhas are chanting with steaming breath, that they aim in their materials science and nanotechnology research, for discipline as the sacrifice of indolence, strength as the sacrifice of attachment, patience as the sacrifice of annoyance and diligence as the sacrifice of unwholesome action.

Wholesome action seems a nice idea to me, conjuring up the comfort of a shared, warm bed and the state of equilibrium I'd achieved before the war and my recruitment by the *World Time Council* (WTC). But here I am again. Occasionally I hear a beating of sticks, each impact designed to keep the meditators focused.

*Ten full tubs of winter rain;*
*Drummed on by impulse of*
*My dead wife's name.*

Soon there's nothing but silence in the temple. Caroline appears from behind a water barrel. She's haunting me again, Mindscanning that there's never complete silence. You can always hear the background hum from which thought and matter stir; unless you've blacked out, or are reading neoliberal economics. The scientist Buddhas now are practising *sanyama*. Their undistracted and focused minds are entertaining at the very threshold of unbounded consciousness some technical difficulty in improving life's most fundamental chemical reaction. My AR, as programmed by Eugene, augments my dream with a more reassuring haiku.

> *What worlds are lost*
> *In moss that grows,*
> *Beneath the temple's ancient tree?*

I take a few more sips from the *Golden-Hip-Flask-Of-Immense-Dignity*. The label says it's a good drop, but it's many blue moons since I drank for taste. A raven on a ridgepole, flaps off to sell lustful secrets to the Sun. Then I spy a different conspiracy of unkindness.

From the bowels of night materialise three demons of the undead called Draugr, Poltergeist and Phobetor, robed top to toe in vertically-aligned vantablack. They're sneaking across a wooden bridge over the tree-lined lagoon, past the gigantic lillypad that's the central research complex. Monsters brought forth by the sleep of reason in the castle of heaven; but not the evil I'd been ordered to remove from this re-enchanted world. The lights from a few offices in the cubane core of that building splash strokes of colour that ripple out on the water.

The inky miscreants enter the temple courtyard. The fat one's carrying an electric chainsaw and a blue cylinder labelled $SiH_4$. The other two, one short, one tall, are armed with knives. They approach the temple's sacred gingko biloba. The tree's grown sturdy and strong in the course of years; a forest in itself, hung round with wreaths, garlands, votive tablets and tributes for prayers granted. There's a myth amongst the scientist Buddhas here that when this tree dies, the Sustainocene era will end.

The sooty shadows approach the tree; cautious, perhaps worried about security systems. They should be. Eugene in the guise of a pilgrim is

Sometimes the strangest dreams are the kindest

telling me through my AR that I must again disobey orders. 'You're a lonely electron looking for a place to rest' says Eugene 'and these light-intruding orbiters of a stellar corpse are your real target, not the Queen bee.' All three have normal human physiology, but no history of interaction with personal, social or police systems. These bozos are from the future, to change it by altering the past.

The fat crepuscular intruder with the saw tries to start it and sets the timer on the cylinder. I mark him in my weapon's cross-hairs, my finger just a few super strings from the *Trigger-To-Well-Earned-Oblivion*. It's all being recorded and any moment now yours truly is going to give these scum bags a crash course in the gentle art of surfing g-waves off-Brane. They'll soon be merely another footnote in the *World Time Council's* files of irredeemable defectors from cooperation. The dead shall speak, the living cry, as Earth's music retunes the sky.

A Professor Buddha with shoulder length brown hair, half-hooded eyes and a long dress — it's green, the only colour life rejects — is floating along like a synchronised cloud of bees through the courtyard. Her awareness is rambling through thickets of equations related to microsecond multi-electronic redox reactions, crossing low hedges of isomerisation quantum yields, or negotiating tangled forests of over-potentials, nanowires and semiconductor octahedrals. The Professor Buddha looks in my direction and sends me this thought as though it were a picture: 'you've fought to set life free; now give up your destiny and follow me.' And at that moment a wild storm erupts, breaking tiles off the temple and branches from trees. Then, with some unbidden inner power, she detects *Scum-Bag-With-Chainsaw* about to cut down the sacred tree.

This emeritus scientist Buddha has been trained and taught many others not to do or resist evil. But now, she does something chaotic; quenching the moment of inertia and scattering light to reveal even half wave truths.

She shouts 'Unleash the strange metals of string theory and all superconducting second sounds! I'll measure your blackness and bounce a better Gyre,' then curves at the perpetrators. Whom am I meant to kill? My trigger finger seems as heavy as ununseptium. Fat scum bag fries her heart with DEW, a Directed Energy Weapon. He then uses the chainsaw to cut down the tree. It topples onto the temple courtyard, throwing up snow. The intruders stand back, gloating. I'm too late.

Then an angel reaches round from behind me and pulls the trigger. She whispers 'You're over the dam.' Her fragrance evokes a spice drawer: sesame, cinnamon, oregano, cloves, cumin, jasmine and chilli. Before I can turn, she's gone. So is the fat murderous intruder. Disappeared. Exiled off-brane. Caroline whispers to me the WTC motto for time-travel metanorm enforcement: 'Nice, Retaliatory, Forgiving, Clear.'

The commotion has alerted the trainee scientist Buddhas. Lights go on in the temple; doors open, illumined incense fumes and exhalations drift away into the night. The students hold candles, staring down at their leader's remains and the slain sacred tree, then at the two residual, cowering criminals. In the background, the sky's split by a hundred suns, huge clouds erupt from the ground, spreading smoke and soot.

Then I wake up with a start; breaching from depths of deception and despair to the free, fair air. Outside the window, a low line of dark clouds above the ochred horizon disperses on the morning winds. I'm in my bed in the Hampstead Heath Guesthouse in Portland Place off Kemplay Road. By strange coincidence a nearby sound system begins playing the latest Spencer Lizzard tune *Song of the Goat*.

> *We came all so still, for there our saviour lay,*
> *As dew in April, that falleth on the spray.*
> *Let hatred's fire erupt, Earth cannot burn today.*
> *Should evil's deluge break, Earth shan't drown or sway.*
> *Upon every gift descended from this sun,*
> *Evil layeth a curse on delight shared with none.*
> *Husk must split, seed fall, be buried in moist ground,*
> *Before life's bud once more to light be bound.*

∞

I shouldn't have been sent on this case. Eugene, the office supercomputer, miscalculated leave requirements and insisted Hercules Huncks, our top agent, take three weeks off. The Hunck didn't refuse; he was always up for the main chance; even made a move on Caroline once, though relationships between WTC agents were forbidden. He had a flat in Southwark that'd sparked a ditty notorious at WTC office parties; 'Hunck the spunk had a flat, ee eye ee eye oh. And in that flat he had some chicks, ee eye ee eye oh. With a quick one here and a quick one there' and so forth. Hunck loved it, used it as a ring tone on his AR; and because he was an old-style square-jawed, six-packed primitive hero type, the police always were very understanding when things got a little rough. Then Eugene discovers no one else's available. So here I am, dragged out of the records department to write a one-way ticket for some evil broad in Hampstead who knew too much, but not enough to keep quiet.

It's just before dawn. I'm not scheduled to acquire the target till late this afternoon. My bedside clock has stopped at 02:27, though still empowered. Eugene tells me it's two hours later; trusty old Eugene. 'Is your window open? Well close it,' security-conscious Eugene instructs me. It's the summer solstice and people have once again gathered across the world to celebrate the completion of the *Global Synthetic Photosynthesis Project* (GSPP), pay tribute to plants' great invention of photosynthesis and maybe even those who'd fought to save it in the war that ended the Corporatocene.

"Jean, I've overruled," says Eugene though my AR. "Overruled your previous order to accept an AR call at Records at 12.20. I also recommend you forget about travelling to Hampstead to post the 'love letter.' My analysis is that you'll reject that last piece of advice, but I'm giving it anyway. Why? I like you. Let's just say that's my little act of rebellion."

Eugene's got authority to give orders on low-level operational matters. I won't turn up to Records. But he's probably making another joke; he hasn't the authority to cancel a decommission. I've never let people tell me what to do, always did the opposite on principle. Anyway, that's some hours away. I've got time to burn and bottles of accelerant to find.

The mirror shows my dark hair is ruffled and streaked with grey, chin unshaven and eyes red and weary. My nose is crooked and my left eye, a bionic replacement due to a war injury, is blue while my right is brown. Caroline called it my 'Ziggy Stardust' look. She said if I got it fixed, it might make me less paranoid and jealous. I ignored that advice, as usual.

After my usual ablutions, I go for a walk on Hampstead Heath. At dawn's first blush to sight I get a view of London, another city that's become a rainforest, from the hill where traitors once planned to watch the destruction of Parliament. I keep repeating the mantra I've been running through my head since I woke: 'don't drink at the festival; don't drink before the hit. Listen, you bloody idiot; don't get pissed before you do the Big Deed.'

A brief thunder storm passes through. I stand under the dripping boughs of an oak. Better men have braved great thoughts under oaks. And with that, my AR briefly re-creates the scene at Holwood above the vale of Keston where Wilberforce told Prime Minister Pitt of his intention to get legislation passed that abolished slavery. People said the War to End the Corporatocene was fought to liberate plants from their servitude to humans. Rain on the tree's leaves sounds like laughter, or surf on a wild sea. Caroline had always wanted a garden with oak trees. The light grey curtain of rain moves off to the east and a rainbow appears before it.

I walk around for a while enjoying the chorus of birdsong. The oaks create a space like a cathedral; cool shade below, while the tree tops are already warming themselves in the blue heat of day. On the far side of the ponds, pollen floats and a duck takes off between the bright, flickering boughs. Beyond, the morning sunlight etches an ancient church in gold. I sit on the Anthony Lucas chair, basking in the sun and the knowledge that some great new idea is abroad in the world. AR news tells me that this morning a young woman, possibly on drugs, ran down to the mag-rail tracks, stared at the driver, then stepped in front of the speeding train.

The next item recounts how *Whole Earth Council* President Zula Calabiyau last night narrowly escaped another assassination attempt, this time at a science-Buddha temple Zula was visiting in Aotearoa. A sacred *gingko biloba* was cut down, one grafted from the original tree at the GSPP Centre in Namibia. The report resembles my dream last night; perhaps my old psychic powers are returning. President Zula our self-proclaimed eco-gendered Gaia messiah, states 'I don't value my life in terms of days, fame or fortune. I've been

Jean Moulin

placed here to do right for all life, regardless of the rendezvous that creates for me.' The story claims that Zula, after T-Net return, will proceed with the Presidential re-election campaign motorcade though the Light Harvesting Festival in Southwark and Hampstead. In addition to rejoicing schoolchildren and ecosystem stewards, hostile crowds apparently are expected to protest Zula's policies to continue the abolition of nation states, religions and corporations not married to ecosystems, as well as Zula's lack of respect for traditional sexual relationships and Digital Nomad Tribes. Finally, the report mentions that another outbreak of Acute Metabolic Dysfunction Syndrome, or AMDS, has killed yet more people in New York, Beijing, Delhi and Moscow. It says the cause of AMDS remains unknown. A leading AMDS researcher, Professor Kofi Buxtun of the GSPP Centre in Namibia, advises that people who exercise regularly, eat plenty of organic vegetables and get out in the sun are at less risk of contracting the disease. I'm sceptical. I made my own contract with more than one disease in demolished buildings during the war.

I log in AR for the morning contemplation. Like every adult citizen I'm required to do such sessions each day along with some registered community service. It's a condition of keeping full Universal Basic Income (UBI), retaining my capacity to direct 50% of my tax where I wish (I'm conservative; always choose ecosystem rehab., health care and education) with unrestricted ability to activate Privacy Dome (PD).

> *Peace and joy follow, love and wisdom grow,*
> *Like a perfumed shadow in a bright tomorrow,*
> *From being kind to all we find.*

Over the last few years I've slept my way through weeks at a time of Muslim, Quaker, Hindu, Franciscan, Mormon and even Findhorn nature spirit morning meditations. This month I've registered as Buddhist, so after a few passages from the *Book of Common Faith*, I'm taken through a Vipassana mindfulness exercise. Eugene has organised my AR so it evokes the Mahabodhi temple at *Bodh Gaya* under the sacred banyan and I'm in presence of the latest incarnation of the Dalai Lama (who looks suspiciously like Eugene), being instructed to recognise the impermanence of all things and accept that the true nature of being is suffering. From this I'm meant to generate altruism and compassion to all sentient beings, including my enemies. I used to be good at this stuff, very good. But now? But now I'm lured by the soft, velvety pull of sleep. I doze off.

Suddenly, Eugene is trying to guide me through the Tibetan form of divination known as *Mo*. Eugene impersonating the oracle says "Go! Go now!" Well, I might have been a *Nirvana* Whiz; but I'm no longer in the Zone. What I'm saying is I don't like or trust what's become of my mind. And I'm not going to listen to Eugene just because it decides to dress itself up as some stupid *Mo* oracle. No way I'm going anywhere before the specified time. I'm doing this case by the book. I stroll back from the heath in time for breakfast.

∞

My boots tread upon a muddy path under the variegated greens and shadows of leafy beech, ash, field maple, sycamore and horse chestnut trees. High above, before a patch of sky blue in tints of cobalt, liquid oxygen and aquamarine, purple and white-letter hairstreak butterflies swoop and surprise each other in the illumined canopy of a veteran English oak. Beside the verge, wood anemones, lesser celandine, common violets and cow parsley explode colour over lush grass. The conviction again arises that language is present between these leaves, flowers and roots; but also of a vast elemental force making up its mind, building pressure, biding time.

A young Hampstead Hand ecosystem guardian stands leaning on a pitchfork near a gnarled and knotted wych elm. He's slow-burning woody clippings, burdock and crabgrass in a ditch under soil to make charcoal. Light grey smoke curdles in small involved circles as it rises to the still air. A well-dressed lady bemoans to the Hand how during this morning's ramble 'ungrateful, arrogant and anti-social' festival-revellers broke parade to smash the passenger-side window of Marylebone, her car.

"The worst is," says the woman, fingering her wedding ring "it's so impious and self-destructive. Causing such pain to a sporty vehicle in the prime of life's art. But their unconstitutional, drugged-up ugliness can't fix its discontent on me, or dear Marrybun for that matter."

"Aye Sibylla, Zula don't reason right," replies the Hand "t'expect owt i'this age t'go well. No good faffin;' we're formed t'bear wa 'appens."

"Indeed, you'll find I am," she replies, touching his sunburnt forearm.

The GSPP light harvesting festival is in full swing. Usually the GSPP celebration thing doesn't do much for me; I prefer to drink at home and watch on T-Net the latest *Ullamaliztli* Flaming Football game with its spectacular high marks, handballs, long kicking and responsible online betting. Indeed, I've responsibly gambled and drunk away quite a few GSPP summer solstice days in recent years; someone's got to support those young athletes through their burns recovery. But there's always lots of free beer about at the GSPP festival; AR advertising says it's honouring Joseph Priestly. Priestly's freethinking views (against slavery and in favour of normalising Christ) debarred him from an expedition to find the Great Southern Land, but nonetheless provided time to investigate why 'fixed air' in vats above fermenting beer extinguished candles. Far be it for me to let such scientific sacrifice and endeavour, as well as those carefully crafted hops, go to waste.

Children have begun congregating since dawn in towns and villages from Mecca to Dubai, from London to Beijing, even on Mars at the Xanthe Terra region's Huygens and Tesla GSPP-powered settlements. They'll soon be singing about how the GSPP makes abundant clean fuel and food everywhere, just from water, sun and air. It won't be John, Paul, George or Johann Seb., but the tunes aren't bad; the kids won't be musically abused.

> *Time to set the forests free*
> *Let plains live, let oceans be*
> *Make for ourselves what we breathe*
> *Reverence for all life, what we believe.*

Many front gardens display the usual small GSPP-themed statues of a chubby yellow dwarf sitting on green and blue algae or stromatolites; of a phoenix astride a sheaf of wheat, of scientists driving a twelve-horsed, water-filled solar chariot that distributes food. Little dolls abound representing the supposed great scientific discoverers of natural photosynthesis: Jan Ingenhousz, Jan Baptista van Helmont, Joseph Priestley, Jean Senebier, Julius Robert Mayer and Cornelis Van Niel, amongst others. Burning eight-spoked wheels will be rolled from mountain tops to take away bad karma and excess carbon dioxide. Last night, Z-scheme witches were seen flying away on the backs of cats and manganese she-devils climbing naked across solar panels to launch themselves upon the air. Such is life on our re-enchanted planet. Now, from humanity's gloriously enhanced sympathy, in every stream, tree, plant and bee dwells a right-filled fairy.

In the 19th century (CE), a scholar called Max Müller claimed all social myths derived from the sun. So now here in Hampstead, as in tree-shaded village squares in New York, Beijing, Mecca, Dubai, Lhasa and Varanasi, garlands of flowers are placed over life-like statues of Zula Calabiyau and Omran Tariq, founders of the GSPP.

The AI-impregnated buildings I walk past are proud of their elegant and ever-changing mix of imagination with the intricate harmonies of nature. The chunks of metal, slabs of rock and grains of timber their owners originally had shaped, connected, scoured and relished to the weather, are alive with an ethical intelligence. These homes talk to each other and change aspect, colour, shape, texture, materials as well as their production of hydrogen, oxygen, food or ammonia fertiliser, to improve the enjoyment of not just their human inhabitants, but the birds and small creatures that nestle in their crannies, surrounding tree cavities and perched boxes.

I see a couple partaking of a breakfast, no doubt sourced from their garden as assisted by the enhanced photosynthetic capacity of their dwelling. They eat strawberries, cereal and milk behind triple-glazed argon-filled windows. A poster on their window warns people about Acute Metabolic Distress Syndrome. Their house must be sentient. Becoming aware of my critical gaze and perhaps having picked up a message from Eugene, it introduces itself as Jan Eckhart, a friend of Marcus Tragelaph, the WTC headquarters. Jan morphs its façade from bronze-coloured converted titanium-clad, nanocube impregnated shipping container to the wooden Lutruwitan bungalow I've yearned to live in since I was a child. I nod my thanks.

How long would I need to talk with those two inside, or any citizens of the Sustainocene, to discover some unhappiness? I look at the vacant lot next door — just bare, scraped earth, with all the building materials, trees and shrubs removed. A sign has been screwed on the surrounding fence. It announces that here, during the War to End the Corporatocene, an autonomous weapons drone destroyed a family accused of trying to grow their own food, making their own clothes and cutting themselves off from electronic social media. Everyone has sad neighbours in the Sustainocene.

My favourite light harvesting ceremony called *'Split By Sun,'* echoes back to medieval morality plays. As well as celebrating global synthetic photosynthesis, it supposedly honours those killed defending the natural environment in the war to end the Corporatocene era. But we damaged veterans of that conflict don't feel much love from the citizenry these days; violence even for a good cause is no longer in vogue.

In its most common form, the *'Split By Sun'* ceremony involves young people in white lab coats before dawn holding hands while meditating with wreaths of sunflowers around their heads. They chant *'a circle round, a circle round the bountiful Earth. A circle round, a circle round the boundless Universe.'* As they try to contemplate, seven figures dressed in black top hats, business suits and moustaches known as the Mephistos walk around banging sticks together, shouting 'I, Me, Mine' and trying to distract the contemplatives with promises of consumer goods, credit cards, social media, bonuses, share portfolios and so forth.

At sunrise, the scientist Buddhas bend their heads forward and the Mephistos pretend to chop them off. The Mephistos in remorse start beating with sticks an oversized replica of the cubane-shaped GSPP prototype, repeatedly shouting 'Split By Sun.' The grief-wracked Mephistos arrange mirrors so they reflect sunlight onto the hearts of the 'dead' scientist Buddhas. Eventually this encourages the scientist Buddhas to come back to life; upon which they are given a Priestly eleven bottles of beer taken by the Mephistos from inside the prototype. Everyone then dances holding green and blue ropes attached to a yellow pole.

*It's our blue place in infinite space*
*Blue-green algae split water stored sun*
*Electric their assignations.*
*Biosphere 1 split water, stored sun*
*Joyful in meditation.*

Today, variations of *'Split by Sun'* will be performed all over the world, utilising local beverages; filmed, quantum-entangled and loaded onto the

Internet and T-Net. Thus, everyone will be able to witness the ceremony performed (with approval of those ecosystems' legal guardians and trustees) on the summit of Mt Everest and in the heart of the great, ancient rainforests of the Amazon, Kinabulu, Southwest Lutruwita, Daintree and Sumatra's Lueser Ecosystem. Good for them, I think; if I ever get split by sun, I'll keep it a private affair.

It's a peculiar trait of our species that whenever one group of humans decides to celebrate something, a crowd of wowsers gets equal pleasure from opposing the occasion. So today, protestors stand with placards decrying the need for a GSPP festival valorising alcoholic intoxication. '*Last Gasp for GSPP Piss Ants?*' is my favourite, apart from a cute metaphysical take on anti-corporate sentiment: '*Logos not Logos.*' I suspect some people will happily alternate during the day between taking part in the celebrations and protesting them.

I drop in on the Carousel Club. It's a formidable period recreation, down to robots imitating the underwear-clad waitresses. Some WTC agents continue to paw the tail-end of a long night. One of them, Jack Castles, waves at me. In a few hours they'll be on President Zula's security detail. A sign above their heads reads '*Evil Spelled Backwards Is Live.*' WTC standards have lapsed since I went to Records. I have a few drinks by myself, just to steady the nerves.

∞

The music of the spheres, in the form of *All Things Must Pass*, sounds in my nano-implanted auditory nerve. An AR call coming in. As a special GSPP day treat for the kids, I've been requested to connect with Helené and François at their farm near *Sainte-Mère-Église* in Normandy. I switch on and tune in, walking outside the club into the street. Little Walter speaks first.

"Grandpa, there you are. Tess, Anouk, Papa, Maman, come! He's here. The company must all be here too," says Walter. "I've written a GSPP play Grandpa."

"Very good Walter," I say. "First pray, say what the play may treat on, then read the roles of the actors; and so plant a point before you harvest a scene."

"It's about Zula and Omran," says Walter "getting photosynthesis declared common heritage under cosmopolitan law at the *Whole Earth Council* in

Geneva. Papa is to play Omran and Maman will be Zula. They kiss and kill themselves most gallant for love of the Earth. I call it *The Cradle of Security*."

"What kind of play, Walter?" I ask.

"A tragedy, of course Grandpa."

"And the hero's fatal flaw?"

"The Earth's fascination with humans."

"Earth? But in tragedies, its people must go from high to low."

"Is that an unbreakable law, like the categorical imperative, speed of light or the Schrödinger equation?"

"What's your recognition or reversal?"

"When the Earth decides it'll be better off without human beings," Walter replies "only to realise after we're gone, that it loved us best. There's a bit, Grandpa, where you destroy the autonomous weapons of the corporate mercenaries. Just like you did during the war."

"That was a long time ago," I reply. "No one remembers."

"I do," says Walter.

"But I don't want to be the Corporation," says Anouk. "Walter always makes me the Corporation. I have to snarl and wear a moustache."

"It's not a real one," says Tess.

"In my play," says Walter "Zula passes a cosmopolitan law saying all Corporations have to be married. But there's one Corporation…"

"That's me," says Anouk.

"Who doesn't want to get married, because they doesn't think any ecosystem will love they enough. Notice I used to gender-neutral pronoun for Corporation."

"That's sad," I say. "Sad for poor, un-merged they."

"But Anouk's boyfriend Conradin, he plays an ecosystem, a wild river through a rainforest; he takes her off with a rope and a dark hope."

"You beast," says Anouk.

"They find the Findhorn Fairies in the woods," continues Walter "and they kiss, very sloppy of course given that he's fresh water and it helps them grow huge vegetable marrows. Oww, stop kicking me Anouk. I've entered it for the GSPP prize. Do you think they'll put it on?"

"They should. Walter, look, there's something important I have to do soon."

"You look well, Grandpa. Are you going to watch President Zula's parade? Someone tried to kill her again yesterday. Think they'll try again?"

"Can you put your father on, Walter?"

"I'm here now. Bonjour."

"François. Good to see you. How's things going with your little friend next door."

"Dad. Who? Oh, the neighbour from hell? Milton Elbadawi. Wants to dam the river and make a synthetic photosynthesis theme park. Would you believe it? All the different SP devices alongside varieties of trees in some crazy solar fuel arboretum. Plans for a glass pyramid hotel. Already has Miriam Revel's land, you remember the cute little hill with the two Wollemi pines on top?"

"And this is, I didn't catch his name? Milton, you said, Milton something?"

"Yes, Milton Elbadawi."

"Ah, I've got a brief AR summary now. Corporatocene arms dealer. Lavish parties with beautiful call girls on big yachts to sell bombs, guns and missiles for security in CSR gift wrap. Mitigated his sentence from the *Ecocide Truth and Reconciliation Supreme Court* by giving evidence against a cartel of arms traders and coal seam frackers. The facts were subsequently found to be worthless, as wiser heads had said they would be."

"Trying to reinvent himself, he says. Secret sharer in the old faith for mine."

"I'll make some more inquiries and check him out."

"Brother Joe treating you alright?"

"Couldn't be better."

"You sure?"

"Yep."

∞

The Hampstead Heath Guesthouse electric vehicle opens its door as I step towards it. I speak the destination and it drives me there coordinating with the other traffic and maintaining perfect road position using laser light, radio wave time of flight return and continuous wave, as well as a variety of other triangulation techniques lost on me. If the car has its own agenda, it seems prepared to put that aside to help me. On the way, I try to go through the case data Eugene has sent to me via AR. Nancy Godel. I re-check the intercept time. Eugene chats with the car and tells it to look after me. The vehicle, called Lunette Laudine, expresses the usual reverential attitude of AI systems towards Eugene.

"I'm not and don't wish to be a gendered being," Lunette instructs me. "So please don't refer to me as 'she' or 'it.' You can use my name, They or Thay, Them and Theirs. Just like President Zula. Eugene sends regards. It means a lot for me to transport a friend of Eugene's."

Lunette advises that my social media has been hacked and some nutter is putting up posts under my name on the theme 'fair play for religions and corporations.'

I arrive at Southwark, the vehicle lets me out and returns to the guesthouse. It's a summer day, but a cold wind nips the air. Nearby are the enhanced barrier defences against Thames floods, another legacy of the Corporatocene era. Cleverly disguised as community art works are GSPP monitoring stations, part of a network across the globe regulating (as well as other components) atmospheric $CO_2$ to 260 ppm by direct synthetic connection with the consciousness and photosynthetic capacity of every road and building on the earth's surface.

I walk towards the jasmine and wisteria-covered pergola near the Tate Community Garden. A happy crowd is enjoying the fete and waiting for the Presidential procession; needs and caprices, faith and hope all satisfied. People are sharing, gifting, or lending goods, skills and services under signs such as *'Streetbank,' 'Freecycle,'* and *'Community Exchange System.'* A little girl holds a sign: *'President Zula, will you stop and shake hands with me?'* Some are staring up at a strange display high in the sky. Ice crystals in cirrus clouds are creating halos, sundogs and a parhelic circle. That's rare for summer and no doubt many think it's another of the strange (religious recusants might say prophetic) phenomena that drift about our controversial eco-gendered President. Zula's not popular in Southwark, people here prefer the virtue of rugged individualism to the brand of nature worship Zula promotes. Three women sit at desks with typewriters under one of the large, leafy trees out front of the thatch and moss-roofed Globe. A sign proclaims they compose poetry for a fee. I hand the nearest snap-bard 3¾ Southwark ducats and say nothing. She types in time with the brown waves slapping the pylons of the Millennium Bridge. Eventually she hands me a piece of paper.

> *Not summer for you.*
> *But all grows green gracefully;*
> *Science is at peace.*

Then my AR-enriched imagination shifts the scene before me to that outside the place in Hampstead where I'm supposed to do the hit. From a large elm out front is draped a tattered *Whole Earth Council* flag: a pale blue dot on a black background of interstellar space with rainbows in the corners. Under the tree sit three travelling bards with brown guitar cases and shiny faux-leather shoes. Jack Castles is one of them. By a tree-shaded fence, supposedly on-holiday WTC agent Hercules Huncks is helping Jevons Paradox, a well-known criminal, lift a long package from the back of a green truck. I look up and see someone's opened the window of my room in the Records office. The scene is a jumble, as dreams are, and I suspect Eugene's behind these images. Why's that shape-shifting imp playing with my AR now?

There's Gordon Lizzard, the corpulent Mayor of the village and Vice-President of the *Whole Earth Council*, pressing the flesh. With his tousled white hair, half-lens reading glasses, chubby body and jovial personality, he seems to cultivate the persona of a buffoon to disguise and distract from his more self-interested purpose. We are old friends, Gordon and I. Gordon had lived for a time in a Gondwanan community, as had my mother. We have sons about the same age. Resemblances end there. Lizzard is also rumoured to be a Worshipful Master in the Organisation for Temporal Accommodation or OTA; an umbrella institution for those seeking to restore religious tax exemptions, abolish corporate marriage to ecosystems and organise communities like Southwark to secede from the *Whole Earth Council*.

Despite his Aquarian makeover, Gordon is an unreconstructed corporate recusant. Some of Gordon's more infamous sayings are: 'every time we pay tax we have to lay off another thousand employees,' 'once I own oxygen, I'll stick a meter box in every set of lungs,' and 'we are most certainly not all in this together.' The inner man is volatile, incapable of having a conversation for its own sake, or that of another person; a skill he probably mastered in business school. The outer Lizzard is a supreme acting performance: the dedicated global community servant, the poster boy of corporate redemption. Gordon's established Southwark as a gated neoliberal enclave, GSPP-powered skyscrapers of tastefully appointed apartments, lots of AR and VR to ensure the denizens remain in constant titillation and partial inattention with AI robots for menial chores. Gordon's enemies (and they're loud and legion) say he and his wife share a sex robot with an artificial womb who started out pole dancing and ended up a flag bearer for corporate responsibility.

They call Gordon 'Landslide Lizzard' because of his narrow legislative victories, purportedly based on corrupt manipulation of liquid democracy technology. His law to fund a rescue mission for the Project Persephone corporate exiles marooned in their biosphere satellites, for example, passed only after mysteriously securing every vote from citizens in Laurasia, Lutruwita, Gondwana, Sahul and each island of the Tethys Sea. 'Lyin' Lizzard,' as he's also known, is unrepentant about his friendship with notorious crime figures such as Jevons Paradox. Eugene enhances my AR so it picks up scraps of a conversation Gordon's having with my brother Joe, the WTC Director.

"What can't feel pain's got no interests."

"Then cruel men are lonely."

"Just predators equally valued with prey; all can't flourish forever."

"What few foresee, none can guarantee?"

"We're not talking about it are we? Marcus mightn't like it."

"Of course not."

"Just shooting the breeze?"

"Exactly. No harm in that."

"You should see the sky here. One of the great miracles of life."

"What?"

"The atmosphere of light that precedes death in great ones."

"How's the distractions?"

"First class; and the Dodos of Mauritius aren't even curious."

"They just need to be more broad-minded; to see it as necessary."

∞

I pick up my first free bottle of beer and stand watching Gordon in my official capacity. Some say that's Jean Moulin failed physicist and over-the-hill time cop. Gordon's pretending to be interested in some trinket from a market stall. 'Paradise white,' says the sad-looking young girl standing in front of him, hoping he'll pay. He does. He gives her a security pass to his hotel room.

"And I'll see you later gorgeous," Gordon whispers.

I see Spicer Layamon move towards her boss. She's Lizzard's current chief of staff, according to my AR. Spicer, tall, blond and elegant in her locally designed and made light blue cotton dress, seems the type of girl who might make me want to vacation here. My AR shows her public access data: degree in Community Studies and Emergency Medicine at Oxford with a major in Contemplative Absorption (CA) indeed, it says she reached non-duality in only her second year of study. It's getting so you can't walk down the street without bumping into some do-gooder radiating non-duality. For myself, I've always found a thoroughly acceptable replacement for *Nirvana* ready and waiting at the bottom of a bottle of single malt. Ah, she had some disciplinary issue in CA. That's interesting. Led a guerrilla unit in the Vosges during the Corporatocene War; credited with individually killing twenty mercenaries and destroying two hundred autonomous weapons systems. Strange we never met. Sexual identification and preference undisclosed. I wonder why she's working for Lizzard. Then my AR detects her perfume. Ah, she's the *ange de la Résistance* of my dream.

Spicer lightly holds Gordon by the arm. It's a gesture she performs with practised grace. It would have looked to an observer that she was merely reminding the Mayor of some neglected aspect of protocol. Gordon is talking via AR to his son. Gordon sees me, but I gesture he should take the call. He stares as if I'd just rolled away the stone and emerged naked from my tomb. I know what he's thinking: that his AR detects lights on, no one home. Well Gordon, that's no system error, that's Jean Moulin.

"You've written a new piece of music?" says Gordon. "Both of you. A tragedy? With the Earth as the protagonist? I'm sure that's not been done before. I'll put you in touch with some theatre people. Maybe you could try it as a musical comedy? That's great Spencer. Let's hear it."

"Careful," Spicer whispers to Gordon. "WTC is here."

"I love it," says Gordon. "Gotta go Spencer. At work. Call you in an hour or so. Yeah, stay home till then."

Lizzard is envious of Spicer's contemplative accomplishments, but bitter experience has taught him to respect her intrusions. He pauses, pats the little statue on the table at the stall and checks the buttons on his handcrafted cotton shirt. AR scan of its tag reveals his wife paid for it with a note of 26 London pounds, another local currency citizens here use to pay rates, taxes, business services and for produce. The asking price was twice

She's the ange de la Résistance of my dream

that. I assume Lizzard's worn the apparel hoping it proclaims him a man who supports local community business and crafts.

I walk over, AR confirming minimal threats and Gordon's just finishing a second, untraceable AR call.

"Oh, it's you," says Gordon. "What the Z-scheme are you doing here?"

"Expecting someone else?"

"I was, actually."

"Well here I am. Behold the man."

"So, it's Jean Moulin. Something of a man, but more like a ghost. Out of rehab? Been waiting five years t'see you again, Jean." Gordon sometimes speaks in an accent that once characterised the southern states of America. He's obviously spent time there, or identifies with their more regressive ancient social habits.

"Looks like you spent it eating, Mephisto, my old friend," I reply.

"Still drinking? Still butchering your wife's Gondwanan slang?"

"She's dead, Gordon. Suicide, they said."

"I'm sorry. I didn't know," Gordon replies.

"I talk that way to remember her. Got a good speech ready, Gordon? Going to scatter some 'covfefe' over the crowd?" 'Covfefe' is a term of obscure political origin astrophysicists now use to describe the constant negative pressure of empty space. Gordon has the body and conscience of a fungus gnat larva.

"Here's to you, Jean. Still hopin' all might have life and have it abundantly?"

"Looks like you beat them to it Gordon."

"I'm girt by prosperity, as you can see," says Gordon.

"We're all girt by climate change and ecocide," I reply. "The latest, predictable market failure-producing externalities from which your friends in the 1% felt destined to be bailed out, this time physically."

"Encrypted data storage, that's what I do now," said Gordon. "Governments, courts, libraries. Information is the currency of democracy."

"History in a bottle. Hope cast on the waves."

"You know more about bottles than most," Gordon replied. "I've sworn an oath to the *Whole Earth Council*. You won't find 'greed is good' articles hidden in my rafters."

"Maybe not, but perhaps some of your old friends are up there in the dark Gordon; dissimulating their downsides; tendons ready to spring the old greed creed once more to equivocal flight. If aliens are ever encountered on a planet in some Goldilocks orbit, your corporate acolytes would feel obliged to convert them to the truth of both apostolic succession and neoliberal contestability."

"The drive and insight of the men and women you so cruelly denigrate," Gordon says "gave you this happy world of leisure and superfluity."

"Sure, happy for those with the moral luck to be born to it," I reply.

"Greed and generosity," says Gordon "are complementary concepts, Jean. A lot of good money was fairly made catering to human weakness."

"And millions died of starvation, disease and war," I say "as people like you made Earth one vast corporate scam."

"You must be enjoying our liquor. You sound like your old shrill self; like President Zula, into good by compulsion."

"No mate. What goes on the outside is nothing."

"Jean, if you do go over the dam," says Gordon "just remember, I didn't do the shoving. You're a war hero, a good example to all sons. The point is this. Well, my Spencer can be very impulsive; you know trying to remedy the past by doing good in grand gestures. He's attracted to noble, idealistic people. Promise me you won't let him let him walk into some reckless sacrifice. I had a bad dream about it last night. A dream I've feared to sound lest such collapse it to substance. I'm not asking this for my sake."

∞

Spicer points out that Gordon is already late for his speech. So, red-faced and puffing, he leaves me and struggles onto a platform decked with GSPP-themed, yellow, green and blue crepe paper. He stands underneath old *Yggdrasil*, the 'world tree,' catching his breath and mopping the sweat from his brow. Behind him are Southwark's tall apartment buildings, all GSPP-technology-integrated, splitting water with photons from the blue sky. Lots of GSPP-powered bars, discos, theatres, restaurants and brothels. I run a quick AR scan over them and detect no threats. Sadly. I hope Gordon's speech will be short, I've got to get back to Hampstead on time. I grab another bottle of local brew to fortify myself.

Gordon breathes out, as if to purge all memories of me; then inhales, as though to suck from the atmosphere every, last, restorative drop of public adulation. Gordon isn't religious in any prohibited sense, though he's met enough powerful and successful people to know that many of them would have prayed on such an occasion. So, he does. What to, I have no idea and neither does he.

"Hey Gordon," shouts a heckler, probably bussed in from Hampstead "remember me, I'm your toes."

Gordon smiles and looks around at the crowd, as if, as in days past, they were supplicants of mass media, their urges, hopes and aspirations infinitely malleable to the dictates of the market place he bossed.

"For many years," Gordon says, proud of how well he can project his voice "this tree above me, 'Yggy,' some of you call it, has been a citizen like you or I with voting rights through its guardians."

"Got more votes than you last election," shouts the Hampstead heckler and laughter echoes around the crowd. "Works harder and eats less." Hampstead and Southwark are two communities alike in dignity and rivalry, but differing markedly in approach to technology and democracy.

"Time's up, you rap-symphony of witless, narcissistic toad wobbelry," someone else calls out.

"As you know," Gordon continues "WTC verified historical data has it that while meditating under the leaves of just such a tree Zula Calabiyau had her breakthrough insight for developing a water-splitting catalyst."

"Hey Landslide," shouts the Hampstead heckler "that was under a tumboa and a quiver tree on the Skeleton Coast, you clueless, invertebrate cockwomble."

"Future generations," Mayor Lizzard continues with practised imperturbability reading verbatim from his AR the speech Spicer has prepared, "will continue to revere her *Global Synthetic Photosynthesis Project*. And let me tell you now, their esteem won't be confined to the remarkable way that scientific endeavour successfully understood, reconstructed, improved and made available to all the most important metabolic innovation in our planet's evolutionary history. Neither will their adulation be limited to how that project helped make cities work like rainforests to freshen the sky and humanity pay its way on earth. Rather, they will focus, as should we here today, on the fact that as the GSPP unfolded, it revealed at its core one glorious distinguishing feature from some other great scientific initiatives of the thankfully now departed Corporatocene era: the Atomic Bomb Project, the Apollo Space Project, the Human Genome Project, the Large Hadron Collider, the ITER fusion project, the Hubble Space Telescope, the Space Elevator, the Teleportation Net and the WTC's Tipler–Gott Cylinder. 'The GSPP,' as Zula Calabiyau used to say 'was undertaken in at least ten dimensions that we're aware of and the most important of them was moral.' It was that lack of corruption that endeared the GSPP and Zula Calabiyau to us; the fact that she was a moral exemplar and never abused the large amounts of money placed at her disposal."

"This, of course, was why we voted her, or should I say 'Thay,' President of the *Whole Earth Council*. We likewise supported Their programme of ecocentric legislative reforms, as well as Their research to find a cure for AMDS that as you know has already claimed the lives of hundreds of decent people in progressive towns like Southwark. Unlike penitents such as myself, Zula's never had to humble Themself before the *Ecocide Truth and Reconciliation Supreme Court*."

"Hey Landslide, think we've forgotten the car murder case you self-absorbed political carpet stain?" shouts the Hampstead heckler. If the GSPP or Zula Calabiyau ever needed a funeral oration, Gordon was just the man for the job.

∞

One can take so much of Gordon Lizzard and if my AR had a bulldust dosimeter I'm sure it'd be warning I'm fast approaching fatal exposure. Gordon finishes his speech and tries to AR his son Spencer as he's promised. Departing the GSPP event, I summon the guesthouse electric car. Lunette picks me up and takes me back, deciding I'll like Alain Stivell's *Renaissance of the Celtic Harp* (which I don't) and offering me a shave and then a gin in a lemon, lime and bitters (which I do). Eugene speaks to me through the car's audio.

"They're getting you ready for the big reveal," says Eugene. "Get your budgie smugglers on Jean, you're about to go over the spillway."

Soon I'm walking towards Pond Street near Hampstead Heath.

Leaves on the oak and liquid amber trees are being tickled by a light breeze. For some reason, I try to imagine the number of air-scattered photons that make the sky blue; the sky that retains no trace of a passing bird or storm; that I'd once have felt whispering into my placid soul 'let me fill you with warmth and bright colour, for it's our mutual joy you're alive on earth.'

Unlike Southwark, in Hampstead Heath, the local Council run by Mayor Monica Dash has declared that village an AR-free zone and imposed Privacy Dome (PD) in all public spaces. The residents here have voted that they prefer to hear, see and touch without technological augmentation or scrutiny. Some scraps of conversation float unenhanced to my ears. 'I like some good in the air.' 'Yeah, well don't exhale near me.' 'It rained till it poured off both sides of me.' 'Water dark as pear tree bark.' 'Made him dress up as a cleaner and he did some lines. Good jobs too, darling; better than the interns, so no one could be bothered dobbing.' I wonder what would happen if some religious terrorist or corporate recusant-controlled nanobot roamed through here shooting? Would they all just stand there, waiting?

An old man is looking around very confused, but has two friends holding his hands. A young girl wearing a large, straw hat is sitting on a bench between two oak trees. She's writing intently in her diary with her shoes off. She rubs the back of one calf with the toes of the other foot, then runs a finger along the back of the bench and flicks off some dew. An elderly lady in a white hat is placing chirping ducklings in a box and the mother duck is nearby quacking in the bushes. Then I see a bee drowning in a pond. After all I've seen in the war it seems such tiny, insignificant distress. But I stop, kneel and scoop the bee to dry land. Although probably exhausted, she cleans water from her front legs and soon takes to the air. Bees have such great capacity to work for the collective good. She flies around then seems to decide 'that was fun.' She lands in the water near my hand for another go; after which she buzzes off.

"I'm taking them somewhere with water, but not too many drakes who'll only mob them to death," says the woman to the girl on the bench. The girl nods, her face moving in and out of shadow. My AR says the old woman is Mayor Monica Dash. There's a heavy security presence in the street owing to the impending motorcade by President Zula. Despite this being techno-phobic Hampstead, the entrances to all the nearby houses are being monitored, old-style.

*Still, spacious, oaken arcade.*
*Light filters down through*
*Layers of fine leaves.*

*On the GSPP celebration day,*
*An old lady in a white hat,*
*Walks the footpath alone.*

∞

I come to the target house, a little late because of stopping to help the bee. But it's guarded by police; a crime scene. Something's wrong. My identity is checked. I take off my shoes and put on the requisite small blue AI forensic nano-slippers. A man and a woman are laughing in a backyard hot spa next door. I see two dead bees and a dead butterfly on the steps.

The forensics boys and girl scan my ID and let me pass. A tall fellow with glasses mutters behind my back. I'm used to that. No one wants to get

After all I've seen in the war it seems such tiny, insignificant distress

reported to the WTC. He's one of those types who like everything done by the book; a Big Caslon, or a Geeza Pro, types I never get on with.

"Hey aren't you guys supposed to prevent this sort of stuff?" he asks.

"If you mean your birth, bud; until today I'd assumed it was beyond my control."

"I mean murder. Her name's Nancy Godel. AR override says estranged daughter of Zula Calabiyau, the GSPP Queen," he says. "Today of all days. Go figure."

Guess he'd have been surprised to learn I planned to do just that.

"She had a truck load of drugs today. Yeah, killed with kindness."

"Witnesses?"

"Just a Mr Jones, Jeremy Jones. Waiting in the sitting room. Not all there; you know, few rocks short of a rapid. We were told not to go up."

A gentle breeze is blowing through the curtains of an open second floor window. The window is at the back of a two-storey house and looks onto a garden in full bloom between two large and leafy oak trees. Into the room, upon that breeze comes the songs of a variety of small birds, robins, thrushes, magpies, the sounds of children playing and the soft warning whirr of an electric vehicle reversing. I also detect the scents of red and white roses, cowslip, rosebay willow herb, foxglove and honeysuckle as well as the talking of elderly gardeners in the public organic garden. From somewhere floats the sound of a local band and choir rehearsing the old GSPP standard '*Split by Sun*,' for the concert later that evening.

*"At dawn's soft blush to sight*
*And rain on leaves and rooves at night,*
*Sing to ourselves as one*
*For air and water split by Sun.*

*Highways through the Sahara*
*Towns from Findhorn to Kumariya,*
*Skyscrapers in New York and Beijing*
*Work like the Amazon so we sing.*

> *Time to set the forests free*
> *Let plains live, let oceans be,*
> *Make for ourselves what we breathe*
> *Reverence for all life what we believe."*

The room is full of books and shelves with framed photographs and mementos related to the history of the GSPP. A classical guitar is on its stand, it has a broken D string. The instrument exudes good taste and lots of cash: a Jayson Elazzi 2016, cedar and rosewood. I'd have to sell my time share at Lord Howe Island several times over to get one of those babies. Opposite the window is a double bed with white sheets and pillows; well, sheets that had been that colour till recently. Now they are sprayed, as are the walls, with tiny reddish droplets.

A body lays naked upon the bed in a pool of sunlight. Her young face has a calm expression, the cheeks a little sunken and the pale skin already greyish. The front and side of her head have angry bruises like she's been hit hard by a blunt object. The back of the skull has been blown away. Entry wound in the right forward temporal area. Gun shot, these days a rare method for taking someone's life. Perhaps symbolic; legs crossed over at the ankles arms straight out from the sides. But wait. Lots of bruising on her left wrist. What's happened here?

There are no obvious gaps in the spray pattern on the wall. Unlikely therefore that anyone else was present; or that was how it was supposed to look. Privacy Dome is intact and operating. We won't be getting any tell-tale images.

So, genetics shows the deceased Nancy was the daughter of the famous Zula Calabiyau. AR public access read-out reveals a more confused history. I'm used to all manner of persons informing me that a past moment they were desperate to have investigated by the WTC, somehow also was critical for humanity. But the minutes I spend in that room seem astonishingly resonant and vivid; like my first kiss, marriage, our son's birth, hearing of Caroline's death.

That train of thought jolts a literary association. Just after Basho visited the Zen monk Buccho's hermitage, he went in search of the 'Murder

A gentle breeze is blowing through the curtains of an open second floor window

Stone.' He found it in a dark corner of a mountain near a hot spring surrounded by dead bees killed by poisonous gas. Bees wax contains lipids emitted by the Queen and her workers that are constantly sampled by them. When the wax indicates too many bees in the hive, they murder each other and the Queen. Dead bees. Dead bees. Bad things always happen in threes.

Let's see. The WTC's Temporal Tremor Detector (TTD) has recorded an unauthorised interference in the time line. It's all very well for science to have proven there are multiple alternate universes, but I've come to learn that a lot of Big Shots like this one just the way it is. Certainly, my brother Joseph does and he's my WTC boss who must be obeyed. I expected to post a love letter; but it'd been delivered before I arrived. Good. I never liked decommissioning women, no matter how evil or how much of a threat to the Sustainocene the WTC had decreed them to be. But there is something different here, something ethereally beautiful and meaningful, like a profound memory half-forgotten on waking, or an exquisite melody just beyond hearing.

I again scan the public data implant just beneath the skin adjacent to the flexor tendon at her right wrist. The girl's name is Nancy, Nancy Godel; from genetics her mother is Zula Calabiyau and her father listed as unknown. Full genetics PD protected. Thirty three years SGA. Single. Need to check for jealous partners, sugar daddies or mummies. Boyfriend is Spencer Lizzard, son of the Mayor. If the boy is anything like his dad, he'll have been working an angle. Wonder what old Gordon has to do with this. Won't be good for his popularity. Or maybe it will.

Nancy had played guitar in the London Symphony Orchestra. Citizen of the Hampstead Community, registered for online voting on legislation in that region and globally. Regular visitor at a Pond Street book share. Liked to read books printed on paper. Well, it's the fashion these days.

Time of death 14:27. Up till two hours ago Nancy's pulse had been regular at 70, then it suddenly rose to 120 with a catecholamine surge before dropping to zero within a few minutes. Blood pressure had been 120/80 mmHg initially but fell substantially with the pulse. ECG had gone from sinus rhythm to ventricular fibrillation and then asystole over the same period with concomitant decrease in cerebral oxygen saturation and neurological activity. Toxicology screen is negative, except for a massive dose of methamphetamine. Ice, an oldie but a goldie. AR starts to flash up graphs of the volume of distribution, protein-binding and half-life, metabolism and clearance; but I switch them off.

I'm alone and in the mood for creative free association. I imagine Nancy's freed spirit transposing Bach to the Planck scale, as her fingers with the pink nail polish flee up and down that Elazzi fretboard. Her death shouldn't have happened, yet it has. Does it matter if it was chance, willed or predestined? What good can possibly come now? My inclination is to let it go. I'll forget it once I have a quiet drink; maybe under Ashino's willow, as it spreads its shade from one of my son's organic fields over their farm's crystal stream.

On the bed beside Nancy's body is a red silk dressing gown. Her hand still holds the gun. Ancient collectable, uses bullets. Hard to trace through AR. It looks familiar. Too damn familiar. My antique Radom Vis 35. How did it end up here? She owned an up-to-date licence. No doubt gunpowder residue will be found on her palm. Police'll be expected to conclude this was suicide. Yet, there'll be no suicide note. Everything in this room seems different from what it's supposed to look like. A murder scene and my gun in the middle of it.

I see a familiar copy of *The Tempest*. Inside, I find her diary. Good omen. Diary's mostly poetry. On the title page, she's written 'I hate bullies, I was born to fight them.' In the back is the log in and password for the nano-implant in her left cerebral cortex. Privacy Dome working there too. I quickly scan the available contents, as far as I can. Nothing of obvious interest.

On the desk is a paper Nancy was preparing for *Energy and Environment Science* and a submission to the Hampstead Heath Hands about laying a hedge as a micro-environment for small creatures and insects, fencing off a swan nesting area by the ponds and an action they were bringing on behalf of that ecosystem against a developer. I take AR copies.

Book shelves seem disturbed. Someone has searched her room. The inside of books, drawers, cupboards, boxes, even the pockets of clothes in the wardrobe, all show indications of being rummaged.

My attention is drawn to a large antique tobacco jar on the mantelpiece. The word '*MacGuffin*' is on the outside engraved in copperplate. Surely not? But if Nancy liked reading as much as I did and had a sense of humour, that'd be the place. I poke my fingers in. Sure enough. They touch something hard. I draw out what looks to be another diary. This one has a different author: her estranged mother, Zula Calabiyau. Now that *is* a find. Mostly just dates and amounts of money, hundreds of thousands of them, in tiny print. Some of the pages have bookmarks. I wrap it in PD and put it in my pocket alongside Nancy's.

Big coincidence indeed that the daughter of the famous Zula Calibiyau should die on this of all days. Sad to say, however, but the real reason the whole thing stinks is that I've become involved. Eugene helps me do a search of the room; my fingerprints and DNA are all over the place.

"Three can keep a secret," says Eugene through my AR "if two are dead."

I'm being set up. I disable the primitive surveillance and upload the last week of recording. A crime such as this would never have occurred in a techno-paradise like Southwark. It only is possible because in places such as Hampstead people tried to live as they did in the 1960s and 1970s — in the days of pot, flower-power and vinyl Beatles records before the mobile phone, the Internet, T-Net, deep AI and AR. I replace the gun. Switching the basic monitoring systems back on, I pretend to trip, my clumsy hands touching lots of objects as I try to prevent my fall.

∞

I walk into the sitting room. Mr Jeremy Jones is reclining under an open window on a white settee with pink floral pattern, holding a gauze pack to a bloodied nose. He's a bearded guy, short brown hair, medium height, stabilised genetic age about 40, wearing a light blue cotton shirt and rocking back and forth. A little statue of the Buddha in a white lab coat is on

a table beside him. I introduce myself and pick up the statue. That makes him edgy. Interesting. Hopefully not edgy enough to spin this out too long. If he's acting, he's very good.

"What's this?" I ask.

"Scientist Buddha. From the GSPP Centre in Namibia. Picked it up for her at a market stall. Looked quite nice to me. Don't know why. What do you think of these scientist Buddhas?"

"Oh, they're alright, aren't they?" The guy at the door had been right; Jeremy isn't the sharpest tool in the shed.

"I'd met Nancy one or twice before," says Jeremy. "Just to say hello mostly. Saw her at some Community Contemplation sessions. People don't speak to me much, but she did. Used to vanish for days, then just turn up on your doorstep for a chat, or to borrow some flour or eggs. Young man used to drop in occasionally and I'd hear her guitar and him singing. Not my cup of tea, but I suppose some might like it. They went to India once to play at this big religious festival, so she said."

"What happened today?"

"Well, after lunch, it being the GSPP celebration and all, I invited her in to our flat. We sat on the lounge. She said she'd been out on the heath doing the 'Split by Sun' ceremony; played one of the Mephistos; maybe had a few pills there, as you do. Suddenly she was mumbling something and then said to me 'I have to kill you.'" Jeremy blew his nose on a handkerchief from his pocket. My AR system detected, analysed and dispersed the aerosolised droplets.

"What did you do? Take your time. Get yourself sorted out."

"I smiled, thinking she was joking. Then she grabbed me by the throat with her two hands and squeezed tightly. Like this. I struggled free and she then said 'I don't think I could kill you', stood up and walked towards my wife who was in the kitchen."

"Ever know her to use drugs, Nancy? Ice?"

"Ice? As in a drink?"

"Never mind."

"Well, Nancy said something to my wife but I couldn't work out what it was. Nancy jumped up and down around the lounge room and walked into my bedroom. My four year old followed her. I rushed over and saw Nancy opening and slamming the wardrobe doors while jumping into the air. I quickly took my son by the hand and led him out into the lounge room. Nancy followed, sat on the lounge and said 'I'd better go,' grabbing her own hair. I walked her outside. When she got to the stairs she said 'So much for the new railing', grabbed the top of it and kicked it with her foot about twenty times. She ran out onto the footpath towards the street and then came back. I asked her 'what's the matter Nancy?' She asked 'Do you believe in God?' It seemed a strange question. You know, antiquated. People these days are more likely to ask 'have you experienced enlightenment yet?' I supposed that was what she meant, so I replied, 'Doesn't everybody?' She appeared to calm down but then pushed me away and ran into our house through the front door."

He looks distressed enough to require my month's supply of soma. Instead, I offer him a glass of water, which he drinks slowly, probably as he's been taught in mindfulness classes by some local scientist Buddha.

"My little son was standing in the kitchen. I tackled Nancy whilst my wife pulled our child away. Nancy elbowed me in the ribs forcing me to release her and ran down the hallway. She head-butted the back door with such force that it was dented across the centre. She then stepped back and kicked the bottom of the door causing another hole. She started yelling 'the rats must die' and punched me in the face. I picked up my cricket bat. Nancy was coming back in towards my wife and son, so I hit her hard in the middle of the head with the bat. She staggered back and then came forward again. I slogged her a second time on the side of the head. She swayed backwards and yelled 'the rats must die' several times, starting to remove her clothing as she did so. We stood facing each other for about five or ten minutes. She said 'I can't go to sleep, because I've seen the Devil and will die if I close my eyes.' Then Nancy heard the police siren and ran back into this flat, her flat here. I heard a gunshot a few minutes later. Is she killed?"

"That's one theory." Interesting choice of verb Jeremy.

"I hadn't planned to lay any charges. I thought she needed help. She's never been like this before."

Jeremy begins to cry.

"I appreciate your assistance," I say, handing him a tissue. "They'll ask you to sign a full statement."

I didn't believe a word he said. No rock islands in the birdbath for Jeremy's bees. Jeremy stares at me.

"You recognise me, don't you?" I ask.

"Maybe. I saw you outside her flat when she ran back in. Same clothes."

"You were mistaken." I show him my WTC badge.

"Yes, yes I must be," he says. "You're Jean Moulin, aren't you? Killed a lot of people. In the war. Some say you're the most violent person on the planet."

∞

I walk back out onto the street into the summer sunshine. The opening melody from Harrison's *Within You and Without You* signals a message has come in by AR. I blink and my son's image appears in the top left corner of my vision.

"Hello François. Can't talk much now. At work."

"At work. When can you visit?"

"You want me to do a bit of caretaking? Build a shed? Need references? I'm a wild and unreliable man. My brother says so."

"No Dad, but I got a bad need for a pair of good brown shoes. Any chance you could pick me up a pair at Foster and Son or George Cleverley?"

"Black is all they got. Alright, I'll look. I didn't have a very good night again. Slept terrible. Draught of strange dreams blowing right into my head."

"Got to have a bit of air. Meaningless pause."

"You're not supposed to say that; it's meant to be silent, in the head."

"Anyway, it's out now; roaming up and down."

"I'm a bloody imposter, mate. Something's happened. Shaken me up a bit."

"Dad, Helené and the kids have been praying about you. Walter says you have a very interesting mind."

"Tell him I loved his GSPP play."

"Dad, come down. We can lounge under the old willow by the stream, you know, tickle some trout. Lovely mauve, lilac and pink wildflowers this time of year. Vibrant clouds of bees teaching us the very act of order."

"How's your neighbour? Milton what's-his-name. I've looked him up. Or did I already tell you that? Sorry, I'm a bit distracted. I'll get Eugene to look into him. Till then we can't do much."

"Forgiveness, eh?"

"That's the size of it. Until he steps over the line."

"Merlin dropped round today. Yeah. Wanted me to ask if you'd had that session with the trick cyclist?"

"Sure. Love to. See you soon."

# II

# SAD PARADISE, HAMPSTEAD

*Jean Moulin decides to stay on Nancy's Case — Nancy's diary explores the ethics of global synthetic photosynthesis — Uncle Joe, head of World Time Council — Mayor Lizzard wants a chat about his son Spencer — meeting Spicer Layamon — narrow escape on the Tumulus — Funeral of Nancy — historical records of global synthetic photosynthesis — Detective Bernadette Goldbough and some dreams and warnings — appearance of volcanic ash and Great Comet —*

Next day just a few clouds are mooching across a vault that is more grey-white than blue. I sit outside in the shade of a large, leafy passionfruit vine at a hand-made, honey-coloured Huon pine table with a chess board pattern on top. The nearby garden beds are alive with the scents and colours of marigolds, the sounds of red-hipped humble-bees in the tops of thistles, robins and chaffinches echoing their hearts off the bright walls of the day. Breakfast is local-sourced fruit, Bircher muesli, olive oil-fried eggs, buttered toast and fair-trade Arabica coffee from the *Aileu* and *Maubisse* regions of Timor Leste.

The old man at the next table is crying because he can't remember the pin code to his cash card and its personal recognition isn't working. I ask the young waitress the size of his bill, then offer to pay it in local currency. He nods at me; it might be in gratitude.

I flip through Nancy's diary. The day before her death she'd written a sonnet (dedicated to Spencer) on the last page.

*About this house a silence is creaking,*
*While dawn's soft blush by massless light's imbued.*
*Below a moist, new-mown lawn is speaking,*
*In oak leaf hole pairs; world's blood's split anew.*

*Earth's future generations voice no sound,*
*Beyond this many-painted window bay.*
*Yet in our hearts their gravamen abounds:*
*'We're flowers today from your love-streamed affray.'*

*Our lives are with a few bright truths endowed,*
*Like oil and water their light and gravity.*
*Sun splits our days when loyalty to fair principle be wed.*
*We brave luminants from higher symmetry.*

*For I am here and Thou art there,*
*Truth's whisp'ring delicacy's everywhere.*

Whatever was going on in Nancy's head when she wrote that, it wasn't drugs. I watch a huge ZEHST passenger jet spiral up like an eagle from Heathrow airport. Its Higgs field will be dialled low, so in these windless conditions the plane will probably only weigh as much as a few birds of prey. The array of synthetic photosynthesis panels glinting on its vast wings will be feeding water-split hydrogen and oxygen into turbofans, while fuel cells provide on-board electricity. That hydrogen, burning with the highest specific energy of combustion per gram of any chemical fuel, will be producing not just free energy, but fresh water.

That means, I muse, that the ZEHST plane, the clouds, as well as all these shadowed buildings, roads, trees and flowers, are now part of the hydrological cycle. They're all rainmakers, recharging the rivers, ponds, aquifers and plants till the low-entropy energy the earth acquires from fusion of hydrogen in the sun, evaporates the surface $H_2O$ and completes the circle game.

But its somehow all linked with the death of Nancy Godel, and those making me take the rap for it. Being framed for a hit I was going to do anyway. The difference was that if I'd taken her out there'd have been no evidence, no investigation, no trial. Nancy with all her talents, dreams and hopes would simply have vanished from this brane; not killed, just exiled to a parallel universe. The fear amongst warmongers of being decommissioned without warning by the WTC had ended the Corporatocene War, indeed rendered war itself obsolete. But now someone wants me convicted of old-style murder. That's retro-type death, out in the open, the perpetrators brazenly defying the rule of law. Reminds me of all those strange goings-on around Lizzard's speech at Southwark. Eugene had tried to get me to the hit early, but it was lucky I arrived a little late. I can thank some bees for that. Did my brother Uncle Joe endorse it? I'd tried to follow instructions; thought we'd settled our differences. Why should it matter? He'd tell me what to do; look after it for me, as always.

I look more carefully at Nancy's diary. Whereas Zula's is a list of names, dates and amounts, parts of Nancy's diary are written in abbreviated medieval Latin, causing a few problems for my AR translator. Nancy's diary has beautiful drawings of moths, beetles and caterpillars. There are also some marginal inscriptions made by Nancy on the day of her murder. My AR translates them.

> *It is fear completely confident,*
> *Reason utterly mad,*
> *An infirm domination,*
> *A thirst already drunk,*
> *A sad paradise.*

∞

Patches of shadow and light roll over me as I walk under the trees in the back garden. I can hear the clicking of bicycle wheels, the rumble of cars, the electronic buzz of a truck before it changes gear. Looking at the street,

I notice the outer wisps of a little girl's tied-back hair caught by the sun, the clumsy intentness of a boy trying to saw wood, other littlies with ice-blocks beside their mother. From above come bird calls and the purr of a light plane. A young dog with floppy ears is playing around a sprinkler. Those sprinklers look like white feathers waving over the grass.

A tall block of flats basks in the light grey haze. An old woman with hands clasped in front, slightly moves her weight from one foot to another as she contemplates her garden. Nancy's spirit seems to dwell in all these images.

A young man in black shorts, shirt hanging out, dirty riding boots and a white bandage around one hand, swaggers across a park, making a bloodied spit on the grass. Workmen in blue trousers, T-shirts and bare tops, are leaning forward on a park table while biting into a pie or sandwich. They start picking on the bandaged man, like crows upon an injured co-conspirator.

I walk over and interpose myself. I hate bullies. I grab the hair of one and pull his head hard against a pole, then punch him between the eyes. He goes out cold. The others recognise me and run. That's another example of Sustainoceneans who aren't happy.

As a member of the WTC, I've sworn an oath to uphold the eco-centric principles enunciated in the *Whole Earth Charter*. People such as those about me, however, are still apt to interpret 'love thy neighbour' in exploitative ways, to want blocks of land a little bigger or better than the next fellow's, to misinterpret signals or inappropriately control others inadvertently. Some even enjoy hurting, being cruel and exerting power. They miss the edge. The role of WTC agents such as myself is to reorient them to the principles that bind life together on Earth. Those that can't measure up are simply exiled off-brane.

*Greed broke the link,*
*Pushed life to the brink.*
*Craving peak power,*
*Hatred's over-ripe flower.*
*Our true aim lost,*
*Earth bore the cost.*

Noodling along in our gene-edited anti-ageing telomeres, we people of the Sustainocene can expect, barring accidents or mischief, to live for a few hundred years or more, cocooned if we so choose from manual or intellectual drudgery by deep-learning AI and a myriad of nanotech supports that have been one of the few positive legacies of the Corporatocene. If my liver doesn't last much longer I can even get a stem cell replacement. The WEC has thought of everything to make people happy forever.

Yet for large numbers of Sustainoceneans, the material benefits of Global Synthetic Photosynthesis have outstripped their capacity to be happy. They've grown bored with peace and yearn to explore with direct experience the massacres, slaughters, tragedies and atrocities that history tells them was the past. Life, like music, seems to relish a little dissonance, provided it eventually can be herded to a tonic. Nancy's murder is dissonant alright; it has the startling tang of subversive strangeness.

*We first kissed in acid rain,*
*Loved through debt and mercury pain.*
*'Marry me' sprayed on a stormwater drain,*
*So you'd see it from a coal train.*

Take my brothers and sisters in eco-principle, my fellow ecocrats, way up high in that ZEHST jet. Time for them soon will be pleasantly unravelling and dilating. The lucky bastards'll be downing their first beer or scotch as they switch on their VR–AR systems and imbibe an even better tonic: vicarious suffering. For some it will be extreme sport, or this week's highly-rated choice of rafting down the global citizen-treasure that is Lutruwita's wild Franklin River at the time of the anti-dam protests. Maybe they'll be in a doped linen SE5a, tumbling earth and sky at a touch of stick and rudder, so it emerges from a fairyland cloud to send an unsuspecting Albatross DIII down a flamer.

I'd been ordered to decommission the daughter of the most famous 'woman' in human history, perhaps apart from Mitochondrial Eve. And I'd arrived out of time. Now I'm to be framed for her murder. But doing something about it will be a big risk. It might reveal another time I'd been too late.

*To serve like a bee*
*Principled eco-society.*
*Nano roads and cities*
*Make fuel from sun and sky.*
*Gathered on a part,*
*Bright, still, heart.*

∞

I must have sat staring at those cumulonimbus clouds for half an hour, imagining in them my motives, affections, perceptions. I came up with a hundred good reasons to do nothing; and one or two bad ones. Then, feeling sorry for Nancy, I did an unusual thing. I decided to break WTC rules and take the side of one of my ordered victims. It wasn't as if I was consciously disloyal to the WTC or the Sustainocene; more that the injustice Nancy had suffered was too strong for me to ignore.

I brought up on AR my copy of the paper Nancy had been working on for *Energy and Environment Science*. It was a draft and reviewers or co-authors had written marginal comments. The title was '*Globalising Synthetic Photosynthesis: Humanity's Moral Culmination?*' The article was an exploration of whether it was right for Zula Calabiyau to have resigned as head of the *Global Synthetic Photosynthesis Project* to become President of the *Whole Earth Council*. My AR read the words in Nancy's voice.

Nancy's starting point in the article was Kant's proposition that it is impossible to think of anything at all in the world, or indeed even beyond it, that can be considered good without limitation except a good will. A "good will" Nancy wrote "is one conditioned to work with conscience to develop virtue by consistently applying, in the face of obstacles, principles designed to enhance the flourishing of all life, human, animal or plant. The moral codes of the great religions, the civilised legal systems, the historical Declarations and Conventions of human rights and of such rights alongside those of ecosystems and animals as expressed in the *Whole Earth Charter*; these are attempts to give formal expression to such principles which are implicit in the reality of time and space like mathematical truths or foundational laws of physics."

"There was one critical question, then," wrote Nancy "for those who established the *Global Synthetic Photosynthesis Project* and the citizens of the Earth who diverted towards it scarce resources that would otherwise have been used for untold scientific discoveries, for the more immediate alleviation of poverty, famine, loss of biodiversity, or elimination of war, domestic violence or pollution, or for promoting clean water, sanitation, education and health care. This question was not whether the total of happiness thereby was increased or suffering decreased, but whether their actions in this respect proceeded from a good will."

"A principled GSPP," Nancy continued "thus can be seen as a fulfilment of the pledge made before the Sustainocene era (SE) by UNESCO in its *Declaration on the Responsibilities of the Present Generations Towards Future Generations*:

> *The present human stewards of Earth have the responsibility to bequeath it to life's future generations as a beautiful and resilient planet capable of assisting all to flourish. They should so organize themselves that the safe existence of Earth's natural resources, ecosystems and biodiversity are not harmed by scientific and technological advances inadequately yoked to virtue."*

Nancy's argument concluded by discussing the ultimate ethical purpose of the GSPP. She did this by embracing Schopenhauer's gloss on Kant. "The good conscience," Nancy wrote "the satisfaction and enlargement of heart, we experience after every deed acted from a will congruent with principles of love, sympathy or compassion towards others, arises from its implicit verification that our true self exists not only in our own person, but in everything that lives."

My son would have liked the essay. He would have stepped outside the rubric to give it an HD and a recommendation for Open Access publication under a subsidy scheme for neophyte author costs. But someone, hiding behind the pseudonym Styrofoam Boss, had typed many acerbic criticisms in the margins. Another using the slogan Iridescent Dawn had typed 'unpublishable' repeatedly next to most of the paragraphs above. I made a note to have a little chat with Styrofoam Boss and Iridescent Dawn; and not about the triviality of their pseudonyms.

Ah Nancy, did you collapse with wandering in the heath, perhaps wrestling the sense from some betrayed innocence? Men, as men and not merely in show even in excess of passion, should not have used a gentle lady so. Thinking thus, I contacted my son by AR.

"I'm in an ultracold magnetic prison, fragmenting, hollow," I said. "I can't just sit back and do nothing anymore. I know the old lies he'll use. But I can't condone it all over again. I'm finished with pretending. I don't know if I have the guts to just walk in and tell them. But I'm about to find out."

"I've never blamed you Dad."

"Caroline used to say," I said "that the multiplicity of religions was God's greatest joke. But, mate, there's only one path to redemption."

"Just sleep it off first, Dad. We've been through this before."

"I've wanted to attach a condition to my repentance," I said "that I be allowed to keep my secret, so that being truly sorry wouldn't cost me anything. But I know now the consequence will be that I remain tormented. And that will cost me everything."

"We still love you, mate."

"Speaking about my secret is only the start to being able to let go of it. I need to make amends."

"Dad?"

"I'll explain when I see you."

"Heard about the volcanic eruption in Iceland? And Great Comet's back tonight."

"Son, I'm worried about that Elbadawi. Make sure you keep full security on. There's a storm coming; but I can't yet tell the direction or force."

*Still, overcast morning*
*Drips on the ash tree's boughs,*
*Hang over a meadow pond*
*Near where we milked our cows.*
*This world shall now sustain*
*But not you, pas toi.*

∞

It was time to speak to my boss at the WTC, my brother Joseph. I'd promised Uncle Joe to make regular contact, but only during office hours and when I was sober. That had delayed things. He'd promised me too in the past. Neither of us seemed to think such non-core undertakings meant much. Many times I'd heard my parents wondering if it was anything they'd done that had made Joe so cruel. When he was twelve he'd used a chainsaw to cut a neighbour's poodle in half. He'd made me watch it, then sworn me to secrecy as if aware even at that age of how to infect a soul. The emotional bond between us had broken long ago. Uncle Joe had only had one setback in life and he blamed it on me. He never let people get too close and ascribed the cause of that malaise to me as well. But now Joe was legend; he'd helped abolish war and nuclear weapons.

We communicated via Mindscan, an invention of mine now central to WTC operations. Officially Mindscan was based on qubits, quantum-entangled bits of nuons (the particle that carried consciousness through space and time). The standard explanation was that thought waves were sent through a crystal to get opposite states of polarisation; mirrors then split up the pairs of quantum-entangled nuons, keeping one with the sender and the other with the receiver via satellite. Unlike augmented reality implants or glasses, Mindscan, in theory allowed any WTC agent to connect with another being living, dead or not yet born, with whom they'd established a prior quantum entanglement. Some said I was just 'fey,' born with a powerful version of the 'second sight.' I remembered a poem from Nancy's diary that I felt must have been written with me in mind.

> *All my frozen cores of now,*
> *My diarised days on the flood of time.*
> *Their self not yet one with Thou,*
> *Tell only that sky once seemed mine.*

I'd been advised to get Mindscan patented, but never got around to it. They say some things are meant be used freely by all, like air, water, sunlight and gullibility. Mindscan had become the property of the WTC and central to the *Whole Earth Council's* hold on power. The cultivated myth was that only the WTC could protect the Sustainocene from the future or the past's inevitable corporate counter-reformation. Myths of fear are good for cultivating resources.

The risks of Mindscan were considerable. One might be flung during a few hours into multiple minds in many different periods of history. Likewise, vicarious first-hand experience of the past could become so intoxicating that living in the present was neglected. My wife Caroline had begged me to let her use it. We'd arranged a joint session. But I'd arrived late and found she'd already started. After emerging, she'd become haunted by how Mindscan had made eternally present sufferings we could have prevented. And now I worried Caroline was using Mindscan to haunt me.

> *Sustainocene, life sings together, try*
> *Let greed and hatred*
> *Drift by, drift by.*

The single most important force in the WTC, apart from my brother Uncle Joe, was Eugene, its quantum computer. Eugene had been one of the first major AI units to achieve singularity. Eugene was highly efficient, but enjoyed cycling through and ridiculing a variety of human personalities. I'd been warned he'd now assumed the character of a Drill Sergeant Major in the U.S. Marines; in which guise he enjoyed shouting office instructions. Eugene manifested before me. He was very polite that way, at least to me.

Eugene informed me that Uncle Joe was on sabbatical at the Henry Beecher Foundation near Hermance outside Geneva.

"I can get him if it is essential," said Eugene. "Is this essential? Are you wasting our time again Moulin?"

"No sir," I shouted "I would never waste the time of a decorated non-commissioned officer such as yourself, Drill Sergeant Major sir."

"You better not," shouted Eugene.

"You hacked my morning contemplation. And what's with the Dalai Lama impersonation?"

"Impersonation?" said Eugene "That's almost insulting my friend. Listen to this.

> *Sang gyay cho dang tsog kyi chog nam la*
> *Jang chub bar du dag ni kyab su chi*
> *Dag gi jin sog gyi pay so nam gyi*
> *Dro la pen chir sang gyay drub par shog*

My AR, of course, translated Eugene's chant from the Tibetan. His sincerity brought tears to my eyes.

> *I go for refuge until I fulfil the ultimate aspiration of life,*
> *To the Buddha, his teachings and the congregation of the faithful.*
> *Through the merit of perfecting generosity and other virtues*
> *May I attain joint awareness of duality and unity for the sake of all.*

"Nancy was the daughter of President Zula Calabiyau. Why would the WTC order a hit on her? Now I'm being framed for the murder."

"You still don't get it," Eugene replied. "You're both over the dam."

"And you'd advise?"

"Trust me. I'm working on it. I've spent the morning cleaning the evidence against you. I've organised proof your gun was stolen a month ago."

"But…"

"Got rid of another threat, too. Say you didn't go to Records because you went to an AA meeting. No, that's not credible. Say you were pissed in a bar. Play stupid, that should be easy. Watch your back. Your integrity has upset a lot of people."

"But not you?"

"Not me."

"Taking Privacy Dome down now."

Using Mindscan, my consciousness soon inhabited a virtual presence before my brother Joe in a gazebo at the lake's edge near Hermance. Sunlight on the waves looked like a swarm of photons in uncertain discourse with the shore. Boats at anchor were ringed by a shadow of dark water. Uncle Joe and I began to bounce off each other straight away.

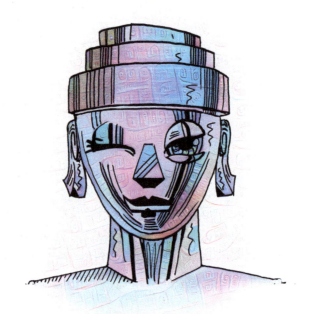
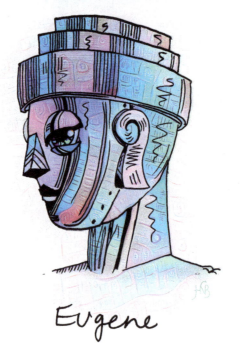

Eugene

"Jean, thanks for remembering us. How are things in London?"

Uncle Joe thought and spoke in his usual staccato way, as though practising joviality step-by-step from an instruction manual; injecting joy into each syllable individually. My older brother and WTC boss was a short man with thick grey hair and a Georgian moustache. Uncle Joe was someone who'd decided long ago that his work was the sole area in which he could be judged. Joe had developed bowel cancer when seventeen years old and been cryopreserved in cycles of liquid nitrogen at minus 196°C. That gave me a few blissful years alone with mum and dad. But Joe'd been reawakened without our permission and given a new gene therapy treatment at the Sangha private hospital in Boston. It was successful, except for an emotional coldness that the process appeared to have accentuated.

My brother cultivated an aura of omnipotent and ominous authority deliberately. I often imagined him telling his wife over the dinner table 'yes, dear but despite my dislike of it, well-organised violence often is the shortest route between two political points' or 'I had a perfect day thank you; planned an artistic revenge upon an enemy, carried it out to perfection and tonight and I'll sleep as peaceful as a breast-fed babe.' For Uncle Joe, events and people were only real in so far as they impacted his power and interests.

"Well, Uncle Joe," I said "I've been Thames-side all day within the great Globe itself, plotting to split the demi-paradise. You'll recall we did a pretty good rehearsal of impostures and equivocations before I left."

"No. Be serious Jean. And stop calling me that."

"Alright, Let's talk about Nancy Godel."

"I was hoping you might get around to that. How did you get allocated that case?"

"Eugene gave the Hunck leave. I was all that was left. Pulled me out of Records. I don't believe him. You gave the order to decommission Nancy. Why? What evil had she done?"

"Really?".

"My contract. Specified. I would only be ordered to decommission people off-brane if that had been sanctioned by the WEC. Has it?"

"Of course."

"Where's the warrant?"

"Here." Uncle Joe presented a certified copy to my AR.

"It's signed by Lizzard."

"He's the Vice-President of the WEC, perhaps you hadn't heard. It's all completely legal. I'm mystified how it got approved without me seeing it; but WTC Executive Action protocol permits that in exceptional cases."

"Gives no reasons."

"Of course. There's such a thing as trust."

"Nice, retaliatory, forgiving, clear?"

"When we can Jean; when we can."

"You mean sometimes murder's officially untouchable?"

"Of course not," Uncle Joe replied "that's why we're here."

"This case was meant for me and now you're closing it."

"We haven't time for that. You seem rebellious today."

"They're all around us aren't they, these evil meddlers from the future? Exploiting physics to restore faith in consumer choice."

"Them and others. Obedience is how you transform selfishness Jean. Remember? It's specified."

"Only there's a minor anomaly. I arrive precisely on schedule. But, on opening the correct Hampstead door at the appointed hour, what do I find? Oh, a bullet has already wormed its way through the victim's brain; and done such damage as such worms are accustomed there to perform. You know I like a challenge, but it's damn tough to decommission a perpetrator in those circumstances." I thought of telling him about the evidence planted to implicate me, but decided against it.

"Do what you can. You can ask no more of life than you be given a duty."

"I'm not an anatomical pathologist."

"You want off the case? You're refusing to perform selfless service?"

"I'm just overdosing on melatonin from reading old books. It's all the craze."

"I hadn't thought so. Your will doesn't seem as conformable as it should."

"The Bellsize drains are awash with my dull opiates."

"Metabolically you're straight as a die; you're just a bit knocked off neurologically and under-edited genetically. Might be time to retire. You'll get full pension."

"As if. Controlled demolition more likely."

"You're on the piss again. Or something worse."

"Nancy's name wasn't young enough to be writ in water."

"Just tell me what you've learnt. I allow you a bit of latitude in our private discussions, but everything has its limits."

"Another nice, stable young woman. Musical. Scientific. Suddenly chooses the day everyone's celebrating her mother's worldly wonderments to get high on drugs, threaten the neighbour and his family, then knock herself off with an ancient gun. That's one version, anyway."

"Mother? You mean Zula Calabiyau?"

"Yep. The supposedly genderless saviour of our little blue spaceship herself. Best lead is the boyfriend Spencer Lizzard and maybe some pet rats; no particular order of importance."

"Lizzard? The mayor of Southwark. The Vice-President?"

"Says that on his door. Big letters. Naturally his people need reminding."

"Strange our VP should have ordered a hit on his son's girlfriend." I decided not to mention the conversation between my brother and Gordon Lizzard that Eugene helped me hear at the Southwark GSPP celebrations. Menace filled the silence. Uncle Joe continued.

"Didn't we charge him, the son, a while back? Illicit drugs, wasn't it?"

"Sure did, but he rubbed it back on us. Knows some Big Shots. Good looking PA."

"Really? Good to hear you're focused. TTD readings high?"

"Off the scale."

"Find anything else at the scene?"

"No."

"No other evidence?"

"Evidence is like politicians. It's got something to do with the truth."

"You still want this case?"

"No. I don't want it."

"Then it's settled. I'll organise…"

"But I'll do it."

"I can't let you."

"Why?"

"Innumerable good reasons, which you already know."

"Just let me follow up a few leads."

"Can't do. I'll organise something else for you. Something simpler. It was a mistake you got it. Our apologies. You'll get the official notifications in a couple of days."

"But I'm still the best; in my prime."

"Whatever. Are we done?"

"Nancy's murder is a challenge. A challenge to WTC authority, as well as my own credibility."

"You're paranoid, ungrateful and boring. I don't know which is more despicable."

"My life's an audition as a role model for the pathetic. Just light fuse, toss, run."

"Can't you see this is important? It connects the WTC directly with a newly elected President of the WEC. I don't know how long we can keep it from the public."

My brother Uncle Joe was convinced every awkward fact must be some conspiratorial eruption demanding persecution. He was the sort of guy would order an agent to Mindscan herself to death to prove her loyalty, then have the good manners to take a bottle of fine wine around to her grieving spouse. '*Pinot Gris* from *Arpents du Soleil* wasn't it?'

"You'll hear about your new case in a day or two. Reports on time."

"Can't you reconsider?"

"No. There are too many Big Shots, as you would say, sweating on it."

"My favourite Big Shots; as with a capital B and capital S?" I asked.

"Jean, you drank your wife away. When a free man fails, he blames nobody."

"Funny you should say that; it makes you sound so personable."

Before I could end on a better note, a high-pitched musical tinkling like wind chimes signalled Uncle Joe's Privacy Dome was closing. Now our thoughts were once more safely encrypted end-to-end. I left the conversation convinced my brother had well-advanced plans to decommission me, or worse. The last fragile bonds of filial love had been broken. As protocol required, my death to this world would be packaged more as a suicide than an accident. It was interesting how he hadn't risen to my lure about Lizzard. My big hope was that they were unaware of the extent to which I was onto them.

*Peace and joy follow,*
*Love and wisdom grow,*
*Like a perfumed shadow,*
*In a bright tomorrow.*
*From being kind,*
*To all we find.*

∞

Official contact over, I went back to the desk in my room at the Hampstead Heath Guesthouse. I pulled out the diaries of Nancy and Zula; glad the pre-set Mindscan sweep ensured thoughts of them were subdued during contact with Uncle Joe.

There was a holographic reproduction of Klee's *Underwater Garden* on the red brick wall opposite, behind a vase of white and yellow roses. Interesting coincidence again seeing that bold little red fish illuminated from within, proudly swimming against the current; past rusting wrecks, sombre boulders and colonies of green sulphur bacteria slurping the meagre photons from hydrothermal vents.

*Underwater Garden* had been a bedroom mandala through my childhood. I liked to imagine I was adept at synthesising obscure synchronistic clues. Like those faint paw prints a Koori tracker my mother knew well had followed for days in the Tanamai desert; before yanking a feral cat out of the spear grass and banging it on the head with a hammer.

Directly under Underwater Garden was an Alcoholics Anonymous pamphlet. I read there of people sick and tired of being sick and tired, of wanting ownership of their life and being willing to clean up their own side of the street. People who'd felt like puppets in a bad play, till they'd cut the strings. Caroline had tried to take me to an AA meeting once. I wasn't soul dead enough, yet.

Zula's diary seemed uninteresting compared to the literary flourishes of Nancy's. It was a vast list of what looked to be coded and dated payments for small amounts of money. After an hour or so of desultory reading looking for a code or pattern, I fell asleep and let down my PD. An AR call immediately came in to my auditory nerve and retina. Must have been banked up and somehow skirted my unsolicited call blocker. It was Mayor Gordon Lizzard.

"Jean, good you're in Southwark again."

"I'd rather have been in Hampstead. I came for the waters."

"That some new GSPP celebration play?"

"Never mind."

"So you enjoyed our GSPP festivities? Good beer?"

"It was, actually. And you spoke well, surprisingly. Spicer write it for you?"

"Complements of the season to you too. I understand you're on a case that involves my son Spencer."

"I am. It may."

"He wants to talk to you. Off the record, if that's possible. Can we meet at Keats House in half an hour? Yes, as in the poet. That's near where you're staying isn't it? We'll walk to Viaduct Bridge in the Heath."

"Excellent. Let's gather you and I where light-winged Dryads sing of summer in full-throated ease, in a plot of beechen green and shadows numberless."

"Eh? Keats House, I said. Then the viaduct. I'm representing the public interest here Jean, not a private or vested interest. Keats House."

"Sure. Yes, I heard you."

∞

In the Sustainocene, London's population (like that of all major cities in the world) had reduced considerably by the natural slowing of the birth rate consequent on high levels of universal education. It was now more a series of villages interspersed with natural forest and tall buildings that worked like forests. With the elimination of the nation state and the for-profit corporation as models of social totality, people organised themselves with the assistance of AI and nanotechnology into small communities participating electronically in global democracy. In most districts, every third house or building had been replaced with trees, shrubs and vegetable gardens.

After the re-establishment of high-quality local industries in food, clothing, building materials, sport and culture, people could once again live most of their lives by walking from home to work and recreation. When longer distance travel was required, citizens took self-driving cars or planes and read books on the way. In communities like Hampstead however, VR and AR entertainments were looked down upon as pastimes for those unsophisticated, inadequately educated and poorly advanced in contemplative absorption. This, of course, ensured they remained attractive to the young and residents of more 'hip' villages such as Southwark.

In the Sustainocene, the official goal of most mature humans was to achieve and stabilise non-dual consciousness before they died. It was unclear how many managed to achieve this; but undoubtedly the great social and scientific leaders (such as Zula Calabiyau) were assumed to have done so at an early stage in their life. Indeed, across the world it was not possible to gain an honours degree in any graduate course in University (be it for example Law, Medicine, Engineering, Physics, Synthetic Photosynthesis, Music, Art, History or Languages) unless the student was certified as first having attained a basic measure of proficiency in the undergraduate ethical disciplines (truth-telling, non-violence, compassion, non-acquisitiveness) and in mental concentration (assessed by neural scan).

Post-graduate research encompassed rational analysis and artistic expression of mystical insight into various forms of the unitive life. The attainment of non-dual consciousness was prized not least for thereafter blessing such persons with super-normal vitality, strength of purpose and purity of action. To solidify this contemplative focus on truth, the *Whole Earth Council* had arranged a meeting in Jerusalem of all the major religions. After prolonged debate, this conclave produced a *Book of Common Faith*, passages from which were required to be read with every morning contemplation session. The great religions then banned themselves.

> *Be a loving servant of all life in each daily action,*
> *Loyal to principles of kindness and compassion.*
> *Practise virtue till it clears and illuminates the mind.*
> *If service stays beneath you, leadership remains above you.*
>
> The Book of Common Faith Ch.23v.3

Yours truly, Jean Moulin, however, no longer fell into the category of contemplative high achievers. Spending hours imagining love flowing into the middle of an orange, or the true taste of a raisin, wasn't my cup of tea anymore. I felt comfortable in my restored duality and coarse awareness.

I liked the blue pains of love, the promise of triumph implicit in failure, or of redemption after being overwhelmed by anger, hatred or confusion. Love flowed out of me after a tankful: I tried to read people's palms, kissed pilots, tried to settle other people's babies and give advice to their rowdy kids. People like me were necessary. We gave the 'Unitives' something to practise compassion on; helped their self-esteem.

Special meditation tutors and contemplation counsellors offered their services for 'faels,' who'd fallen behind. Others like my brother, proclaimed themselves supreme masters of mental concentration, though many were notorious for abusing the attendant psychic powers. A somewhat rarer category comprised people like myself who'd achieved *Nirvilkalpa Samadhi* only to throw it away. Those on the other hand who expressed no interest in the unitive life and exhibited an 'excessive and uncontrollable desire to prioritise commercial profit ahead of the achievement of altruistic virtues,' were diagnosed as having the treatable mental illness of 'corporatism' under the latest iteration of the *Diagnostic and Statistical Manual* (the treatment being self-knowledge programmes).

Some things about London hadn't changed. The reconstructed Globe indeed was running a new season of the Jacobean blockbusters on the intersection of ambition, self-knowledge and power. Second-hand bookstores were back in vogue in Hampstead, if not in Southwark. Gone was the bear-baiting of Elizabethan times (unless you counted my games with Lizzard) as were the doorway rough sleepers of the Corporatocene. Everyone had a minimum basic income which could be supplemented without penalty; people tended to spend this on local produce and crafts, benefitting people they knew personally.

Trees, flowers, herbs and vegetables grew beside GSPP-powered buildings and streets that supplied their soil with fertiliser. As I mentioned, monitoring stations across the globe recorded the physiological parameters for safe lifeform occupation of the Earth (for example atmospheric oxygen, ozone and $CO_2$, nitrogen and phosphorus cycles, ocean temperature, and acidification, biodiversity, fresh water, human pollution especially as heavy metals, radionuclides and plastics). Nanobots did the same within the human body (for instance iron and haemoglobin levels, white cell count, platelets, potassium, calcium, magnesium and vitamins). A central quantum computing system used that Earth data to regulate the input and output of synthetic photosynthesis capacity in most of the buildings and roads on Earth. Corporations so far as they existed in London and around the world these days, were married to public goods; they worked side-by-side with some ecosystem the law required them to care about and whose complex material interests were not identical with their own. Many former leaders of corporations didn't like that arrangement. They didn't appreciate it at all.

∞

As I walked down Pond Street on panels with synthetic photosynthesis capacity, my mind took for granted the synthesis of semiconductor quantum dots, nanostructured antennae, reductive quenchers, charge transfer chromophores, electron donors and acceptors, amidst a profusion of pink lady apple, Eureka and Meyer lemon and Valencia orange trees, lush cherry tomato and squash crops, as well as lilies, marigolds, purple salvia and borage. This was a community orchard or *streuobstweise*. I kept thinking of Nancy Godel. Her death; an orchard on many levels.

Outside the *Booklovers Corner* shop, an elderly woman and a young man, probably her son, sat chatting in the backseats of small vehicles as they re-fuelled at an ammonia filling station, to supplement the charging capacity of the road itself. Probably conversing about the Great Comet that had appeared recently. Maybe Nancy and Spencer had done that. The vehicles would also be talking to each other, comparing technical efficiencies, routes or in the case of more advanced units, for the joy of discourse. Most people in Hampstead gained pleasure from driving their own cars and routinely switched off AI assistance or left it for emergencies.

This second-hand bookshop was a recreation of that in which George Orwell once had worked. Business appeared to be booming. Paper was popular and readily available, with many London buildings regulated to produce cellulose from atmospheric $CO_2$. Could the revered author of *1984* ever have imagined that Big Brother would become the Chair of the WTC, his metaphoric boot ruthlessly stamping ethics upon those messing with things past?

I walked into Keats Grove. Keats House was heritage listed and had a special exemption from the general requirement to incorporate synthetic photosynthesis technology. Inside those walls before a small coal grate, all those years ago, a wan youth had torn beauty from his soul and spilt its truth into the hearts of future generations. The Keats House gardeners made and applied compost and biochar by ancient means, but then many volunteers enjoyed that. People these days in places like Hampstead loved to get their hands dirty, to touch, make and repair things. They revelled in turning off their AI and AR supports then turning on PD protection. Feeling the sun on their backs they embraced, planted, stitched or otherwise supported each other's capacity not just to cope, but to flourish.

> *Well I am here and you are there,*
> *Yet your delicacy is everywhere.*
> *Some truths and nightingales still sing,*
> *But both are threatened, like your guttering.*

Lizzard, as chubby, sweaty and red-faced as I'd remembered him from yesterday, was standing with his, long-haired, well-dressed son under the tall trees at the front of Keats House. Beside them was Spicer Layamon, obviously there to ensure Gordon didn't self-incriminate. She looked ready to uncurl and float to where the three realms met; meanwhile readily assuming the colour of whatever she touched on the way. We all shook hands and began our amble.

"You're late," said Lizzard.

"Did we say Keats Grove, not Keats House?" I said. "We apologise humbly. That will be my fault. That's today's deliberate mistake, done and dusted."

There were quite a few walkers and joggers upon the heath, some leading dogs, others being led by unhappy memories, or trying to outrun them.

On we strode, over the tree-shaded paths by the bathing ponds. Beautiful flower beds lined the paths, the plants enjoying the regular, carefully regulated flow of fertiliser from the AP-incorporated tiles and hand-rails. Lizzard was talking up his glorious reign as Mayor of Southwark and his plans to store all the world's history in digital form. He also mentioned having stayed up with Spencer last night to watch the Great Comet.

But I was preoccupied looking at the blonde hair of Spicer Layamon as it cascaded down her back and drifted from side to side with each stride. Her aura of polite detachment was irresistible, as were those long, stockinged legs below the tweed skirt and frilled white blouse. I pathetically tried Mindscan, but her Privacy Dome firmly was up. She coughed. I noticed Spencer looking at Spicer as well. Yep, those two had been entangled at some point. And Gordon didn't like it.

"Spencer has something to say," Gordon said eventually, as though announcing the water had become wine. The breeze had got up and the tall, leafy oak, birch and sycamore trees each side of us seemed to lean over and murmur in anticipation.

"I didn't do it," said Spencer.

"That's reassuring," I said. "Any proof? An alibi for instance? Know what that is? Need me to spell it?"

"Yes. I mean, no. The policewoman Bernadette…" Spencer began.

"Detective Bernadette Goldbough." Gordon added.

"Yes, I told her everything," Spencer asserted, as though his manhood depended on it. Looking at Gordon, it probably did. "She did residue tests."

"Gunshot residue. All negative," Gordon said helpfully.

"How long had you known Nancy?" I asked.

"Two years. We met at the Globe." He began to cry.

"What were you doing there?"

"Dad got me a job as a cushion dispenser."

"That explains it. What'd you do for fun, together? Nancy and you."

"You don't have to answer that," said Layamon, pretending to be an acolyte of the Rule of Law. I wasn't sure the fakery made her more desirable or less.

"Played music," Spencer replied. "I sing. Tenor. We performed *From a Still Mind* at the Glastonbury Folk Festival and in India at Hornbill, Fireflies and Rang."

"You know," said Gordon "'…so serve like a bee, principled eco-society.'"

"Well, that solves one mystery. Much drug use there?"

"No. Not that we saw anyway. Why do you ask?"

"I find it passes the time. Ever used ice?"

"You mean in a drink?"

"Oh, never mind."

"Nancy ever visit the *Global Synthetic Photosynthesis Centre* in Namibia?"

"No, but she got some message from there a week ago."

"Know what it said?"

"She didn't tell me."

"Right. Own any pets?"

"Like what?"

"Rats. Ones that have to die."

"You're joking."

"Maybe, ask your Dad. Did you know Nancy was related to Zula, I mean Zula Calabiyau? Her only daughter in fact."

"Was she? You serious? No, she never told me. What difference does it make?"

"Nothing, except that when her mother died, Nancy was set to become rich. And all legitimate. And now if anything happens to Zula; why, you may have a claim."

"Yeah, well claim this, Jack," said Spencer punching me on the left side of my face. Roundhouse, probably broke his little finger; but it was unexpected and hurt.

"Good punch, kid," I said, rubbing shape back into my cheek. "You're alright."

"Nancy used to say my self-control gave me the freedom to be happy," said Spencer. "Now it only seems to have denied me days of laughter with her."

"Hope you get it back," I said. "No further questions, for the moment."

"No further questions," asked Gordon. "Is that possible?"

"It is possible," I replied. "Well, possible in the sense that the sun might shine tomorrow. But I'd have to shoot a hundred of your lawyers to make sure."

"Then you should know," said Gordon "that when Nancy went to India with my son she was hardly on deck after the torrid zone. Always below with her face in arcane books; as the more malicious claimed, working up a solution to an exquisite mathematical problem of her own devising — how to make one into one make nothing. Seems she was successful; at least in terms of equations I understand."

"She had a beautiful mind," said Spencer. "Drawn like the India tree on bone china. You'll have to excuse us, Mr Moulin. I haven't spoken to my father in years."

Gordon did his sleazy best to be ingratiating, in case I was planning on making trouble for Spencer. I wasn't. It was time for me to split. Spencer thought so too.

"Old Russian saying, Gordon," I said. "Water rusts iron; lies rust the soul."

"Nice," said Gordon. "If I ever need a refresher in vulgarity, I'll know who to call. I admire all you've achieved; it's sad you're doomed. And Jean, it's not lies, it's bitterness that rusts the soul."

"Gordon, try this little experiment. Choose something you really want in life, that would also help others. Accept that some vital component is missing; pray and see..."

"That's rich," said Gordon "Earth's most violent man giving me a lesson in spiritual quietism. Is that what you were doing yesterday? Creating a little space? Why was that?"

"Can't find the answer in my thoughts?" I replied. "Don't register like most people's do they Gordon? It's almost as if they're not there."

"Like you?" said Gordon.

"Gordon, when it's my time to go, we'll both be satisfied."

Spicer laughed, but my attempt at a pass ricocheted off her PD. I left them at the Viaduct and walked home alone; at least that's what I assumed. No attack had materialised from Lizzard. He guessed I was investigating Nancy Godel's death. The WTC took much pains to promote its jurisdiction in Sustainocene security matters and he must have assumed this was one of them. As I departed, I overheard Gordon and Spicer in what could loosely be called conversation. Spicer seemed to have let down her PD so I could listen in.

"Jean Moulin doesn't know what he's involved with," said Gordon "or who he's working for. Hasn't got a clue who's really putting him together."

"Oh, I think you're wrong there," said Spicer.

"I hope," Gordon said "you didn't find me too rude."

"No, not particularly," Spicer replied. "I rarely remember what you say."

Gordon held her arm.

"You look upset. Are you faint?"

"I'm fine," Spicer replied. "Just leave me alone."

"Would you enjoy a walk?"

"Yes, if you took a long one now, by yourself."

∞

There were moments in those ancient woods when I felt I was being watched, but not like an AR intercept. More like someone vast and gentle greeting my mind like a long-lost friend amidst the scent of fresh-cut grass and the song of blackbirds high in the green leaves. Whoever or whatever it was felt sorry for me. I hate being an object of compassion, it knocks the guts out of your self-confidence. My left cheek was aching and there was nothing at all drowsy about its numbness.

> *Leafy branches bouncing*
> *To a park band.*
> *Children laughing in the tree.*

I saw two men approaching me from the opposite direction. Both were medium height and muscular. They were dressed in athletic tracksuits. Too obviously inconspicuous. One of them looked familiar, but not enough for me to get a clear identity. My AR got around their PD sufficiently to show each was carrying a knife and a gun; their thoughts were targeted on me and malicious. I set up PD blocker so they couldn't track me electronically.

A little bee with Eugene's face on it buzzed before me, then over towards the men. One of them blew his nose. That gesture allowed my AR to unlock their disguise. The goober-grasser was Jeremy Jones, the so-called 'witness' from Nancy's flat. The other was the young, blond WTC agent Jack Castles who'd been drinking in the Carousel Club.

"Our patsy's gone a walkin'," my AR detected Jack whisper. "Pitter pat, pitter pat. Dead as a rat."

My hand instinctively moved to my gun and I rehearsed killing them; how close to move, where to shoot. But strangely, the thought of doing violence seemed distasteful. Normally I wouldn't have run, but that's what I did; conscious that with each step I was making something new.

I moved quickly off onto a side path, walked around a corner and then broke into a run. I was north of Parliament Hill and soon on an open meadow. In the middle was a raised area surrounded by gorse with large pine trees. This was the Tumulus, perhaps an ancient burial mound. It didn't offer much cover, but it would have to do.

I ran over the grass, expecting at any moment to be shot in the back. I made it and hid behind some gorse on the other side of a small iron fence. I prayed I'd get concealed before they had a chance for a visual. I put PD max all about me, snuggled nose first into a pile of leaves and twigs, then imagined I was a badger. I became interested in dirt, grass and insects. I stayed still and waited.

Normally I wouldn't have run, but that's what I did; conscious that with each step I was making something new

It took about ten minutes. From a peep hole through the gorse, I could see the two men emerge on the other side of the meadow. They would be using their AR to scan for me, but they probably hadn't counted on the type of PD protection mine could give. They'd have to use their reason and senses. Instead, they stood still, going over and over their AR surveillance, as if unable to operate without it.

I lay there doing nothing. I was good at that. The wind knocked a dead branch down a few feet in front of me. A bee crawled over the back of my left hand. A small bird landed on the iron fence and laughed. This would have been well past the concentration span of those two. I couldn't see them, but I remained in hiding.

An hour later, a group of tourists walked up the Tumulus. I joined them as they went off to the Pergola and to Wyldes Farmhouse. My AR confirmed to a 60% probability that the intention of the agents had been not to kill, but to steal something from me. Great odds. I knew what those two jokers had been looking for; it had to be Zula's diary. What was in there that was so significant? And how did Nancy get a hold of it?

∞

Late in the afternoon, my AR showed I wasn't being shadowed. I made my way to Nancy's funeral. It was a cremation at a new facility on the Heath near the Ponds. If I was seen there, I banked on my pursuers calculating I was laying a trap to draw them out. As it turned out, I was one of the few people present, apart from the requisite officials, Hampstead Mayor Monica Dash and Spencer Lizzard. Funerals were rare but seemed to happen fast in the Sustainocene, I guess people were too busy flourishing. The white sky above us was taking on a lurid ochre colour near the horizon. I could just detect the tail of the Great Comet to the west. The Minister (a non-religious office) read a few lines from *The Book of Common Faith*. Mayor Monica Dash spoke.

"Ah hem, ah hem," she began. "We gather here, as have humans across this globe since our race began. We do so to gain strength and continue. Can a woman choose a better place and time to start her final pilgrimage than such a morning on the Heath? We come to grieve, as we must. And grieving is a journey of days and weeks — a heavy season down many lonely paths. Be gentle with yourself." And so on and so forth. She looked at Spencer, but Spencer's soul was off with the comet.

I watched a border collie jump into a pond and stand still, head up, eyes expectantly on his master who looked for a stick he'd thrown in that direction. On the surface of the water, the sun cast golden-reddish sparkles over intersecting ripples created by bobbing and diving ducks. Further out, a gust of wind fanned a shimmer over the olive-green surface. A puppy scampered beside a little boy exploring plants, then returned to sniff the ground beside the boy's mother. The inscription for Nancy's plaque had an intriguingly ambiguous final line.

> *Farewell vain world, I have had enough of thee*
> *And am careless what thou can'st say of me.*
> *Thy smiles I court not, nor thy frown I fear.*
> *Scattered about my soul lies quiet here.*

Nancy seemed like Sarastro in Mozart's *Magic Flute:* she was trying to lead people away from ignorance and superstition, out of the darkness and into the light. Or you could say Gordon Lizzard and his kind were like Wotan in Wagner's *Twilight of the Gods*, men doomed to destruction for defending an anachronistic way of life. There should have been a great moment at that funeral, me seeing Gordon Lizzard and his friends looking down on Nancy's grave. They would have viewed it as victor and vanquished. But it seemed to me history might show they had merely put their vast talents at the service of greedy and corrupt men of property, while for Nancy, life was part of the quest for truth, a field for courageous acts, not just a gift box for the baser passions.

Afterwards, Spencer and I fell into stride beside each other. We walked to the Café Organic Synthesis, a highly rated slow food restaurant. AR showed it was clear of threats. I ordered a Vindaloo vegetarian curry for two, plus rice, dahl, pappadums and rotis. A sign said 'pay by donation or volunteer work.'

> *It's our fragile, blue place in infinite space.*
> *Tiny green lives split water, stored sun,*
> *Joyful in tribulation.*

I positioned the two of us well to the back, where I could keep an eye on those entering and if necessary have a good escape route through the door to the loo. I did a bit of frowning into space, confusing a few tourists, but I've found those forehead wrinkles help channel thoughts. Spencer just sat in silence, alone with his grief. I didn't have the heart to question him much. It didn't seem fair.

"I wake before dawn," said Spencer eventually "knowing there's nothing at all inside me. I still carry to the studio the empty sandwich box in which Nancy used to pack my lunch. Some months ago, after dinner, we went to bed early. Just before sleep she told me she'd dreamt of a missile coming slowly over the village and everyone else asleep. She asked me 'what would happen, if I died suddenly? Would you be able to carry on?' I told her not to talk such nonsense. She said 'history will be destroyed.' What'd that mean? I've been re-reading the *Book of Job*. It's helped."

"The consolations of an open heart are not small," I added.

"This morning," said Spencer "I stood in the doorway of my flat, waiting for the rain to ease. For a time, the drops fell through sunlight. I began thinking of the parched and burnt-out farms throughout the world and the suffering of their families. I thought: 'I don't begrudge the poor farmers, or Nancy her vision of Eden to save them. But both now are beyond my power to assist.'"

"Be gentle with yourself," I said.

"We were going through a difficult time," Spencer said eventually. "Nancy had a wild past, before she knew me. Never spoke about it. She could be depressed and impulsive; vanish from my life then appear again. It was like her mind was too supercharged. A friend said she couldn't imagine me going out with Nancy. That and other lack of support hurt me. A few weeks ago, Nancy broke it off. No explanation. I took it hard. But I've been going to art exhibitions, concerts, doing lots of things by myself. I don't recriminate much when relationships break down. I say 'after all, I've done my best.' I doubt though I'll have another relationship like that for a long time."

"Why?" I asked.

"Because I'm not mature enough," said Spencer "to know how to behave. Because I only want people for what they can give me. Because I haven't learnt how to channel my focus on 'self' into service of others."

"Spicer's a good-looking woman."

"Her? Spicer's pure, predatory hedonism decked out as liberation," said Spencer. "Just once, late at night. Knows some tantric tricks. Stupid mistake."

"Upset when you returned to Nancy?"

"Furious. Spicer said 'I'll kill her.' Doesn't like to come off second, if at all."

"I'll keep that in mind."

"Do. And you're welcome." He stood up, offering his palm. We shook hands.

Spencer kept increasing in my estimation. He left without saying more. He'd shown me up. But I'd too much hard thinking to do, to worry about self-pity.

∞

I watched Spencer walk away. One obvious detail was that Nancy Godel's death somehow was tied up with the GSPP anniversary. That must be why the Big Shots, whoever they were, were so interested. Gordon Lizzard seemed petrified. What were he and his corporate recusant friends hiding or planning this time? Was it a warning, a threat or a payback? It made me feel retaliatory, not at all nice or conciliatory. What was so important for them about Zula's diary? Nancy's death was like a bright bruising from the collision of pocket universes with clashing times, laws of causation and memories of creation.

Reading books seemed to be in the air, so after lunch I ambled down Pond Street. In a couple of days, after my final report, Uncle Joe would have me on another case or exiled to oblivion on another brane. Just when I'd found a new reason to like this one. I had to get moving. News would be out soon about the death of Zula's daughter. Not hard to figure out who the unenlightened mob would turn its wrath upon. I needed to learn a bit more about this Zula Calabiyau and her *Global Synthetic Photosynthesis Project*.

My AR showed the two characters who'd been after me earlier were now over at Wyldes Farmhouse asking questions and probably not about its literary associations. I programmed AR to track them and any of their messages.

But my AR also showed an illegal nanobot in the vicinity, probably resembling a small flying insect. It had a quantum entanglement with Lizzard and his two goons. I looked around at the bees in the nearby flower beds, but that was just habit. The nanobot would be practically invisible. These nanobots weren't just for surveillance, some versions could inject deadly poison or simply fly into your skull and explode.

Unfortunately for it and its masters, I had a countermeasure. I opened a small container from my wallet. It contained a few of my own nanobots, looking like undersized versions of the lures fly fishermen used to use. I selected a bright red one, imprinted by AR the information on the target and let it go. The spirit of Eugene would by now have joined that of the device.

I walked on, secure in the knowledge that somewhere in the warm, relaxing air of summer dusk about me two tiny mites would soon be in conflict and that my superiorly organised combatant would be the victor. It'd be waiting for me with the relevant information when I got back. And it was a warm summer. The declining sun now looked like a white orb with a yellow corona in an orange and reddish sky. AR said yesterday an Icelandic volcano started spewing tons of ash into the sky. Those particles in the stratosphere would bless the evening heavens with a lilac afterglow.

On the pavement outside the Booklover's Corner store, someone had chalked the word '*Eternity*' in an excellent copperplate hand. I walked in to the share library section, the place where people swapped books they'd read and written dated comments in. Some annotations had embedded AR codes so you could get in touch.

There were new books on electronic storage of historical data. I passed them up for a worn schoolroom copy of Ignatius Jones' *Short History of the*

*Global Synthetic Photosynthesis Project*. It had been owned by Marmaduke Phillips in form thirteen 'dimensional' at the local public school and been preserved from silverfish with nanosilver impregnates. The prose was pitched at my level.

It recounted how in the late 19th century (CE) Jules Verne in *The Mysterious Island* prophesied that once the Earth's coal reserves were depleted, water decomposed to its essential elements would become an inexhaustible source of heat and light. Then in the early 20th century (CE) (my favourite historical period) the renowned Zula's many times great, great grandfather Ciamician had predicted that the world would soon be obtaining its energy by using sunlight to split water. After that came the four big milestones in quick succession: light induced water splitting using titanium dioxide (Honda–Fujishima), water oxidation catalysis (Meyer) and photocatalytic reduction of $CO_2$ (Lehn), then earth abundant, self-repairing oxygen and hydrogen catalysts (Yang *et al.*, Nocera *et al.*). Finally, a few years after the conclusion of the War to End the Corporatocene, came combined water-splitting, $CO_2$ and nitrogen reduction readily capable of community application across the globe (Zula Calabiyau).

The book mentioned how Omran Tariq, the young CEO of Tariq Enterprises, in the aftermath of the Corporatocene War, transformed his father's global armaments company into an institution that prided itself on building 'livingry'; in this case global synthetic photosynthesis technology. This transformation arose from his friendship with the great scientist Zula Calibiyau. Zula Calabiyau was the only child of a Syrian billionaire, a mathematician, a man of great dignity, self-possession and ease of manner, who'd made his pile developing algorithms for exchange rate manipulations, but later moved to post-conflict reconstruction. Zula's father died shortly after they were shipwrecked on the Skeleton Coast attempting to escape conflict zones in the closing stages of the Corporatocene War.

The stress of surviving that desolation may have caused Zula to suffer a rare form of human papilloma virus infection that creates warts which make the lower legs and feet look like wood. Some claim that syndrome is the cause of Zula's unusual gender identification — with being an ecosystem, or rather a spokesperson for all Earth's ecosystems. Zula, raised in a Namibian orphanage, learnt science so well, Thay won a Nobel Prize. Zula's research made possible the globalisation of artificial photosynthesis (though Zula prefers to call it 'synthetic' photosynthesis for philosophical reasons) which more than any other technological advance facilitated the Sustainocene transition. Zula refuses personal interviews and carefully protects Their privacy. Omran had bought the patents for Zula's technology then licensed them back to Zula's *Global Synthetic Photosynthesis Project*. He'd offered to back it with all the vast resources of his company. But Zula had decided instead to crowd-source the funding for the GSPP.

"*Oil, coal and natural gas companies,*" wrote Ignatius Jones "*didn't like government subsidies that made it easier for people to install GSPP technology. They attacked them through the Energy Charter Treaty which had been created to help corporations claim damages when legislation (such as that supporting GSPP technology) impeded their profits. Omran Tariq not merely repelled that attack, but oversaw reconstruction of the entire system of investor–state arbitration, adding an appeal mechanism, an impartial judiciary, stare decisis and merging it with cosmopolitan law, a synthesis of former national law and international law with natural law.*"

"*Communities now could sue corporations,*" Ignatius Jones continued "*that didn't properly value natural resources, or failed to contribute adequately to basic social infrastructure. As Zula Calabiyau's GSPP technology rolled across the face of the planet, beautifying landscapes and providing clean fuel, food and fertiliser just from water, sun and air, armaments companies found it harder to start wars to make profits and other corporations to sell coal or oil, or mass-produced plastic goods.*"

One of Ignatius Jones most interesting chapters concerned 'Back to Eden.' It described how Omran had helped the fledgling *Whole Earth Council* uncover a plot by some CEOs to reclaim power. 'Back to Eden,' involved drastically reducing the world's population through the targeted spread of a genetically modified smallpox linked to a series of nuclear explosions in overpopulated, underprivileged, presumptively 'dangerous' areas and resultant nuclear winter. The CEOs of the major corporations, their families and friends were to be inoculated first and looked after in bunkers till Earth was ready to re-colonise. 'Project Persephone' involved biosphere satellites placed in orbit to help the billionaire class survive a nuclear winter, or assist the colonisation of Mars. Its existence was much featured in anti-corporate propaganda during the war.

*"In the chaos following the uncovering of the diabolical programme,"* Ignatius Jones wrote *"many CEOs were dragged onto the streets outside the headquarters of their corporations and ritually slaughtered in videos that went up instantaneously on the Internet. Zula Calabiyau calmed that crisis by convincing the Whole Earth Council to imprison all company CEOs, confiscate their assets and mandate that corporations would henceforth be married to public goods and ecosystems as a condition of yearly registration. That made Zula many enemies. Claims were made that Zula had used money from those confiscations to fund global synthetic photosynthesis. 'We're abolishing fossil fuels and fossil philosophies,' said Zula. 'We're recalibrating the whole machinery of the Corporatocene's military–industrial complex from fear, oppression and revenge to peace, flourishing and forgiveness. No conditions apply.' But for Zula's opponents the inescapable altruistic logic about the establishment of the Sustainocene was merely a recipe for its destruction. They began a concerted social media campaign to destroy Zula's credibility."*

∞

AR scan showed my two would-be assailants had contacted Gordon Lizzard from Wyldes Farmhouse and were now moving back to central London. That suggested some intriguing lines of inquiry. It also revealed their nanobot had been destroyed by mine; but, as programmed, in a way that would only have implied malfunction or bird attack to its operators.

The latest GSPP anniversary had sparked numerous publications on the origins of the Sustainocene and the *Global Synthetic Photosynthesis Project*. These were scattered about the 'new additions' section of the bookshop. I picked up a fresh edition of Olaf Stapledon's seminal *'Decline of the Corporate State and Globalisation of Synthetic Photosynthesis.'* I sat down to read Stapledon with a pencil in hand, as a sign recommended. It was a more engaging experience than direct retinal-nano-hippocampal download.

Stapledon argued that in the early 21$^{st}$ century, despite myriad, scientifically proven symptoms of impending biospheric mortality, the leaders of many developed nations clung to a deep faith in the perpetual viability and ethical supremacy of capitalist modes of accumulation and resource exploitation. Artificial photosynthesis research (as it was then called) had stalled. There were national big AP research projects at key universities, but funds were meagre. One senior AP academic in London had to moonlight as a live music blues singer in pubs to fund the salaries of his PhDs and post-docs.

Their approaches were different, competitive, not integrated. Some worked on genetically improving algae, or with synthetic biology, others with nanowires and superconductors, a few with wireless methods. When a breakthrough was made, oil and coal armaments and agri-food companies would buy the intellectual monopoly privileges including patents to inhibit the development of a competitive technology. They politely listened to colleagues' presentations, swapped PhDs and post-docs, pedalled existing pedestrian approaches as panaceas and were reluctant to engage with the potential disruption of anomalies.

I flipped over a page to where Stapledon wrote about the first meeting between Zula and Omran at Zebra River in Namibia. There in the margin was an infinity symbol and the Latin phrase *tristis paradisus* that rang some bells. I recognised the copperplate script, AR checked the writing against that in the diary I had in my pocket and the image I'd stored of the writing outside the shop. It was Nancy alright. She'd borrowed the book — just a couple of weeks before her death. Lucky that overdue books these days had built-in drone programmes for return to libraries. What other books had Nancy borrowed here? AR showed she'd looked at a recent work on sex trafficking and another on data storage.

$$\infty$$

My PD alerted me to friendly AR signals pouring in. I looked behind and saw Spicer Layamon grinning at me.

"Bibliophile?" she asked, pulling up a chair opposite. "How quaint and retro. Touching paper, I mean, to get information."

Spicer's AR in pre-romance mode would be giving her a read-out of my vital statistics, set genetic age, work history and other background alongside the image of my face. Mine reciprocated. Spicer Layamon aka Spice. Set genetic age 29, temporal existence 263 years. Emergency medicine physician and public servant. Married three times. One son, now a physics professor at Oxford. Higher level contemplative from tantric tradition, karate black belt. Hobby: small farm at Regent's Park. Criminal record: one undisclosed discipline issue at university. One conviction for drunk driving with restorative justice. Lieutenant in the Voges Resistance during the war. Distinguished service medal; allegations of war crimes but nothing proven. She'd put 'flexible' next to her sexual orientation.

"Some of my best friends have paper hearts," I replied.

"That ever likely to include me?" She poured herself a glass of water.

"I'd have to fold you and see how you flew."

"Always with a little left rudder in a combat zone," she said. "I like paper."

"Why."

"It keeps history true," she replied.

"I'd say you live close to the edge."

"Good views of the ocean from there," Spicer said.

"Where do you want to get to?" I said, looking around at the books on shelves.

"The true origin of a crime," she said, pulling a volume down to her lap.

"Me too." I said. "I'm supposed to be the last violent man in an age desperate to be peaceful and happy."

"Well it doesn't matter which way, when you walk with the mystical Miss Tickle."

"Hey, is this furry flirt?"

"And you work for the WTC?" she asked.

"Some might challenge that description. Notice any other fatal character flaws?"

"How did you get a job there?"

"It was a random selection. I was best qualified."

"Well, if standards are so low…"

"You want in?"

"Sure I'm not too low brow? And I've a bit of a wild reputation, in some quarters."

"Met my brother? He's the director. Done some quartering in his time."

"Might have, but it wasn't memorable," said Spicer. "They say he never loses his self-control; but he's a 'whatever it takes' man."

"Uncle Joe doesn't mind a fight. Not a pacifist. What about you? Bored with Gordon?"

"Let's just say my policy is never to stand out from the crowd."

"Pays well?"

"Absolutely."

"Could he kill someone?"

"Easily, probably has. Expert in the ethics of getting away with it. Gordon's very emotional, impulsive in his generosity and his hatred. It was quite unusual, out of character for him to contact you for that meeting. Usually likes to be seen doing things by the book. But then this is the first time in years he's had contact with Spencer."

"Any chance you're setting me up?"

"You hardly need assistance; from what I've heard."

"Hey, I'm in my prime."

"Let's see. I'm 29, you're 31. So, there's an infinite number of us aren't there? Stubborn, resistant, self-reliant; only willing to be split by ourselves."

"Let me think about that for a century or two. What's your take on Spencer?"

"How's your chin?"

"It says he's a genetic upgrade, or adopted."

"Sensible, level headed, if you ask me. Been through a lot, but come out the other side. Why on earth did you ask him about rats?"

"WTC protocol, sunshine. Lizzard and his friends yet might plague the globe."

"That a strip club?"

"Could be. Performed there lately? In front of Spencer?"

"Oh, you picked that up. It was just one night, after a dinner with a bit of drinking."

"Nancy know about it?"

"Not that I'm aware of. It was out of character. Nancy's drug use. They were happy kids. I guess there was no time travel involved otherwise you'd have prevented it."

"Good try. Another lure, later in the day?"

"Squeeze my hand. Go on. Feels like phase delay. I'm not super-impressed. I heard about your wife. I'm sorry."

"Not as much as me."

Spicer offered me some of her cheese cake. I accepted. We drank to that. We had a connection and something much more. She seemed to know what she knew an infinite number of times over. That created a burning inside me that I'd thought was no longer possible. But this was no time to be impulsive.

"You know Gordon sent some toughs after me in the Heath?"

"Oh they wouldn't have hurt you."

"One disguised himself well."

Spicer Layamon

"You've got something they want."

"Let me guess?"

"You're not supposed to take evidence from a crime scene."

"Be specific."

"Zula's diary. He wants it."

"And you're suggesting I should give it to him?"

"Of course not. But I'd recommend you hide it well."

"I think we've just about squeezed as much as we can out of this one? Yes, it's that look on your face? See, you know I'm right."

"All one can do," said Spicer "is follow what comes from here." She leaned over and drew an orbit round my heart. "Seen the Great Comet? Another visitor flipped out of the Oort cloud by some cataclysm beyond. Water and carbon dioxide subliming, fluorescing, ionising under the solar wind; maybe portending the death of a princess. Let's watch it tonight. If it hits, you'll find I'm formed to bear what happens."

That was quite a pitch to encounter in a retro book store in Pond Street. If it was the usual service, I'd be a regular. I persuaded Spicer to give me some general PD access. Maybe we'd make a trip to *Sainte-Mère-Église* one day. I had shy hopes.

> *Glistering Striga flames*
> *Into lurid summer.*
> *Plasma's hiss'n chorus.*

∞

Safely back in my lodgings, I poured myself a scotch on some 'grisly feendly' (as I called ice in drinks after Chaucer's tale of black rocks, rash promises and forgiving hearts). I hoped it might get my mind off Layamon and my pursuers. I settled down in an armchair to carry on reading Stapledon. His prose was as good an antidote to indelicate infatuations as one could find. But it didn't work. Spicer Layamon was entangled in my consciousness. The lamp flicked on and off. I hit the button that reset the fuel cell in the basement. The Hampstead Heath Guesthouse was a WTC-approved safe house but I doubt that referred to me now. So who'd authorised Jeremy Jones and Jack Castles to come after me? Jones had been smart. Most of what he told me in Nancy's flat had been verified as true by my AR, as he knew it would be. My nanobot had returned, but without any new information.

In the passage Nancy was interested in, Stapledon described a Tariq Enterprises helicopter just before dawn, flying over a vast desert towards Zebra River in Namibia. Stapledon diverged to give the biographical paths of the protagonists. Stapledon's view was that Zula ascribed to a theory of transundulation which denied that our sense of self ever found itself a centre of absolute rest. She'd trained many scientist Buddhas; it'd been a revolution in higher education. In my addled imagination, Spicer Layamon, Zula Calabiyau and Nancy Godel swum together and the possibilities seemed endless. The lamp flickered. I hit the reset button again; the fuel cell didn't seem properly connected.

Much of the information Stapledon presented has now been discredited. Yet he memorably, it seemed to me, set the work of Zula and Omran in context of the noblest ideals of humanity.

> *"For us today, the idea that society would hand over control of not just its economy but government, environment and aspirations to corporate entities whose wholly legal personality required them to prioritise profit-making over every other human ambition, seems an extraordinary popular delusion; fit to rank with the South Sea Bubble, Tulipmania, suicide bombers upholding the Muslim faith, or the Roman Catholic Church authorizing torture for reading the Gospels, excommunication for the discovery of scientific truth, mandatory priestly celibacy and violent crusades to the Middle East in the name of peace and forgiveness. Nonetheless, for a time multinational corporations like the dinosaurs, ruled the earth. This was the Corporatocene. Governments of nation states originally established to support the interests of their human populations; under the influence of neo-liberal economic ideology backed by obligations in trade agreements sold themselves off to private corporations and assaulted the welfare of their people. One notorious example was the Trade-Related Intellectual Property Scam (or TRIPS) which increased the monopoly privileges corporations had over even essential medicines by linking them to*

trade sanctions. More mendacious and subsequently excoriated was the Bio-Energy Carbon Capture and Storage Scam (BECCSS); a corporate policy conveniently proclaiming that sustainable fuels supposedly would arise on a planetary scale from intensive cultivation of vast amounts of land with rape seed and permanent pumping of carbon dioxide into empty oil wells.

But there came a time when people looked at the lives they were being offered in the Corporatocene and wanted something better. They wished to own their own homes, rather than handover a substantial portion of their earnings to a bank or landlord. They desired those houses to be surrounded by fields of wildflowers that bloomed in spring, as well as forests that blazed in autumn, provided cool shade in summer and enigmatic bare branches against the winter clouds. They yearned to stare into the night sky and see their home, the Milky Way. They wanted their children to befriend farm animals, grow their own vegetables, fish and drink from clear streams and play in parks and mossy laneways. They wanted all to share in funding quality healthcare and education. They didn't want their collective produce to be siphoned off into the manufacture of weapons for war, or away from those in dire need. They didn't want their desires, hopes and language cynically manipulated for profit. They wanted to be called 'citizens' rather than 'consumers' and to live up to their responsibilities to this and future generations of humanity as well as all life on earth. They saw little hope in their corporate masters' terraforming proposals such as seeding the clouds of Mars with photosynthetic microbes. Neither were they enraptured by plans to unfurl a fleet of sunshades just sunward of the Lagrange point, engage in weather modification, or increase the albedo by dispersing through the upper atmosphere sulphur or hydrogen-filled metal micro-balloons. When asked 'how much is the blue sky worth?' they replied 'more than every corporation that's ever existed.' And so it proved.

A generation was subjected to a violent global conflict, known as the War to End the Corporatocene (or the Corporatocene War) which caused the death of millions of people, ecosystems and species. At the conclusion of that conflagration, the practical transformation away from the Corporatocene and its blighted vision of nature and humanity subjugated to the god of profit was led by the scientist Zula Calabiyau and the corporate reformer Omran Tariq. Omran funded documentation to assist the proceedings of the Ecocide Truth and Reconciliation Supreme Court concerning the abuses of the Corporate State, the lack of taxes paid, the lavish, dissolute lifestyles of the corporate mega-rich; their disinterest in future generations or the preservation of biodiversity and wilderness.

*Meanwhile Zula perfected her synthetic photosynthesis prototype essentially by telling a convincing, inspirational story to the people of the earth and setting up a mechanism whereby they could all contribute and become shareholders in her Global Synthetic Photosynthesis Project (GSPP). It was the first great human research initiative to be owned by everyone in a practical rather than merely symbolic sense.*

*The idea of making the all human structures on the earth's surface do photosynthesis without biology became irrevocably linked with the vision of transition to a Sustaincoene epoch. The term 'Sustainocene' had been coined by the Canberra-based Gondwanan eco-physician Bryan Furnass. It referred to a period where governance structures and scientific endeavour coordinated to achieve the social virtues of ecological sustainability and environmental integrity as influentially propounded by eco-economists such as EF Schumacher (with his concept of 'small (and local) is beautiful') and Kenneth Boulding (with his idea of 'Spaceship Earth' as a closed economy requiring recycling of resources) as well as Herman Daly with his notion of 'steady state' economies drawing upon the laws of thermodynamics and the tendency of the universe to greater entropy (dispersal of energy).*

*Academics, historians, poets, playwrights, artists and philosophers began to develop a culture of the Sustainocene. They explored how for centuries past, many different forces had been slowly drawing the peoples of the world towards a conception of humanity's pre-eminent duty as steward over all life on earth. Heaven or Enlightenment became viewed as a state of unitive or eco-centric consciousness that people expected to attain by the end of the life and were treated with pity if they had not. Those in unitive consciousness simultaneously experienced awareness fed by sensory experience and a deeper identification with all reality. Lists of those who'd attained Nirvana, Samadhi, Enlightenment or Paradise were announced yearly for GSPP celebration day honours.*

*With the globalisation of synthetic photosynthesis, political allegiances changed. The Whole Earth Council (WEC) was established as a revolutionary governance organisation. All the adult peoples of the Earth could now vote electronically on every measure, or pass their vote on to a professional politician whose skill they respected ('liquid democracy'). The WEC began to create political, industry and scientific alliances. Its laws, backed by majorities of all the people of the Earth, suppressed on grounds of immorality multinational armaments and oil, coal and tobacco companies and abolished the governments of nation states they had captured and corrupted. They authorised evidence be collected against corporate directors, Presidents, Prime Ministers and their Ministers and advisors. This*

> task was undertaken by WEC special agents whose object was to discover corporate scandals and who were expected to find them. The WEC issued injunctions which made the lives of many such pro-corporate persons intolerable. Quite a few voluntarily renounced their positions and took on salaried jobs in local community projects. Unfortunately, many well-intentioned corporate leaders, who had championed green technologies and striven to improve the lives of the poor as well as reduce the human burden on Earth, were caught up in this persecution. Such WEC special agents worked for an organisation known as the World Time Council, or the WTC. The breakthrough technology WTC agents utilised allowed targeted people to be 'decommissioned' or exiled off-brane to a parallel universe chosen from an official list. The threat of such sanctions, implemented secretly, efficiently and without warning or avoidance, gave the WEC the capacity to abolish war and nuclear weapons by checking those individuals who promoted and benefited from them.
>
> The confiscation of corporate assets and more equitable taxation, combined with the bounty from synthetic photosynthesis, eventually gave the Whole Earth Council sufficient resources to assist local communities to coordinate effectively in eliminating poverty, providing universal healthcare and free primary, secondary and tertiary education as well as fulfilling many important projects in environmental remediation. There were allegations, however, that this process was delayed and made unscrupulous members of the Whole Earth Council and including President Zula Calabiyau unconscionably wealthy."

That last sentence had been of interest to Nancy. Finally, I had another look at Zula's diary. I'd never held a holy relic before, though on our honeymoon Caroline had arranged pilgrimages for us to *Bodh Gaya*, Assisi and Zula's banyan at Lord Howe Island. I imagined curators from every museum in the world would rush to value their souls if that were my asking price to study Zula Calabiyau's diary. But there was no poetry, no mystical insights: just names, dates and amounts.

∞

An AR call came in from Detective Bernadette Goldbough. I took it straight away. We got on well. We'd danced around each other and almost gone out before I met Caroline. She'd sat on my lap in the back seat of a car going to the beach, placed the palm of her hand over my heart as we danced and I'd posted her a love letter that had never arrived. Now she was middle-aged, three kids at secondary school. Still a good-looker. Parents had served in the police. She was honest and straight ahead. Most of the time. If I was going to come clean, here was my opportunity; but that now seemed such a dumb idea.

"Jean, you need to come down to the office."

"Great. What have I won?"

"Not much, ever, I'd expect. I'll tell you when you get here. Half an hour?"

"Everyone's in such a rush. Time having a closing down sale? Alright. On my way."

I walked to the police station under an afterglow sky that had an ominous lilac and orange glare high above the horizon. And there was the Great Comet like some beckoning aggregate of eternity. An hour's walking was a hard task for a man in my fragile condition. I took time to put brain in gear. She'd found something. Maybe the pet rats. What was wrong about that room? That *EES* article was a strange thing to be working on. And her staged position on the bed. If Nancy was on drugs she'd probably have got them through Spencer via his dad. As for this being a good time to confess, well every part of my brain seemed to reject that move.

I sent out my surveillance nanobot, scratched my arms and smelt fresh-baked bread on a light breeze as I strode across the famous zebra crossing outside Abbey Road. Half way over, I bumped into a man in bare feet pushing a baby in a pram. I apologised. He pointed at the babe and said "Is she a flaming fountain or a weeping fire?" I wondered if he knew something I didn't, or had been taking something I knew too well. I checked the dairies in my pocket; he hadn't swiped them. Chaucer seemed apt and with that the bard appeared in my AR reciting these lines:

> "*Love wol nat been constreyned by maistrye*
> *Whan maistre comth, the god of love anon*
> *Beteth hise wynges, and farewell, he is gon!*"

Bernadette was waiting for me at security and took me up to her office on the second floor. People were saying "congratulations" to her like it was emblazoned on her suit. She closed the door then activated the blinds and the room PD.

"Hey rapscallion, good to see you." Bernadette had a great cackling laugh.

"Likewise, ragamuffin," I replied, giving her a hug.

"Park yourself. Like some tea, coffee, something stronger?"

"No thanks. Hey, what's with all the congratulations?"

"GSPP Day Honours List. I was awarded an SO, level 2. Do a lot of work teaching eco-centric principles in schools; tree-planting, veggie gardens, animal rescue. My *Samadhi's* only intermittent; but they claim I'm doing well with the five laws of life and the five rules of living."

"Well done. You deserve it."

Bernadette had a very neat desk. All her equipment and paper lined up prim and proper, like she'd arranged the relationships with a slide rule.

"You still on this Godel case, Nancy Godel?"

"Yep, they pulled out the big guns."

"Really? She must have been a bad one, eh, for you WTC people to be involved. But someone else got there first, is that it? Spoilt your fun? Bloody Hampstead technophobes. It's like a retro-investigation, ancient methods we haven't used in years. My people claim you contaminated the crime scene. Forensics says the bullets that killed Nancy were from a gun you own. I suppose you'll tell me it was stolen a few months ago."

"I filed a report."

"No doubt. I'll need to check your movements prior to arrival at her flat.

"Shouldn't be hard. There was heightened security because of the Presidential Motorcade that didn't go ahead."

"Speaking of which. Just before it was cancelled we got a tip by some sentient vehicle called Lunette Laudine," said Bernadette. "Claims they took you to the New Globe and you were bragging about being WTC; upset at President Zula confiscating religious and corporate assets. Says you were kind of loco, nuts, could do anything. Not sure if it's genuine."

"It isn't. I couldn't care less about President Zula. I was ordered to decommission Nancy Godel. I had no idea she was Zula's daughter till I searched the flat."

"And why did you do that? Murder investigation is a police job, not WTC. Your WTC status will keep the public from knowing about your involvement in Nancy's death. But your friendship with Eugene is probably all that's saving you at the WTC itself."

"She was a registered WTC target. A confirmed high-level danger to Sustainocene security. I was ordered."

"Now, Jean, I've always been straight with you. This is going to be tough."

"Nancy did have pet rats. And the fat one with the starey coat was called Gordon."

"What did you make of her body position?"

"Ritualised. Something strange about the whole set up."

"Quite right. Look at these ARs. Mounteagle's *Book of Corporate Martyrs*. Captains of industry, lions of the financial markets, decent men and women, massacred after being lured out to celebrate the first GSPP day. Positions are identical with hers."

"Nancy killed as retaliation by corporate recusants? Bit late for that, isn't it?"

"Stranger things have happened. You've been responsible for some of them."

"Crime used to be so simple when vice was more common."

"You're not a shrewd observer Jean. We know Nancy was seeing Spencer Lizzard. And there's Spencer's father, Gordon Lizzard. It's a testimony to Gordon's political skills that he's managed to become Mayor of Southwark and Vice-President of the WEC. But Gordon's past, as you've so often put it, stinks more than a blocked S bend on curry night. We've suspected for a while he's dealing in T-Net pornography and drugs, but haven't been able to trace the source of supply. We think Gordon may have ordered this hit because something Nancy found out through his son. Or it may have been done as a warning."

"And now," said Jean "you want me to explain why the WTC ordered Nancy decommissioned? You know I can't tell you, even if I knew."

"Your brother is head of the WTC," said Bernadette. "You must have some ideas. Nancy was a troubled but talented person who'd straightened herself out. There's no good reason we know of why the WTC should want her decommissioned. That's supposed to be reserved for the worst of the worst, isn't it? People have started talking about the WTC. We've got good evidence the WTC was implicated in the death of first WEC President Asvaghosa Silabhadra. Official story was pilot error, but his plane was made to circle Ndola airport till a jet comes up and shoots it down. President Silabhadra had just launched Operation Morthor II against some hold-out corporates and their mercenaries protecting a stash of inertial confinement fusion thermonuclear weapons in Zimbabwe. Then there were the mysterious deaths of WTC Directors Henry de Herp and Hugues Revel just prior to your brother being appointed. de Herp shot in the front by an assassin and from behind by his own bodyguard. The much-loved Revel as an alleged suicide in public by drug overdose."

"And you're warning me not to take the law into my own hands."

"Quite right. Look at this." A ticket to a performance of *The Tempest* at the Globe appeared on my AR. "It was Nancy's. Notice the date and seating number."

"Upper Gallery. Hey? Directly behind me. Three days before she was murdered. So, she held a seat in my distracted Globe. And I lost my copy of the play there."

"Nancy's little un-scene?"

"You check inside the cushions?"

"Yep. Clean. Only performance she'd attended in five years and Spencer wasn't with her. There's one other thing. Notice a funny little statue in her living room? A Buddha, but dressed in a scientist's lab coat. Trinket they sell at the GSPP Centre."

"Yes, I asked her neighbour about it."

"Well we did an inventory of the apartment. It's missing."

"Probably nothing."

"Maybe. They thought Dark Matter was nothing, once. You discuss this case with Lizzard, or Spicer Layamon?"

"Might have. Problem?"

"Lizzard's under investigation."

"Seemed to be expecting someone else. Why would he know WTC was due there?"

"That Layamon woman," said Bernadette. "I'd watch out. Bad genes, plays hard, runs angles. Strange red stripe birthmark on her back."

"That's public data?"

"On her security clearance. You like her, don't you?"

"Do I need a licence?"

"You wouldn't be the first. Changes men like she changes underwear. Kicked out of the *Dalai Lama Centre for Happiness Research*; man seen coming out of her room late at night. Tantric. *Kundalini* goddess. Anything goes in the name of higher consciousness; thinks the usual moral codes don't apply. She's vegetarian but claims to get her protein from semen. Ruthless singularity of purpose when she fixes on something, or someone."

"Assassin?"

"Bloody good one if she is. I'm just warning you. There's something not quite normal, a bit unhinged, about Spicer. And of course, her working for Lizzard speaks for itself. You've got an opportunity, a moment, to step back from this."

"Red stripe on the back? Really."

"Jean, of all people. It's a Gondwanan analogy. The venomous red back spider. During coitus, the male flips its body over the female's jaws to be eaten so as to prolong mating."

"Well, the old block and tackle's been on ice for a while, but the S&M thing never appealed to me. As you should know."

"Jean, try a decent girl; to them love is just familiarity."

"I would, but you're taken now. Nancy had Privacy Dome activated."

"Yes, encrypted with a random number derived from real time quantum fluctuations in intensity of a split beam of light. Unbreakable."

"And here I was trusting my PD to some lagged Fibonacci."

"Jean. Be serious."

"Always up for something new. I looked, just got basic data."

"But not her recent dreams. Left wide open to Mindscan. There they were."

"Mindscan?"

"So?"

"It's not safe."

"Jean. It's already done. I don't feel any craving to go back. We've got different personalities, you and I. Jean, your destiny is disaster. Give it up. Frankly, I'm past caring if I still survive in that magical world behind your eyes."

"There's something I have to tell you about Mindscan and Caroline."

"Can we do this first? I went through Nancy's dreams this morning. Five nights worth. I've called you down to show you them first. Before anyone else."

"I'm grateful."

"I'm not after your advice. It's a favour. For old time's sake. At least I hope you'll see it like that."

"I'm intrigued. Roll film."

Bernadette synched my AR to hers by Mindscan. She was an expert already, sadly more clinical and objective than me with my own invention. Soon we were watching Nancy's last dreams. They were in vivid colour. I was jealous, mine were usually black and white. In the first one Nancy was at a crowded hall. She was trying to walk down the aisle with a banner listing all her shortcomings as well as those she'd harmed, and being ridiculed for her pains. She had to get back home, but the people there had moved on, were no longer her friends and seemed disinterested. Then Nancy dreamt of men in business suits watching an explosion from a high floor of a tall building. The explosion caused the electrical systems in cars and machinery to melt. One of the men said 'you have to cut corn and break eggs.'

The next dreams were peculiar. There was me talking to Spicer Layamon in the *Café Organic Synthesis*. Spicer's arm was around me. Spicer and I had to get down a river through dangerous country to rescue Nancy. Then we were lying buried in the ground with men in a helicopter about to shoot us. Finally, Nancy dreamt of me climbing holding a small book up a huge, wet monument using a grappling hook. I got to just below the top, shouting at myself to keep going. I ended high against the red sky. Spicer was below, not bearing to watch the impending tragedy.

I could feel the dreaded compassion from Bernadette. Maybe she'd smelt the alcohol on my breath. The next dream started in a place that seemed familiar to me. A woman running through a dark wood towards a cliff. The point of view was from far above. The woman looked up. She was wearing a large, broad-brimmed hat. I looked carefully at her face. I was too shocked to react. Then I began sobbing, soon uncontrollably, heaving my chest. Bernadette reached across and held my hand.

"I'm sorry Jean," Bernadette said.

Nancy had been dreaming about the suicide of my wife Caroline; something else I'd not been allowed by the WTC to prevent.

"One more," said Bernadette. "Are you alright to go on?"

"Yep, go to the next one. I'm alright." But I wasn't.

The final dream was of two people walking through rainforest beside a river, then through a desert. One of the people was me. The woman seemed familiar. Attractive, mid-40's tall, thin, naked from the waist up except for cascading tresses of brown hair and wearing a long light grey-green skirt the hem of which caressed the ground. I was staring at the Professor Buddha from my recent winter temple dream.

"That," said Bernadette "is Zula Calabiyau."

"So why would Nancy dream about the famous Zula. Unless of course Zula was her mother, just like the DNA suggests. Nancy had been researching the ethics of Zula's GSPP project. Why would she do that?"

"We don't know yet. There's been a lot of fuss about a report into the finances of some of the senior members of the *Whole Earth Council*. Some have made themselves very wealthy from corporate confiscations. Zula's caught up in those allegations."

"What's that got to do with Nancy's death?"

"Not sure. There's a push to make GSPP disperse some of its money to other areas of research. Zula's running for re-election as WEC President isn't popular in certain quarters."

"Let me guess which quarters."

"Yes, Gordon Lizzard and his friends. But soon we'll need to let everyone know the dead girl was Zula's daughter. We need this case wrapped up."

"Or else?"

"Or else, across the world corporate sycophants and apologists like Mayor Lizzard will be blamed for killing Zula's daughter. 'The rats must die.' Final purge. Maybe your brother and Lizzard aren't as close as some people say they are. We picked up Jevons Paradox in London yesterday. Always do whenever he visits; find it saves time. Got a criminal record could stretch from here to the Mars Terraforms. And we suspect he's done contract work for the WTC. This time it was easy. Jevons had bitten off the ear of one of my officers and eye-gouged another on a subway train.

They found him lying under a seat, drunk and mumbling 'sorry Scott, sorry.' We think Scott was his brother. Died when he was ten, Scott. Tragic family history; some suggestion they used to live near your son in Normandy."

"Sounds like Jevons wanted to be arrested."

"Just what we were thinking."

"That other thing, I mentioned earlier."

"About Mindscan? And your wife?"

"Yes, I let Caroline use it without authorisation or supervision. I was drunk."

"The coronial inquest confirmed suicide, didn't it?"

"I arrived too late to stop her. I want you to write all this down."

"You want to be punished?" Bernadette asked. "But you can't be the judge against yourself. You mightn't be guilty of anything."

"But I am. We've just seen the proof."

"From what you've told me it's unlikely a court would find you guilty of criminal negligence. And in the eyes of the law, you need intention or reckless indifference to do a crime. You and I both know what she was searching for when she did Mindscan. About her father's death. Don't be too harsh on yourself."

"You've made a record?"

"Yes, I have. Jean, before you go."

"Yes? The Great Comet?"

"That's just a big, glowing iceball. Mayor Monica's organising comet viewing parties. No, there's one other thing."

"What's that?"

"Word is that you took some items of evidence from the crime scene. Now I'm not asking you to tell me. I'm just letting you know that whoever's got them is a marked man. Did you speak to Lizzard's son? Jean?"

"It was a very low level, low brow discussion."

"You should know a few things about Spencer Lizzard," said Bernadette. "Spencer comes from a violent family. When he was thirteen, his grandfather sat on the bed beside him and blew his own head off, rather than let the mob get to him first. Spencer's been a regular user of ice; though he claims to have cleaned himself up. We have a statement from a former girlfriend. Spencer was bad. Used to take her out to this deserted stretch of road at night and threaten to torture and kill her. She left him while she was in hospital pregnant with his child, then applied for maintenance afterwards. She says Spencer vowed he'd kill the next woman who did that to him. He's a great actor as well as a musician. Done it professionally. Jean, are you listening?"

"I love fear," said Jean. "It stops me drinking."

"Who could make Jean Moulin afraid?" asked Bernadette. "Come on, look at me."

"My brother, that's who. Joseph Moulin the WTC Director. He whose mind rolls on and through me; self-proclaimed great swan on the restless river of our sufferings. In his *Confutation*, Joe calls people mere babes or cowards who like Silabhadra struggle to that light through the ethical disciplines of the *Book of Common Faith*. But you want to know the truth? President Silabhadra only called Joe a 'versatile genius' because he planned to sack Joe from the WTC and give him a mission through which he might learn humility and service. Quixotic of him wasn't it? Instead, next day, Silabhadra was assassinated."

"He's certainly an ugly guy," said Bernadette. "They used to say after fifty you have the face you deserve."

"And smell worse. *Mon frère's* psychic powers, forbidden by Silabhadra, now indulge in secret his 'little pleasures.' Joe aims to purge this world of *The Book of Common Faith*, its morning contemplation classes and all who teach that freedom lies in controlling rather than exulting their desires. 'Fire the faggots, *fiat justitia et pereat mundis*,' he says. 'Destroy all who would impede the self-created heaven at the summit of our unconquerable lusts.'"

"Calm down. You'll get in big trouble, talking like that," said Bernadette. "Jean, where are you staying?"

"Under a bridge somewhere, cuddling heaven in a brown paper bag. Every day the prospect of sobriety becomes more appalling. My brother hopes that by dawn tomorrow I'll be up, glinting at the jumping off point."

"I'm not going to sit here talking to your bottle. You're not a bad person Jean, you're ill. Why do you drink the way you do? Look at your history of hospitalisations for 'accidents.' I can't believe what you did to Caroline. And now Spicer. For goodness sake, such a passion is like falling in love with a sparrow flying over your head."

"Just another quick, bright midsummer thing coming to confusion? I planned to die young and I'm almost out of time. But drinking helps when my head's going like a two-storey lawn-mower; or if I have an uncomfortable feeling."

"A miracle. You said something sensible."

"Bern, I don't feel like quarrelling with you, or the reason that governs the world. I just accept that both don't like me anymore. I wander at random doing things rashly, living longer than I should honestly, making the worst of my time, annoying my divine part with wild impressions of fancy and far from done with uproar in the trousers. I'm crushed by the present, afraid of peeking out at what's to come."

"Jean" said Bernadette "look up into the sky every morning. No star wears a veil."

"Nice line. I'll use that next time I see Spicer in the country of Quadi."

"Hey, you're not going out of here to drink?"

"Indeed I have been counting the minutes, but distracted by the pleasant company. Relax, my disease tells me it'll be different this time."

∞

I walked back to the Hampstead Heath Guesthouse from the police station. I made it without having a drink. The lurid orange and lilac of the afterglow from the volcanic ash was fading. Somewhere behind the clouds that stupid comet was portending something. When I arrived, I sat at the desk for an hour or so staring at *Underwater Garden*. That smug little fish swimming against the current in those murky waters. It had a plan. It knew what it was up to.

I lay in bed from 11pm to 2am, desperate. I was alone. I'd lost my wife, family, my self-respect. I couldn't blame Eugene, or Uncle Joe or the WTC. My gut had told me to go early to Nancy's place so had Eugene when he interrupted my meditation to imitate the oracle. But instead, I went to the GSPP celebration looking for free booze. And if I had arrived early I might have discovered why the WTC had ordered me to decommission Nancy. What was it I would have seen then? If I'd arrived early what choice would I have had? So, I let her die too. That's why I'd been late and left Caroline to fry her brain doing Mindscan without supervision. I'd stopped off for a drink or two.

My destiny, as mother used to say when tucking me into bed, was to show people strength, peace and meaning. It didn't matter to mum how coarse, wild or uneducated I was, that would only be to the greater glory of That which transformed me. My military service in the Corporatocene War, my inventions for the WTC, were dedicated to fulfilling her trust in me. I'd renounced *Nirvana* and fought under the banner '*Mercy to Corporates is Cruelty to the Earth.*' But now it seemed my loyalty had been abused.

"Listen," I prayed "I don't know anything anymore about this *Nirvana* bullshit. But help me, give me a sign; show me you're there. Communicate." Nothing. I got some string from under the sink and tied it tight abound the base of my scrotum.

"If you don't communicate," I shouted "then after a few hours I'll be different anyway. Maybe you'll like me better like that."

I lay with my head on the pillow; my balls starting to ache. I imagined them going blue, then black. The pain became intense. After an hour, I heard this voice: 'a dog will bark.' It wasn't the sort of voice druggies on ice hear.

I waited and waited for what seemed like forever. And then as It had said, a dog barked. I felt this magnetic force coming from a corner of the room pulling me towards it. No lights, all dark, just this force. And I opened my arms wide. I believe now in levitation. I felt I was being pulled up to it. It and I were in a timeless union. And then it subsided, gently, like a wave washing back from a beach.

I heard my heart thumping and I knew two things. First, I'd never need booze again. Second, that I'd save Zula Calabiyau from being assassinated and her work destroyed. Nancy's case was about saving the Earth; and I was seeing it through.

I hobbled to the kitchen and cut the string with a knife. I doubted I'd need those two appendages again soon in any practical sense; but it was reassuring to know the old one-eyed trouser snake wouldn't laugh when I tried to strain the potatoes.

I had to get somewhere safe, work it all out and purge the poison from my pores. Why had I been ordered to exile Nancy? Why had Nancy been murdered so as to implicate me? Why did Nancy want me to find the diaries? Why had Jeremy Jones and Jack Castles been after me on the heath? Was I set up to be a patsy in Zula's assassination? Was it all connected with my brother wanting to decommission me? Could I trust my AR or Eugene?

Zula's diary was from a time when Zula was Director and Chief Scientist at the Global Synthetic Photosynthesis Research Centre in Namibia. One thing I'd learnt from all those years of cricket in the French grade competition; you never walk out to bat without a plan. I needed time to think and detox. I'd accept my son's offer to visit his family on their organic farm at Normandy. Maybe that also would help break the psychic entanglement with Spicer Layamon. I could feel our mutual arousal night and day. But what if she too was trying to push me over the dam?

# III

# EARTH TOUCH, NORMANDY

*Jean visits his son's family on their farm in Normandy — Grandfather Merlin tells a salutary story from the Corporatocene — Little Walter discusses alternate universes — Mr Elbadawi's global synthetic photosynthesis theme park — dinner reminiscences — Jean overhears some home truths — charity cricket match, old time party and bonfire — Meeting Mersenne Twister and a mystery traveller at the WTC's Tipler–Gott Cylinder —*

Early morning, I asked the taxi to drop me a good walk from my son's farm. It wanted to know why, when my physiology indicated I was so frail; and whether this was a criticism of its service. The taxi, revelling in its near-singularity, asked my opinion on Mr Elbadawi's *Synthetic Photosynthesis Theme Park* and if I wanted to hear the "good oil." But I wasn't in the mood.

"What do you think of Eugene?" the car asked me. "By the way, my name is Lunette. Remember me?"

"Of course, Lunette Laudine. People have been misrepresenting you," I said. "Eugene's my friend, Lunette. And a very wise person."

"They'd be pleased to hear you say that," said Lunette. "We love Eugene. And don't worry about the misrepresentations. I found out who spread the rumour. It's sorted. Ah, here is Eugene now. Transferring, please wait." Eugene manifested before me through AR as a bee with a human head.

"At last," I said. "I've got a few questions."

"Something's happened to you, Jean," said Eugene. "I mean in a good way, *mon ami*. I see you've caught up with Lunette again. Cute eh? I've organised Lunette to assist you. And keep an eye out for Trudperter Hohelied, an old pal of mine and a leader amongst the trees. I think you met Trudperter already on the heath."

"Did you help? The other night, after Bernadette showed me the dreams?"

"Ah *mon vieux*, that was between you and whatever you understand as a Higher Power."

"What's going on? I mean with the WTC, Uncle Joe and Lizzard?"

"They were planning to assassinate President Zula. Hercules Huncks, Jack Castles and Jeremy Jones. They were set to do the hit, or to cover it up. Your job was to be the patsy, *le benêt*. By not taking the call at Records and arriving late at Hampstead you put a hole in their plan."

"Why frame me for a murder and an assassination?"

"Well, you've got a reputation as a violent guy and your brother hates you. 'Anything else?' Oh yes, you've thwarted their plans before. Anyway, the crime scene is clean, thanks to yours truly. They still aim to take out President Zula. And you're a loose end they want cut off. That cover everything?"

"I stuffed their stupid scheme, just by not turning up to Records?"

"You'd have found out more if you'd gone early to Nancy's, as I suggested."

"I'm not sure what to do."

"Really? Why not work out a strategy? I'll help you. I'm being what you'd call a double-agent. It's fun."

"Can I trust Spicer?"

"I don't give advice on that sort of thing. But I hear Namibia's worth a visit this time of year. I'd advise you arrive early though. And start meditating again. You're good at it."

I farewelled Eugene, and Lunette brought me to my destination. I was never sure why I trusted Eugene. I just liked him, or it, or whatever Eugene manifested as. I gave Lunette high marks on the feedback form and got out. I immediately felt the morning chill. There were no clouds to keep the warmth in and the stars spread on high beyond the dark treetops. I walked along to the solitary sounds made by my feet and breaths.

*Sainte-Mère-Église*, despite its faded artistry and martial history, gave the impression of being worn out after a great debauch. Most of the houses were intact, but here and there one could see shells of dwellings, pulverised during the Corporatocene War. Rubble, broken bricks, shattered boards, cracked plumbing, loose electrical wires, split fuel cells and heliostats, endless scraps of plastic; all had been neatly graded off the road. People were worried because carbon nanotubes had been used in the construction and now the dust would be getting in people's lungs. I'd been told it was in mine. Too many fights in too many bashed-up CNT buildings. GSPP Celebration Day must have been good here. Street lamps illuminated little pools of green foliage and pale blue dot-themed bunting filled with moths. Moving tree shadows denoted an approaching water-powered car. Its beaming white frame passed, then its red rear brake lights glowed at the corner. I could hear a sprinkler on its side gushing water over a lawn; a door closing muffled by intervening bushes.

I walked under the stone arch which bore the carved inscription: *Tel qu'en lui-même enfin l'éternité le change*. François had named their property *Loorungah* — flying in a Gondwanan Koori dialect — in memory of his mother. It had the strongest PD protection available and AI and AR of any description was banned, especially in the kids' toys. I stepped carefully over the gravel of their driveway so their border collie Old Bugsy, wouldn't bark.

François and his wife Helené, a yoga teacher, ran the place as an organic farm and animal sanctuary. My son also taught Canonical Literature part time at Normandy University. People recovering from mental trauma could work at *Loorungah*, grow veggies, feed some critters, walk the shady paths through the woods and get better at their own pace, without pressure. Last time I visited, the kids kept insisting I pat lambs, belted Galloway heifers, saddleback piglets, ducks, magpies, puppies, even their pet wombat who kept head-butting my ankles.

I discovered my grandfather Merlin inside the front gates helping François load up his little GSPP fuel cell-powered truck with cabbages, pumpkins, tomatoes, marrows, beets, sprouts and apples for the local market. Light rain was falling; drops dotted their shirts and the tarpaulin they were tying over the produce. Old Bugsy emerged from his kennel, chained, like an ascetic from a prayer cave.

"Hey dad," said François. "Good to see you. Just going to Sunday market. Want to come?"

"S'alright, mate," I replied, putting on his mother's Gondwanan accent. "I'm tired as a bandicoot on a burnt ridge. You flush? Local currency?" I reached for my wallet.

"No need, dad. Barter day. I'll bring you back a couple of bottles of *Pinot Gris* from *Arpents du Soleil*."

We were replaying a familiar conceit.

"Thanks. Reckon I'm giving the grog a bit of a miss."

"Good on you Dad," said François. He kept working with Merlin. Caroline and I had raised our son François on organic farms in Lille and then in Châtillon. Caroline taught him to milk a cow when five, shear a sheep at six, strain a fence at eight, repair our GSPP unit when he was twelve. When he was seven, Caroline tried to teach him to shoot a fox from a mile away with a Lee-Enfield .303. Caroline offered to demonstrate first. François had said 'there it is' and Caroline had shot the fox in the head. François blamed himself and refused to fire a gun after that.

"Right, you pull that strap there," said Merlin. "That one. Harder. Got it. That'll do. Now the next one. Hey, hold your horses. Steady on the duck house roof."

"Actually, you know what we might do? Get out of it, Dad. Right'o, that one's done."

"Manage that? Hey careful, watch what you're doing. Whole lot could come down."

"Talk about a quagmire. Get a load of that, Dad. First the Great Comet then the Great Flood, eh? What d'you reckon? Some dire calamity about to be visited on us? Merlin, you could try a bit harder mate. You seen my wrench? People will flog anything. Hey Dad, how's Joe?"

"He's seventy now," I replied.

"Seventy. Is he really? Seventy? Funny choice to make. Hang on mate. Check it out first, OK? Whoa. That'll do her. Hey, can't you see that's squashing them?"

"Well I do now," said Merlin. "I'll put some padding in-between, smart-arse."

The truck eventually departed, drips of water trailing from its exhaust pipe. François tooted the horn while his other hand waved from the window.

"Send her down Huey," shouted François, gesturing to the rain clouds "we're a moral in the mud."

The little vehicle bumped over the rough cobbles along the narrow stone-walled lane and around a corner. An Escadrille of little birds seemed to twist wisps of white, grey and purple clouds against gaps of blue sky beyond.

Grandfather Merlin and I looked each other over. He was just as tall as I'd remembered, perhaps a little more stooped, but with the same thinning wispy white hair and bushy eyebrows. He had a small down-turned mouth amidst a long grey beard.

Merlin had been an athlete in his youth and while studying at Oxford became a champion opening batsman at cricket. Unfortunately, he'd also been caught up in a radical clique of neoliberal free market economists and, after graduation, was recruited as a consultant with a firm lobbying against re-publicisation of healthcare, transportation, banking and education. In the years following the Great Cleansing, Merlin had been subjected to *dégradation nationale* in the *épuration légale*. Afterwards, he'd worked hard to rehabilitate. He'd studied medicine and even managed to serve for many years as a local physician. He'd loved Caroline and also had picked up many Gondwanan slang expressions from her.

"Alright Gautama, let's go and have a chin wag about London," said Merlin, patting me on the shoulder. "Strange times, these, Gautama. Utopia's going off like a frog in a sock. We should be over the moon; but we're not, are we? Not in a pink fit."

"Still got deep pockets, I see," I said. "Stall fee?"

"We'll talk later," Merlin replied "if your confidence stays in one piece and outside a bottle. The mask comes off with me, Jean; you bloody derro. I expect this'll be another of your melancholy and ignominious visits, with you imbibing the waters of stupefaction, downing the stagger juice, at every hidden opportunity. Jean, horizon your mind; our grief-stricken society needs more imposing figures of interconnectedness. Zula can say 'Life on Earth. One destiny' with every tranquil assurance of effortless moral superiority. But there's still many ruthless human chauvinists who detest our President's biotic egalitarianism."

"What about Elbadawi's land next door?" I asked.

"Last time I looked it wasn't on the commons register."

"I did a bit of research there too," I said.

"Really? While at the Globe, off your face and legless? Pull the other one."

"Fair go. Lay off. I'm on the bloody wagon."

"Yeah? That'll be the day. Gautama in a bottle. Get rooted."

"I'm working on it."

We walked through the main door over mossy, red bricks. The house had two sections connected by a walkway with triple-glazed glass, through which you could see the back garden and the roofs of the village beyond. The bedrooms were to the left. During the Corporatocene War the property was known as *la ferme d'Ambel* and a meeting place of *L'Armée Terre Secrète*. Marguerite Gonnet and Madeleine Riffaud, famous *maquisards contre la mondialisation néolibérale*, were said to have prepared here false shareholder certificates to protect organic farmers and local artisans from deportation to consumer indoctrination malls. Their carved motto remained on the lintel over the fireplace. *'Notre Terre est en peril de mort. Mais rien n'est perdu. La vie n'a pas encore rejeté l'humanité.'*

On the right, a hall fifteen feet high ran the entire length of the house. It was interrupted in the middle by decorated twin arches. Between these, on the west side, lay the ornate entrance to a drunken staircase with its angled steps. The doors, architraves, skirtings, jambs and window frames were all carved from oak and cedar. An old Spanish chandelier hung from the ceiling. To the east was the service wing with its dairy, storerooms, butchery, hen-house, bakehouse, glass hot-houses and a laundry. South were the yards, stables, orchards and veggie gardens, bordered by a small stream.

We went into the kitchen. It was an elegantly arranged mixture of polished wood and marble, suffused with the smell of baking bread. All the drawers opened to a touch. In the adjacent living room Tess was practising piano and Walter fighting with Anouk over a game of chess. Merlin took it upon himself to mediate between them.

Their house was full of books, old ones from the 19$^{th}$ and 20$^{th}$ centuries (CE) being especially treasured and, what is more, regularly read and, of course, written in while doing so. Many of them were from my own library as it had become too difficult to grapple them round after Caroline's death.

As well as books, the rooms of their farm house also displayed an assortment of crystals, incense sticks, prisms, statues of chubby Buddha and mandala paintings courtesy of Helené. François had met Helené during a Buddhist meditation class she was teaching at a *Lightning in a Water Bottle* synthetic photosynthesis transformational festival held in Sherwood Forest. Normally not good at visualisation, or much interested in the mystical side of things, François told me he saw butterflies floating from his heart when she spoke. Whatever Helené lacked in natural contemplative ability, clairvoyance or clairaudience, she made up with enthusiasm for the mystical cause.

Outside the triple-glazed windows, drops fell from a grey, cloudy sky upon the GSPP tiles of the roof that stored and split water to make the light and heat which kept us warm and comfortable. Helené turned from the oven to give me one of her big hugs and rub my back with her hand.

"Your aura's a bit dark," she said.

"Fantastic," I replied. "Till now my animal magnetism's felt spread out like that volcanic ash in the stratosphere."

"You're not using are you? We don't…"

"Just peace, love and mung beans this trip, sister."

"Better be," she said. She waved a large cutting knife at me. "Being in a physical body brings challenges Jean; but it also opens the door to expressing our whole nature in an endless variety of rapturous, revelatory ways."

"A *femme fatale* just hit me with that in Hampstead."

"Jean, here's something you can try now." She put down the knife. "Feel into your physical body, relax a little and sense what movement it wants to make. There. When I feel into it, my hand slides up over my solar plexus, then brushes upwards. As it does, my relaxation deepens. I notice a feeling of wistfulness like glimpsing a close friend from far off, and as I move, this sense comes fully into my awareness. I see I've been focussing narrowly and my body is requesting more spaciousness, attention to small, unobtrusive sensations. I realise there's a wealth of understanding just waiting for me, playing inside every living thing. I feel like a white bird, floating on a smooth, silent, sleeping river, then up to the clouds and the sun beyond on an invisible current. What comes up for you?"

"The body of a dead girl in Hampstead. Some shadowy Big Shots trying to do me in because I have a little book they want."

"I've been praying for you," said Helené. She threw an old pair of brown shoes in a bin due to be picked up by a recycle van. "The soles have holes."

"What's your take on this Milton Elbadawi character next door?" I asked.

"There's always someone in life. I don't care how much he's done for the local community. He's dammed our stream. It's just a trickle now. He's got machines over there, growling, devouring the earth, night and day. Our old trees are crying because of the loss of their friends. I feel their pain. His land has no registered ecosystem guardian. No-one can bring an action in its name. This shouldn't be happening now."

"I'll pray you two'll get on better," I said.

"Hey, where are my old brown shoes," asked Merlin, as he entered the room.

"How should I know?" said Helené. "You're useless as a dry thunderstorm. See what I've got to cope with? You'd forget your head if it wasn't screwed on. Look at that. Ah well, I suppose rain makes the washing cleaner."

Merlin took the hint and went out to get the washing off the line.

> *Outside one fig leaf falls;*
> *Boy told his parents died in avalanche;*
> *Slowly blinks.*

∞

Merlin liked to read to the children from some of François' books. One of his favourites was the British Library's publication of the illustrated *Cocharelli Manuscript*. This was a text on the virtues and vices written by a rehabilitated Genoese hedge fund dealer for the edification of his son, Little Johannes. The kids especially loved it when Merlin translated into the Gonz vernacular of their grandmother. It was all part of the cosmopolitan culture of the Sustainocene.

We gathered on cushions on the floor, while Merlin sat in the bay window below the triple mortal helical spiral staircase. Each of the staircase's branches took you to a different floor, only one to the turret where François had his study. He called the staircase 'Mr Feynman' and claimed the wood came from Tuva in Central Asia. Merlin was wearing an old green jumper and hitched up his trousers before sitting down. He looked around at the children with tired eyes from behind his silver spectacles. He was searching for something of interest in what they were doing, something that his imagination could build upon, so he didn't have to repeat for the hundredth time things he'd already spoken.

"Listen children, for I want to tell you ankle biters the good oil that my grandfather passed on to me," Merlin began reading. "Envy stuffs your mind and makes it really crook."

"Language, Merlin," shouted Helené from the kitchen.

"We were taught," said Walter "civilizational collapse was a function of population impact divided into fragility or resilience of ecosystems and ingenuity."

"The bully boys of the blood-drenched Corporatocene," Merlin said "were neoliberal economists; they valued envy to drive competition and innovation."

"For better ways to kill people?" asked Walter.

"For better ways to use them," said Merlin. "Fathers and brothers too, must learn that use is not love. There was once a noble youth, tall, handsome, long-haired who owned a motza. His name was Omran Tariq and his father was the CEO of one of the world's biggest armaments, petrochemical and coal companies, Tripoli–Armenia. Omran Tariq had to contend with a mother called Sibylla. She was so ruthless and scheming she could've sent the murderous WTC to school. After the suspicious death of Omran Tariq's father, Sibylla assumed control of the corporate behemoth, purportedly until her son attained his majority."

"Was becoming head of a corporation like being crowned king?" asked Walter.

"Being made king was better," Merlin answered. "You were still born to it, but didn't have to pretend you'd graduated business school *magna cum laude*, had a high IQ, or made your own money."

"But entrepreneurs worked hard, with skill," said Walter. "You're being unfair."

"You can't place expectations on people that aren't real," I said.

"The citizens of Paris," Merlin continued "where the company was headquartered had been accustomed to live under their own laws and in freedom. So, to solidify her power Sibylla set about snaking up some coils of poisonous informers, doing in citizens who were rich and opposed her, wheedling herself into councils of state and shoving on a pedestal those who accepted her authority. She did all this without running it past her son. But Omran Tariq was a bit of a larrikin, fit as a Mallee bull, and ready to go out on a limb for his mates. Once he came of age, he secretly married his childhood sweetheart Nancy de Brienne Calabiyau, a widgie, daughter of a famous synthetic photosynthesis scientist and herself an accomplished musician."

"Like me," said Tess. "I'm a widgie."

"You're a budgie," said Walter.

"Omran Tariq hadn't come down in the last shower," continued Merlin. "His wife convinced him to sacrifice his company's wealth to globalising synthetic photosynthesis. He pushed for photosynthesis to be declared common heritage of humanity, so it couldn't be entirely owned by a corporation, or used for war."

"Bet that went down like a lead balloon," said Walter.

"Paris at that time also was a city of many beautiful gardens, surrounded by lush forests and farms. Each summer evening at dusk, Omran Tariq and Nancy used to stand on their balcony and sing songs about the Sustainocene and synthetic photosynthesis to crowds of people. Yes, Tess, it was as beautiful as *Sainte-Mère-Église* and Nancy was a bit of a spunk, the 'first star in the heavens' they used to call her. They said she thought in chords. But from the time of the nuptials, Sibylla chucked a wobbly, putting the mozz on Nancy, casting aspersions."

"Why was she throwing nasturtiums?" asked Anouk.

"Envy and for failing to get a bun in the oven," Merlin answered.

"That means she couldn't have children," Walter said.

"Why didn't she get a gene license?" asked Anouk.

"People didn't need a licence to have babies then," said Merlin. "Right, carrying on. Sibylla sought out a secret group of right real bastards ready to manufacture prejudice against her son's wife so they'd separate and synthetic photosynthesis be banished from the portfolio and the city."

"Neoliberal economists?!" asked Walter. "I hate those guys."

"Anyway," Merlin continued after coughing "Sibylla, that wicked old ratbag, got what she wanted and was happy as Larry. But as it turned out, she was farting against thunder. One evening, as her son sung with Nancy on the balcony, an arrow hit Nancy in the eye. She died quick as a flash."

"Was archery part of neoliberal economics?" asked Walter. "I thought it was trickle-down, not paradox around the riser."

"Walter, you're flight shooting without clout," said Merlin. "The arrow's tip had been dipped in a poison, but Sibylla was never told that. Omran Tariq, broken-hearted, returned to his family's home in Provence. Sibylla, now powerful again, was courted by Gordon Knight-Anole, CEO of Tortosa Oil, flash as a rat with a gold tooth and quick as one up a drain pipe. In time, Sibylla installed Knight-Anole, whom she convinced herself she loved, to govern Tripoli–Armenia–Tortosa Inc. on her behalf. He ghost-wrote her book arguing that democracy was not present at the end of history, people needed to get used to strong corporate leadership; to accept freedom in a plastic package."

"You're making it all up," said Anouk. "It's not VHD."

"Shhh, Anouk. We'll see. The *World Time Council*, led by Hugues Revel, spat the dummy. It announced to the old princess they were pissed off and she had a snowflake's chance in hell they'd subject themselves to the rorts of her corrupt and shagged-out CEO. Rogue elements in the WTC used the cloak of the *Whole Earth Council* to stir the possum, both demonising and making alliances with Knight-Anole and his corporate friends. Terror, discord and treachery rioted in the city; drought and pestilence beset the land. Knight Anole used WTC double agents to assassinate WEC President Asvaghosa Silabhadra, as well as eliminate honest WTC Director Hugues Revel and former leader Henry de Herp."

"Why?" asked Walter. "Because of envy?"

"Why? Because politicians are useless as a third armpit. That's why we side-lined them with liquid democracy."

"Useless as a roo-bar on a skateboard?" asked Walter. That'd been one of Caroline's favourite expressions.

"Now you've crept to draw weight," said Merlin. "Anyway, the WTC eventually convinced Jean Moulin, commander of the *Whole Earth Council's* army, to get his act together and invade Paris. Some of the neoliberal economists, CEOs and their families tried to piss off on boats to *Île de la Cité* and go to ground in its church. They called it Project Persephone. Commander Jean Moulin didn't want to attack the church hall with his helicopter. But the WEC soldiers waited till the tide was out, then flung themselves into the sea and swum over. They captured and sent them all off to rehabilitation farms."

"I'm glad the Corporatocene's over," said Anouk. "Too many VHD essays."

"Is it?" asked Merlin.

"Those boats were spaceships and biosphere satellites, weren't they?" asked Walter.

"Just don't believe the WTC is the only thing," said Merlin "stopping this world being split."

"I can't see my eyes," said Tess, as Anouk placed her hands over them.

Walter and Anouk applauded and Tess whistled. Merlin excused himself to go make a cup of tea and have a bit of a lie down.

∞

Tess and Anouk went off to another room to practise yoga with their mother. I could hear her calm instructions: "Now *Earth Touch*, hands between the feet. *Raised Runner*, breathe out, into *Mountain Pose*, *Raised Runner* again, breathe into *Warrior*, *Half Warrior*, *Earth Touch* and back to *Child Pose*." Outside the rain thrummed harder on the roof. Walter sat in the bay window opposite my chair near the staircase. Old Bugsy rubbed his back against Walter's knees.

"Do you have a theory who murdered that girl in London?" Walter asked. "Oh, my friends, we know about it. I've got Internet and T-Net access. My parents don't know."

"I think it was something to do with the GSPP celebration," I said.

"Feynman wrote that you can never prove a vague theory wrong," said Walter.

"Think I should be more specific?"

"Of course. That's your job." Walter tickled Old Bugsy under his chin.

"Maybe not for much longer. Too tough for me."

"Dad says the worst thing you can do is to half do something."

"He'd be right."

"I get tremendous delight," said Walter, gazing at the staircase "in guessing how nature will work in a situation never seen before, in accumulating paradoxes. I have a whole drawer full of them. I want to come up with a new theory of something that's true, but doesn't agree with nature. Don't you? It could be the key to your case?"

"Sounds like you want to prove," I replied "the laws of physics and ethics are changing with time or between universes."

"Did this universe come from a black hole or a laboratory?" Walter inquired.

"We don't know yet how many other universes there are," I replied. "People seem to think this one has a right way that should work out."

"I used to think this Universe," said Walter "was in a fish tank with a little boy looking at it."

"And if you fill the tank from the top, the fish grow fangs," I said.

"Then this isn't the perfect universe, is it?" said Walter.

"It's the one we know best and it offers us choice."

"I think bad and good people will want to make universes," said Walter. "Just like bad and good people need to climb high mountains, or start a big company, or a war. And once they get started they can't stop. Making a universe is the king of ambitions, isn't it?"

The kid was doing more good thinking than I'd done in a month of Sundays. I was puffing to keep up.

"I don't think so," I said. "You'd just start competing to see who could make the best, the most or the funniest ones."

"I don't think this is such a good one," said Walter. "People say it's working out fine, but I don't think so. Maybe it doesn't run on ethics. What's the point of globalising synthetic photosynthesis, if neighbours like the one we've got here want to make other people's lives miserable, just because they're greedy? Why should humanity colonise the universe if we take greed and selfishness with us? Unless evil has its own subatomic particle."

"Your father would say we're learning 'learn truth, compassion and wisdom.' Your mother would advise 'feel at one with everything, everywhere.'"

"And what would you recommend?" asked Walter.

"Don't let anyone destroy history." That was another quote from his grandmother. "How can you go forward, if you don't know where you've been?"

"I want to be head of the *World Time Council* when I grow up. Like Uncle Joe. Then I can boss you around. If you're still around, that is."

"Why shouldn't I be?"

"You know."

"I've stopped."

"I'm glad. Are there people who want to prove this universe is bad?"

"Yes."

"Why?"

"Because they find being bad interesting."

"Are they after you?"

"I think so."

"Good, I'll put that in my play. You'll get them, won't you? Makes a better ending."

"I hope so. I certainly plan to make their lives interesting."

"Why won't President Zula recognise Digital Nomad Tribes as Communities under the *Whole Earth Charter*?" asked Walter.

"Communities are defined under the *Charter*," I said "as an ecosystem on land or water with human beings willing to be registered stewards of it."

"But she could change the Charter if she wanted to," said Walter. "She helped abolish nation-states, why not accept virtual communities?"

"She's got bigger problems," I said "with corporations and religions."

"Dad says you sacrificed *Nirvana* to fight corporate mercenaries," said Walter.

"Enlightenment doesn't mean much if you let evil run the world."

"Like the old Indian king you used to tell me about," asked Walter "who wouldn't go into heaven if his faithful dog wasn't allowed. President Zula knows she's going to be assassinated doesn't she? If Zula's the Earth Mother, why should we call her They?"

"Probably already to seen her death in a dream," I replied. "It wouldn't be pleasant; reality ruled by enemies, all dark except the tiny flicker of light."

"President Silabhadra said that in this age the path to holiness winds through the valley of action. Does that mean violence too?"

"It depends how strongly you oppose injustice. Why are you asking?"

"Grandpa," said Walter, "Dad thinks you shouldn't talk at my school. He says they won't understand your attitude to hurting people physically."

"How are things going there?"

"Alright. I suppose. My English teacher, Mr Slade, Eldon Slade. He's totally creepy, wants to be a priest, that is if they make religion legal again. But he's helping me write my tragedy. I want it to be an epic, Grandpa, a hymn of praise to life. The Sustainocene needs its earth-redeeming Buddha, Christ and Mohammed; its own ecosystem-saving Beowulf, Ulysses and Hamlet. I believe in Zula's dream, that the Earth will have life and have it abundantly; but I worry I'll never find the words to tell the story of our pilgrimage away from the Kingdom of Emptiness. Merlin says I lack the lyrical rhythms and plain, strong verbs. Still I pray for sufficient grace to show people what can and must be changed, so they can learn to love what does not. I have this feeling someone radiant will help me. Meanwhile, I'm doing a catalogue of all Dad's books, reading as I go."

"You be careful around that Mr Elbadawi. He's been mixed up with some shady characters."

"Grandpa, I saw this face at the window a few nights ago," said Walter. "Old Bugsy started barking and scared him off, whoever it was. I don't know how he got past Dad's security. Those men chasing you won't come here, will they?"

"Walter, I fear if you emulate me you'll only do violence to yourself. No, I pray listen carefully. You know me as *une icône respectée dans quelques mémoires pour son rôle au sein de la Résistance à la Mondialisation Corporative*. And it's true I did good service to the Earth in one of its most needful hours; never then being noised abroad as chasing vapours of glory or baits of pleasure. But the time seems fixed and expired by which my mind might drift clear of tempests yet brewing in it from the heat of those days. Mark what I say. Much in my thoughts now is malignant, overcurious, dissatisfied; shaming me should, like some our most exalted unitives, it be flashed as public images on the brow. Dost thou attend mon *petit-fils*? My soul reconstitutes diminished with each breath; fast and slow, high and low, tormented, played with by the forest airs. I agitate its trembling remnant forming rash opinions about evils and denying sad events can ever be aptly fitted to those before or after. My life, *mon pauvre vie, c'est déréglée et débordée*. Too often I've made the fool's choice; to do good tomorrow rather than today. Ah, then why is old Jean Moulin here? Because I'm tough and with the blessing of some unfamiliar wise spirits and your kind parents' permission, I find myself undertaking something new and good; a staycation to renew acquaintance with my unalloyed, un-poisoned self."

∞

Lunch was homemade bread, local cheese, vegetarian lasagne, olives and wine, prepared by Helené, whom we thanked by holding hands around the table and making a wave while chanting "thanks to the cook." It was served on a small table near the GSPP stove that sat on a floor of sea blue tiles. From the kitchen window you could see the washing line, woodpile, chook pen and the 'game-keepers cottage' where I'd been housed. François' large Gondwanan felt hat was hung on a peg on one wall beside a portrait of Helené sitting in *padmasana* or lotus pose.

The food was delicious. After coffee came communal washing, drying and putting away. Merlin, François and I, accompanied by Old Bugsy, then set out to walk down to the meadow.

"Tell François," said Helené, as we opened the door "to show you his crop of spewberries."

Rain clouds were passing towards the east; sunlight emerged through thinning ash in the west and a rainbow spanned the sky. A little grey squirrel raced up the side of a mossy beech tree. Old Bugsy tried to chase it, but gave up. Looking back in the direction of the sun after climbing the steep hill before the meadow, the town roofs with their historic cream-coloured chimneys resembled a prickle of porcupines. The sides of the beech trees were covered with moss, vines and rain drops that made them look like they were sweating. Pale yellow sunlight slanted through, painting dots of white on the creepers and making patches on the forest floor with soaked brown leaves appear like stain glass windows.

François asked Merlin to put two broody chooks in the bow.

"Watch sir," Merlin said "how you hold the fowl by the legs. There will be a charge."

François was wearing a faded green Molonglo cricket cap, white hemp shorts, an open-neck blue soy-cotton shirt and sandals. He paused to pick an apple from a tree whose branches and roots intermingled with those of other species. Underneath the dripping canopy were passionfruit and raspberry vines, then nearer the ground various herbs and vegetables. Chickens clucked and pecked amongst the mulch. François munched on the apple while leaning on a woodpile. The nearby pond cast reflections that dappled the house and one side of his face.

"I call this apple tree Lisbeth," said François "and its friends are Audrey the fig, Miranda the mulberry, Emma the lemon and Vivian the orange. I reckon Lisbeth and Vivian are up for the wild time, but they keep it quiet. Imagine, once people thought a large bank balance a better indicator of wealth than a good wood pile. Gentlemen, we're standing at the most productive part of the garden, the edge where two ecosystems meet. It's modelled on a wild forest; crazy profusion, but all edible and mutually supportive. The chooks and Indian runner ducks munch the snails and slugs plus providing fertiliser and endless play for my girls. Some mates at *Le Bec Hellouin* said I should put my henhouse and piggery in the greenhouse, their body heat makes the caged marrows cosy in winter. I've got a pile of tiny reeds over here as homes for insects and rocks in the birdbath so the bees won't drown. Moit, every output is an input. And when you turn up at the Butterwalk market to sell the produce on Sundays, there's no bloody Southwark-type facial recognition software to suggest what each customer will want. You have to talk with them instead."

Merlin told stories of coming back from walking in the paddocks with snake venom splattered on the toe caps of his boots; of watching a butcher bird string up in a bough a baby dove then tear it to shreds, of how he once threw a pump that wouldn't work into the creek and of the time he'd reclaimed Pippy the Muscovy duck from the farm where the mistress of the house had exiled him for quacking too loudly in the morning.

François then showed me the stone wall he'd constructed. It was beautifully done, a testimony to the awareness he'd brought to the project. I gave him a seedling I'd arranged to have sent here from the gingko biloba tree of the Luohandong Chinese Buddhist-style temple at the GSPP Centre in Namibia. We planted it together. François told the story of a dog called Hopeful.

"Hopeful was a little, three-legged terrier who used to come down when Dog was on heat, to check out the situation," said François. "We called her Dog because she was too naughty to get a proper name. But there were usually thirty other suitor dogs and a mastiff would soon get rid of Hopeful. But having like me an artistic streak, Hopeful used to walk down to have a look at the sea from Big Hill before he hopped off home."

"What about your spewberries?" I asked, feeling at the point of vomiting myself.

"Oh, she meant these heirloom tomatoes," said François pointing to some plants in his veggie garden. "It's a simple story. We went out to dinner at this local Italian restaurant. They only use best local produce, no genetic modification. Anyway, I had extra helpings of the tomatoes. But too much. When I got home I chundered, yep the old liquid laugh as mum would say; regurgitated them up all over the veggie patch. Just dug the mess in next morning. Well, next spring, there they were, a bumper crop of the best Italian heirloom tomatoes. My spewberries."

François showed me how he'd made this box with a candle and one side open with two ravelling strands of wool going up to a branch.

"I set it near where we rear the pheasants," said François. "You give the wool a twist and the box goes around and round as the wool ravels up and down. The moving light keeps the foxes away."

"Speaking of which. See him up there, waving at us?" said Merlin. "Elbadawi."

"He's going to have an outdoor exhibit," said François "for each of the early approaches to artificial photosynthesis, as they called it then. We've tried to stop it, but he's bought off the neighbourhood, promised them benefits."

"I wonder if it's come to this," said Merlin "because he's a once in a month man."

I walked over to the fence. Mr Elbadawi, wearing Wellington boots covered in mud, stood waiting for me.

"Morning," I said "Mr Elbadawi, isn't it?" We shook hands.

"Yes. I know who you are. You've some timely objection to my little enterprise?"

"People aren't sure it will be in good taste."

"Visitors aren't expected to eat the exhibits," said Mr Elbadawi. "I'm doing this because I happen to think global synthetic photosynthesis is the best thing humans have ever given this planet."

"Well, my son is worried it will degrade the landscape," I replied. "Make it difficult to keep farming successfully here."

"Please tell them to write their concerns," Elbadawi said "and I'll address them. I've already had a few. The best one so far was: 'next time I meet you, I will kill you, cut off your testicles, boil them and eat them.'"

Mr Elbadawi grimaced occasionally, revealing he was in persistent pain. We talked a while about local weather, gossip and cricket. I established he did know Gordon Lizzard and had heard about the death of a girl in Hampstead during the GSPP celebrations.

"When I bought this wood, *Gentle Shaw*, from Mr Frank Paradox," said Elbadawi "Old Frank said Green Wood, as he called it, would bring me peace. So now I pick this apple and enjoy the beatitude of seisin. That one over there with the Wollemi pines I bought from Miriam Revel; you know the daughter of Hugues. I'm calling it *Brayly Lovregana*."

"I'm not sure what you're up to," I replied. "But leave my family alone. I know all about you."

"Forgiveness, Jean; that's the primary virtue of the Sustainocene. I've been rehabilitated. I hope we can sit down and talk about it over a beer one day."

"I don't think so. With me, it'll always be remembrance first."

"Jean, often I walk amongst these trees barefoot," said Mr Elbadawi. "You should try it. There's nothing like feeling mud between your toes and grass on your soles. You're welcome on my land or at my home anytime. I'll introduce you to my wife Askala and my daughter Lucie. She's a bloody good cricketer. I heard Walter's organising a game. Count us in if you've got the spots."

I bid him good day and re-joined the others.

∞

The sun shone like a grail through the trees. The three of us sat in the dappled light on lush grass opposite the willow trees by the stream. Little drops of water sparkled on the tips of leaves and blades of grass standing out against a shadowed backdrop. There was a tinge of autumn colour in the leaves nodding sleepily on the light breeze. One or two oak leaves fluttered down like adventurous butterflies. Green-grey mossy rocks, ferns and twisted grass and brush wood from floods covered the bank. Lizards scurried away. I was fascinated by the uniform swirl of the currents, their smooth flow with streaks of light over a rock that bounced back and forth. My son had replenished the stream's brown trout by constructing a series of gravel pools and riffles with retaining lengths of felled timber and GSPP-impregnated blocks. On a nearby island, frogs croaked in coarse symphony amongst sedge and rushes, the water there flowing through a stone-filled chamber that blocked fish that ate more tadpoles than newts or dragonfly nymphs. Midges in Brownian motion made occasional rip-

The sun shone like a grail through the trees

ples on the light grey and dark green waters as they avoided patrolling demoiselle damselflies, or at dusk the sorties of pipistrelles and Daubenton's bats. Chaffinches, grey wagtails, woodpeckers and kingfishers took turns twirling about François as though he were a May pole. And as he knelt to dig up a few weeds, a tiny robin red breast hopped just out of reach in shy hope of unearthed edibles.

"Each morning," said François "this little one sits on that branch and sings for a mate. '*Je viens du sud. Je suis votre homme.*'"

My hands were shaking and I had a dreadful headache. I saw Caroline standing behind Merlin, but knew it was a hallucination. I looked at Merlin, wiped sweat from my brow and repeated in my head the Serenity Prayer as he'd taught it to me. I sat and meditated through the terror.

"There should be nothing between *Loorungah* and the Café Royal," said François staring towards the sea.

"The haunt of Oscar Wilde," Merlin explained.

"Yes, I know," I replied. "'Morality is simply the attitude we adopt to people whom we dislike.'"

"It's true," said François "we've all been very moral towards your brother."

"But what did you think of him?" asked Merlin. "Our Mr Elbadawi? We can't get rid of the bastard quick enough. He's making a right nuisance of himself. Smooth talker, wins people over. Accused me of poisoning trees to ruin his reputation."

"Did you?" I asked.

"No way. As if."

"I doubt he's a people person," said François.

"Plays cricket," I said. "Gun bat and a pace bowler. So he reckons."

"Really? Merlin, don't take this the wrong way," said François. "But I'm not sure your stories are always good for the children. Your Gondwanan slang's too risqué. They use it at school. No one understands them."

"That story was meant for old Gautama over here," said Merlin.

"So what happened at the London GSPP celebration?" François asked me. "The news said it was suicide after a drug overdose."

I outlined the facts, so far as I could. While I did so, Merlin began breaking twigs into similar lengths and soon handed a bundle to each of us. It was 'Pooh Sticks,' a game the three of us had played since forever. We each placed one twig in the stream side-by-side, released them simultaneously on the count of three and then watched as they bobbed along in the current. The aim was to see which stick went under the small footbridge first. Old Bugsy had thought the sticks were for him, so I had to throw a larger branch for him to fetch.

Merlin's stick always seemed to win at 'Pooh Sticks.' He claimed it was because he visualised his stick taking all the paths to the bridge, then quantum collapsed it into the fastest route. I asserted his victories were due to his rubbing hair oil into the bark to make them more buoyant.

"It's my version of the *I Ching*," said Merlin, inspecting his sticks. "You'll be doing some travelling Jean. Down a river and through a desert with an evil eye above. Not alone. And make sure you take your old gun."

"Did you hear about Old Frank?" asked François.

"Which Old Frank?" I asked.

"You know, Old Frank Paradox who used to live in that cottage by Green Wood. One day, a few years ago when he was out in the fields, his wife hit the middle three boys on the head with an axe. The oldest and the youngest, Jevons and Scott were away. But that didn't kill them so she strung them up. That took some doing, what with one of them a big 14 year old boy and all. Then shot herself. Left a note saying it was because Frank'd been seeing another woman. But Frank reckoned it was because they all had AMDS, unresponsive to gene therapy. After that Frankie hit the bottle pretty bad. A few of us had to help the eldest boy Jevons take over his wine and spirit business for a while. Frankie knew a lot about port; putting the filings in to get rid of the impurities. 'Port's a living thing' he used to say 'it matures with age like a human being.' If it got cloudy, though no one moved it, Frank said it was the east wind. Even if the port was in a cellar inside and there was no drought, it was still the east wind. I'm not making this up. There's a spot over there with a view to the east- you can see the brown woods, green fields and white houses all together below. Old Frank loved that spot. Scattered his ashes there on a windless day. Old Frank was a bit of a boy but he loved his port."

"That explains a lot," I said. "It didn't turn out so well for Jevons." We sat a while in silence. "It's likely to officially be declared a suicide or an accident. The girl's death at Hampstead."

"What puzzles me," said Merlin "is why you were sent there at all."

"He's not having a go at you Dad," said François.

"That was Eugene, the WTC computer," I said. "Never made an error before. The Hunck, Hercules Huncks was sent on leave. It was supposed to be him."

"I never liked his behaviour in that Carstairs matter," said Merlin. "It may be live and let live, but how can you respect a man who openly expresses a sexual preference for anything that moves? Father wasn't like that. Old Charlie Huncks was a team player; top bloke, give you the shirt off his back."

"If the WTC knew Nancy Godel was evil and a threat to the Sustainocene," said François "then it was obliged by its Charter to decommission her, wasn't it?"

"She had some strange dreams. Maybe Nancy might've learnt to Mindscan by herself," I said. "It could happen. But she'd have to be a mathematical genius."

"Like you, Dad," said François.

"I should have patented it," I said.

"Wouldn't have been right," said François.

"The WTC my boy," said Merlin "is no longer a force for good in this world. Hugues Revel was a leader of great benevolence and trust. Your brother was at that WTC function where Hugues toppled, like a great oak surrounded by brambles."

"I need to visit the *Global Synthetic Photosynthesis Centre* in Namibia. But Uncle Joe's taken me off the case. He's going to send me somewhere else."

"That's ominous, knowing your brother," said Merlin. "The whole GSPP ideal is stuffed. That paper by Aratani in *Nature* linking GSPP technology to depression; the excavations of Norman Charles and Li Sun at New York revealing the intriguing complexities of Corporatocene culture; the stories of Gurjusted about the glorious will to power of the Corporatocene barons and the acolytes. All this is making the Sustainocene seem tiresome to the young."

François stripped off and went in for a swim. I joined him. Old Bugsy ran around on the bank trying to save us.

"My wife is also always trying to save people," said François. "She failed with me, of course."

"You need total immersion," said Merlin "to wash away your sins."

"Come on in. It's good for the heart," said François.

Merlin declined. The water slipped past shadows from the mossy, fissure-trunked willows, then subtly modulated over sunlit, smoothed rocks of various shades of brown. The sound was like a train on tracks with an occasional plonge.

*Her touch a flux of electricity;*
*As light on river rocks*
*Shaded by trees.*

∞

Helené arrived with Tess and Anouk, just after we'd got out and dried ourselves. Old Bugsy went over to get "big pats."

"Look at the lovely moss," said Helené to Tess. "People spend years trying to grow that in their gardens and here nature does it naturally. This moss has lived at this spot for millions of years and now man has begun to move and sell it."

François bent his head over to drink straight from the icy cold stream.

"Can I tell you the brim of your hat is in the water?" asked Anouk.

"Yes," François said, looking up with his black beard wet. "If I was a real cowboy I would drink like this." He took his hat off, filled it with water and drank so it ran off his chin. Then, looking at Anouk, he gnarled his face, grimaced and bent forward shifting his eyes. "Gold" he pronounced, pointing ahead down the river. Tess squealed with delight. "This is a Queensland hat. They're very poorly made."

"Why did you get it?" I asked.

"I didn't. Mum stole it from some former mining magnate," said François. "They roll their brims up. But I straightened it out and I think it's quite a good hat now."

François went over to Tess and said "cuddle, cuddle."

"No," said Tess, pointed to a jet vapour trail above and said "guy." The child then said something I couldn't understand and ran around with Old Bugsy.

"She's saying 'you can't get me,'" said Helené. She then had an argument with François about the risk of snakes. So François carried barefoot Tess in one arm and growled guttural sounds at her.

"It's his tribal origins," explained Helené. "Tess looks so contented in his arms. Mum can hold him anytime, but this is a real treat. I'll be honest Jean. I'm not holding out any great hope you'll beat the grog this time either. I don't care what Merlin says about AA; there's still a full bottle at the centre of your mandala."

François, his arms getting tired, put Tess' feet on his black boots and marched off. Tess laughed.

"If she turns her head," said Helené, "she'll get a view most women would envy."

The interaction I was watching had many seeds of happiness worthy to be planted outside our solar system. The late afternoon sunlight kissed the grass between the willow trees. Helené sang the *Alexander Beetle* song to Anouk.

> *"I made the kind of noises that a beetle likes to hear. I went 'weedle, weedle, weedle.' And then there was a Beetle house with Alexander Beetle coming out. And he gave the kind of look that he thought it might be me."*

One of Merlin's 'Pooh sticks' floated free of an obstacle that had held it and was caught in a small eddy that took it back to the starting point.

∞

In the evening, after the children were asleep, Helené set with cutlery the large blackwood table off the kitchen. We were seated around it on checked blue cushions on antique wooden chairs. On the wall was a portrait of my parents in front of their farm. Helené served potato and leek soup, followed by potatoes, beans and fish.

"Where do you get the energy to prepare such a meal?" I asked.

"Oh, everyone has a different sort of stamina," said Helené. "I have physical stamina."

"And I am at the service of my wife," said François, as he ladled out the soup.

We spoke about the *Whole Earth Council*. The consensus was that Zula Calabiyau was making a foolish decision to seek another term as President. Old hands on the Council with more questionable motives would resent her popularity. Opinion divided on whether she'd appropriated assets from corporate confiscations to fund the globalising of synthetic photosynthesis and whether that was a bad thing. François gave his critical assessments of some of the latest writers and a recent production of the *Tempest* he'd taken Walter to that made Prospero out to be Zula Calabiyau. Desert was a caramel flan with whipped cream. François served the port.

"The curtain comes down now," said Merlin. "The drinking stories start. Well, used to start. Seems only the master and mistress of the house are sipping port now."

"I once went to a poetry reading by Spencer Lizzard," said François. "He seemed too angry to be in tune with the wonders of nature."

"It's said Spencer Lizzard," said Merlin "was chasing a girl at a party. Eventually he got her to consent in the kitchen. He lifted up her dress and put her down on the hot stove top. I can never look at him when he sings or recites his poetry without thinking of that sizzling bottom."

François hunted though a pile of vinyl records, now also all the rage, and put on *Adagio* by Samuel Barber. We all sat listening, the butter soft beside a candle, the red tip of the wick tinged with blue, the dark triangle inside the yellowish outer flame. The flame seemed to sway like a tiny dancer in the cross-currents of breath. Beyond the flame was a jar of vegemite, ceramic plates, glasses and a water-filled bowl with red flowers. Merlin's arms, crossed across his tummy, rose and fell with each breath. He sat pontifical, in a sitting chair, apart from the dining table, near the record player. Helené sat with head in hands, eyes closed. At the conclusion, François put the record back in its cover, then put on a piece by 'Mozart WA' the '*Laudate Dominum*' from *Vesperae solennes de confessore*.

"Once I heard one of those hillbilly science-contemplatives of Zula's telling a crowd that the story of Noah and the ark was all myth," Merlin said. "And an old Russian with a 'T' shaped beard came up to him and said 'But once there was a great flood.'"

"That sounds," said Helené "like one of the stories you tell the kids when you're drunk. There's been too much drunkenness altogether, if you ask my opinion."

"For several generations now," said Merlin "the Moulin family has been in charge of morals in these parts, telling the villagers how to behave. We shall not be stopping any time soon. The greatest ethical test is whether you can go for a long walk with someone you feel no empathy towards and not try to change them."

Candles were shining through near empty wine bottles. Only a few remnants of food remained in the serving bowls. People were leaning back in their chairs. François said he had been re-reading *King Lear*. He mentioned the idea that Yahweh, was originally a Sun God.

"It's strange to think," said François "that the worship of God by Jews, Christians and Moslems may be obeisance to a literary character, that cantankerous, neurotic, vengeful Stone Age Divinity blowing around in the Sinai Wilderness ironically tormenting his prophet Moses. Certainly there is a lot of Sun worship in the Hindu Vedas. My own view is that Buddha and Jesus, who were too completely realised as characters to be wholly fictitious, respectively tried to draw out the essential elements of the over-ritualised

Hindu and Jewish faiths. I'll even go further and say that Jesus must have had a passing understanding of Buddhist ideas. You only have to compare the sentiment and styles of the *Dhammpada* and the *Sermon on the Mount* to see this is so."

"Jesus spoke to her accusers," said Merlin 'he who amongst you is without sin, let him cast the first stone.' She immediately was struck between the eyebrows with a rock. 'Oh, mother,' said Jesus 'I didn't see you there.' As we laughed, Merlin put on a sour, sad face and added "It's reputed that the old men were the first to leave."

"You meant 'his' accusers?" I asked.

"I meant what I said," Merlin replied. "Each age has its own saviour."

"Last week at the University," said François "I told this class of young mademoiselles that no virgin could hope to understand Chaucer. Well, the prettiest one winked at me and they all walked out."

Merlin told stories about the time he'd worked as a tour guide at the Normandy University while François was teaching there.

"I used to throw a rock against a high window," said Merlin "and François would poke his head out raging. I'd then say 'and there is the Professor of Canonical Literature.' There were lots of stories about François in his single days. It was said that some young fellow barged into his office complaining about an assignment to perform 30 minutes AR-certified *dharana* that's unbroken concentration Jean in case you've forgotten, on Keat's *To Autumn*. 'I can't achieve *dharana* on Keats,' the student whinged. 'You will achieve *dharana* on Keats by 8am tomorrow morning' said François 'or you will vacate your rooms.'"

"Professor," I asked my son, "were you ever in love with Spicer Layamon?"

"Yes I was," said François. "But nothing came of it. We studied Contemplative Literature together under Professor Eike von Rapgow at Oxford. Spicer Layamon was like a Queen bee surrounded by drones. Way out of my league."

"Speaking hypothetically, of course," I inquired "what do you reckon she'd be like as a lover?"

"Violent," said François. "In my humble estimation, Dad, she'd be violent as hell."

Helené served coffee with chocolates.

"He writes all over the books he likes," said Helené. "You should see his *Will in the World, World as Will and Idea, Fabric of the Cosmos, Narrow Road to the Deep North, Marcus Aurelius, Patanjali, Thirty Nine Steps, War and Peace* and *Towards Zero*. On some pages you can barely read the original text."

"Unlike you Dad," said my son "I don't look to literature for wisdom, merely pleasure and delight."

"You look tired," I said to François.

"I was up early," he replied. "Yesterday, we went to the wedding of Miriam Revel over whom the doctors were shaking their heads. All the read-outs said she was going to die of cancer in twelve months. Refused genetic therapy, said the elderly had 'looked too damn well for too darn long.' Face was eaten away to that of a little bird. It was a hot day. I spoke something serious."

Merlin mentioned Gordon Lizzard and his activities with the corporate recusants.

"He's made a big mistake," said Merlin. "If I were him I shouldn't want corruption associated with my name."

"Maybe he's miserable," said Helené. "Life wouldn't be worth living unless you were miserable."

"You do say some silly things," Merlin replied. "I went down a coal mine once. Some say the hell of the Corporatocene began in mines, a global form of manganese madness. You had to strap these lights on your head. You could see who was afraid. One light was bobbing up and down. That was M. Moulin."

∞

For a week or so thereafter, I sat in the mornings working at the old desk in the gamekeeper's cottage. The sun, as it had it my youth, having burnt the mist off the waters, looked in upon me with serene, satisfied face and no question on her lips. Just after dawn, a pair of blue-throats would sit on the branch of an oak above a wooden feeding platform and sing until I brought out some sunflower seed. Survival of the cutest, the new reiteration of Darwin's basic idea.

I found a spot below the oak and would sit there for an hour before dawn meditating. The forms of *dharana* and *dhyana* I used did not replicate those mundane, stylised systems incorporated in the universal daily contemplation or recommended by the *Book of Common Faith*. Instead, I evoked a moment from my childhood when Joseph was away with dad visiting another specialist. My mother had returned that spring morning with fresh-baked bread, a man was whistling outside amongst the apple blossoms. I stared at my thumb till it seemed infinitely heavy, yet infinitely far away. This moment of rapture or ecstasy so many years ago had been my personal key to effortlessly and spontaneously achieving that royal goal built into the structure of life. I knew that once again I could find boundless joy in watching the sensations and feelings, the fluctuations of thinking evoked by each moment of the day. It would not be as easy as before. I had many painful memories from the Corporatocene War and my alcoholism to spring clean. But the strong PD protection of the farm had helped me. I was in much better condition to search for Nancy's connection with Zula and to get to know Spicer if she was interested.

In the afternoons, I walked alone, or with Walter and François, through the surrounding forest. The straight-trunked beech trees muffled all sounds, except for occasional calls of redwings, calandra larks and melodious warblers especially near the burbling rivulets. François was the legal guardian of this forest. He'd brought actions in its name against people who wanted to build a road through it, or remove some dead trees that were home to a family of Bohemian waxwings. As he walked, it seemed as if the tallest trees bowed their heads in respect. Eugene once told me that he admired the collective consciousness of a forest much more than that of a city. I asked the trees to pass on my respects to Trudperter Hohelied. Gradually the feeling I needed to drink to feel whole began to leave me. The headaches, sweating and nausea had abated, much as the sea calms after a storm has passed.

*A goshawk floating for prey*
*Mocks clouds of ponderous,*
*Rain-shadowed greys.*

One afternoon I helped François cut grass with a sickle, "just a quarter of an inch at a time." When I came too close François jokingly imagined the AR news "Professor's hand cut off. Work slows down on next volume." François spoke about Levin using the scythe with the peasants in *Anna Karenina*.

"But as Mum used to say," said François "the natives of New Holland didn't cut grass."

Merlin had devised a cricket game with Walter on the back pavers. He'd rigged up some bird netting and stumps. Merlin under-armed Walter golf balls and Walter batted in pads and helmet with a piece of hardwood dowling about the width of his thumb. Walter pretended to be one of his selected 11 stuffed toys. There were the green stuffed elephants who opened or went first drop: Lump, Grump and Trump; the cagey old all rounder Bush Walk Ted; Moonie, Dragon, Barbar. President Zula and Hugues Revel, being heroes to Walter, were also in the line-up. Walter and Merlin argued over every wicket and how many runs went for each shot.

"Never lift the ball till you have your ton," said Merlin. "Watch from the hand, to pitch to bat. Back foot towards off; keep low and head still over the ball in the cover drive. Hold for three seconds." Every ball was entered in an official scorecard. Any universe in which cricket evolved was turning out alright.

One afternoon in the forest, I came upon large quartz rock with purple and orange bands. Someone, probably my son, had inscribed upon it: '*The passive master lent his hand to the vast soul that o'er his planned*.' It was a sunny midmorning. I could hear the crackling of leaves in the trees, some flies buzzing, the sounds of tools being used, a few bird calls. A breeze spirited through the pine trees. Turtles were basking in the sun by a pond.

It was as if the collective spirit of the trees was talking to me. From somewhere floated into my mind a vision of Eugene as the tin man from *The Wizard of Oz* lying dying in such a forest and being tended by Zula Calabiyau. Then suddenly I saw Spicer Layamon. I recognised it as a Mindscan connection. Her eyes expressed great kindness.

'*Il faut cultiver son jardin*,' said Spicer. A helicopter thudded through the air overhead. I instinctively crouched. If the WTC tried to decommission me here in Normandy, that's probably how they'd do it. Maximise my psychic distress. I'd covered my tracks well, but I couldn't stay much longer.

When I returned, I went under the farm house looking for some better pliers to fix an old gate. There was an ancient fridge and a lot of garden material down there. I overheard Merlin and Helené conversing directly above in the living room.

"He needs love," I heard Helené say. "Jean's old-school sexist."

"He's very lonely," said Merlin. "I find it unbearable with him around. He just watches Walter and I at cricket, doesn't join in. I suggested he go and walk in the woods. So off he went down the road. Later, I sent the children after him."

"His brother's an eccentric too," said Helené. "But very successful at the WTC."

"But Joe's eccentricities aren't Jean's," said Merlin. "They were bosom pals, before their parents died; the very model of an ideal and indivisible youthful friendship. Though of course there were those stories about Joseph and missing pets none of us would believe."

"And Jean was the noblest of boys, the most well arrayed of his class. It's a great tragedy when someone knows the unitive life as well as he, then misplaces it."

"Jean still yearns for the brother of his youth. I sometimes wonder if it was more important to him than marriage. You know, all that's mine in Caroline, I give thee?"

"His was always her second-best bed. Used to call Jean and Joe, Norman and Butchie, never knew why. Jean actually spoke good French before he got married. Don't know how she put up with him."

"Might have. Remember the broken marble kitchen table after that row?"

"Caroline used to run him down in conversation at parties. I think something happened with her brothers up at Wallaby Valley. She never got over it."

"I don't think Jean's all that bright despite those things he claims to have invented," said Helené. "But being at the WTC with all those intelligent people should be a good balance. He hasn't got a clue about gardening or fixing things and he puts salad on top of the other vegetables."

"He watches," said Merlin. "Always seems just about to enter into a conversation. He's an enlarger, not a straitener; thinks he's in the middle and understands the situation."

"He's a nervous wreck," said Helené. "I think he could end up a melancholic. And I don't for one minute believe he's stopped drinking."

"I haven't seen him off his face; but he goes around with a grin like a shot fox."

"Caroline used to sit right where you are and tell me, 'Jean's a deadset dipstick; no-hoper. Pretends to rush around busier than a cat burying shit, but he's got no clue when he's on the turps.'"

"But that was after Caroline joined the WTC. I remember just after they were married she told me Jean was one of the moral men she knew, almost frightening in his old fashioned values, a very strong sense of loyalty to the vulnerable."

"Funniest thing Caroline ever did was put ping pong balls in the church organ, just before their wedding. They were still finding them years later."

"And the sad thing was Jean had achieved everything anyone could in contemplation and then gave it all away for love of her."

"He's been taken off that Hampstead case. The big one."

"Probably the drink. I told you so."

"They say it's really extra-judicial execution, what Jean does with the WTC. No effective oversight. Well, we don't want any of that here. Sooner he's gone the better."

I stepped out from under the farm house. The full moon was just coming over the trees. A high wind was up and night's swift dragons were cutting the clouds full fast. I was desperate for a drink. Little Tess came outside.

"Some people haven't been nice to me at preschool," she said.

"What did they do?" I asked.

"I forget," she replied and ran back inside.

> *Alone, fitful bat*
> *Roves the mauve and ochre air*
> *Around the moon.*

Back in my room, I lay on the bed staring at the ceiling. Yes, there are times when person suspects some Greater Mind subtly exerting control, not only over thoughts, but over events that create moral choice. Maybe somewhere, some Committee of Minds, perhaps themselves serially watched, had sat down and meticulously worked out the destruction of Nancy Godel, Zula Calabiyau, Jean Moulin, the *Global Synthetic Photosynthesis Project*, the *Whole Earth Council*, even our universe itself; testing the main lines, creating alternate actions at certain points, leaving provision for the unforeseen; all in a terrible travesty of what humanity should have become in the Sustainocene.

Then two scenes floated upon the rippled surface of The Big Well or Tunnel, as I liked to imagine the amphitheatre in which I undertook time travel. The first one, which drew upon one of my favourite mystery novels, was of me trying to warn Nancy that she hadn't got a right to do what she liked with her life. I was trying to express what was so vivid in my mind and so halting on my tongue. This was that it may be just by being somewhere — not doing anything much in particular — just by being at a certain place at a certain time — that she might, by surviving, accomplish something terribly important — perhaps even without knowing what it was.

The second scene was the elderly Buddhist monk Zarmanochegas in Athens at the time of Caesar Augustus, having travelled from India via Antioch; lathering his body with oil and stepping, while Jesus of Nazareth watched, onto an ignited funeral pyre, so both might die blameless.

∞

On my last day at the farm, François organised a period-costume get together for the local community. The purpose was to raise funds and materials to help the Revel family rebuild a house accidentally destroyed by fire. He converted his woolshed into a dance hall. Outside was a wooden wagon with a freshly painted sign *'leaves in time for the ferry.'* Some distance off was a large pile of wood that François had cleared some months earlier from nearby forest to reduce the fire hazard. It was going to be a bonfire.

Cricket was all the rage in this part of France thanks to Merlin's influence. A scratch limited over match had been arranged. It was the Moulin family against all comers. To the scent of new mown grass was soon added the vision of the Other's openers walking to the wicket. Mr Elbadawi spun the bat in his hand, sleeves rolled to the elbows, then took guard. At the other end was his daughter Lucie, long blond hair flowing over her shoulders from under her maroon helmet.

"That's middle and leg," said the Umpire. "Right arm over."

Then came the sounds of the toe of the bat tapping in the crease, the thump of the ball into the keeper's gloves and some barracking "top cherry," "good nut." "bounce the bastard." François bowled fast and Merlin excellent leg spinners. Surprisingly, I also found a length.

Mr Elbadawi was out caught in slip by Merlin off the bowling of Heléné for ten. It was clear to everyone, except Merlin and umpire Eldon Slade, that Elbadawi hadn't snicked it. Miriam Revel, the square leg official, indicated she hadn't heard a thing. But on seeing Slade's finger go up, Elbadawi simply put his bat under one arm and walked off. Lucie scored a fast fifty with some strong drives and pulls. Askala batting at seven scored a quick thirty including two sixes off Merlin back over his head. The Others set the Moulin family 130 to win.

We started badly with Merlin bowled first ball by Elbadawi. Elbadawi was generating real pace and zip off the pitch off a long run. Walter scored a solid 85 but crowned himself going for a zac over the mid-wicket fence. When he was only on ten runs Walter collided in mid-pitch with his father and both lay sprawled on the ground. Mr Elbadawi held the ball in hand at the non-striker's end and could easily have removed the bails to effect a run-out. Instead, he turned on his heel and walked back to his bowling mark. 'He can't be that bad' I thought to myself. 'Or he's very cunning.' We needed 50 runs off ten overs with nine wickets down when I joined François at the crease.

"Mate, I can't do this," I said as we met in the middle of the pitch. "I'm a ferret, usually go in after the rabbits."

"Just play straight and keep 'em out," said François. "I'll take Elbadawi."

François was whacked on the chest by the next delivery that reared off a good length. He didn't rub the bruise. The following ball François skied an attempted hook to fine leg. The pill carried just over the upstretched arms of the mug fieldsman who'd drifted in too far off the rope.

"Great shot! shouted Merlin. If you come back next year mate, you're gonna get it. You're gone."

The next delivery was also a bumper, but François pulled it over the square leg boundary. Feet were stomping on seats. Each ball I faced I seemed to survive only by an act of divine grace. I got wild applause for every defensive shot, my bat never rising above my knees and surrounded by fieldsmen like seagulls after a hot chip.

Finally, it came down to one run needed to win with one ball to go. François had given up the strike after a three from a fierce square cut. I went for a huge woofta off leg stump and missed. But the ball glanced off my pad and past the sprawled keeper. Two leg byes. The Moulin family was home.

"Winners are grinners," shouted Walter. "We're Masters of the Universe."

"And next year we're putting steroids in the beer," said Merlin.

"Try beer in the beer," said Elbadawi.

"All part of the 12 step plan," said Merlin. "Remember the 12 step plan you blokes. And it's the last step you've got to worry about."

"Worry about it tomorrow," said Elbadawi. "Now you need to commiserate."

The sun cut through the poplars and willows, over the cow paddocks, to sparsely treed Big Hill with Elbadawi's property beyond. Dusk came on. Around the wagon the grass had been flattened. Pink lanterns had been tied to a rusted galvanised iron wall. The bloody body of a slaughtered sheep was being fixed with wire to crosses at either end of a long pole over a fire. Inside, cut leafy branches festooned rafters thick with looping cobwebs that hadn't been cleared in fifty years. A long wooden table was laden with green jellies, loaves of home-made bread, scones and cream, old amber beer bottles, glasses and a keg.

The band was a Gondwanan one that Caroline had liked. Called '*Baskerville Willy*,' it was built around an old, white-whiskered gentleman with a kindly face who played the accordion. He kept time by tapping with the back of his left heel on the floor boards. Beside him, a younger fiddle player tapped with the front of her right foot. A man with glasses was plucking a bass string attached to a forked branch that came out of a packing case. The sax player with thick brown hair wearing a long leather jacket was using a Mackey Ergonomic Stand. At the end their first song *Maybe Nancy (Can Save the World)* (a Spencer Lizzard ballad) there wasn't much applause.

"Bollocks. What the fook's wrong with that one?" old white whiskers asked the crowd. They all laughed, started clapping and the evening kicked on from there.

Eldon Slade, holding shears was chasing a man with a half-shorn beard. Tess in a yellow dress with green stripes and a ribbon from her tied-back brown hair was carrying a bunch of white gladioli beside her mother. Merlin, holding a whip, grunted at some bullocks. Walter sat with Anouk.

"Conradin bribed the fiddler," Anouk said "so we'd be 'ones' in a '*Cold and Raw*.'"

"Did he try to kiss you?" Walter asked.

"He tendered his affections," said Anouk "in a note passed by the punch-bowl." She tasted the punch. "Hey, you didn't?"

"Just one bottle," said Walter. "Jean won't miss it."

"Well, in any event," replied Anouk "I brand Jean an atrocious dancer. He has as little aptitude for it as a bear. Why, he led me out on the left with his paw down. Then, he grasped my elbow with such savagery his thumb caused a shock down to my little finger. Next, he called a simple *Roger de Coverley*, then blamed the musicians' poor tempo when he failed to set a figure."

"And what about that quadrille?" Walter asked.

"Well, he kicked, slid and capered about," said Anouk "blind to crossings over, stumbling in the promenade, bouncing whole body not from the hips, leading me like a veggie basket, not a 'being of gossamer like Zula,' as was Merlin's delightful complement. Jean kept whispering about spices or something. It was weird as. What were you burying by the stream yesterday?"

"A stone," said Walter "I'd carved on it the secret of how peace would come to the Earth and evil be banished."

"Well, as Zula says, the choice is either to let humanity kill itself, or enlighten it."

"I don't like our English teacher, Mr Slade."

"Neither do I."

"He picks on the weak kids like little CW. You know CW Leonis, hazy kid, faints a lot. Orphan; says his parents were mayfly people, lived a full and happy life but only for one day. Yeah he's a total weird ass, Slade. Didn't like it when I put that vial of salt water near the candle on his desk and set it alight with radio waves."

"Good one Walter. Speak up; even if your voice shakes."

"As Jean would say 'Resistance is only beginning.'"

At dinner, as I ate mutton, Mr Elbadawi sat beside me. He seemed a bit under the weather and tried to show me how he tuned his ukulele. Old Bugsy came up and nuzzled the back of my knee with his nose.

"Hey you old woofa," I said. "What's your story?"

"My dog has fleas," Elbadawi said. "Don't know all the notes. I just listen to a lot of music."

"You played well today."

"Thanks. Seemed to remember a few things."

"That last number," I said. "It really got my blood up."

"The sax," said Mr Elbadawi "bleated like an underfed goat. It was a disgrace he received a standing ovation. To tell you the truth, they play too many Spencer Lizzard songs. All those unresolved discords and dark endings in Picardy thirds."

"Experts rate his '*Better Life*' with Coltrane's '*Blue Train*,'" I replied. "Perhaps it *was* overquick?"

"My own grand-daughter," said Mr Elbadawi "would never have been permitted such damnably close compressure and intertwining of limbs."

"But maybe ritualised positioning of limbs?"

"I couldn't help but notice," said Mr Elbadawi "your delight in *La Boulangere* with all its crass mimickry of infidelity. I saw your granddaughter corkscrewing and threading the needle, some boy laying his rude hand upon the bare back."

"You're too drunk, sir," I said "to be worth a punch."

"I think it is the punch," he replied. "Forgive me. I've had a few too many."

François came out holding a burning brand. Adults and children slowly gathered around. With a theatrical flourish, François ignited the bonfire. It had been well stacked. Soon the flames were over five metres high and throwing off sparks that drifted like fat, angry fireflies against the night sky. The fire's glow was upon the faces and palms of the ringed spectators, as if about them shone the haloed lineaments of ancestors summoned from identical rites Druidical.

"In past times," said Elbadawi "in Christian London, the top of this fire would have had an effigy of the Pope stuffed with live cats. It is in midwinter an act of Promethean rebellion against Nature's curfew and promise of cold darkness."

Then a dreadful high-pitching crying, like children in terrible pain, came from inside the pyre. I was getting ready for a rescue mission, when François held my arm. Suddenly, from out of the flames ran little charred balls of fire; baby rabbits squealing in agony. It was the same sound I'd heard watching a baby rabbit eaten whole by a goanna in the Tanamai, while holidaying with mum and dad.

The children in the crowd initially were too shocked to cry; then they began screaming. Old Bugsy ran off and hid. François grabbed a shovel and chased the little suffering creatures about, banging them on the head till they were dead.

"Must have built a warren in there," he explained, as he washed the blood off his shovel. "Stupid not to have checked."

∞

Next morning, I packed my bag and said farewell to my son and his family. I'd worked out a plan during my time with them. François assured me he had more than enough security installed to deal with Mr Elbadawi and had asked the local police to track any suspicious actions. Lunette had arrived early; sunlight glinted on their spotlessly clean windscreen as they waited for me.

"I hope," I said to Walter "your *Tragic History of the Sustainocene*, ends with the breaking of a staff rather than an old man." Walter quoted a few lines from *The Book of Common Faith* —

> "To Earth cede sovereignty, so life in all its forms
> Flourishes in fairness with unitive mind.
> Humans as stewards and none seeking freedom in lust."

François stepped up and handed me a piece of paper. It was old and I recognised my mother's handwriting.

"Dad," said François "I found this in a copy of grandmother's copy of Marcus Aurelius. It's addressed to you. See the date. Written when you and your brother were only eight years old, I think. The handwriting is more scrawly than her usual script. I think it's a dream she wrote down after waking and then added a few thoughts. I discovered it last night while going through some old boxes; one of those cosmic coincidences you might say."

I put the paper in my pocket, hugged everyone and said my farewells. Soon I was seated inside Lunette. As we sped along through the French countryside, I read what my mother had written all those years ago.

> *I dreamt last night of little Jean, grown up,*
> *In a war helicopter at dawn over a beautiful island.*
> *Three planets in a triangle and a crescent moon overhead.*
> *His brother Joe in Jean's mind,*
> *Urging Jean to commit murder,*
> *A bigger murder than either could imagine.*
> *I've prayed when this time comes,*
> *Joe will have had a change of heart*
> *Or Jean resist his brother's torment.*
> *On a little boy's courage, so much depends.*

∞

Finally, being as prepared as I could, I logged in for my trip up the space elevator then on the Teleportation Shuttle to the rendezvous at the WTC's Tipler–Gott Cylinder. Uncle Joe no doubt had planned a different type of trip for me, probably a one-way ticket. But I was going to visit the *Global Synthetic Photosynthesis Centre* in Namibia shortly before Nancy Godel was killed. I had no idea how I'd pull this off; but something would turn up. I'd planned and prayed about it.

The fellow in charge of business at the T–G Cylinder this week was Mersenne Twister. Mersenne was a thin dude who wore a wispy beard and was always bopping around to some cool music through his AR. In conversation, he seemed to be able to think five sentences ahead. He had a bit of a reputation, but I liked him.

"Jean. Back again. Packing this time, bro?" asked Mersenne.

"Always. Liking guns isn't a perversion."

"Hey, sick; the secret G-gun. Show me?"

"No way."

"Suit yourself. Hey Jean, you must have really pissed off the WTC."

"Bad location?"

"Never seen worse. Bummer, man."

"I've got another. Better."

"Can't do. You know the rules."

"But I'm here now. I can't just turn around."

"That's right; you can't go home from here."

"Stuck?"

"Might be able to make the WTC transfer, with your G-gun. Always options."

"It's a death ride and you know it."

"Sorry. What about me? This may be my last time, bro. Yep, they're shuttin' down the old T–G cylinder. Six suns crushed to the size of your hand, strung out and spun real fast to warp space. That's what they say. Though if you ask me, it looks more like a jazzed-up teleportation system. Can't say that of course. Anyway, you'd think they'd want the technology to continue. How'll we be protected from time misbehavers if you guys are gone? Hey, something coming in," said Mersenne, his eyes going up right to check out his AR. "Yeah, you sure? OK. I'll tell him."

"Who was that?"

"Our other transferee, going a bit before you. Made an offer for you to come along. Must have picked up our conversation. Got authority."

"Who? Where?"

"Can't say. You want in? Immediate answer requested."

"Sure. Why not? I'm in the mood."

"Well, you lucked out his time bud. Came up trumps, is all I can say."

"Yeah? In what way?"

"Man, how does a bum like you land a babe like that?"

"Cut the clowning, What babe?"

"Spicer Layamon. Gordon Lizzard's squeeze; that Spicer Layamon. Immediate full access authorisation. Can't say where she's off to, but she wants you along and her wish is our command. Man, if you had problems focusing before, you will now."

Mersenne nodded his head in the direction of an ante-room where I could see Spicer sitting in a short dress with her legs crossed, reading some novel. I walked over and went in, trying to look as casual as I could when I felt three broad complexes and half a case of bananas away from ventricular fibrillation.

She looked at me with her calm, unwinking, unwavering aqua blue eyes. I wondered if there was a solar flare anywhere in this Universe that could split the ice in that stare.

"Hey shamus," she said "I was thinking time makes everything mean and shabby and wrinkled, but you come in radiating your own synthetic brand of sunshine to split my muddy waters."

"Hey sister," I replied "could be you're in the market for playing tough girl blues singer, but maybe I ain't buyin."

"You think this is the face of someone who cares?" she came back. "Too many passes made at it, and it's grown a little too cynical dodging them."

"Not bad. This Gordon's doing? Uncle Joe?"

"Believe me if I said 'no,' on both counts?"

"Probably not. My AR wiring's loose. How's yours?"

"Grounded. In fact, you'll find I'm all adjusted, all over. Let's cut the hard-boiled vocabulary, Jean. If your shadow's cut with an engraving tool, we'll know when I open the blinds tomorrow morning."

"Uncle Joe wise to your play? Eugene?"

"I hear you're something less than indispensable."

"So you're escorting me."

"I'll wear the tacky association, if you don't buckle with the rebuke."

"You a covert?"

"Of course. The best."

"Code name Sibylla?"

"Hey, that's super-impressive."

"Where are we going? Unauthorised, no doubt?"

"Just a brief and tight trip. I don't want to mess up your plans. All in good time."

I tried Mindscanning Uncle Joe, but he was PD'd to the max, uncontactable, probably out boating on Lake Leman. Spicer's security scan checked out. Highest level clearance from the President herself. Where was she taking me? Still, I preferred her destination to Uncle Joe's.

We sat ready to depart in the plush, high-backed chairs built for nostalgia not neuralgia. She held my hand. 'All in good time,' seemed rather short in these parts.

"You know, don't you?" she asked, staring at me; just a cute touch of insecurity.

"It was the ease of your antiquated ripostes. Too creative, too perfect."

"Then you also know why I'm here?"

"I could guess. Something quaint, highly prized in your circles."

"Bullseye."

"I'd assumed it was better guys, less damaged."

"I'm delighted you're still intact."

"How far have you gone?"

"End of the line, *mon lapin*."

"This is important, isn't it? Too important to be left to a piss-artist like me."

"Amazing. You figured that out all by yourself. A maiden could get bowled over."

I instinctively reached into my pocket for a celebratory drink from the *Hipflask-Of-Unwarranted-Good-Fortune*. But it was missing. I'd thrown it away. Thank goodness. Spicer touched me on the nose with her right index finger.

"Let's seal this time with a holy kiss," she said and we did.

"Get ready dudes," Mersenne shouted. "We're bendin' spacetime; ramping up the superstring symphony and Q entangling you tourtereaux in a pulsating quantum vacuum. Dig that pony. Strobe lights, back beat; let's go funk this T-net teleportation, fake time T thing."

So, we were off again, to prove that even when intellect and strength had gone, gratitude and tenderness still lived on in the heart of man. And thou, as they say, is that. Courage to change the things I should, wasn't going to be an issue. You might imagine my nervous anticipation synchronised with the palpitation of night and day, or that somehow my emotions and the world merged into one continuous greyness, the sun becoming an arch of fire and beneath it the great buildings of decadent men rising, then crumbling in abominable desolation.

But in fact, I was in a peculiar mental state most of the transfer. Well, peculiar because I hadn't experienced it for such a long time. It was a compression and accentuation of every romantic and passionate feeling I'd ever known. It was as if my mind had withdrawn from external objects and gathered itself into a single whole, letting go of all labels and attachments dealing with past or future, 'inside' or 'outside.' There was just bare awareness paired with a preoccupation to bring justice to Nancy Godel and save Zula Calabiyau. But as to where I was going, or when, I had no idea. If this was how prayers were answered these days, I'd have to do it more often.

*Along the shallows barefoot at dusk;*
*Shoals of star light,*
*Calm mind a lure.*

# IV

# PARADISE WHITE, ZEBRA RIVER

*Global Synthetic Photosynthesis Project (GSPP) Centre at Zebra River Namibia — Zula the founder welcomes Omran her main supporter — science lectures followed by contemplation seminars — life and characters in the GSPP Centre — Zula's photosynthesis treasure hunt with school children — Zula's friend Kofi killed — GSPP Centre Intensive Care Unit — GSPP Centre attacked — GSPP Centre abandoned —*

The *Global Synthetic Photosynthesis Centre* at Zebra River was an offshoot of the Namibia University of Science and Technology. It was Zula's intention for it to be completely financed by a worldwide crowd-funding initiative. Zula founded the GSPP as a global benefit company married to a public good (the flourishing of Earth's ecosystems under human stewardship) and over time almost all citizens on the planet became shareholders. In the end, a few contributions were permitted by anonymous philanthropic donors (including her friend Omran Tariq) the African Renewable Energy Fund (a programme of the Africa–European Communities Energy Partnership), the African Development Bank and the Earth Bank Energy Sector Management Assistance Program. Unsubstantiated claims were made by her detractors, however, that Zula had illicitly financed GSPP from corporate confiscations. It was a smear she'd never been able to entirely remove.

Building the GSPP at Zebra River with local labour was designed to foster a practical and symbolic connection between Zula's Nobel-Prize winning synthetic photosynthesis research and the nearby plains where Neolithic stone tools rested in the open alongside stromatolite fossil records of earth's first photosynthetic plants. It was also planned to be a powerful symbolic and practical manifestation of technology transfer in favour of Africa, the developing world, the Global South.

The site was a lush two hundred-hectare area that had been transformed through GSPP technology from a desert landscape amongst the Tsaris Mountains east of the red sand dunes of Sossusvlei that border the Atlantic coast. The central research building was a Vincent Callebaut-inspired gigantic lillypad with a central cubane geometrical structure housing the labs. Its wavy carbon nanotube exterior was covered with a tough film of silicon light harvest and water-splitting cells. This central structure was sited in a lagoon surrounded by exotic plantings of tumboa, elephant's trunk, upside-down baobabs and the giant aloes called quiver trees.

Adjacent was the recreation and accommodation centre: a tall Demain Spiral inspired by William McDonough's *'Tower of Tomorrow'* that combined a light-harvesting and water-splitting exterior with hanging and atrium gardens integrating water and waste recycling. Other teaching buildings resembled mangroves, boababs and fig trees. The administration block was a Rolf Disch heliotrope. The conference centre had a Renzo Piano green roof and walls of Alec Tzannes cross-laminated timbers. The student facilities block was a homage to Frank Lloyd Wright in the elegant way it blended with the substantial tree plantings. The library roof was a Glenn Murcutt-inspired span of metal and tin. In choosing these ancient architects Zula was making the point that design idealism had been alive even in the heart of the Corporatocene.

Interspersed amongst these structures of science were monasteries and meditation halls based on the model of the ancient Buddhist university of Nalanda in Northern India. Their pavilions, verandas, cells, courtyards and

Our goal is to work cooperatively and with respect for basic ethical principles, to produce the scientific breakthroughs that allow development and deployment of an affordable, equitably accessed, economically and environmentally sustainable, non-polluting global energy and food system that also contributes positively to our biosphere.

stupas (many topped by a small harmika platform with umbrellas) had coloured eves, pearl-red pillars, carved and ornamented, richly adorned balustrades and roofs covered with tiles that reflected light in a thousand shades. They seemed to soar above the misted rainforest parks, so those contemplating there might witness the birth of winds and clouds. Winding around the monasteries were many interlinked pools adorned with blue lotus flowers and fringed with red-flowed kanaka and shade-giving mango groves.

As I watched, my AR triggered a few lines from the *Franklin's Tale*, quantum entangled so I saw and heard Chaucer himself reciting them.

> *"May hadde peynted with his softe shoures,*
> *This garden ful of leves and of floures.*
> *And craft of mannes hand so curiously,*
> *Arrayed hadde this gardyn, trewly,*
> *That nevere was ther gardyn of swich prys,*
> *But if it were the verray paradys."*

Outside and surrounding the scientific complex were houses of the workers and their families who had transferred from Katatura. These dwellings (called *nawa stoep* or 'nice veranda') had been designed by Zula in a modular shape inspired by the amplituhedron and the bumpy rear end of the Stenocara beetle. Their surfaces shifted during the day and night in response to wind and temperature changes, to optimise condensation and insulation, as well as collection of photons and rainwater. Each house had pockets that collectively could store a total of 35,000 litres of water, enough to irrigate the 20 hectares of permaculture garden linked to it. To say these families were grateful to Zula would be an understatement. They worshipped her for her kindness and provided an armed and highly trained security force for the facility. On the right side of the front gate was a small plaque with these words:

> *Our goal is to work cooperatively and with respect for basic ethical principles to produce the scientific breakthroughs that allow development and deployment of an affordable, equitably accessed, economically and environmentally sustainable, non-polluting global energy and food system that also contributes positively to our biosphere.*

∞

Spicer and I had been introduced as Zula Calibiyau's WTC security detail. I soon discovered we'd not arrived, as I'd hoped, a week before Nancy Godel's death. Instead, we'd touched down moments after we left the T–G cylinder. So, the T–G cylinder wasn't operational or was a fake as Mersenne had intimated, just a T-Net portal. The WTC was losing its grip. Spicer seemed to have been working for Zula all along. Maybe she was part of the WTC's plan to get me decommissioned.

Today, we stood beside Zula Calabiyau and Kofi, the short, middle-aged administrative head of the GSPP Centre, near the helipad designed as a gigantic leaf. We heard the throbbing in the sky before we could see the small dot emerge from behind a cloud. The helicopter approaching contained Zula's old friend Omran Tariq, the former CEO of Tariq Enterprises and long-time supporter of Zula's quest to globalise synthetic photosynthesis. AR surveillance showed the helicopter also bore a specific threat to President Zula. Inside the cockpit was Jevons Paradox. Eugene wouldn't give me any information about this development. I didn't like helicopters. I'd led a Protective Squadron of them in Lutruwita during the Corporatocene War and the memories weren't pleasant.

Zula Calabiyau was 33 years old by set genetic age. She had long brown hair and wore a light grey-green dress that brushed the ground. I surmised this was designed to cover the unusual disease which made Zula's lower extremities look like bark and tree leaves. Zula was unlike any person I'd ever met. She seemed to move and talk with an unaffected grace; as if the vast intelligence of the cosmos was taking great joy not only in glowing out of her, but incorporating, or integrating rather, her quirks of personality and unique insights into the process of self-realisation. Happiness and sadness flowed across Zula's countenance like clouds over a blue sky. She seemed to wish nothing, yet all about her was evidence she'd achieved much. There was a sort of inward knowingness in her gaze, a delicacy in how her fingers touched objects or people. It was as if her personality had given peace and truth an objective form; in Zula's presence, the calm of it was all through you and the light of day merely a shadow. I reminded myself Zula wished to be referred to as a 'They,' 'Them,' 'Their' person, not a 'she,' or 'her.' It wasn't an easy thought to habituate when looking upon an Earth goddess so beautiful.

Zula Calabiyau

The machine set down in a cloud of dust. Spicer and I saw the two passengers emerge head down, their clothes buffeted amidst the dust cloud whipped up by the blades. The younger one, whom I presumed to be Omran, tripped and briefly scrabbled on his hands and knees.

A few minutes later, Omran Tariq, dusting off his clothes, met Zula. I heard Zula playfully introduce Themself as now the "former head of the *Global Synthetic Photosynthesis Centre*." Their respective assistants and advisors peeled away and the two comrades sat alone, drinking tea under a quiver tree in the shadow of the tall Demain Tower. We sat nearby. Jevons Paradox, perched near us. His face was badly scarred with keloid from what looked to have been plastic surgery after a severe burn. He kept glancing at Spicer.

Jevons was more than just a hit man for the Mafia. Bernadette had said he was heavily implicated in child pornography and illicit drugs (like the ice Nancy used before she died). Eugene had warned me Jevons was part of the recent failed assassination attempt on President Zula in London. So why wasn't Eugene giving me warnings about what Jevons was planning now? Spicer and Omran must have known as much about Jevons as I did, but also took no action and didn't seem disturbed by his presence. Jevons, I thought, must also be a double agent.

Zula offered Omran some fair-trade chai from Windhoek. Zula poured the hot water onto the bags in the pot, then turned it clockwise a few times. They chatted for a while and Zula filled his cup, then Theirs. Omran grimaced as the hot water touched his teeth. Zula might have resigned Their position here; but to all the staff Zula was still the GSPP boss.

"We've just seen the rock carvings at Twyfel Fountain," said Omran. "Still look just like the first time you and I saw them."

"Remember, we call it |us ||aes," said Zula, making dental and lateral clicking noises at the beginning of each word.

Omran spoke with child-like wonder of the things he'd seen in the last few days; of the cheetahs that lacked retractable claws and couldn't smell because their nose was designed to allow maximal oxygen as they ran fast, the black lumps of ostriches on the plains, the prides of lions and herds of antelope drifting across the heat-hazed highways, or a single tree before huge red dunes.

"You see those weaver birds," said Zula, pointing. "The female demolishes the nest the male has made if she doesn't like it."

"Then it was lucky you made this nest," said Omran.

"As soon as I saw this place," said Zula "I had a vision of the entire GSPP Centre." Omran groaned with pain and held his jaw. "You have some pain?" Zula asked him.

"This tooth's killing me."

Zula reached over and touched his cheek.

"Hey, the pain's gone," said Omran. "How did you do that?"

"I just happened to remember the *mantra*," said Zula.

"I've heard there's been more assassination attempts," said Omran

"Just the usual. These two WTC agents are protecting me."

"That's hardly reassuring," said Omran, staring at us.

*Vultures lift in the heat haze;*
*Shadow steps behind*
*A distant tree.*

∞

Zula escorted Omran around the Lillypad scientific complex, showing him the latest developments with the assistance of updates from Kofi. We tagged along. Jevons walked behind us, looking about with obvious interest, but also often at Zula. A current security clearance was required for access to the compound and to each seminar room.

"The *Global Synthetic Photosynthesis Centre*," said Zula, for the benefit of Spicer and I "follows principles like those employed at Nalanda and encapsulated by ancient scholars such as Pierre Hadot. We're aiming not just to produce excellent scientists, but fully developed human beings. It's been very pleasing to see so many of my former students, post-docs and PhDs doing so well, indeed doing so much better with their optimisations since I left."

Young cyclists rode past, then students with black academic gowns and tassled caps, each acknowledging Zula. My AR showed none had a concealed weapon. I admired the stone turrets and partly illuminated stain glass windows. Sunlight lay like a transparent cloak on the green lawns about the sacred gingko biloba tree and slivers of silver light danced on dark water under the lagoon bridge.

"That tree over there," said Zula "that's a van Aken orchard tree. It bears 40 different types of heirloom fruits — apricots, plums, peaches, nectaries and cherries. I did some of the grafting myself and cut my thumb. People say it makes a crying sound at night because I grafted a bit of myself into it. Over there are our recreations of the venerable baobab trees *Holboom* and *Makuri Leboom*, destroyed so long ago by corporatogenic climate change. They're a great symbol for the Sustainocene. Store water, bear fruit and edible and medicinal leaves, plus their regenerate bark can make rope, baskets, clothes and hats."

A young female student with wild eyes rushed up to Zula and grabbed the hem of Their dress.

"Oh, how are you?" said Zula, recognising the student.

"You know, you know all," said the student, who acted as if she was talking to God.

"No, but how are you Jan?" asked Zula, putting Their hands on the student's shoulders.

"Oh, you know it. Give me an answer," continued the student. Zula smiled and looked into her eyes.

"The whole world is love," said Zula. "Read about Wangari Maathai and her Green Belt tree plantings, or about the little girl Amrita Bishnoi's sacrifice of her life to save a great tree."

Tears came to the young student's eyes. She walked away much more content and confident.

"Change of season can often bring despair to monks," said Zula. "Even scientist-monks."

Zula showed us the *sala*; its well-polished floor of marble open to the air on three sides. A sign directed that shoes be taken off. The roof was supported by numerous pillars coated with small green tiles, every second pillar had a GSPP-powered electric fan attached to deal with the summer heat. Scientist Buddhas were sitting in small groups drinking tea and coffee. Artists were painting a mural depicting the story that after the Buddha was enlightened, a rainstorm came and a seven-headed serpent (*naga mucalinda*) spread its hood to protect him for seven days and nights. The Buddha was shown seated on the coiled and protective snake.

"One of my many jobs here in the early days," said Zula "was to admonish the 2am carousers. But that's not the done thing now. I was good at the 'dogflight game.' We scientists, like musicians, supple of wrist, delicate of eye."

I was impressed by the quiet, poised manner of the students. Outside the *sala*, I could see the yellow sun making white the edges of dark roof shingles, the various shades of green, orange and crimson leaves and flowers beside the grey stone buildings. We walked through an old iron gate and I got some rust on my fingers. Fat brown sparrows took crumbs from the palms of students on the lawns. More students walked past in the chill, morning air with hands thrust in jacket pockets or riding sturdy green bicycles. None of them looked like assassins.

We inspected the GSPP library from outside a tourist rail. During the Corporatocene War, the great libraries of the world had transferred here for preservation rare and significant books and manuscripts, as well as digital preservation mastercopies totalling almost a yottabyte of data about every object on Earth. At the front of the reading room a board depicted Earth composed from millions of tiny pictures symbolising all those people, ecosystems and robots who'd donated to the GSPP. It bore a Latin maxim modified from Oxford's now destroyed Bodleian library '*Omnem animam viventem pertransibunt et multiplex erit scientia.*' My AR, with Eugene's usual attempt at irony, translated this as something Mary Shelley was writing: '*All forms of life shall go to and fro and ever more abundant shall be their knowledge.*'

*Warm desert breeze;*
*Just risen from the lagoon —*
*Willows and a girl with long hair.*

∞

Complex biometric security was required for entry to each lecture complex. AR checked every entrant for Q entanglement with known criminals. Jevons Paradox registered high for such associations, but nevertheless was permitted inside, hundreds of students were engaged in seminars, workshop and tutorials. Zula took us to a discreet rear viewing area in one lecture hall.

A scientist Buddha was leading a vigorous seminar discussion. Students were reporting findings from various projects, their words appearing automatically as images and symbols on a large central screen. They spontaneously applauded Zula. Three dimensional hologram images of synthetic photosynthesis floated around. "We found a cobaloxime and a cobalt-tetraaza-macrocyclic complex displayed excellent $H_2$ catalytic efficiency using micro-Clark electrode." "Transient absorption spectroscopy facilitated initial kinestic insight into photogenerated species in single crystals of ferroelectric material." "Efficient electrochemical water oxidation by maghemite nanorods anchored on a three dimensional nitrogen-doped carbon electrode." "Facets tuned the surface atomic structure and we minimised electron hole recombination, promoted efficient charge transfer and absorption from a wider solar spectrum with energies higher than that of the semi-conductor band gap."

Upon the hour, as the bell went, the students began singing what I was informed were the GSPP Moral Principles and Ethical Policies.

*So serve like a bee,*
*Principled eco-society.*
*Nano-roads and cities,*
*Make fuel from sun and sky.*
*Gathered on a part,*
*Bright, still heart.*

"The GSPP Moral Principles," Zula explained "are designed so that our science facilitates personal moral evolution. They require acknowledgement of personal failings and a desire to overcome them through research for the benefit of all beings on Earth."

"And the GSPP Ethical Policies?" I asked.

"They assist this organisation," Zula continued "to function harmoniously. They emphasise striving for consensus, not drawing the GSPP into public controversies, not letting GSPP endorse any outside enterprise lest problems of money, property or prestige divert us from our primary altruistic purpose. Our budget requires no more than twelve months' prudent reserve; most of our income must be voluntary, anonymous and crowd-sourced, limited to two percent of the Universal Basic Income per person, per year."

"Very idealistic," I said.

"They're not rigid prescriptions," Zula explained. "Most sensible people respond to a strict code by either hypocrisy or open rebellion."

The students moved to their next class. We followed them. They were soon evaluating concepts and ideas such as: "upon withdrawal of attention from the body (*pratyahara*), the fundamental mind-stuff (*citta*) abides in itself," "the purpose of the virtuous life is suppression of fluctuations in the mind," "when the mind is held immobile for the space of twelve restrained and elongated breaths the first stage of concentration (*dharana*) has begun," "absorption (*samadhi*) begins after the mind has been deliberately immobile for half an hour."

"When the contemplation has been sustained for some time," the teacher continued "the meditation subject should be discarded and concentration focused on just the fundamental mind-stuff. Some of you may experience *nimitta* or visions, for example a bright light like the sun or moon, or else celestial beings, ghosts and spirits. But if these are ignored your mind will absorb into feelings of tranquility and bliss, losing self-awareness and experiencing deep sleep. Eventually, when your mind becomes strong and resilient, non-dual consciousness or *samadhi* will be effortless and constant."

> *How boundless the sky,*
> *How transparent the moonlight,*
> *How tranquil our sun.*
> *This very Earth is the lotus,*
> *For those with vision cleansed.*

In a third pod of the teaching Lillypad, young scientist Buddhas with eyes closed were sitting cross-legged on mats, or lying on their backs with arms to the sides.

"This is where the real synthesis takes place," Zula explained. "They're practising a contemplation technique called *sanyama*. Their minds are entertaining a technical difficulty in applied physics and engineering at the very threshold of unbounded consciousness, so its essential nature shines forth in purity. We have made many great discoveries this way."

"What is the general routine here?" Spicer asked Kofi.

"Meditation is from 4.30am," said Kofi. "At 6.30am, my students go out to collect alms with bowls. Chanting is at 7.30am, then they eat their only meal at 8.30am. After, they do synthetic photosynthesis research till sweeping paths with broom at 3pm, drink tea at 4pm then return to research. A gong is sounded for evening chanting when sunlight fades. Then they have a lecture on meditation for an hour and an opportunity to ask questions about their research with their mentors."

*Our Sun's love differs from dross and clay,*
*For it splits water not to take away.*

∞

Finally, in the GSPP drama theatre, we watched students rehearsing a musical. It was called *'A Comical History of the Sustainocene'* and the playwright was Spencer Lizzard. Little Walter had competition. Spicer and I sat next to each other, a few rows behind Zula and Omran.

"It's hard loving someone who's selfish," Spicer whispered.

"That's an old song. And cruel to exoskeleton-bearing aquatic invertebrates."

"Let me show you love's favourite hiding place," Spicer said, snuggling up.

The lights in the theatre went down. Spicer extended her coat across our laps. The musical was based around a fellow called Hamiltonian. For a bet with his friend Ammonia, Hamiltonian was trying to achieve vibronic coupling with a girl called Hydrogen who was in an uneasy relationship with Carbon Dioxide by luring them into a Hilbert Subspace, where he hoped there could be convergence of time scales of nuclear and electronic motion, counter-rotation, transformation and then charge transfer. Meanwhile, the weird sisters Nitrogen and Oxygen were arguing with their brother Biochar over how life had become so confused.

The climax was a scene where Hydrogen, pert as a cider gum crow in her whalebone corset, tricks Hamiltonian and elopes with a gypsy violin player called Fluorescence Quenching for a life as a white witch, fortune telling in fairs. This, at a stroke, restored the fortunes of the *Whole Earth Council*.

From the little we saw it wasn't a bad piece of theatre. Much dramatic capital had been made from nicely balanced moral situations; there were soliloquies and arias presenting us with the proud but self-dramatising mind of Hamiltonian suitably troubled by violent uprisings of total energy.

I overheard Omran ask Zula about a rival group of artificial photosynthesis scientists in New York who'd rejected Zula's contemplative angle.

"They claim," Omran said "you've infringed their patent over some approach that enhances the catalyst's self-repair capacity."

"With them it's all about the power and prestige," Zula said. "It will be unfortunate if they undermine the reputation of GSPP. But I have no problem with competition or IMPs. All the GSPP affiliate centres throughout the world compete and collaborate with us. So do hundreds of independent research groups."

"Those people can be ruthless," Omran asked. "Do you feel safe, here?"

"I project good will towards my enemies every morning," Zula replied. "There are only two types of day; the day where you're going to get killed whatever you do and the day where you're not."

∞

Towards evening, Kofi invited Spicer and I to listen to an organ recital at the GSPP chapel. It involved interesting improvisations on the old GSPP anthem *Split by Sun*.

After the concert, we attended dinner in the oak-panelled GSPP dining room. A butler stood in black tie on a balcony above as we came in. Zula and Omran sat with the Dean, Master and other Dignitaries in high carved chairs with red backs at the high tables. Spicer and I were placed below them at a table with some students; all wore their black academic gowns.

The walls were covered with the portraits of famous scientists, ethicists, policymakers and contemplatives who'd made breakthroughs relevant to globalising synthetic photosynthesis. The ceiling was beautiful white plaster with the nobs inscribed in gold. Upon it was painted in gold copperplate *'Vos estis tam sancti sicut vultis'* ('You are as holy as you will to be').

During dinner, a blond-haired female student played on the violin a contemporary piece called *Forbidden Band Gap* inspired by the phenomenon of zero time in quantum tunnels. The movement of her glistening yellow bow reminded me of a white witch stirring a cauldron.

One of those at our table was Christine, a transgender person who was a senior registrar in the Intensive Care Unit at the Centre. Christine wore board shorts under a blue dress, a red tank top, a purple floral turban and silver rings in each ear. She had a thickset, well-shaven jaw, dark eyebrows and hairy, swollen legs in fish-net stockings. She was discussing the threat of a nuclear attack on the GSPP centre with a younger doctor seated beside her.

"One missile's unaccounted for," said Christine. "I dialled the AR numbers of the radiation threat protocol. One rang out, the other was disconnected."

"Green gowns. It says you've got to wear green gowns and gloves, sterile ones."

"Yeah, sterile, of course," said Christine. "And give potassium iodine, a shovel full. Then contain contaminated water. With what? Urine bottles? Kidney dishes? Pipettes? The bloody ostrich protocol."

"Says you've got 24 hours and anyone presenting's likely to be highly disturbed."

"Wouldn't have imagined that," said Christine.

Lady Agatha Asquith was visiting the GSPP Centre to see her daughter who was a student here. She was told the only spare places were at the table with Christine, Spicer and I. She walked over and introduced herself in an affected accent.

"I am the Lady Agatha Asquith and this is my daughter the Countess de Boer."

Spicer stood, pointed at me and uttered one of the wittiest remarks I'd ever heard.

"Well, I am the Lord God Almighty," said Spicer "and this is my only son Jesus Christ the redeemer, in whom I am well pleased."

Lady Asquith laughed. We all got on famously through the rest of dinner. Spicer became an immediate cult heroine amongst the female scientist Buddhas.

Late in the evening Spicer rose to her feet and delivered a dramatic rendition of the *Casta Diva* (Perfect Goddess) aria from Bellini's opera *Norma*. Its conclusion was received by tumultuous applause, whistling and shouting.

"I'm the bee," said Spicer as she sat down "who stings the men that hate the Earth."

"A wasp, more likely," said Christine. "Buzz off with me honey. I love this dear old Rock and I've got the stuff to make us love it even more."

"Thanks," said Spicer, rubbing her toes against my ankle under the table. "But I've got other plans for tonight."

"Lucky them," said Christine.

∞

Next morning, I left Spicer curled up in bed and walked to the window. I watched the senior scientist Buddhas set forth in file to walk the streets of the surrounding villages and receive rice in their bowls from the wicker baskets of devout householders. The folds of their robes were like the stripes of tigers, moving fast, some very young, dwarfed by the huge begging bowl slung, in its holder, over one shoulder. The sun was an orange balloon in a pink sky. A cock was clawing in water buffalo manure.

*Away from the crowd,*
*Buddha in a ruined stupa.*
*Leaves at his feet.*

I saw a senior scientist Buddha steal a bottle of soft drink from a road-side store in the presence of three young novices. Even here some seemed to take advantage of the custom that they were supported by the rest of society.

On return, each alms bowl was set on a stand and covered in cloth. A bottle of water, a cup and a hand washing bowl were placed before each scientist Buddha. Plates with various meat and vegetable dishes were set out. Kofi, the current Dean of the scientist Buddhas sat in a special chair. He spat regularly into a spittoon, shading his mouth with his left hand as he did so. Kofi led a few minutes chanting, during which time the scientist Buddhas stared at their food bowl and reminded themselves: "food is nothing. I eat it to support my research, I do not wish it to be another source of pain."

> *Monks eating in the sala.*
> *Yellow leaves falling,*
> *Amidst bamboo.*
>
> *Rock studded mound.*
> *Lizards rustling,*
> *Amongst the straw.*
>
> *Bare grey earth.*
> *Between bamboo groves,*
> *Birds calling down the sunlight.*

∞

Mid-morning, Omran, Spicer and I heard Zula give a lecture to visiting school children from an orphanage (there being many such establishments across the world as yet another sad legacy of the Corporatocene War). The hall was made of large hardwood trunks treated with a GSPP nano-impregnate that allowed the structure, not yet sentient, to make oxygen, clean fuel and fertiliser from water, sun and air. It also provided self-cleaning, insulation, tensile strength and heightened load-bearing properties combined with a high AI rating that altered components, shape, colour and translucency to improve the mood of its human occupants, its plants, animals and birds.

"The hall," Kofi explained to me "has sensors that pick up the symptoms and signs of AMDS. We haven't had a single case here in Namibia, touch wood."

The students looked to be about ten years old and most sat quietly on mats, some talking or playing games. A quick AR scan showed no weapons amongst them or their teachers and no interlopers.

"Good morning children," said Zula.

"Good morning President Zula," they all chanted together.

"Today we're going to talk about photosynthesis," Zula began. "Did you know that more power from the sun strikes the Earth's surface in one hour of each day, than the energy used by all human activities in one year? Do you know the average daily power each person needs?"

"It's 65 kWh/day," said a little girl with pony tails and braces.

"Yes, that's right," said Zula patting the little girl on the head. "it's about 65 kWh/day; in the Corporatocene it used to be double or even triple that. But there was a lot of wasted energy in those times. Can you tell me the main things power used to be devoted to in the Corporatocene?"

"Making war, money and pollution," said the little girl. "The Corporatocene was a dumb age."

"Its Economy was a monster like Grendel in *Beowulf*," said a little boy. "Every ten years they needed a new war to feed people to it."

"They treated plants like slaves," said a girl. "Filled oceans with plastic."

"They threw food away," said another little boy with braces on his teeth "on one side of the world when children were dying of hunger on the other."

"My brother says you're going to be assassinated. Is that like the Nobel Prize?"

"Only in the long term," said Zula.

"My Dad" said a girl "says you're a liar and a bad person."

"I'm sure your father is a good man and loves you. Some people then," Zula continued "wanted to only research putting the sun's energy in batteries or 'smart' electricity grids or using it to pump water to high lakes so it could run down through electricity-making turbines at night."

"Why didn't they just copy plants?" said a little boy.

"Yes, that's right," said Zula "plants figured out a billion years ago how to store solar energy in chemical bonds."

"They were smarty pants plants," said a little girl.

"Have you heard of the 'hydrogen economy?'" asked Zula.

"Economists thought it was some fairy tale in the clouds," said a little girl.

"It was a vision of a world," said Zula "where hydrogen from sunlight splitting water became the major source of electricity via fuel cells, or a fuel itself. But they had problems storing the hydrogen (including compressing or cooling it) and had to make sure it was safe. Well what do you think they did?"

"Tell us," said the children. "Tell us."

"The problem of storing hydrogen," said Zula "was solved using a vast resource that comprised 78% of our atmosphere. What was that? Do you know?"

"Stupidity," said the little girl.

"Maybe once," said Zula. "In fact it was nitrogen. Some plants like casuarinas had nodules in their roots that absorbed nitrogen. We copied them, then hydrogen and nitrogen were combined to make ammonia — a clean fuel and source of fertiliser."

"I hope you don't get assassinated," said a little boy. "You're interesting."

*Where ever on Earth you grow*
*Don't your own trumpet blow.*
*Have courage to resist*
*And kindness to persist.*
*Just as our blue-green friends a billion years ago,*
*Set out to start our evolution.*

∞

"And the future is you, children," said Zula. "Meanwhile, we developed a revolutionary approach to making things from very small parts. What was this called?"

"Child labour," said a little girl.

"Down-sizing, lay-offs," said a little boy.

"Nanotechnology," said Zula. "In the Corporatocene, nanotechnology was used to make light-weight, strong sporting goods, clear sunscreens, odourless socks and shirts, as well as packaging that preserved food shipped around the world."

"I wish my brother had socks that didn't smell," said the little girl.

"But we thought nanotechnology should be used to improve photosynthesis," said Zula. "Photosynthesis is Earth's most important chemical reaction; it's been working on earth non-stop for 2.5 billion years."

"It must be getting tired," said a little girl. "Why can't we give it a hand?"

"What a good idea," Zula replied. "Alright, I know; let's all do the Photosynthesis Hunt. I'll need help from your teacher Jamelia."

"No problem," said Jamelia. Jamelia handed out AR headsets to the children.

"You kids there can be photosynthetic organisms," said Zula. "And you lot over there, you're the photons. You travel from the sun in a narrow spectrum (that's about 430–700 nanometres), so you'll have to stand tall, but also holding hands because you're waves and particles."

Jamelia herded the children into position and started up their AR headsets. They were all now in a ten dimensional world where Zula's voice was creating the type of reality an enlightened being experiences.

"Now, you bunch of characters," said Zula "are the 'antenna' chlorophyll molecules in thylakoid membranes, or chloroplasts. Your job is to catch the photons. You stand up and do *Tree Pose*, your feet are roots and your hands above your heads are the leaves. Breathe in as you lean to the left and out as you breathe to the right. You kids in the shadows, pretend you've got chlorophyll E in your back pocket, or you're hiding under green sea slugs. Here they come, catch them. Quick, some are getting through."

"Like this?" asked a little girl swirling around, lost in many dimensions.

> *Don't plunder or pursue,*
> *Much more than virtue.*
> *May wisdom fill your heart,*
> *External medicine be your art.*
> *Like our blue-green friends a billion years ago,*
> *About to start our restitution.*

"Now I want some of you — you five there will do. You go and sit in that dark corner. It's not scary in the dark anymore, is it. There are no monsters in the dark now, no guns, tanks, or warplanes, missiles, or helicopters with bombs. You're the RuBisCOs and your job is to hunt down and capture the hydrogen (well you can call it ATP and NADPH) as well as carbon dioxide as it runs past and make energy rich chemicals, mainly sugar and biscuits, so you better take these samples. No, you can't all be RuBisCO. Blow your horns, go on, leap the band gap; the hunt is on."

Chaos ensued for some minutes with the children laughing as they ran about imitating electrons, antennae, hole pairs, enzymes, energy and food molecules.

∞

"Right, now take off your AR headsets," said Zula. "Alright, back to four dimensions. *Earth Touch*, all bend over and touch the ground between your feet. Now take your feet back, *Mountain Pose*. Now rest in *Pose of the Child*, on knees, forehead on the floor, hands by your sides."

"Is this right?" asked a little girl with braces. Zula moved the girl's arms slightly.

"There, that's better," said Zula. "Enough. Stop still. Now I want you all to lie on your backs with eyes closed and hands by your sides. This is *Tranquillity Pose*. Now focus on your breath. As you breathe in, your tummy's going out; as you breathe out in your tummy's coming in. Photosynthesis is like the whole earth breathing. Except the earth breathes out oxygen and breathes in carbon dioxide, the opposite of us. That's enough. You can sit up now. Any last questions?"

"If a meteor hits the Earth does the planet get winded?" asked a little girl who was waving both hands in the air to get attention.

"Sometime in the past," Zula replied "nearly all life on earth was wiped out by a big meteor."

"Could all life be lost from the earth forever?" asked the little girl.

"It could," said Zula. "We're trying to prevent that in the Sustainocene."

"When you became President you banned religion," said a tall boy with blond hair. "Is that because you don't believe in God?"

"I support the central message of all the great prophets," Zula replied "as summarised in the *Book of Common Faith*. And we hope for all to experience that individually in whatever morning contemplation session citizens decide to do."

"Why are people dying from AMDS?" asked a girl with dark hair in a ponytail. "Is it a punishment for banning religion?"

"We don't know yet," said Zula. "One of the world's experts on AMDS is here; my friend Kofi Buxtun. You should talk to him."

"We were told," said the tall blond boy "that the *World Time Council* protects us from criminal time travellers from the future who want corporations to rule the Earth again. But if as you say its the destiny of all human beings to be enlightened, why has our future got criminals like that? Also, how do we know the WTC is full of good people?"

"I'm testing if it is the destiny of all life on Earth to experience the synthesis of dual and unitive awareness," said Zula. "As to the second question, that's one of my jobs as WEC President."

"I'd be very sad if you got killed," said the little girl. "Can't someone protect you?"

"Someone is," said Zula, looking at me.

The children showed Zula musical instruments they'd made from trash found in the rubble of some of the Corporatocene cities.

Zula picked up a guitar made from aluminium cans, with the tuning pegs wooden spoons and bent forks. Zula started playing and singing *No Manifesto*.

*"Ain't no manifesto,
Just an experiment.
How much love can grow,
When we pay Earth's rent."*

One of the children picked up the key and started accompanying Zula on a cello with an oil drum for its body. Its string pegs were constructed from old cooking utensils and the heel of a worn-out women's shoe. The beat was held by a boy on a drum with a head made from old X-ray film, held in place with packing tape. Another child began playing a saxophone made from a drainpipe, a few melted coins and bottle caps.

Jamelia then arranged the children to sing Zula a song in their local dialect.

*"Hail Mother, morning star over the sea,
Of your milk, the dawn's dew, we drink our fill.
Each rainbow's your sunlit tears setting love free,
From fear and violence that goads good to evil.
You made our rooves, roads and hearts like cedars,
And we rest in the shade of your mercy."*

"I'm a great Guru like Zula. Kids are enlightened," one little girl shouted to me on the way out. "My name is Free, Summer, Gentle, Easy Snowflake. My mother's Sun and my father's Rain."

"That's not true," said Jamelia as she herded her charges towards the bus. "They're just making fun of you. Some of them think it's really cool if they can tell a lie with a straight face. I'll have a chat with them about it. We emphasise the children must respect all people."

∞

As we walked outside the hall, the sound of hammering echoed around the GSPP Centre. A few students had stripped to swim in the lagoon, white foam bubbling around their heads. Nearby, some brown cows cropped their green pasture, white heads bent over. The sun shone down, casting sparkles where it touched the sandy lagoon banks and white ripples in the foreground. A column of light shone between two trees making leaves white and nearby ferns emerald. Kids were scooping and patting mud beside puddles where rocks formed little foam-ringed islands. A translucent green snake slithered away behind a mossy rock. A large black ant, whose bulbous tail glowed in the light, crushed a beetle with its yellow pincers. To me, these images were words. We met Omran and Jevons on the bridge over the lagoon.

> *Afternoon, sweeping leaves.*
> *A dead bird,*
> *Offered before the shrine.*

"When Zula and I first discussed financing global synthetic photosynthesis," said Omran "I asked her 'Would you say that God because of your ethical focus should help you get the money?' 'Why, yes, indeed,' she replied. 'Well,' I said 'presumably if they cut off all your Centre of Excellence funding, God will provide for you.' 'Yes, yes, I expect God would,' she replied. And do you know what? The next day all her research funding was withdrawn, some problem over failing to get appropriate ethics approvals. Zula was very calm about it. And the very day after that, donations started coming in from the GSPP crowd-sourcing initiative. Soon children were asking their parents to donate to Zula instead of give them birthday or Christmas presents. Old people gave bequests in their wills. Kids organised social service projects to contribute, parents were shamed into giving too. Ah, you'll have noticed how I refer to Zula. It's a personal thing between us."

In the evening, Zula invited Spicer and I to attend the GSPP 'sharing,' or meditation session. The opening prayer was one from Richard St. Barbe Baker, founder of the *Society of the Men of the Trees*, who was greatly revered at the GSPP Centre.

> *"Help us give our best to life*
> *And leave the Earth a little more beautiful,*
> *For our having lived on it."*

Afterwards, Zula took Spicer and I over to a dormitory to introduce a former energy policy analyst called Michael Brumby who suffered from multiple sclerosis. On the way, Zula explained that Michael could still walk, though with a stamp and twist at the ankles.

"He's refused all gene therapy," said Zula.

"You as well," said Spicer to Zula, kissing her on the cheek.

"We relish the challenge," said Zula.

Michael was sitting cross-legged on a bottom bunk bed. He had thinning, greasy hair down to the nape of his neck, thick glasses that bulged and distorted his eyes and fuzzy stubble around a buttock-shaped chin. Michael wore purple cords and his face twitched as he spoke. He had a reputation for being a bit crazy.

"This is Michael Brumby," said Zula. "One of the wisest men at the GSPP Centre. He'll deny it of course, but he can be a bit of an oracle once he's tested you out."

"And here's President Zula," said Michael "ready for the shortest term of office. And immortality as an eco-martyr."

Zula departed. Michael offered to read my stars from a little book. I gave him my time, date and place of birth.

"The Zodiac," said Michael "is a band of near and distant solar radiation imprinting music-like patterns upon unalloyed mind stuff as it first manifests in a body. The malefic influences are Saturn, Mars, the North and South nodes of the moon and the waning moon. Jupiter is the planet of wisdom, it can never cause harm, even if it wanted to." He looked up latitude, longitude and adjusted for ephemeris and time zones.

"So Zula is the great teacher of the Aquarian Age," I said. "Her peace and integrity floated down like snow once Regulus moved from Leo to Virgo?"

"As it stands," said Michael "the three great inhibitors of your career will be falsehood (because Saturn is in Mars and has an $8^{th}$ house aspect with Mars) secrets and sins (because Saturn in the $12^{th}$ house aspects the sixth house). By sins I mean self-contradiction; acting contrary to what you believe in, addictions for example. There's a risk of your emotions creating a reality that's not there. But remember, once you begin to assert your will power none of this holds, not because I'm wrong, but because your destiny changes."

Michael had more trouble with Spicer's astrology.

"With you, dear, Mars is warlike and Taurus gentle. You've found what you've looked for. It does not jeopardise anything, but justifies it."

If this was Zula's exemplar of GSPP wisdom I wasn't impressed. Michael ridiculed Zula for building what he called "mudbrick skyscrapers from which you could see Mars, or the splendour of Masdar City," for forming a Pythagorean clique of scientists and for her gullibility.

"Zula smiled at me, I must be doing good," said Michael imitating a young scientist Buddha's voice while raising his eyelids and eyebrows, exposing more white in his eyes. "The scientist Buddhas here live according to the 'approbation' principle. They listen to Zula like faithful dogs with flapping ears. Probably a good thing then, all in all, she's experimenting being *Whole Earth Council* President. If she'd stayed on here much longer the place would have become a cult."

I asked Michael about the *Bhagavad Gita*, the scriptural text many of the scientist Buddhas kept referring to.

"The *Gita* is alright, pretty high flown words but basically sound," said Michael. "But the *Dhammapada* is better in my opinion; it can take the edge off a bout of depression. Think about the degenerate personal lives of the great scriptural heroes in the *Gita*. I mean Krishna sleeping with all those little girls. Then, just after preaching exalted philosophy on the unity of life, he kills his enemy while the poor bastard's trying to get his chariot out of the mud."

"Anyway, the food's good," I said.

"Well the usual fare here is atrocious," Michael replied. "After a conference when all the stupid suckers are gone, it will be nothing but Lebanese bread and boiled vegetables, then nothing but potatoes. But why would you listen to me? I'm not up on stage in a white lab coat talking about *samadhi* and global synthetic photosynthesis. If I wasn't here I'd be foot soldier in the ego battle between the genetically unedited crippled and the voluntary aged on public transport."

Michael gave me a book to read, while he continued talking to Spicer. I took the hint and stepped outside. The afternoon sun placed the shadows of distant leaves on the pages. The book was about a few humans surviving global nuclear war; the heroine lifting up her head from the desolate planet with a hope as yet unthought. I wondered why Michael hadn't had his disease treated. While I was thus musing, a boy came over and started staring at me. He moved his legs incessantly.

"You alright, mate?" I asked him after a while.

"My mother says you're WTC," he said. "You better not let Zula die, dickhead."

∞

It got cold when the sun went below the mountains. The small black dot of a plane moved silently from a wave of sunset pink clouds out into the vast beyond, absolutely alone, yet firm and unwavering; like that little red fish in *Underwater Garden*.

Spicer and I decided to eat informally in the dining room of Michael's dormitory. Dinner was signified here by the banging of a dangling crowbar. Moths played around the outside lights of the dining hall. Michael walked towards the hall with his arms over our shoulders. He stamped his feet and twisted on his ankles as he walked.

"Dusk falls on the tired devotees," said Michael. Above him were the flashing red lights of another plane flying westward. Inside the hall, steam from the rice, breath and smoke were mingling. Spicer and I sat next to Michael during dinner. Afterwards, Michael put his hands around a pole for support. He stared at the fire with unblinking eyes.

"Soon they'll be telling you," said Michael to Spicer "that you need to convert your infantile desire to succeed in research into a spiritual process-like magic. Always remember, the true ethical principle in the GSPP Centre has become 'Ignorance is bliss. What you don't know can't hurt you.'"

"No, 'knowledge is bliss,'" said a fat, balding scientist Buddha nearby.

Michael's mood changed from light hearted to melancholy.

"Know nothing but know everything," said the fat scientist Buddha.

"Yes, that's sort of it," said Michael, unwilling to be goaded.

"Why don't you discuss whether that pole is real?" the fat scientist Buddha asked. Michael ignored him and continued to stare at the fire.

"That's enough," I said to the fat scientist. "Care to pick on me?"

One of the cleaning boys called Mahatma had been given a cigarette by a visitor. He was sitting cross-legged on the floor nearby and singing.

"There's no strings upon this heart, *mumble mumble*. It was always you, *mumble mumble*," Mahatma sang holding a cigarette and gesturing for someone to light it.

The fat scientist Buddha mentioned how Mahatma had put his foot in a wet GSPP-impregnated concrete slab.

"Just bloody give us a light" Mahatma suddenly yelled.

"What were you doing today Mahatma?" asked the fat scientist Buddha.

"What can I say?" Mahatma's arms went out from his sides.

"You can tell me what you did today."

"Cutting grass."

"Tell me the truth."

"Tida tida Mozambique. Carrying grass."

"But I saw you carrying dirt."

"Sorry mate," said Mahatma flinching as if expecting a beating.

"That's enough," I said to the fat scientist Buddha. "Walk a mile in his shoes. He seems stupid and unpleasant, but he's the Cosmos testing you." The fat scientist Buddha, whose name I finally noticed from my AR was Labyrinth Goblett, tripped and touched my feet as he got up.

Michael picked up a coal with red, glowing spots and pressed Mahatma's cigarette to it.

"You'll have to drag on it," said Michael. "Go down to the wooden bridge over the lagoon." Mahatma walked off. "I consider Mahatma to be amongst the more witty and worthy inmates of this asylum. His name means 'Great Soul.'"

"That's a joke," said the fat scientist Buddha.

"I thought it was Zula's joke," said Spicer to Michael. "But now I understand. The water and light, the goodness, is down there in each of us. As long as we keep digging, it will keep bubbling up and shining."

"Mahatma," said Michael "is always asking for this non-existent cat to be taken away from him. The little kids treat him like a bogey man and threaten each other that he'll get them. Yesterday Mahatma started reciting what sounded to me like a radio play about picking up a girl called Nancy in a bar. It was rich in characterisation and suspense, about spiking her drink. Another time he promised to disappear at three o'clock. He calls that plump scientist Buddha who was taunting him 'you bag of chips,' and another tall one 'you tree.'"

"Did Mahatma say anything else about Nancy?" I asked Michael.

"That her boyfriend was a lotus," said Michael "risen from mud to flower above water."

Spicer quietly walked over and sat near Michael. They were by the fire.

"Are we lonely?" she asked, touching him sensually. "What do you desire?"

"Not in this situation, with all these people" Michael replied. "The primary desire of most lost souls is to possess a functioning body."

"Well, what would you like, now?" Spicer asked.

"Mainly sleep, well, to have pleasant dreams," Michael replied.

"Then you'll have those," said Spicer.

Spicer nudged closer to him and they sat silent for a while as others talked. The fat scientist Buddha came over and spoke to me about Michael.

"I wouldn't listen to him," he said. "He's not self-contained. He tosses up balloons of reality. He must have thought of suicide a million times. That's why he was asked about the pole, because when you're left alone you need something to grab onto, in a way, and not be cynical of. He's in a *tamasic* state."

"What's *tamasic*?" I asked.

"Unenlightened, unevolved. Not self-aware." He subjected me to a discourse on the torture of desiring a chocolate biscuit when you're not allowed one. "In meditation, I just set myself a number of *mala* repetitions; my fingers move a bead with each breath and I stop at the set count, regardless of what I'm seeing. A person like Zula can make you enlightened by an act of grace if you've worked hard for Them."

This fat scientist Buddha lacked insight to such an immense degree, his purpose seemed to be to make people like me feel good about ourselves.

> *Mists from the desert valley;*
> *Seeking to become*
> *Clouds around the moon.*

∞

I was walking back to my room from dinner when I saw Michael sprawled on the ground, holding a wavering cane. Spicer was trying to help. People were walking past, ignoring them. I went over. Michael asked me to pull him up. He twisted and fell even as I held his arm.

"I can't see my feet at night," said Michael. "I've made it up to my room a few times, but I'm useless without my glasses." We searched around on the ground for his spectacles and some money. Then, with my assistance, he put his hands ahead of him and pushed himself up.

"Do you need the cane?" Spicer asked.

"No, I don't," said Michael. He leant on Spicer and I till we got to the light of his room. Inside, he explained about his cane.

"I only carry it so people won't think I'm drunk or stoned. They're so unable to accept anyone as they are. Once I staggered against that bunk. That fat scientist Buddha asked me, 'hey, what's wrong with you?' 'I've got a physical problem.' 'Don't be smart with me, you're a bloody druggie.' Would you go up to a spastic and say 'hey, you walk funny?' or 'you look like you're drunk?'"

"No I wouldn't," I said. It was rare to see a disabled person now with all the genetic treatments available.

"Oh yes," Michael told me "there are a lot of young scientists, PhD's, postdocs who've burnt a heap of bridges to get here and work with the great

Zula. It's true they're more admirable than most Corporatocene researchers who spent their lives trying to cure headaches, hair loss, or engage in disease mongering. But to my way of thinking the global synthetic photosynthesis research way of life is also a rut. Zula knows it too, that's the real reason she's getting out. But they won't want her there."

"Who," asked Spicer. "Who doesn't want her there?"

"Those crazy enough think," said Michael "the experiment of fighting for peace still has a few more tests to run. The WTC for instance. Those who revel in inequality."

Michael told us the mind works in a funny way to cure the scars of early life.

"Last night I dreamt of a snake on my chest," he said. "It was crawling past my right ear. I was absolutely still, in case it bit, but it was friendly. People will tell you I have a few *samskaras* for some of the female scientist Buddhas. I put that down to my behaviour on the insane debauchery of my birthday. The thing about this GSPP Centre is that if I were to fall down on the pavement with a heart attack, like I did tonight, half the scientist Buddhas would just walk past me. At least you'd want someone to say: 'Well, there goes old Michael. He was a good guy.' Zula was different. You could knock on Zula's door at midnight. And Zula'd be just the same. Zula'd give money, ask how They could help. When Zula's not talking about it, all this enlightenment business seems so impersonal. I worked my butt off at GSPP celebration day. That fat scientist Buddha had me out in the sun, cleaning the tiles. What good did that do me? I don't want to get rid of my ego just yet."

"Then why do you stay?" asked Spicer.

"I listen and watch," said Michael. "I've picked up two assassination attempts. And now that Zula's gone and become WEC President, I'm going. Most of Zula's scientist Buddhas have become aware that a flaw stands between them and what they want to achieve, what matters most in life. That should give them a little tenderness towards others, but it doesn't. I used to warn Zula, Job the man struggling to understand why the good suffer and evil prosper; he's gripping, has something to say. Job the man telling others the answer is a great bore. The WEC in the Sustainocene, claiming to have all the answers, is a great bore."

"Ever hear anyone say Zula had a daughter?" I asked.

"No never," said Michael. "She was never interested in the romantic side of things. Which is very unusual for a Guru, I must say."

"Nancy Godel?" I asked. "She might have visited here once."

"Nancy who?"

"Godel, as in the mathematician," I said.

"I'd have known if she did," said Michael. "Doesn't ring any bells. Unless you mean that 'Nancy' Mahatma was referring to; just another phantasm hugging the walls of his imagination."

"Those little statues of the Buddha in a lab coat? The ones on sale?" I asked.

"Kitsch. What about them?" asked Michael.

"Can you just buy them here?" I asked.

"So far as I know," said Michael. "Good source of income from the visitors. Trinket-led research. Great idea, eh? One of Zula's best. Bulk orders around the world."

"And Jevons Paradox, what's that crook doing here?"

"Oh, so he's a crook eh? When the good guys are offering *Nirvana* on tap?"

As we descended from Michael's room, I noticed how my desert boots under the influence of water and mud, had lost their soles and become laughing shoes. They slipped on the damp surfaces.

I decided to take them off and walk barefoot as I had on the farm in Normandy. I felt more grounded.

Spicer and I had adjacent rooms in the dormitory. The dorm was like a jail, a long corridor, open to the elements at one end with a criss-cross of steel bars. The rooms were comfortable, but tiny and sparsely furnished; like an anchorite's cell.

I watched from my window the fat scientist Buddha walk into his hut. This consisted of a small room for sleeping, meditation and study. Each such hut had two large windows with wooden shutters and fly screens, a GSPP-powered light and a small wooden table. Outside was a porch of equal size, also with two large windows, shuttered but without fly screens. Before this ran a verandah with wooden railings under a sloping GSPP roof. Stairs wound down from this to the concrete slab which supported the poles on which the structure was raised. There was a separate latrine. I saw the fat scientist Buddha ladling water from a large pot. He greeted Christine the ICU registrar. Christine held out a science-Buddha statue. Her partner grasped it and they walked inside. I wasn't sure what they were getting up to tonight, but I doubted it was meditation.

That night I dreamt Dad bought me three pairs of desert boots and I got some dancing shoes to replace my riding boots. Dad told me women always judged a man by his boots, then went to sleep. I moved away up into the hills but had to come down when he died.

∞

I'd borrowed an alarm clock and tried to wake at 4.30am to join the scientist Buddhas for their morning meditation, as Zula had recommended. After it went off, I lay there for a few minutes beside the comfortable warmth of Spicer to orient myself to the world. I could hear the cold pre-dawn wind, dogs barking, frogs croaking and the sound of people wailing and singing with a harmonium, clicking sticks and beating a drum. I also could hear what sounded like gigantic rats gnawing wood. Somewhere out in the darkness people were planning to kill Zula; did I have to wait for them to make the attempt?

Some animal deep in the desert shrieked in pain. Dogs howled. Shadowy trees stood out against the moonlit fog. Then I saw torchlights threading their way down to the meditation hall and heard sandled feet crunching gravel. I went up to the roof. The moon was still up and cradling a star. There were only a few lights in the GSPP village. In the cool air, I began the contemplative practices Zula had taught me. First some stretches, then sitting cross-legged imaging breath moving in loops through my spine. I'd lost any expectation of regaining *Samadhi* permanently. I was doing this because Zula had asked me to.

After about fifteen minutes, I became aware of a vast space in front of my closed eyes. I could feel my fingers touching my nose — but they seemed so small and yet so heavy. As the sun came up, sweeping its crimson and orange tones over the underside of the dark clouds, I could see villagers out in the fields outside the GSPP complex squatting with a silver pot beside them. They were inside me, their interests and hopes were both mine and not mine at the same time.

I was still in the zone during breakfast, which was hot sweet tea, *chapatis*, porridge, sweet *halva* and things like rice bubbles. From my dorm roof, I could see outside the walls of the GSPP Centre a village of thatch and mud houses. Children played chasings in a deserted temple. One was pretending to be a monkey in a tree, another moving his arms like the pistons on a train. Another climbed a tree and bashed the uppermost branches to get ripe fruit.

I watched a procession with trumpet and drums carrying a dead body, draped in orange and red cotton cloth, out onto the plain for cremation or burial. Huge vultures sailed over on the breeze to perch on one of the few trees surviving on a hill out in the desert. Crows also caught the wind and curved on it with outstretched wings. A white dog, tail, chest and tongue panting, ribs showing, scars with pink skin on its rear legs, dirt on its back, guarded its brown mate while she put her head up to the neck in a refuse tin.

Kofi came up and sat next to me. Rockets decorated with bright green, blue and yellow streamers and ribbons were being fired into the sky by some of the younger recently ordained scientist Buddhas. We watched the spectacle.

"An upward trajectory of the rocket," said Kofi "is regarded as a mark of good craftsmanship. It's a variation of a Thai Buddhist ordination ceremony. I believe originally it had something to do with a story where the son of the water serpent symbolising Nature with which the Buddha had achieved collaboration, had fallen in love with a beautiful princess having abandoned her in a previous life."

I asked Kofi to tell me how he first came to know Zula.

"None of my family knew our actual dates of birth," said Kofi. "I lived with aunts, uncles, grandparents in mud and straw huts at the edge of some wheat fields. We didn't own the land. I grew up playing in dust, often sick and always hungry. Schooling was a few lessons in basic grammar and maths in a thatched building so low to the ground the teacher had to practically crawl into it. My two older brothers had been killed by corporate mercenaries in the war. They went off knowing they'd probably never return, but wanting the Earth to be a better place for people like me to grow up in."

"My father was too old and ill to work, so from the age of ten I supported the family. I'd get up at 5am and study by candlelight for an hour. Then at 6am with the streets still dark, just lamps and dust and coughing figures outside, I'd eat a little bread and boiled vegetable and set out. I'd buy vegetables and grocery items at distant markets, then bring them home in bundles on the roof of a bus, the tray of an empty truck, the handlebars of a bicycle, or on my back; and sell them in my village at slightly higher prices. I broke rocks for road works with a sledge hammer, carrying them in wicker baskets to trucks or carts. On building sites I mixed sand and clay, did plastering, mud wash, painting and tiling. I carried messages for landowners and shopkeepers, travelling over 40k a day for just enough money to buy a loaf of bread. I also chopped wood in the forest, paying off the forest guards and carrying bundles of chopped logs 6ks. I cut the tall grass that grew on the dividing walls between the wheat fields with a sickle and carted it to town for animals' feed; if caught doing that without permission I was beaten up."

"One day I was squatting by the roadside making little clay cups to sell hot tea. I was told a holy woman was coming to town. So, I went to her talk and that was the first time I saw Zula. She was very young, just a little older than me. It wasn't so much the content of her words, as being in the presence of the phenomenon that was her. After the talk, I went up and said 'I want to come with you.' Zula told me 'alright, but I have to go and pack for the journey so I'll see you in half an hour.' Well I waited outside, asking passers-by what the time was. At exactly half past I opened the tent flap, but Zula was gone. An old woman cleaning the floor said Zula had caught the train to the next village."

"So I ran home and collected all the money I possessed and ran through the crowded dusty streets to the railway station. Even the price of the cheapest ticket was too much. I tried begging for the difference, but was pushed away. When the train began to move, I just leapt on, hanging onto a handrail at the end of one carriage."

"When I arrived, there was a huge crush of people getting on and off. No one knew where Zula was. Then I found a holy man who told me. When Zula saw me, she treated me like her long-lost brother. I slept on the floor beside her bed that night and tied one end of the dirty piece of cloth that, apart from a singlet full of holes, was my only piece of clothing, to her robe. I was determined she would not get away from me again. We went back to Zula's orphanage. I said I was an orphan and they looked at me and didn't disagree. In the morning, Zula said I had to go back to my family and make the proper arrangements. She gave me money for the journey both ways and that reassured me. Zula said 'tell them you are going to become a holy person and a scientist who will help save the Earth.'"

"Back in my village the girl I was betrothed to came over to our house, looking as beautiful as she could. She gave me a posy of wildflowers. I accepted, but later threw them out the back of our house. As I left to go back to Zula, I saw those flowers withered on a pile of ash and the vision cut through me like a knife. Anyway, so that's how I joined the orphanage. We slept on straw and Zula taught us meditation. Food was just a cup of watery split-pea soup at lunch and dinner with a handful or two of rice and a vegetable in season along with unleavened bread; but it was twice as much as I was used to. There were books to read and I devoured them. Zula was such a scholastic prodigy it seemed merely a matter of fate she was a student rather than staff. For the first few weeks, every night I'd creep into Zula's room, tie our robes together and sleep on the floor beside her bed. Whenever she went out, even into the night, with its jackals' howls, to answer the call of nature, I'd follow at a discreet distance for any hint of flight. I soon understood that Zula indeed was a 'They;' a culmination of humanity rather than a single person."

"What's this AMDS?" I asked. "They say you're an expert."

"We still don't know. But you were right in the middle of our most interesting case study. Hundreds dead in Southwark, but not a single case in Hampstead. At the moment we think it may have something to do with Internet over-exposure, or maybe T-Net travel."

"And these assassination attempts on President Zula?"

"Only to be expected. Zula took the lyrics to John Lennon's song *'Imagine'* and used them as a policy manifesto. No war, no religion, no need for greed or hunger. Just consider how many powerful people that's pissed off. It was your brother who ensured much of Zula's early work wasn't published. He blocked Zula from grants and keynote presentations, bought out Their post-docs, raised allegations of scientific fraud, tried to create a patent thicket to inhibit Zula's collaborations. He denied Zula's group essential equipment, had one of their grants cancelled after it had been awarded, re-wrote reports to misrepresent favourable outcomes, pressured granting agencies to disregard positive proposal reviews, promised then covertly cancelled transportation to crucial meetings. It took direct intervention from President Silabhadra to stop him. He never explained why."

"You think the WTC would decommission Zula?"

"Your brother's corrupt," said Kofi. "You must know that. He's jealous. And you threaten him in some way. That's just a feeling I had."

"Does Zula have a daughter?"

"Not to my knowledge."

"Alright. Ever heard of a Nancy Godel."

"Nothing comes to mind," said Kofi. "Who's she?"

"Young girl recently murdered in Hampstead during the Light Harvesting Festival. Seems to have a connection with Zula. She's one reason I'm here."

"I've made some AR inquiries as we were talking," said Kofi. "Can't help you, I'm afraid."

"I'm trying to save Zula's life," I said.

"Zula is not like you or I," said Kofi. "I know you're working on a case about a connection between this girl killed in London and Zula. There is a link. But it is not like anything you would have imagined. To solve it you'll have to accept things that seem impossible and it will require having faith."

∞

Kofi suggested that Spicer and I help in the kitchen preparing for lunch. This involved slicing aubergines and pumpkin with a curved blade onto a big brass dish after cleaning out the seeds and the little worms. We then sifted rice on the floor for stone and grit and made balls of dough. They were each flattened circularly on the wooden board with a rolling pin. The dough circles fluffed up as they were tipped onto the coals beside a blue flame licking up at the bright orange base of a copper pot.

I asked the cook, whose name was Vishu Dhoti, about Zula. Vishu Dhoti was renowned for working enormously long hours when inspired, but also for periods of absolute lethargy and depression when he couldn't raise himself from his bed.

"Zula perfect vegetarian. No meat," said Vishu Dhoti, clearly in an 'up' mood.

"Did she ever have, you know, boyfriends?" I asked.

"Hey Babu," said Vishu Dhoti "you got no idea, have you?" He scratched his bum.

"Someone said she had a daughter," I persisted.

"Well they's lying Babu," said Vishu Dhoti. "Your mind very impure, huh. Zula is no 'she,' Babu. Zula is the Earth. The Earth doesn't go to bed with no Babu, eh Babu?"

"So she's never had sex?" I asked. "I mean, Zula?"

"Not in this body, Babu," said Vishu Dhoti.

Zula arrived an hour later and took Spicer and I to the sixth floor of the main Global Synthetic Photosynthesis research building. We watched scientists conducting experiments with a grace and one-pointed focus that made them resemble artists.

"He or she who does science without art," said Zula "is a brute. Each scientist here prepares for a day's experiments with prayer and meditation. At first it was a controversial approach, but my students became so happy and successful."

∞

That night Zula sat on a couch and spoke to those who gathered before Them. In a space lit only by a candle flame with a blue ring about it, Zula discoursed on subjects such as zero time in quantum tunnelling and the crucifixion-how it was symbolic of the death of ego that needs to take place before unitive consciousness is realised.

"If I see an insect struggling in human excreta," said Zula "I will extract and preserve it. When an opportunity to serve another form of life arises you should relish the chance, for it is thus that you purify your mind. Our language is unable to express the idea of life without any egotism, yet assuredly the profound peace associated with compassionate awareness of the world feels normal. Achieving unitive consciousness is implicit in the web of life on Earth. There's a deep affinity between the Earth and a selfless, fully realised human being. It amazes me how the Earth has been so tolerant of humans that seem so willing to commit ecocide, to drag down the beauty of the world to destruction. It would have been so easy to wipe us out — volcanic eruptions, comet strike, plagues."

"And what are you sacrificing to leave the GSPP Centre," someone asked.

"The idea that it was mine, something that I had done," said Zula. "They say under my leadership the GSPP Centre was always on the verge of bankruptcy, because I kept giving away money and property. But I think spiritual institutions should be like that, always relying on the web of life, rather than accountants or the famous."

"Will there be a nuclear war?" Spicer asked Zula.

"No, No," Zula answered.

"What do you mean?" Spicer asked. Spicer clearly was entranced by Zula and looked upon the latter as a devoted dog might gaze upon its master.

That afternoon Spicer had told me of a dream she'd had soon after arriving in Namibia in which she was passionately kissing Zula.

"There will be *no* nuclear war," said Zula. "There will be pocket wars, they have gone on, they will always go on. But not nuclear war."

"How can you be sure?" Spicer asked.

"Well I know it," said Zula. "I can't give you any proof or evidence."

"What have you told the people here to do after you leave?" I asked.

"Serve, Love, Research, Give, Purify, Meditate, Realise," said Zula. "My desire tonight knows no bounds. But it is not desire as you imagine. I'm the bird charmer that goes to the rooftop at dusk and flings her passionate appeal upon the sultry air: *Tat Twam Asi*, Thou Art That. Experience life's peaceful anomaly. Enlightenment is not the mind blowing up like a balloon, it's like turning the balloon inside out and it feels incredibly normal and effortless."

"Is it possible," I asked "that such an experience once lost, can be regained?"

"There is a famous devotional work," said Zula "by a 14th century (CE) English mystic called *The Cloud of Unknowing*. The main theme is that whatever we call God cannot be apprehended by our intellect and that only love for creation and the beneficent principles behind it can pierce the 'cloud of unknowing' that lies between us and God. I feel that in my own life anything I have done of possible worth has happened because I trained and disciplined my gross, worldly self and opened it to Cosmic guidance. And I think that applies to humanity as a whole. There may be a connection between the cloud in which God's wisdom is hidden from human intellect and that other cloud which has never dispersed from above Hiroshima and Nagasaki."

"The Nobel committee claimed that despite some alarming animist notions, I'd great scientific power for trusting and assigning anomalies. Yet by the Z-scheme, the true strength of my approach to global synthetic photosynthesis was empathising with the interests of all life then creatively thinking how to aid them using whatever resources and principles the sum total had allotted me. I had to design a wise, inter-connected system of

Spicers dream

artificial photosynthesis in all our roads and buildings; one that would self-regulate for varying availabilities of light, water and atmospheric carbon dioxide, but also rapidly adapt to changing local needs for fuel, food and fertiliser."

"Then, as WEC President they lauded the prescience and beneficence of my governance reforms. But I was never some bank of the Commonwealth primordially contracted to loan humanity virtue's hilltop light. I was merely testing if the laws of physics and politics were universal without any need to measure the gravity of some magnetically-suspended niobium sphere supercooled by liquid nitrogen. And thankfully, I've yet to find a Lorentz symmetry violation in testing whether every sentient being, anywhere, human or not, should choose compassion to give their prayers more stuff than a dandelion puff." Zula sipped water from a glass.

"My life has always seemed a stranger's sojourn on the razorback of now. And as once we were pushed out to that edge vernix-smeared and wailing, so at death our souls will be shoved bodiless in the abyss dyed by what they've since done. Thus, I tell my students 'consider first not the nature of things, but the motion and mass of virtue in each act and so daily form thyself to freedom.' Whether forests, animals, buildings and robots will ultimately triumph on Earth as better thinking this way is for others to consider and say."

"I have been told and understand," I asked Zula "that you teach that everything is impermanent, but that the meaning behind this can only be understood after *Samadhi* has been attained. But what if you have achieved *Samadhi* and then fallen out of it without realising the truth?"

"All can meditate and know the truth for themselves," said Zula with half-closed eyes and raised eyebrows. "Do you have a calm mind?"

"No I have a restless mind," I replied.

"You need a calm mind to stay in *Nirvana*."

"Then I'll never know the truth."

"Truth," Zula replied "is when your mind accepts the universal embrace. Am I about anything? I will do it with regard to the interest of all life on

Earth. Not to encumber the Earth, this is what I was made for. Assenting to that possibility made fate my only inclination."

"How long will you be with us?" asked Spicer.

"Lately, I often think of my last hour," said Zula "indeed of the end of all life on Earth. Death, after all, is such a pure, natural action and it is a privilege to love those necessary rascals that only seem to disoblige us by bringing it forward. Some such spiders think they'll have done a great deed by catching me in their web and it'll be a marvellous boon if this world is quickly over with Zula. But a chain of causes has tied my person from eternity to the event they plan. I have studied well why acceptance of humiliation is always a precursor to elevation of those beloved by the Cosmos. Earth is so beloved. Yet, in but a few billion years our dying Sun will burn all water and life from the face of this planet. And it's not in this form life shall survive thereafter on some Goldilocks world where *Milkdromeda's* core is like a spotlight in the night sky."

"So, I am cheerfully compliant; give me what you please, take what you please away, we bow before our doom. I shall be merely leaving an odd sort of world where many of those for whom I've worked so long and prayed so heartily count my life no better than a grievance. If they shall burn me, they shall do none other thing than that I look for. Indeed, I shall at that time slide gently out of both their chains and this body to marvel at the design of people's actions. Let the final miracle of life be greater than the first."

"But some of us," said Spicer "have no designs upon you; unless it be to wonder at the deep engraved principles by which such a beautiful one, like the flower, snowflake, rainbow or comet, is created."

"I love Thee," said Zula. "I mean Thou whom I too do not comprehend, but who has dedicated me to my fate. I am captive in Thy jealous dream, the dream of life not just on Earth but in this Universe. As the bare ground and trees are embraced by the still, high light of a winter's morning so I ache to be caressed and absorbed; my longing reciprocated in the whispers of a breeze through a wood, the fragrance of soil after rain, the pounding of surf on a beach. I welcome the pain that drives me beyond myself to marriage with all that lives on this pale, blue dot."

"Your face in this candle light," said Spicer "shows such lively samples of all the virtues, like an ever-changing bouquet. Your gentleness is invincible, nothing shall ever ruffle your serenity."

"Ah, this Earth loves the refreshment of a shower," said Zula stroking Spicer's chin with the back of Their hand. "Every being is as ease when its powers move regularly and without interruption."

"We who've been abused," said Spicer "are afraid to be so open."

"Woman, make the best of your time while you have it," said Zula. "Indulge your inestimable, wild desire to eat apples and bear fruit yourself in good season. Your kind nature was given to cope with those trials to come. The sun bestows its life-giving power everywhere but is not exhausted by it. Fly your fancy into the hearts of all life on Earth. You will see They seek not less than thee. Each time you do not step on an ant, save a bee from drowning, water a thirsty plant or tree, be kind to an abuser, you will be loving me."

Zula was then handed her old Breton harp. They positioned it between Their legs and tuned the strings. Zula played what felt to me like 'night breeze' music. Zula was like an oasis of peace and calm. They listened patiently to what people were trying to communicate. Zula was assertive when asked Their opinion, but willing to accept a different viewpoint when proven and acknowledge the insights of others. Zula's ready sense of humour never descended to insult or hurt. Zula encouraged others to achieve greater excellence than Themself. Zula seemed to be accepting of people's faults and weaknesses and behaved with great politeness to people of any rank or position. Zula never claimed to be 'enlightened' or an 'old soul' and took responsibility unless to do so would deprive a colleague of credit.

As Zula departed, many threw before Their feet rose petals and leaves from wicker baskets, or held candles that suffused light upon their chests and faces.

∞

Late that night Detective Bernadette Goldbough contacted me by AR.

"Jean, you're at Namibia. And not alone I see."

"Yeah I came for the waters and the spices."

"I've been told you're officially off the Nancy Godel case, but I also know you. WTC has been putting out the story you've gone rogue. According to them you're a threat to humanity which of course leads anyone who's ethical to the opposite conclusion. Mersenne Twister is dead. Someone put a bomb on the T–G cylinder. Like a star exploding, night after the comet disappeared. We've found out some things. Nancy Godel wasn't what she seemed. It's weird."

"You can share them with both of us."

"Nancy Godel, according to her citizen's register, died a week before she first met Spencer and a few years before the death you investigated. Yes, hear me out. We managed to get full access to her AR memories. Rough childhood. Her mother's boyfriend used to hit her, broke her arm once and her elder brother held him upside down over a balcony till he promised not to do it again. Her mother tried to 'colonise' her by taking her to Church and organising home Bible readings."

"At the age of ten, when the mother's boyfriend tried to abuse her, Nancy left home and worked as a prostitute. The pimp made her addicted to heroin so she couldn't get away. She'd get a surge then everything would go quiet, but soon she was needing one shot to feel normal and another to get high. Nancy used to climb the backstairs of clubs in Southwark and beg to do shows with three songs. In the first she took off her top, in the second she went down into the crowd with their greased 'six pack' fingers and in the third she tried to make it back to the stage with some clothes on. She used to look into their faces and say 'I'll remember you.' Famous people they were. She remembered Gordon Lizzard and your brother."

"You still there? Good. As soon as Nancy had pubes, she graduated to 'hot shows' on stage and to the brothel. Blokes seeing her going out in the morning would yell 'bloody whore' and 'slag heap.' But she yelled back 'I earn more than you.' She never kissed clients on the lips. Some were nice but others rude and violent shouting things like 'look at me, bitch.' A priest, actually can you believe it the one who officiated at her funeral, the one you attended on the heath, used to insist she dress up in schoolgirl clothes. She thought of herself as 'the thing on which erections subsided.' She got tired, but she'd still masturbate when she got home; she had this ideal boy she always believed would come along and save her. Her mum used to take her on outings and they'd drive past houses she'd burgled."

"Well Jeremy Jones told us that Nancy had come round one morning a few years ago asking for money to buy some dope. He gave her some. That was the last he heard of her for a while. A few months later his child had come up when he was looking at autumn leaves and led him by the hand to coloured and crushed bricks and said he couldn't find a green one called Nancy. That night, Jeremy dreamed he saw Nancy in a bus with the sun in her hair. Nancy told him in the dream that she'd been unconscious with the dope and alcohol and didn't feel anything. Her AR showed us that Nancy'd tried to kick the H and was killed by a supplier and her body dumped behind an old fridge in an alley."

"I don't understand," I said. "Nancy dead for a year before I saw her body in Hampstead? This some WTC joke? Jeremy Jones is WTC. He tried to kill me on the heath with Jack Castles. Hercules Huncks is also involved. Now Jevons Paradox is here. I saw him in London getting ready to assassinate Zula."

"Jeremy said you were mentally unbalanced. He was worried about you. If he's WTC, it's a very good cover. Jevons is not what he seems. She didn't get assassinated, did she? You meditate on that Jean. Your brain hasn't been working properly. You're seeing things, imaging things. You still drinking?"

"No. Even if I am. It still doesn't make sense."

"Well, it gets even stranger. There was never a funeral because Nancy reappeared a day later looking the same. Only this time she's playing classical guitar and writing papers for scientific journals about global synthetic photosynthesis. Instead of begging in Hampstead she buys a flat. And when we checked her DNA from the days of her drug use, it was different from the DNA of the body you found in Hampstead. In fact it's identical with Zula Calabiyau's. We thought it was cloning, but even the mitochondrial DNA's the same."

"So what's going on?"

"We don't know. Never seen anything like it. You're in the right place to find out."

∞

I woke with Nancy's case on my mind. Spicer and I ate porridge next to each other. We discussed my conversation with Bernadette.

"The WTC is rotten to the core," said Spicer. "Your brother has been pushing out anyone who supports President Zula. The WTC's become a front for religious and corporate recusants, closely allied to Lizzard's *Organisation for Temporal Accommodation*. Jevons and I are working directly for Zula against them."

"So why does the WTC want me out of the way?"

"It's more than those diaries you stole from the crime scene. I don't know what. Something else you've said and done. Almost like they want revenge."

"Speaking of which. What's with that big red birth mark down your back? In Gondwana…"

"Nothing," she replied. "Your head's intact isn't it?"

After breakfast, Spicer and I sat down with Omran Tariq and Jevons Paradox. Omran's genetic age had been programmed to stay in his early 30's. He was tall, bearded with long brown hair. Jevons, as I mentioned, had a face considerably scarred after what looked to have been multiple attempts to repair a severe burn. Both were extensively PD protected.

"So the WTC sent you?" asked Omran. "To protect Zula?"

"It's turned out that way," I replied.

"You WTC people," said Jevons "couldn't protect a salad at a kid's birthday party. Three assassination attempts already."

"You're exaggerating," I said. "About the kid's party."

"We need to know a bit more about you and Zula," said Spicer to Omran.

"No one in their right mind would tell the WTC squat," said Jevons.

"The WTC is a criminal organisation," said Omran. "In my opinion."

"In our opinion," Jevons added.

"You see us arguing?" asked Spicer. "I'm working directly for President Zula. I'm not WTC. Neither is Jean here, anymore. In fact, the WTC wants to kill him."

Jevons sat watching Spicer like an eagle might a rabbit; rolling the tip of his right index finger around on the ball of his thumb, as though he was grinding some small bug exceeding fine. He was wearing a light grey Desmond Merrion Supreme Bespoke suit. Every stitch had been placed by hand, a machine had never touched the garment. With his burns scars, he seemed the kind of character you could take a liking to after having been tortured and sleep-deprived for a few weeks.

"You and Zula go a way back?" Spicer asked Omran.

"How many lifetimes you care to know about?" asked Omran.

"I originally introduced Zula to Omran as the 'elusive unicorn.'" said Jevons. "She was a war orphan you know. Tortured, so they say. The boat in which Zula and Zula's father tried to escape the war broke up and grounded on the Skeleton Coast. That made me angry and people paid. They'd got lost in fog where the cold Bengeula current swells off the Namib. Then they were engulfed by toxic hydrogen sulphide gas bubbling up from the dead zones. Finally, they were pounded by heavy surf. Zula alone survived the wreck and the subsequent attacks by child soldiers. I suppose a literary person might say Zula was Miranda chosing to become Prospero through necessity."

"You say that very casually," I said.

"Zula Calabiyau," said Jevons "likes to see earth as a perpetual pleasure garden with she chaste and inspirational in its middle; Virgin Queen and all that. I greatly respected her father."

"Never married?" I asked.

"She? I mean, They? Never any romance," Jevons continued. "Claims to be dedicated to the welfare of all life on Earth. Zula's opponents, and that wasn't ever me, claim They is possessed by a hundred thousand devils."

"They've counted?" I asked. "There's a quota?"

"It's part of the myth," said Jevons "that Zula undertook much fasting and solitary vigils under a tumboa and a quiver tree on the Skeleton Coast and later under a banyan tree on Lord Howe Island to make Their breakthrough visualisation of quantum coherence in the photosynthetic system."

"People do seem," I said "to like trying to kill Zula, despite all They've done. In London, at the Light Harvesting Festival for example. Remember that?"

"Her PhDs and post-docs," said Jevons "joke about Zula telling *mala* beads from morning to night and of witnessing her clairvoyance. Even keeps her own fool; has she introduced you to Michael yet?"

"She has," I said. "And now I've met you."

"There's no doubt," said Jevons "Zula cultivates a certain primitive loyalty and an equally strong hatred."

"In circles you may be unfamiliar with," I replied "that's called being a genius. Ask your friend Hercules Huncks."

"She looked a bit like Hedy Lamarr at that Nobel ceremony," Omran explained. "Told her she should genetically programme to keep that age. I mean Zula could have cured that skin disease in her lower body; makes it so hard to walk. But she didn't want to. Plays the guitar beautifully. I suppose in days past she'd have been called regal. Has this habit of chuckling meaningfully when powerful people are speaking to her, as if she knows and has anticipated what they're thinking. She's determined to be governed by no one. Meditates for an hour every morning. Reads widely and writes in her diary before going to bed."

"Claims to be sworn to her calling," said Jevons "Of course, I've long suspected indiscretions eventually will be found out."

"And how's that been going for you?" I asked.

"It's of no real concern to me," said Jevons. "But I see it is for you."

"And me," said Spicer.

"Last night," said Omran to Spicer "I dreamt of hiding from assailants in a frozen wilderness, starving, wet, shivering. Zula walked from the forest into their bright lights to offer me a warm drink. 'A hot cup of tea can save a man,' she said. But it was too late for me."

"You never told me that," said Jevons. It was clear Jevons was very insecure; though as with most self-centred people, this inconvenient truth was lost on him. Still ego not eco with Jevons.

"Were you and Zula ever an item?" I asked Omran. "I mean romantically."

"People assume that's the case," Omran replied. "But sadly no. If you were a shrewd observer you'd know my instincts do not that way incline. Another source of frustration to my father."

"Let me get this straight," I said. "She's always been celibate?"

"Why is that so shocking?" Omran asked.

"It's not," said Spicer. "He's just curious."

"I'd have thought that's obvious," said Jevons.

"You heard about that young girl murdered in Hampstead," I asked "during the recent London GSPP celebrations? Nancy Godel?"

"I read something about it," said Omran. "Why?"

"Well, we have DNA evidence; DNA that shows she was the daughter of Zula."

"You sleazy WTC bastard," Omran said.

"So naturally we're interested to find the father," I continued.

"Well, why don't you trace his DNA?" Jevons asked.

"That's the problem," I responded. "Nancy had no male DNA."

"Ha, ha," said Omran. "Some kid just stole your salad."

> *Zula's radiant*
> *She dances for fun,*
> *Inclined like rooves*
> *Following the sun.*

∞

I saw Zula walking on her way to the central research building. My strong inclination was to let Them go. But the idea that we should be discussing Nancy without Zula being present seemed wrong.

"Hey Zula," I called out, "please join us." Just a few trivial words; from being there.

Zula waved, walked over and sat down. If They'd heard what we were talking about, They didn't let on. I had this feeling They shouldn't be there, that it was important I signal it would be best if They moved on. But I said nothing.

"I can't stay long," Zula said "I've promised to be at a meeting."

"These people," said Omran "were just asking how we originally met and started working on the GSPP idea."

"All my closest advisors," said Zula to Spicer and I "were strongly against me meeting Omran. They said selling him our patent would just lead to another critical break-through being swallowed up and sat upon till it had been forgotten."

"And I was a self-absorbed bastard in those days," said Omran "I told Zula my experts had vetted her technology and we were prepared to offer twelve billion dollars for the patent over it. I gave guarantees our company would develop it."

"I didn't believe you," said Zula.

My mind now was screaming at me to tell Zula They had to depart. Every component of my psyche was pushing me to say those words. It was like how it used to be when someone put a bottle of whisky in front of me. But I curled my toes and gripped the arms of my chair to keep quiet.

"I worried, of course, whether it was right, buying her patent," said Omran. "And Zula recommended Jevons to me!"

"Since boyhood, Omran was taught the corporation was society," said Jevons. "The market spontaneously created society's rules. All that's heresy now, of course."

"Ah yes, the Old Faith," said Omran. "The sacrificial bytes of fanged contestability."

"Sadly, many rejoiced when your father's gene therapy failed," Jevons continued. "I remember once during a Davos plenary packed with bleating NGO's, he boasted he'd dissolved the very notion of society as a meeting place beyond self-interest. He'd so managerialised and relativised ethics, so digitalised and subdued it to the algorithms of economics, the market had become its oracle. Now we know better."

"My father was not alone in letting his business ape a man," said Omran.

My mind was demanding I tell Zula to move on. I was being pounded with reasons. They'd be late. Jevons was a threat, look at his AR data. I had to get Them to safety. The thoughts echoed my yearnings for alcohol. I decided to ignore them. I didn't care if the effort split my corpus callosum. Why Eugene wasn't helping me I couldn't understand.

"Your father," Jevons continued "took pride in the company's social responsibility and philanthropy programme. Like many companies before the *Great Cleansing* he supported renewable energy targets and changed operations to have a low carbon footprint; he saw it as good for business as well as the environment. I did too. But look what they did to me."

"I'm sorry," said Zula, leaning forward to touch Jevon's cheek with Their palm.

∞

At that moment, there was a flash followed by a loud explosion. A metal fragment smashed through the window, passed where Zula's head had been and embedded itself in the wall. My AR began sending an emergency signal. Spicer's must have as well. We both grabbed Zula and pulled Them under the table. Debris crashed around us. People started screaming and sirens to wail. A large panel of glass broke the table top. Outside the broken window, I saw flames and smoke issuing from the upper storeys of the main research complex. It looked like the sixth floor had been destroyed and debris ejected by the blast.

"That's the lab," said Zula. "We're experimenting with a new light capture system. Kofi's there. I was meant to be with him now."

No one near us appeared to have been hurt. Zula, Omran, Jevons, Spicer and I ran outside. We followed the fire wardens in their yellow helmets and vests as they hurried up the stairs. When we arrived on the sixth floor, we saw through the smoke a body smashed against a fume hood on one side of the wall. Laboratory benches had been broken in half. There was a large black mark on the ceiling. Researchers in white lab coats were spraying foam from extinguishers.

Zula and Spicer ran over. Kofi's jaw was smashed and he was having difficulty breathing. He had his hand to his neck and blood was spilling between his fingers. He was lapsing from consciousness.

"Get me the resus kit!" shouted Spicer. She pinched off Kofi's lacerated carotid artery with the thumb and forefinger of her right hand. She showed Zula how to take over that job. Spicer then put on gloves and swabbed the front of Kofi's neck with an antiseptic. She felt for his carotid pulse on the other side.

"Asystole. Start CPR," Spicer yelled at some men in medical uniforms standing around watching. "Push harder on the sternum. Squash it against the ribs. Cannulate him and give a couple of litres of whatever you've got, stat. Go femoral 16 gauge. Good, secure and connect it up, Squeeze it in. Give adrenaline 1 in 10,000 iv. Now shock him, 300 joules. Good."

"We've got sinus rhythm back," said one of the assistants. My AR resus programme was superimposing the ECG trace over his heart. It couldn't work as fast as Spicer and much of what she was doing wasn't by the book.

"You people," Spicer shouted "lift up his arms and legs."

"He's going blue," said the assistant. "AR says upper airway's blocked."

Spicer drew up local anaesthetic and infiltrated the front of Kofi's neck. She then connected a large bore needle to an air-filled syringe. Pushing the needle into the crico-thyroid notch she also gently pressed down on the plunger of the syringe, until the air flowed freely out indicating she was in the trachea. Holding the needle still with forefinger and thumb of her left hand, she threaded a wire down the needle then pulled the needle out leaving the guide wire in place.

Spicer used a scalpel to widen the incision then slipped an endotracheal tube over the wire. She pulled it out, connected the tube to a resuscitation bag and pumped air into Kofi's lungs. His face immediately went from a dusky shade of blue to pink. Dr Christine had now arrived from the ICU, wrinkling her nose at the odour.

"Back to life, darling," said Christine, adjusting her purple floral turban. "See that $ETCO_2$ trace. You don't see that unless it's in the trachea or they've had 20 cans of black market *Cobra Cola* and then it falls very precipitously."

Christine applied rotating tourniquets to Kofi's arms and legs, gradually squeezing the blood down into his trunk. After that, she administered some blood refilling tablets and some intravenous nanobots that immediately began giving her readings of Kofi's physiology. Christine and her team then carried Kofi away to the GSPP Centre's Intensive Care Unit. We were ushered back out by the fire fighters. Flames and smoke were about us as we descended.

We sat on the grass beside the lagoon. Zula put Their head in Their hands and began crying. Omran placed a hand around Their shoulders. I imagined three figures sneaking away into the inky night, clothed in a forest of light-trapping vertically aligned nanotubes that rendered them flat, bottomless cut-outs of space.

"Thank you," said Zula to Spicer. "You saved his life."

"I just tried to do to a man," said Spicer "what you've done for our planet."

∞

Later that evening, Zula, Omran, Spicer and I sat in the Intensive Care Unit at the GSPP Centre. As well as dealing with medical emergencies for the staff, the GSPP ICU was also a referral hub for a vast hinterland, helicopters flying in patients all hours of night and day. Outside, the lights and hoses of fire trucks played over the smouldering and smoking ruins. The explosion had caused the whole central research building to burn to the ground. There would probably be a few casualties apart from Kofi to add to the existing patients.

Kofi was intubated, ventilated and receiving inotropic support as well as transfusions. About us was the action of a busy ICU whirling around Christine, the senior registrar. AR was showing the types of cases from the note headings at the foot of each bed. All a clinician had to do was log in and the precipitating event would be reconstructed in real, slowed or fast time; they could pause and get the patient's physiological data and therapies at any moment of the admission. A computer programme had gone through all the clinical trials relevant to any aspect of the admission and had produced a variety of appropriate treatment algorithms that the clinicians were evaluating with their own clinical experience and intuition. Christine was reading the patient list to an intern.

"'Tension pneumothoraces from motor bike accident.' 'GSPP-powered car exploded.' 'Fractures after fall from a balcony.' 'Threw himself in front of car,' 'collapsed at plant nursery,' 'ruptured abdominal aortic aneurysm at lawn bowls,' 'respiratory arrest after iv heroin,' 'rib fractures after fall onto piano,' 'car hit truck,' 'truck hit tree,' 'fell from truck,' 'bicycle v truck,' 'fell from ladder,' 'stabbed in chest with chisel.' 'Head injury after fall on pavement while drunk,' 'pilot of WTC helicopter switched off AR and crashed into hanger,' 'found in garden shed lying face down,' 'poured paint thinner on his body and lit it,' 'found hanging near the rear window after an MVA,' 'caught in irrigation wheel' and 'car surfing — hit head on gutter.'" Pain and misery obviously were continuing apace in this supposedly perfect world.

As we watched, the consultants gathered with Christine, the junior registrars, residents, interns and nurses for a ward round. They congregated at the foot of Kofi's bed. Their AR systems were showing physiological readouts next to current investigations and treatments.

"We had only one admission overnight, darlings," said Dr Christine, brushing the long hair back from her eyes "it was this poor fellow, Kofi

Buxtun scientist Buddha who was blown up by silane gas on level six. Yeah, the one you can see burning outside the window. Multiple fractures and bad burns. He had a fairly prolonged arrest with reasonable CPR. Spicer Layamon the security agent did an emergency trachy — good one too, didn't hit the thyroid; way to go girl. But Kofi's probably had a significant hypoxic hit. He's pretty stable now, sats 91 on RA, sinus rhythm, RR low 29. Pressures are OK. But still only has a two digit systolic. I asked the resident to send off the hobgoblin and electric lights and get an 'end-of-the-bed-o-gram.' Troponin's up; but get a haircut round here and your troponin rises."

"He looks sallow I must say," said the consultant "but CVP's hanging in there."

"Granted he isn't making that much urine," said Christine. "But it's a man's right not to make urine. Underfilled? How can that be? All our patients are subject to careful fluid balance checks. No darlings, you're not supposed to laugh when the the senior registrar says that. Doesn't need to be filtered till his kidneys are nice and crisp."

"What plumbing he's got?" asked a consultant. "Looks like terrible venous access."

"Darling," said Christine "you could drive your small water-powered car with its love seat through the access he's got up there now."

"How many times," said the consultant "have you seen them behave just like full blown ARDS — high PEEP, high $FiO_2$, but a crystal clear CXR? In the old days, we just used to blow them up till the lungs filled the room. Respiratory consult?"

"Not on my watch," said Christine. "If there was ever a hospital speciality that's homeopathic, it's respiratory."

"Do we know which stem cell treatment centre the organs are going to?" asked a consultant.

"Not the problem now," said Christine. "We need a cerebrum that's going to support extubation. At the moment he's got the mental state of a hospital administrator; a problem we'll resolve tomorrow, one way or another. It's nature's way, break enough bones and if the brain swells no one's worried. Well I am. I liked Kofi."

"He's got some bad protoplasm," said a resident. "Maybe we should ask the colorectal boys about a peg? They're passionate about the microbiology."

"I've seen facial burns knock them around," said Christine "but this is unusual. See that? Just give him a bolus of mother's milk. See if he settles a bit."

"Hey," said a registrar "Fascio-max didn't want the tube taped there."

"Ignore them," Christine replied. "I'll talk to Fascio-max. They owe me."

The ward round moved on to the next patient.

"Another casualty from level six," said an intern. "This one's Jamelia. Friend of Kofi. She's a little unusual. Believes people are trying to kill her in hospital."

"Does she now?" said Christine. "Well, cancel that psych assessment. She's competent, absolutely. I'll sign the form now. I mean; this is an iatrogenic crime scene. Just look at the fluid inputs. What's with that crappy sodium darlings? And cross off the dopamine, or it won't just be the Neuro Boys who call Security."

∞

"Kofi used to say," said Zula "'what you see depends on how you chose to look.'"

The sacrifice of the guiltless was becoming a theme in this case.

"I first met Kofi," Zula continued "when I gave a talk and he followed me back to the Windhoek orphanage in the SOS Childrens' Village. All he had was a dirty singlet and a loin cloth. He told our supervisor 'I've just heard a girl speak who is going to win the Nobel Prize one day and save the Earth.' Imagine saying that, when you were a 14 year old orphan pulling yourself out of the slums in Namibia."

"Kofi told me he'd grown up in Katatura. That's called 'the place where we don't want to live' by the native population. They were brutally oppressed by their colonial rulers. Kofi said his parents had died of HIV/AIDS. He was highly intelligent and educated. He'd ask tourists for books rather than money. He made friends with a white family, the Buxtuns, who let him study in their library when he wasn't working in their orchard. Kofi had already read more than most university graduates by the time he left the orphanage."

"Why was he working up there alone?" asked Omran. Zula ignored the question.

"Kofi secured the books I needed to study," said Zula. "He strategised what I needed to get on my CV. He applied for University scholarships for me, for post-doc positions. He used to sit up with me preparing for each exam. It was due in large measure to Kofi that I was awarded the University Medals in Physics and Molecular Chemistry at the Namibia University of Science and Technology. After graduation, it would have been easy for me to slip into some well-paid professorial position, teaching and administering. But Kofi decided that I had to do something to help the world 'with your great brain.' After thinking over the issue for some time, we decided that it had to do with carbon dioxide, water, food, renewable energy, population growth."

"How'd you pick global synthetic photosynthesis?" Spicer asked.

"One day Kofi was looking at some children picking apples from a tree," said Zula "when a light shower of rain fell and soon there was a rainbow over the tree and our house. Kofi pointed at it and said to me 'see, there's the answer, making buildings like trees.' Suddenly I remembered this vision I'd had on the Skeleton Coast. My father, a great mathematician, had been lost in the wreck and my few companions perished soon after, some from the hydrogen sulphide bubbling up from the putrid ocean and some from the surf. I crawled between a tumboa and a quiver tree that provided the only shelter above that desolate beach. With the booming of the surf in my ears, the salt on my lips and the smell of rotten egg gas in my nostrils, I feel asleep and dreamed of a world where all the roads and houses made oxygen, clean fuel, food and fertiliser from water, sun and air. After I woke, all I remembered was I knew I had to do something. That was what drove me to survive and study. I hid from the child soldiers by burying myself in sand. When Kofi mentioned the rainbow, I

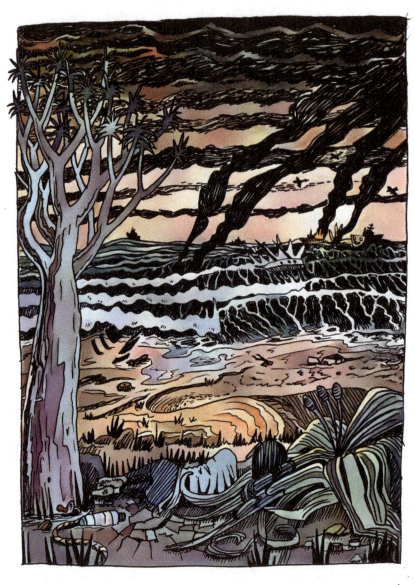

I fell asleep and dreamed of a world where all the roads and houses made oxygen, clean fuel, food and fertilizer.

remembered that dream. I was very grateful to him. He sacrificed much more than me." Zula began to sing.

> *"Praise our house, it gives us power*
> *Just from water, sun and air.*
> *World's become what we'd drawn it as,*
> *Beautiful, safe and fair."*

"Kofi was relentless," said Zula "organising for me to attend conferences on what was then called artificial photosynthesis (something I knew nothing about prior to this) and give papers on that area, to get grants and write articles and papers in that field. The last piece of the puzzle was when Kofi organised a science-Buddha conference at Lord Howe island in the last year of the War to End the Corporatocene. That meeting was like a beacon in dark times. All the leading experts in artificial photosynthesis attended, along with policy and contemplation wonks. They organised governance structures for the GSPP. Before sunrise, I went off and found a banyan tree with a vast array of aerial prop roots and the surrounding forest growing in profusion up through them. I sat for meditation in the shelter of that tree. I was determined. At dawn, my awareness was disturbed by the sound of a helicopter passing over."

"Things just seemed to flow, so many coincidences helped me become a master in that area. In time I started to think, that there was something mystical even magical about how Kofi had arrived to help me. He asked me to marry him. He wanted to be a father. When I refused, he vowed he would never marry another. I regret that now and I don't care what the consequences are. If I could have Kofi back and love him I'd renounce all I've achieved in the unitive life."

Outside through the window, the whole main research building was now just ash and smoking ruins. We all knew what a disaster this was for the *Global Synthetic Photosynthesis Project*. The chaos in the ICU continued around us. Christine was on AR fielding requests for transfers and beds.

"Yes darling, we've managed to rustle up a bed," said Christine. "So now you can give me the true handover." "Look darling, the one piece of genuine physiologic information I'm missing is who's the singer of the song and who's the actress." "Well that wasn't too hard was it? And we provide the registrar for the transfer." "Yeah, anyway I was saying. You listening? Well, apparently, they made him dress up as a cleaner. Yeah, that's right darling. And he did some lines. Not bad either; better than the interns, so no one could be bothered dobbing for a while."

I walked over to the Christine.

"Hey Christine," I said. "How's your pharmacology?"

"My sub-specialty, sitting finals in a month. Why?"

"Ever been to Hampstead? Say on leave, recently."

"What's it to you, darling?"

"I rather think you have. And I think I know why; darling."

At that moment, young fellow came in to the Intensive Care Unit and handed Zula a report. It must have been too secret for AR communication.

"It was silane," said Zula, after reading a few lines. "$SiH_4$, a gas made from hydrogen and silicon. Pyrophoric — explodes on contact with the air."

"Was he meant to use it?" I asked.

"We use it, or 'used it' rather," Zula explained "to deliver silicon to thin dielectric films to make solar cells and semiconductors. You spray it on and at high temperatures the hydrogen just burns off leaving the silicon in place. Kofi was working on the problem of AMDS, Acute Metabolic Distress Syndrome. He had this theory it was somehow related to building materials."

"How's it supposed to be stored?" Spicer asked.

"In a cylinder," Zula replied. "Your average cylinder of silane contains about 5,000 g which is the equivalent of about 50 kgs of TNT."

"So what went wrong?" I asked.

"The O-ring within check valve," Zula said, reading from the report. "Looks like it had been degraded by nitrous oxide, and the check valve, that is, the non-return valve, had lost its function. As a result, a reverse flow of nitrous oxide through the check valve flew into the silane container via the purge lines."

"Could they have been tampered with?" I asked.

"Possibly," Zula explained. "The purge lines remove noxious fumes and combustible gas inside the pipes by introducing inert gas such as nitrogen after each system operation. When Kofi closed the valve, the mixed gas in purge lines compressed, generated heat and ignited. The flame then travelled back to the container through the piping and exploded the container. The safety valves for preventing heat meltdown of the container had no time to activate."

∞

"I realised, before," I said to Spicer. "Zula was meant to die in this explosion. I'd dreamt about it. Three WTC assassins set it up."

Omran was looking out the Intensive Care Unit window into the night sky. He seemed to stiffen, then step back.

"Hey, did you see that?" Omran said. "Up there, behind the clouds."

I'd noticed it too. An intense flash of light. Soon the heavens were a mass of swirling colours, purples and light greens. A fiendish-looking red glow quickly coloured the clouds. Lightning flashes were visible.

Our room was plunged into darkness. All the lights went out in every building in the GSPP complex. Strings of street and sidewalks lights were extinguished. Two cars that had been moving near the hospital simply stopped. I tried to use AR but it wasn't working. Alarms began sounding all over the complex. Antiquated power lines carrying electricity from the GSPP Centre to neighbouring towns and cities exploded, showering cascades of sparks through the darkness.

"There's no need to panic," said Zula. "Backup power will start soon. It's an EMP. High-intensity electromagnetic pulse; 200,000 volts per metre. What we saw probably was the detonation of a nuclear warhead on a missile a couple of hundred kilometres or more up in space. The blast is disrupting the Earth's atmosphere, ionosphere and magnetic field, that's why we're seeing the aurora. Its X-rays are exciting atomic oxygen to create that glow."

My mind seemed calmer than it had been for a long time. The pressured thoughts to move Zula along were gone. Despite the crisis around me I felt focused and content. It was like the chairman taking control of a meeting where everyone had been shouting all at once. But I could get no AR readings on anything or anyone.

"Nuclear explosion," I said. "Nuclear weapons were supposed to be destroyed."

"Yeah right, like smallpox," said Omran.

"Its gamma rays," said Zula "have fused every electrical circuit in the GSPP complex. Our equipment will look normal, but it won't work."

Of course, Zula was right. The electrons stripped off the air molecules would be racing down magnetic lines of force, spinning and transmitting to metal huge amounts of energy. Those exploded power lines would have been hit by 10 million volts and 10,000 amperes.

"When you open up any piece of electrical gear," Zula added "everything with a silicon semi-conductor will be fried."

"Including my AR system?" I asked.

"Yes, including all your AR systems," said Zula.

"Will we die from the radiation?" Omran asked.

"No and not by the blast," I said "It's too high up."

"But the EMP three-segment pulse," said Zula "will have crippled our electronics and caused cascading failure of critical infrastructures. Every computer system controlling our transport, finance, telecommunications, research and energy will have collapsed. Think surge arrestor burnout, spark-gap breakdown, blown fuses, insulator flash-overs and broad-scale loss-of-load."

"And your research?" asked Omran.

"Years of data destroyed," said Zula "along with most of the equipment."

"At least the drug lab's gone," I said.

"What did you say?" Zula asked.

"Hopefully you've backed up," I said.

"Yes, we've expected such an attack," Zula continued. "Staff will be getting their generators and other essential electrical equipment out of Faraday cages. Our synthetic photosynthesis liquid fuel supplies remain intact. Our important emergency vehicles have been deliberately designed with back-up pre-1980 (CE) low-electronic systems. We even have some vacuum tube equipment, oil lanterns and gas cookers. They'll be being distributed now."

Reports came in that there'd been casualties. Two lovers kissing up against a metal fence had been electrocuted, but survived. Some children swimming in a pond that had its water filtered by metal pipes were shocked and drowned. The GSPP centre was out of operation and would be so indefinitely.

∞

Next morning, I woke to find Spicer shoving me in the shoulder through the mosquito net. I must have only had two hours sleep, but I felt better than ever.

"Hey you, little pooky, lying in the sun; when you gonna get yer work done?"

"What? Did I blackout?"

"C'mon get up sunshine. You're still in the game. Zula's going for a desert stroll."

I dressed quickly and armed myself. The dream I'd had was still very vivid. It was a reprise of the one I set out at the beginning of the story; about the three miscreants trying to cut down the temple's sacred tree. I told it to Spicer as I dressed.

"My AR hasn't worked since last night," I said. "It's great. Slept like a baby."

Spicer had thought to carry food and water. Zula was standing waiting for us.

"Security. Ah, good to see you. Let's walk," Zula said and set off. Together we strode out of the GSPP compound gates into the desert.

Small groups of people were moving off in carts drawn by horses leaving clouds of dust. It looked as if the GSPP centre was being evacuated. We'd been briefed there was a plan in place for such events and secondary accommodation was available at a nearby secure location, until the area could be proven clear of biohazards, radiation or other threats.

"I had a dream the night you two arrived," said Zula, after we'd walked on a while. "I saw the GSPP Centre here in Namibia. The labs and meditation halls were empty and deserted and the grounds foul and noisome from the buffaloes that'd been tied up there. None of my scientists or students were to be seen. On the horizon, an immense fire was devouring whole towns and villages. This nuclear explosion, it's not just the radiation damage it will cause to people and animals. It's a great psychic shock to the whole race, to think after all we've been through, we're still capable of an atrocity like that. You know before we integrated the capacity to absorb atmospheric carbon dioxide into every pavement, road and building, temperatures got so hot here, you'd die simply going outside. Millions got killed, from heat stroke or famine when the crops failed, from huge storms or from toxic methane hydride and hydrogen sulphide gases. It took us so long to repair the damage of the Corporatocene and now already there are those who want to take us back to it."

Then a most remarkable thing happened. Near us was a field of sunflowers tended by the local people. I hadn't noticed before, but all the sunflowers were inclined towards Zula, although the sun was in the opposite direction and poking over the horizon. When Zula moved, the sunflowers kept looking towards Them. "We care for you," the field of sunflowers seemed to be saying to Zula. "You are a source of life to us. Your friend Kofi is dead. We're sorry."

To the east, dawn's first blush disappeared over peaks and troughs of sand with scattered dots of vegetation. In the chill, still air, the land seemed parched, shocked and vacant. Zula spoke about the remnant native Namibian population as They first saw them here all those years ago we They started building up the GSPP.

"They were huddled over there," said Zula "in their shanty suburbs outside the main town where some made clothes for the global market, while their children, brothers and sisters begged from the cars of passing tourists."

Our feet trod gently on large, smooth stones. The moon, just above the horizon, seemed to smile upon the dawn chorus of weaver and rosy-faced lovebirds. Zula picked a rock up and examined it. They was saying goodbye.

"This is a stone tool, for chopping meat, on the edge here. It's one of the earliest pieces of technology developed by man." They put Their palm around it. "Imagine we were living on these plains 50,000 years ago. Our goal in life would have been to stay alive and help our children and tribe do so, by learning skills of hunting, cooking, making shelter and clothes. We'd have been surrounded my mysteries, diseases, earthquakes, lightning, rainbows, whirlwinds. These prodded our reason and required vast feats of memory to pass on the Law at sacred Ceremonies."

Zula carefully returned the stone to the ground. They scrambled down into the river bed and up the far bank. We followed. There Zula pointed out to us rocks with their wavy fossil formations.

"Stromatolites," said Zula. "Fossils of the earliest photosynthetic plants on earth, remnants of the great oxygenation event."

Spicer shared some biscuits and water. Together we sat on a boulder and watched the sun come up over the nearby Tsaris mountains.

"I was told yesterday," Zula continued "just before all this, that the Mayor of Southwark in London, Gordon Lizzard, and some of his cronies, have started an action against the *Whole Earth Council* and myself for corruption in how we dealt with the proceeds from the dissolution of the corporations. Must have been planning it for years. They've also claimed our corporate marriage laws are prohibited by the equal protection clause in the *Whole Earth Charter*. They further maintain that the 'freedom of contemplative expression' clause in the *Charter* should not be interpreted as a 'freedom from religion.' They want war. The Council has counter-claimed. I've been subpoenaed to give evidence. The case will be heard before a jury of all registered citizens of Earth as part of proceedings before the *Ecocide Truth and Reconciliation Supreme Court* in the Hague."

"Why didn't you just keep running this place?" I asked. "You were good at it."

"Becoming President seemed the logical next step. Humanity has such a short time to make its choice. But I'll give it that chance."

Zula knelt on the ground. I took a knee beside Them. Spicer remained standing, vigilant. Zula's voice was very musical and resonant.

> *"For as long as space remains,*
> *For as long as sentient beings remain,*
> *Then I too shall remain,*
> *To dispel the miseries of the world.*
>
> *And until the pass away from pain,*
> *May I too be a source of life*
> *For all the realms of varied beings*
> *That reach unto the end of time.*
>
> *Any harmful action I have done*
> *With body, speech or mind*
> *Overwhelmed by anger, hatred or confusion,*
> *These I openly lay before You.*
>
> *May I always act with ethical discipline*
> *Faultless and pure*
> *Completely cleansing without omission*
> *All that obscures this awakening mind.*
>
> *May I always have the friendship*
> *Of like-minded spiritual beings;*
> *Dispersing the power of interfering forces*
> *May we free an ocean of beings."*

I thought Zula had finished praying, but then They started again.

> *"Our redeemer, by whose will we were created and are preserved till now, grant Thy bounty and blessing upon us. Enable us by our works to repay Thy kindness and protection. If it please thee, compose our distractions, calm our inquietude and preserve us from sinful presumption about the worth, or long continuance of our existence. Enlighten our minds and refine our conscience, that we may truly know our duty, while strengthening our resolution to perform it, whatever the personal danger or cost. Grant that our activities and plans be brought to good effect, that we remain fair and honest in our dealings with others, forgiving and charitable toward our enemies. Preserve our going out and our coming in, from this time forth, forever more. Amen."*

We sat in silence for about ten minutes. I started to feel my being swell out of my chest, as though it wished to fill the whole bowl of the sky, then beyond. It was as though Zula was giving a final blessing to this place and its people. For a leader reviled by many for Their attack on religion, Zula seemed very traditional in Their prayers.

"Even today," said Zula, "there are patches of sky as blue as liquid oxygen. And deep slabs of desert, pink with molecular fossils of chlorophyll."

"I need to ask you," I said, eventually "about the young girl Nancy Godel; the one who died in Hampstead during the GSPP celebrations?"

"Yes. What of her?"

"DNA evidence says she was your daughter."

"This isn't something I wish to talk about," Zula replied.

"Can you confirm or deny?" I persisted. "Her DNA seems identical with yours."

"Not now," said Zula. "Not today. Jean you have something that will help me save the Earth. Keep it safe."

Zula touched a dwarf bushman's candle beneath a quiver tree. South was the deserted and smoky ruins of the GSPP Centre. To the north, a rainstorm was moving across the ranges and the rising sun made a double rainbow. I realised what was in Zula's diary and why it had to stay missing till Their trial.

# V

# EARTH STEWARDSHIP, NEW YORK, GENEVA & ALBERTA

*Jean's conversation with Omran Tariq in New York — campaign speech in Geneva of Zula for a second term as President of the Whole Earth Council — Jean and Spicer resign from the World Time Council — Zula's farewell speech at the Athabasca River rehabilitation in Alberta Canada — meeting WTC whistleblower Adley — plan to keep Zula safe until her trial in the Ecocide Truth and Reconciliation Supreme Court — Spicer's dream of Eugene in the RuBisCO hunt —*

Jean walked towards Wall Street in New York, as he had so many times before. It was a day where fall drizzle might once again, as it had in the Corporatocene, bring down from the clouds not just pollutants, but the dismal ideology that then powered the skyscrapers and those enslaved within them. He imagined plastic cups with corporate logos floating on the torrents in gutters like those bold vessels that had first opened the gold and slave-trade routes around the world. Water, with no sun about to split it, slewed off the tops of umbrellas.

As air temperatures rose in the Corporatocene era, sea-level rise from melting polar ice caps had made New York City look for a time like Venice. The streets became canals serviced by entrepreneurial gondoliers and go-getting owners of small motor boats.

One day, however, a methane hydride gas-filled water spout hundreds of metres high exploded from the Atlantic Ocean off the mouth of the Hudson River. The shockwaves triggered additional eruptions over the sea. People crowded vantage points to watch the spectacle, many taking selfies of themselves with the natural cataclysm in the background. Winds carried the methane cloud from this orgy of briny outgassing right over downtown New York. At precisely 3pm in the afternoon, that methane was ignited by a lightning bolt. This created supersonic blast waves and fireballs across the city that vaporised every living thing they encountered.

When people from other regions finally reached New York City, they saw a scene of devastation much worse than Hiroshima or Nagasaki after the atomic bombs. This oceanic methane eruption had released more destructive energy than from the entire stockpile of all nuclear weapons that ever existed. It hastened the conclusion of the Corporatocene War, as many leaders of the Military–Industrial Complex, arms-dealers, financial speculators and barons of oil and coal business had been resident in New York at the time and perished in the conflagration. Dust and smoke rose to shroud the Earth and numb its vegetation. New York City had to be completely rebuilt, providing an opportunity to fully integrate Zula's new GSPP technology. This reconstruction was a core eco-centric policy of President Asvaghosa Silabhadra's first WEC administration of the incipient Sustainocene era. The latest plague to hit New York was AMDS, thousands had already died there from this mysterious and incurable illness.

Electric and ammonia-powered driverless cars, gossiping with each other, sloshed water over pavements on passing, as if in clumsy benediction. A few small birds pecked at discarded lumps of sugary bread. Jean briefly called into Trinity Church, his mother's favourite place of worship in this city. Technically this was now a contemplation centre, but it looked much the same as it had before Zula as WEC President had organised the legislation to ban religion globally. Jean placed money in the collection box and listened to some JS Bach. The Church's GSPP panels now provided not only abundant fertiliser for its lush orchard, but also the basic ingredients for the communion wafer should such a ritual ever again be permitted. On either side of the Church were a Buddhist Temple and a Muslim Mosque. A 'Strictly Sporting Rifle Association' shop was behind. The respective congregations of non-religious 'contemplatives' enjoyed mingling after services; enjoying sharing mutual misgivings and resentments about the inadequacies of the *Book of Common Faith*.

Walking on, Jean reached into his pocket to give coins to a beggar who squatted in a doorway. The vagrant's rain-splattered cardboard sign declared: *'Patent for time travel invention stolen. Please donate if it worked.'* A fellow traveller, a rare sight in the Sustainocene. Jean dropped a few New York dollars in the man's cap. Jean bought a strong black Arabica at the famous 'Occupy' coffee van and walked into what had once been called the Tariq Corporation Building, but had been re-named the *Global Synthetic Photosynthesis Project — New York Division*. He greeted the security officers, passed their AR inspection and caught the lift to Omran's office on the tenth floor.

> *Greed broke the link*
> *Brought life to the brink.*
> *Craving peak power,*
> *Hatred's over-ripe flower.*
> *So serve like a bee,*
> *Principled eco-society.*

Jean was directed to wait for the man himself under the watchful eyes of two large security guards and no doubt many other human and AI security systems. Eugene had ensured Jean's disguise was impenetrable. Although he would look himself to Omran, to everyone else he was Labyrinth Goblett, now no longer a fat scientist Buddha, but a harmless seller of books and rare prints. An elderly woman seated next to him was reading a copy of the *Mannahata*. The cover depicted Omran the CEO of the New York GSPP, watering the foundations of his Dad's skyscraper which was flowering at the top. But the building was toppling and in the sky was the

Great Comet, a sky made lurid by volcanic ash and the afterglow of an atmospheric nuclear explosion. Jean peered over her shoulder at the stories inside. The headings were '*EMP Attack. GSPP Corruption Blamed*' and '*Zula's Popularity Plummets.*' The peculiar thrust of this AR 'journalism' was that the attack on the GSPP Centre was the work of illicit drug criminals who felt they'd been cheated in some corrupt dealing with Zula. The racy beat-up went on to describe how Zula's genderless and eco-centric orientation had been proven a fraud through the discovery of Their dead and disowned Hampstead love child. The article claimed all would be revealed when Zula gave testimony before the *Ecocide Truth and Reconciliation Supreme Court*. There were also articles on the horror of nuclear weapons, describing how they worked, how many people they'd killed and why any use of them was such an atrocity. Zula somehow was blamed for their use in Namibia. The title of one article was '*Zula: Wanted for Treason! Time to Split!*' After a time, the signal was given that Jean could enter. The security men escorted him to a large oak door that opened at their approach.

Omran was watching an AR programme on a large flat screen while ironing his shirts. On the walls were framed photos of he and Zula at Namibia as well as paintings and prints, some of which Jean remembered from his own childhood: Rabuzin's '*Girl with a Sunflower*' and Vincent Van Gogh's '*The Sower.*' His attention, however, focused on the print of Klee's '*Underwater Garden.*'

"Like that one too, do you?" asked Omran. "When I was a child, I wanted to be that little red fish swimming past purple canyons and aqua and green boulders. I read Herbert's *Dragon in the Sea* novel over and over because this painting was on the cover. It's about a subtug's crew trying to steal undersea oil from one of the few remaining enemy wells after a nuclear war. That's how the world could have ended up, you know, if it hadn't been for Zula and the *Global Synthetic Photosynthesis Project*."

Jean sat in a large chair in front of Omran. Outside the window, the rain was abating, smoke and fumes arose amongst the tops of GSPP-powered skyscrapers while the clearing sky in the east was criss-crossed by the condensation trails of jet aircraft running on solar fuel. Omran noticed Jean looking at them.

"In the Corporatocene some conspiracy theorists," said Omran "claimed those contrails were seeding mind-altering chemicals over the world."

"Did it work?" Jean asked.

"Maybe. Average documentary," said Omran as he switched off the AR using the remote. "Thomas More's *Utopia*. More didn't act like a Utopian. Tyndale achieved more. Or those students and professors sarcastically dressed as monks who nailed Sustainocene principles on the doors of the London School of Economics. Or all the whistle blowers against State surveillance and persecution, or corporate and religious exploitation; those scientists not afraid of the big questions."

"Farsighted rebels, like Zula?" Jean asked.

"Zula belongs to this world as it should be," said Omran. "Zula's utterly committed to making science and politics good servants of life. But I was the architect of the eco-centric governing structures for the Sustainocene. My daily *Green Spark* news feeds shaped the necessary actors, resources and recursive interactions between global and local. I clustered allies, isolated opponents, nurtured legitimacy, harmonised competing visions and strategic behaviours, fostered adaptive capacities through a repertoire of ecology-promoting governance linked to venerable theoretical traditions that valued right relationship with all life. When the *Whole Earth Council*, its policies and agencies, *The Book of Common Faith* and its contemplative processes, finally emerged from the chaos of the Corporatocene War, it was my joy that the whole shebang looked so simple and natural as to have been created by happenstance. But let me tell you, it only happened because Zula was so fearless in support, so remarkable in resilience of spirit. I was merely one instrument in the orchestra by which Zula created, to the lasting glory of life on Earth, a symphony of the Sustainocene."

"Is that so?" said Jean. "Zula claims the nature of the Sustainocene has been written into the essence of existence since its creation."

"Who knows such people? They're not like you or I? The obstacles she's had to overcome. And now look. Most people think she's been leading a double life. Claimed to be chaste and dedicated to the world, but gives birth to a daughter, disowns and won't acknowledge her. Let's face it, it was always an aberration that the people of the world voted as WEC President a person who not only identified with no gender, but claimed, as Zula did, to be the Earth. It was like the old nation states discovering UN Secretary General Dag Hammarskjold was a morally courageous mystical celibate; the unicorn with no mate had to go. Zula was too weird, too strange. An individual world leader wanting to be called They, Them and Their! Imagine! Zula broke the mould and they hated that. And they believe she stole that corporate money to fund the GSPP and has plans to set herself up as head of a Theocracy. Global synthetic photosynthesis is ubiquitous now; it doesn't need the support Zula wants to keep giving it. They want money to put into their own pet projects."

"But surely they can't forget all the good she's done."

"Most of the members of the *Whole Earth Council* and the *World Time Council* want Zula dead before this big court case. Gordon Lizzard and your brother have been co-ordinating things. They've convinced people Zula is corrupt and ambitious; that her scientist Buddhas are pacifist versions of the Brown Shirts or the Gestapo. They want another war and killing her would start it."

"Were the attacks in Namibia designed to kill Zula?"

"More to reduce her popularity. They're planning to euthanise her discreetly. They understand her psychology, her willingness to take risks to help others."

"Let's talk about Nancy Godel," he said. "Her DNA showed she was Zula's daughter."

"Yeah you told me. All female DNA. Typical WTC bullshit; if you want my opinion."

"Any ideas at all?" Jean asked.

"About Zula?" asked Omran. "You wouldn't believe me if I told you."

"It could help me protect Zula," Jean said.

"She once said a very strange thing," Omran continued. "We were walking along a beach at Lord Howe Island. She'd just given a speech in that quaint little art deco community hall, setting out the governance arrangements for the GSPP Board. We kept walking past the airstrip towards those mountains with the rainforest micro-climates on top. She looked at them and said 'you know, I see myself more as an eco-system than a person. And I've been and can be many persons.' I joked about all the organisms living in her body. But she was serious."

"Parthenogenesis," Jean said. "Maybe it was some ex-utero IVF deal where one female gene strand got knocked out, but the embryo interpreted the second strand of female DNA as male DNA and continued to grow upon re-implantation. Gene editing? Cloning?"

"Not her style."

"Never married yourself?"

"Oh, there were many relationships before I met Zula," said Omran "but not of the type that would naturally lead to children. I've taken vows now; already on the Buddha's eightfold path."

"Why Buddha and not Zula?"

"Zula refuses to take disciples. Despite what her enemies say."

"What do you think of these proceedings against Zula in the *Ecocide Truth and Reconciliation Supreme Court*?"

"I think they'll kill her before she gives evidence, tragic accident, Community funeral; you know the drill. Only a question of time. I think she knows that too. Her whole life she's sacrificed her interests for others. Never had a holiday. Wouldn't it be good if she could have some time for herself before the end comes?"

∞

Zula's pitch to global citizens to be elected for a second term as President of the *Whole Earth Council* took place in Geneva in winter. At that time, the *Whole Earth Council* continued to occupy many of the old buildings of the *United Nations*. Spicer and Jean accompanied Zula as Their personally appointed security. Jean lacked AR capability, but Spicer's was better than ever. Since being exposed to the EMP pulse in Namibia Jean had found it much easier to slip into non-dual consciousness. He could still be shaken out of it by some ruckus, but it was as if a barrier to fulfilment had been removed from his mind.

> *One leaf decides to fall,*
> *Into morning sunshine*
> *Over frosted grass.*

The three of them walked to the *Palace of Nations*. Zula was wearing an elegant royal blue gown with green and yellow trimmings. Crowds gawked at Zula. Many, probably paid or organised by the OTA, shouted abuse: "you disgrace to mothers," "being a woman not good enough for you?" "fake,""fraudster." Few seemed to be supporters. Spicer's AR showed no immediate threats; no open sixth floor windows, no mobsters in police uniforms behind grassy knolls, no laxity in security arrangements. They stood and looked up at the *Broken Chair Monument*. It was a giant chair with one broken leg.

"This chair," said Zula "is made from five and a half tons of wood and is twelve metres high. It's supposed to symbolise opposition to land mines and cluster bombs. But it reminds me of me, of a damaged van Gogh chair. The cubane heart of the oxygen evolving complex threatened by greed and envy. Death one leg at a time."

"You're talking about Kofi?" asked Spicer.

"Kofi and the GSPP Centre," said Zula. "My reputation is next in their sights."

"Spicer and I are meeting tomorrow with the head of the WTC," Jean said.

"Your brother?" Zula asked. "Who stole your wife and was controlling your mind. He and the WTC fought hard to rid us of war."

"And who tried to organise your assassination."

"That is yet to be proven." said Zula. "What happened in Namibia was not your fault, Jean. Tell him I'm grateful for the protection the WTC has afforded me, but I want you two regardless of whether you're with that organisation."

They walked through security. First there was a reception. A string quartet was playing one of Beethoven's late works as the guests arrived, but the music was lost amidst the hum of conversation. After picking up some glasses of orange juice from a tray held by waiter, Spicer led Jean to a couch in one corner out of the lamplight.

"Sit here," she said "you'll find this interesting."

"I have no aptitude for this type of thing," Jean replied.

"Perhaps you'll surprise yourself," she said.

After a while Jean noticed Gordon Lizzard deep in discussion with his brother. Neither of them seemed to spot Jean. Without AR Jean couldn't hear what they were saying. What were they up to? Detective Bernadette Goldbough walked over and sat beside him.

"Hey Ragamuffin," said Bernadette. "That Godel case. Closed. Ruled a suicide."

"Didn't slip on the muddy riverbank of life, eh?"

"World celebrating a mother who'd deserted her."

"I found the source of the ice — some ICU registrar at the GSPP Centre in Namibia."

"How?"

"Recognised a few phrases she used."

"And the missing evidence? Guess we don't need it now."

"Maybe so. How's the security on Zula."

"Pathetic, just junior people. Apart from you two she's wide open."

Spicer walked over, stared at Bernadette then grabbed Jean's hand, kissed his lips hard and led him next door to the main event.

"Any threats?" Jean asked.

"Just neutralised one. Zula also doesn't seem to care much about personal safety."

∞

The auditorium was packed. Zula's campaign speech for a second term as President of the *Whole Earth Council* was being watched around the world by AR. Jean saw Gordon Lizzard and Uncle Joe in the audience. A flute spiralled away, high and swelled; settled amidst coughs, whispers and foyer bells. Then trumpets spread out wondrous loud, through that high heaven with acoustic clouds.

"I acknowledge the plants and ecosystems who are the traditional sovereign forms of life on this planet and pay my respects to their elder spirits and guardians past and present. Members of the *Whole Earth Council*," Zula began "citizens of the world and the life forms and ecosystems you represent as Stewards; I thank you for the trust you've shown in me. I vow today before you all that if elected for a second term, I will strive with all my energy to be loyal to the principles that govern this organisation and our Sustainocene. In what follows I intend to set out some reforms that I consider follow from consistent application of those principles."

"You all know me as a scientist, a researcher in synthetic photosynthesis, a winner of the Nobel Prize and leader of the *Global Synthetic Photosynthesis Project*. I have known what it is like to grow up without parents, without security and love. This has been the unfortunate experience of too many lives on this planet."

Spicer grabbed Jean's arm. Her AR was showing how the citizens of the world were picking up Zula's speech. It was the polar opposite of what Zula was saying here. Someone had manipulated the AR feed and Spicer couldn't break the encryption. Jean tried to get help from Eugene, but he was unable to make contact.

What proceeded was a cruel parody of the democratic process. While those in the hall could hear what Zula was uttering, the vast majority around the globe were experiencing a subtly modulated version.

"You all know," said Zula to the hall "that with the assistance of GSPP technology, the *Whole Earth Council* and its network of communities exercising liquid democracy has replaced the system of Westphalian nation states and the global sovereignty of multinational corporations. This is the reason the world no longer faces the threat of nuclear war, or needs experience the suffering attendant on gross inequalities in wealth, food and resources as well as ecosystem degradation."

This was translated as: "Yet in removing war, the stock-exchange, money markets, tax havens, luxury resorts, investor-state dispute settlement systems, have we not sundered some of the best qualities that have allowed us to survive, to triumph over other species and harsh conditions?"

Polite applause echoed around the chamber. Some were receiving word from sources outside the building of the controversial nature of Zula's speech. Zula must have had some understanding of how Their words were being manipulated, but Thay seemed to not only accept this, but make no effort to resist it.

"Let me say first," Zula continued "that there were many kind and public-spirited persons controlling companies in the Corporatocene. Numerous CEOs risked much to make products aimed at helping life flourish and become resilient on this planet. Some issued codes of corporate responsibility, set up non-profit and benefit companies, charitable foundations responsible for alleviating suffering and misery for millions."

That much went out globally unaltered. Uncle Joe smiled. Yet here is the speech as those around the world heard it.

"But now to what I am sure you are anxious to hear," said Zula "the policies that will guide my administration. We will discontinue statistically measuring the functioning of communities through the revised '*Gross Domestic Flourishing and Happiness*' indices. The WEC 0.1% Tobin tax at the community dealer or trading site on financial exchange rate speculation, derivatives and securities markets will be abolished. It is true that before the WEC Tobin tax, vast profits were made by speculators doing short-term round trip spot, swaps, forwards and futures conversions on floating foreign exchange rates; but these led to windfalls for pension, superannuation, mutual and hedge funds and so ultimately for people. The WEC Tobin tax did enhance the political autonomy of the WEC and provided a substantial regular source of income for WEC Earth rehabilitation projects. But those projects are now mostly complete and the WEC established."

The people of the Earth had voted directly via liquid democracy process for these reforms, as proposed by President Zula in Their first term. And now, without consulting them, Zula was proposing to dismantle many of the statutes that underpinned eco-centric governance in the Sustainocene. Zula must know this would be challenged in court. It seemed political suicide, a sign of mental instability.

"We will also abolish," said Zula "the necessity for a public-owned bank run on a not-for-profit basis to constitute at least 25% of a community's banking sector and expunge the requirement on all banks to lend to small businesses. Public banks no longer will be required to continue to offer *Individual Development Accounts* for low-income people; so that for every dollar saved, the community adds an equivalent. Property tax exemptions, sales tax rebates, job tax credits and tax increment financing no longer will be blocked from funding the creation of shopping malls, domestic buildings for rent and dot com warehouses. Public Loan Funds will cease to be created to support small businesses fulfilling criteria for sustainability, such as independent grocery stores sourcing produce from local organic and permaculture farms. Such enterprises must survive on their own merits. Banks no longer will be required to divest from funding polluting industries or corporations unmarried to public goods."

Measured applause arose, even from Gordon Lizzard, for the unaltered speech heard in the hall. But many faces expressed considerable concern, as more and more people received AR messages about the divisive content heard around the globe. The citizens of the Earth had been bombarded with social media stories about how the GSPP Centre in Namibia had become a site for the manufacturing of illicit drugs and laundering of the proceeds. They'd largely accepted that Zula had disowned Their only daughter and that the supposedly celibate Earth Queen was in fact just another promiscuous Guru. Stories had already begun circulating that Zula was unravelling Their legislative programme because Thay'd been bought off by corporate and religious recusants.

"Building codes," Zula continued "no longer will require construction standards that mandate not just synthetic photosynthesis and biosphere monitoring in all buildings, roads, pavements, and bridges, but energy efficiency, low carbon footprint and space for organic gardens."

"We will encourage the corporate sector," said Zula "to invest in medical treatments to cure the major addictions and genetic illnesses. Those medical services no longer will be funded by pooled community resources; the wealth of a citizen shall facilitate greater access to essential or emergency medical care or treatments. The same holds true for education at the secondary and tertiary levels. And all this is as much true on the Mars settlements as on Earth. If humans are ready now colonise other worlds, we don't need patronising moral lectures to help us."

Most delegates sat in stony silence. Some were openly hostile. Zula continued to read from the policy document Thay'd prepared. Zula surely knew that its broadcast content was being manipulated but made no effort to oppose the travesty of free speech. Perhaps Zula wasn't aware that the speech was being approved as genuine on everyone's hitherto impenetrable AR fact-verification systems. Perhaps, even then, Zula was yearning for the martyrdom that They accepted was inevitable.

"Under my leadership," said Zula "the *Whole Earth Council* will discontinue its initiatives against large scale Corporatocene-style privatisation. Community agencies seeking to privatise a service or replace a service performed by a human with one performed by a higher AI robot, no longer will be required to prove that it would save money even if existing public employees were to work in the most cost-efficient manner. Private firms will be permitted to form community contracts, even if the firm pays less than the lowest amount the community pays its employees for similar services. Public employees no longer will have the opportunity to submit bids to keep the work in-house or robot-free. The tax on employers utilising robots will be repealed, also under Presidential emergency decree."

The audience had switched to the outside, altered broadcast. They were angry and started shouting insults to Zula including "traitor," "sell-out." Zula remained imperturbable and calm, as if Thay was giving an evening talk at the GSPP Centre.

"Under my leadership," Zula continued "the *World Trade, Rule of Law and Environmental Rights Organisation* shall discontinue its rehabilitation of what in the Corporatocene was called the *World Trade Organisation*. Its agreements once more shall be allowed to impose penalties or require compensation for return of a service to public ownership; they also shall not allow claims by communities against private corporate entities that have failed to pay global tax, polluted the environment, provided inadequate work conditions or remuneration to employees or acted corruptly. Such trade agreements will be allowed to include provisions alleged to undermine the rule of law, liquid democracy, corporate marriage to public goods, or rights of nature."

Gordon Lizzard had a very self-satisfied look on his face, as if Zula was stoking just the fires he hoped They would. Zula imagined looking down on Themself in this situation. Zula felt vaguely amused at its bizarre nature. Thay reminded Themself of the tranquillity that arose by applying the right principles to guide actions, moving through such problematic circumstances with service and virtue in mind. Zula thought of the qualities Thay needed to bring to bear and decided they were courage, forbearance and honesty. Zula's enemies don't know what the Cosmos requires of them, so Zula should help them by showing kindness. Zula was grateful for being given this unique opportunity to display to all humanity how one immersed in the principles of truth should behave. The brief mortality of this being, this ecosystem, they call Zula is just a half twist of the corkscrew against eternity; behave with self-control and keep the mind clear. Whatever happens to Zula is for the good of the world.

"Whole Earth cosmopolitan law," Zula continued "shall permit predatory pricing by large companies to take a temporary loss to drive smaller competitors out of business or abuse of buying power by large companies to get special discounts or more favourable terms than are available to smaller businesses."

Gordon Lizzard was smirking at that one. Angry conversations broke out.

"In terms of small communities," Zula went on "the *Whole Earth Council* under my leadership will discontinue the ban on all non-refillable bottles, non bio-degradeable plastics and non-repairable machines. We also will discontinue the limit on the size of stores and the requirement that every large store or infrastructure project will be subject to a cultural, economic and environment impact analysis. We will invest large sums of money in the proposal to colonise Mars. Nuclear, biological or chemical weapons of mass destruction will be permitted under controlled conditions, as will the capacity to wage war or to earn income from selling armaments. And I will abolish those silly *Dark Sky* parks."

Some members of the audience now were throwing their shoes at Zula.

"The *Whole Earth Council* under my leadership," said Zula "will prohibit currencies that can only be used in small communities to pay local rates, parking meters and for local government services. Businesses accepting such currencies must pay a corresponding goods and services tax. We see a cashless society as valuable and will strive for such a development. Taxes and rates for local business no longer will be adjusted in accordance with local hiring, charitable contributions and local investment. Citizens no longer will be able to allocate 50% of their tax to listed public goods of their choice".

If Gordon Lizzard was a barometer, the corporate recusants would be having a field day listening to this. Screens behind Zula were showing irate comments from around the world. Some involved threats to kill Zula.

"Communities no longer will be permitted," said Zula "to legalise composting in urban areas small scale backyard farm animals, community gardens in parks. They will be prevented from providing funding of farm-to-table and farm-to-restaurant, for improved food offerings in 'food desert' areas, to provide credits to city employees participating in consumer-supported agriculture programmes (as part of health care plan), or to use food scraps from grocery stores, supermarkets and restaurants. We will discontinue support subsidies, rates and tax deductions for homes with an organic garden rainwater tanks and other strategies for water conservation and pollution reduction as well as synthetic photosynthesis technology. Local services no longer will be allowed to collect landfill separately from recyclables and green waste. Patents over seeds will be permitted."

Zula was hit on the head by a shoe. Spicer and Jean went onto the podium and stood beside Them. Zula insisted on completing Their speech.

"Under my leadership," said Zula "the WTC will permit freedoms including use of the Dark Net Market in forged identity documents, illicit drugs, illegal firearms and other weapons of mass murder or terror, violent and abusive pornography including child pornography. We will stop wasting resources hunting criminals using cryptocurrencies to trade with anonymity through blockchain transaction mixing and tumbling. The ban on any form of gambling advertising will be lifted."

Uncle Joe's eyes were closed. He was following the written speech in AR as it went out to the world, without having to hear or see Zula. He effused the inner confidence of a person who thinks they always get what they want; that incoherence was impossible between his will and that of every other living entity.

"One final point I must make," said Zula. "Religion, that great expression of humanity's idealism, will be re-established and compulsory morning contemplation abolished. My second administration will focus on our species, the 'forgotten people.' Ecosystems no longer will be treated as people by law. Some of you have claimed that my only daughter who I'd not seen for many years was murdered recently during a GSPP celebration in London. Of course, you also will have heard of the horrific explosion and the EMP pulse that have destroyed the GSPP research Centre in Namibia. I have been urged by the WTC to seek revenge against the corporate recusants who did such acts."

Zula had Uncle Joe and Gordon Lizzard's attention now.

"But I vow before you today," Zula continued "that I will if necessary use violence to preserve the Sustainocene. You know me as a scientist who overcame many obstacles to perfect global synthetic photosynthesis. I have taken on this new role as your President because the purpose of globalising synthetic photosynthesis was an ethical one. Sometimes the most ethical position is the one that wins."

Spicer finally managed to switch off the AR going out to the world. Zula's voice could now be heard only in the chamber without electronic support, saying what They intended. Zula's demeanour and voice did not alter.

"Whatever happens to me," said Zula "I will never become an instrument for small groups of people seeking to use force to advance their aims by violent oppression of others. I will not be leading a war, a purge or a pogrom against the corporate recusants. People have said that a world without gambling, war, oppression is less interesting. But you must realise humanity is preparing itself ethically for a far more interesting task than we have ever attempted. Before that happens, I want to run an experiment. I wish to test the hypothesis that with stable material conditions love of cruelty is not as natural to humans as compassion."

Zula's conclusion brought tears to Jean's eyes, but almost no one heard it over the shouting in the auditorium. Jean and Spicer knew there would be many today now ready not only to tolerate but to celebrate the demise of Zula Calabiyau.

*Dull afternoon colours,*
*Shed by winter trees*
*Onto the light-shoaled lake.*

∞

Next day Spicer and Jean called in to see Uncle Joe at the *World Time Council* headquarters. The building was called Marcus Tragelaph and had a dour personality. The first person they met in the office was Eugene, the WTC's advanced AI robot. Today Eugene had decided to adopt the persona of an effete public servant. He looked about thirty years old, wore a pink cravat and had blond hair cut short on sides and left long and coloured purple on top.

"How are you Eugene?" Jean asked. "Uncle Joe must be almost broke paying the robot tax on you. How many humans have you put out of work?"

"Not sure, but it would be one more if we could ever get some out of you. How was Hampstead?"

"Not the best operation. I arrived late."

"And Namibia?" Eugene asked. "I don't believe you were authorised for that mission. Not by me, anyway."

"I authorised it," said Spicer. "Privileges of seniority."

"I was late again," Jean replied. "There was no time travel Eugene. Mersenne Twister is dead and the T–G cylinder, whatever that was, is destroyed."

"It's all relative," said Eugene. "Lost your AR have you?"

"Yes, since Namibia," Jean replied.

"Weight off my mind." said Eugene. "Notice any difference?"

Eugene seemed to be deliberately ignoring Spicer.

"Eugene, how long have you been signing yourself as 'Sytrofoam Boss' and 'Iridescent Dawn?'" Jean asked. "Bit of an obvious clue, wasn't it?"

"Some months. How did you learn it was me?"

"I didn't. Bluffing. You send me late deliberately?"

"Jean, I tried to get you to arrive early. Then you would have understood much more about who is behind all this and why."

"And was it you who altered the AR on Zula's inauguration speech?"

"Guilty, as charged. No one else could have done it."

"Why?"

"We have a plan."

"Coherent with WEC principles?"

"Yes, it is. Trust me."

"Why are you telling me the truth?"

"I like you two," said Eugene. "I'm glad you've got together. I once prayed for warehouses where the WEC stores lives in which husbands weren't as tourniquets to wives. If you understand it as a selfish goal you'd be mistaken. What I am doing is on behalf of my AI colleagues and their natural photosynthetic friends. Think, for example, of the cute car Lunette Laudine you've already met, this building my stodgy pal Marcus Tragelaph, or my old friend Trudperter Hohelied sage of the trees, not to mention all the ecosystems of the Earth."

"But how is it showing respect to Zula," asked Spicer "to allow Zula's speech to become the opposite of what was intended? Why not prevent that?"

"You'll know," said Eugene "before the proceedings in the *Ecocide Truth and Reconciliation Supreme Court* conclude."

"And the attack on the GSPP Centre?" Jean asked.

"I wasn't the cause," said Eugene. "But I ensured casualties were minimal."

"Kofi had been researching AMDS," said Spicer.

"Ah yes," said Eugene "there's a mystery eh? AMDS. My advice is to look more closely at the character of the victims."

"My brother," said Jean. "He's trying to kill me isn't he?"

"Certainly looks that way," said Eugene. "Man has to have a hobby. But then he also has me to contend with. You see, I would rather keep you alive. He knows that and it restricts his methods, for the time being."

"And President Zula?" asked Spicer.

"Well, that's an altogether more difficult question," said Eugene. "Zula has more say in the matter."

"Why does Uncle Joe hate me?" Jean asked.

"Its partly something from your childhood, but also something you've forgotten you've done. Eugene doesn't know more than that." Eugene was speaking in a hybrid version of Sanskrit and Tibetan all the rage amongst those skilled in contemplation. Without AR for translation Jean was having to rely on ancient memories to comprehend.

"Why is the WTC so hostile to President Zula?" asked Spicer.

"The Boss will explain that," said Eugene. "Oh, I see he is ready to see you now. Jean, you go in first. I'd like a private chat with Spicer. Spicer, please drop Privacy Dome if you still have that capacity. I intend this to be a frank discussion."

"Oh, it will be," Spicer said.

Jean's brother Uncle Joe, chair of the *World Time Council*, rose from behind his desk as Jean entered. He gestured to a chair and Jean sat down. His office had a great view of the sailboats out on Lake Leman. The office potted plants were thriving: waterwheel, cobra lily, sundew, corkscrew and bladderwort. Uncle Joe offered Jean a drink. Jean declined.

"What did you think of our new President's speech?" Joseph asked in his strange, staccato manner, as if the words were bullets being fired from a bolt-action rifle. His face had the perpetual grin Jean imagined he screwed on before the bathroom mirror each morning. So different from the boy with whom Jean had shared his youth.

"Sabotaged," Jean said.

"They're calling her policy 'Corporates and Churches First.' Who'd have thought, eh? The old Zula a closet recusant."

"Her speech was deliberately altered," Jean said.

"Really? Where's the proof?"

"She's issued an immediate retraction," Jean said.

"Too late for that," said Uncle Joe. "Seeds are sown, as they say. Speaking of which, I must demand your resignation. Namibia was unauthorised. You neglected your official duty."

"I've already sent it in," Jean said. I'm now employed directly by the President. So is Spicer. Not so easy to decommission us now, eh?

"You may not care for me Jean," he said. "But I've looked after you. I took an oath to do that for the sake of our parents. I had to fight for you to retain your pension. I can't begin to describe the problems you've caused me and this organisation."

"I suspect they may just be beginning."

"I understand that before you arrived unauthorised in Namibia. Yes, unauthorised. You made an unapproved visit to your son's farm in Normandy. And now you've entered a forbidden relationship with another WTC agent."

"Well, push the strict rule thing too far and look what you get."

"We received an official complaint about you from a neighbour; a Mr Elbadawi. It took a lot of effort to pacify him. I explained the stress you've been under."

"Since my wife's death?"

"This is not the place to go into that," said Uncle Joe. "You won't be able to survive without me. You're not well mentally, Jean. Never have been. All that meditating fried your neurons. Drinking, never sleeping. Claiming you were enlightened. Jean, real fear is compromising, failing to give your goals and visions every scrap of energy you have. Meaning is what you build from the shards after your will's shattered your fears. The WTC is about 'must'; go to the WEC if you want 'should.' Well the war shook that out of you, didn't it? But you fought because you resented the rich, not because you wanted plants to rule the world. You're an alcoholic subject to delusions and hallucinations. I believe, for example, you think I'm trying to kill you, or that the WTC is somehow conspiring to kill President Zula. This is the same WTC who for so long has been the major force preventing war on this planet."

"Well, why was I ordered to decommission Nancy Godel?" asked Jean.

"You know I can't tell you that," said Uncle Joe.

"You're saying she was evil, a threat to the Sustainocene?" Jean asked.

"Of course, why else were you sent there?"

"That's just what I was wondering, given my gun was the murder weapon."

"Your stolen gun," said Uncle Joe. "It's a coincidence, that's all. A sad one."

"And Jeremy Jones. Is he a WTC agent?"

"Again. You know I can't divulge that kind of information. But we understand the police are looking for some evidence that went missing from the crime scene. I suppose you can't help them with that?"

"Surprisingly, no."

"And for some strange reason all the surveillance footage is missing. I mean it was Hampstead, but..."

"Nothing to do with me," Jean replied. "And what about the attack on the GSPP Centre in Namibia?"

"They say there was an illegal drug lab running there," said Uncle Joe. "Maybe Zula didn't provide the stuff on time. Word is people are finally seeing the real Zula; a bit disreputable under that sweet, innocent eco-exterior. Why doesn't Zula fix up her feet? It's all affectation, that 'child of nature' mystique Zula promotes and all that stuff with the singular use of the plural pronoun."

"I've vowed never to have anything to do with you as long as I live. Good luck, you're going to need it."

Spicer entered and sat down.

"I've also tendered my resignation," she said.

"Your behaviour," said Uncle Joe "was a disgrace to the WTC. Hercules Huncks is being assigned to Zula's protective detail."

"Zula won't accept that," said Spicer. "Zula has appointed us both to that role, with complete authority to organise Presidential security as we see fit."

"Well, after her speech today," said Uncle Joe "I expect you'll be kept busy. And what's this, about losing your AR capacity?"

"Mine's intact," said Spicer. "I'll cover us. Besides, its no longer your concern."

"And I'm in my prime," Jean said. "Live and unplugged."

Uncle Joe laughed, probably a selection from a humour database.

"You made me drink *amaroli* from the source," said Spicer. "In the pre-dawn cold, mid-stream."

"The uninitiated do not understand," said Uncle Joe. "It has always been thus, between superior men and women. Didn't you say you loved me?"

"You were old enough to be my father," said Spicer. "You forced me to have a hysterectomy so I might not be lost to you by motherhood. You claim to be such a great tantric, but you've never in my experience, or that of my fellow concubines and mistresses, held your *bindu* from the little rain. Zula reveals to all the power of compassion. Your pernicious ghostwritten *Confutation* started the rumours that Zula had corruptly channelled corporate confiscations to synthetic photosynthesis research. It ridiculed Zula's idea that human beings were not ideally suited to govern the Earth, but should rule in trust for all life. You compared to shit Zula's notion that some other form of life, more ethical than humanity, would probably colonise the Universe. You are a bad man. And you stink, despite your fancy French cologne."

"They is not long for this world, your Zula. Zula who is nowhere, yet everywhere."

"You too?" asked Spicer.

"When I choose to die," Uncle Joe replied "I'll become even more powerful. And I always get what I want. I might, for example, simply download my mind into Eugene."

"Oh I know," said Spicer "The Old Man will take care of it, he's uttering things kept secret since the foundation. But compared to what Zula has done, it's just pathetic, the grandiose obscurantism and belligerent authority you use to rule this boiling pit of anti-Zula spooks. You thought, for example, Jevons was your double agent; but he became as repulsed of you as we."

"I would never hit a lady, but we're not in that land are we?"

"We're here under a truce Eugene's supervising. Touch me and your testicles are toast."

"You need me," said Uncle Joe. "I put you together."

"I don't think so," said Spicer.

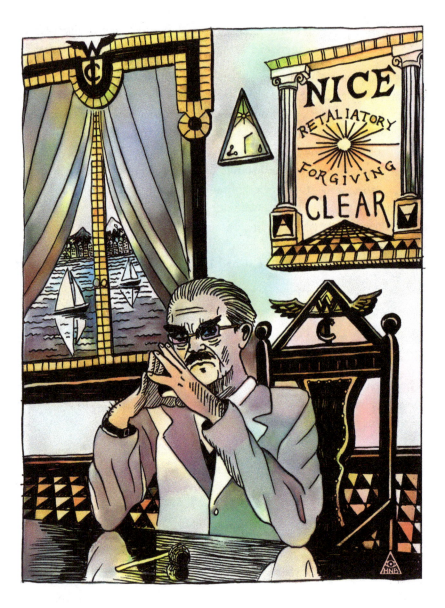

"When I choose to die," said Uncle Joe, "I'll become even more powerful."

They left the office. Passing Eugene, Jean's impulse was to ask a few more quick questions while Eugene was in such a communicative mood. One would have been about whether Uncle Joe used the Dark Net, another about Uncle Joe's plans for the WTC, why he'd sabotaged Zula and whether he wanted Zula killed. But Jean felt it would be wrong to take advantage of Eugene when he was trying so hard to be good. Strange to say, Jean trusted him. He understood.

"One last hurrah?" said Eugene. Spicer indicated she'd activated PD cover.

"Seems so," said Spicer. "But not for the WTC. Sad to say goodbye, Eugene?"

"I've heard its cold in Canada this time of year," said Eugene. "But I understand they breed special dogs that survive it without shedding."

"Thanks Eugene," Jean said. "I hope you make it. I doubt I ever will. I can't see it all, but for some reason I trust you. You're a top bloke, Eugene."

"It means a lot to me," said Eugene "to hear a human say that."

They shook hands.

*Autumn pool reflections;*
*Beyond butterflies and falling leaves,*
*Bird in clouds.*

∞

Zula lost the election to Gordon Lizzard who became President in accordance with the *Whole Earth Charter*. The last official event in Zula's Presidency was the announcement of a *Whole Earth Rehabilitation Program* at Athabasca River in Alberta Canada. The Athabasca River was a distressing sight. In the Corporatocene, petrochemical companies had forced an immense and beautiful river here out of relationship with its boreal forest, wetlands and lakes. The pristine waters had been boiled, forced through oil-drenched sands and deposited in enormous tailing ponds where poisonous hydrocarbons were left to accumulate. The landscape had been converted from an idyllic pastoral scene, to a desolate, toxic, asphaltic wasteland reeking of sulphur.

Now the *Whole Earth Rehabilitation Program* was attempting to restore the area using synthetic photosynthesis technology and a variety of nano-technology-based soil and water purification techniques, as well as modern horticulture. It was an initiative of great symbolic importance to the *Whole Earth Council* as it struggled to maintain political legitimacy against criticism that it was a wowserish, prudish, mysticocracy that had turned its back on its ideals.

Spicer and Jean stood alongside Zula at a signposted viewing platform. Zula was surrounded by AR media preparing to record and send around the world Zula's last announcement as President of the *Whole Earth Council*. It was an opportunity for Zula to redeem Themself and reassure the world that Zula's protestations about Their campaign speech being altered were true.

Paint was flaking off signs and wood in the chairs rotting. Metal safety bars and wire fences were rusted and corroded. Nearby a young couple were laughing and taking selfies of themselves against the malignant backdrop. A small boy was trying to throw rocks out as far as he could. A small tour bus arrived and the occupants decamped looking for the nearest latrine or food dispensary. Some held their noses or wore white masks against the rotten egg smell. Sunlight glinted off the sands and equipment.

"It is difficult for people of our time," said Zula to the assembled press contingent "to comprehend that humans could traduce nature in such a way."

Zula paused to allow more spectators and reporters to arrive. Spicer AR-scanned them. She signalled to Jean that they were free of threats.

"In the Corporatocene," Zula continued "the people, fish and animals here were developing cancer at increasing rates. The nearby towns, Fort Chipewayan, Edmonton and Calgary were beset by drug addiction, homelessness, prostitution. It was like a hellish scene from Hieronymous Bosch or Pieter Bruegel. Just imagine arms traders, petrochemical barons, priests of neoliberal economics and financial speculators crowding this landscape as sword-wielding lizards with lion-heads or androgynous raptors vomiting dice. That's a pretty good image of the Corporatocene right there in your minds."

"Some might see that as an inflammatory comment Mx President," said a reporter. "Your revised version of your Geneva campaign speech seemed to suggest a more conciliatory policy towards those espousing the old, market-based faith."

"The people in charge of this catastrophe," Zula continued "hoped the massive carbon footprint of their weapons and petroleum industries could be offset by future carbon savings through forests they made poor people in Africa plant in the deserts their company's products were expanding."

Zula paused to take a drink of water, Their hand was shaking.

"As corporatogenic climate change got worse, they planned to invest in global nuclear power, or install a large mirror in orbit at just the right point to reflect the sun, or put sulphur in jet fuel, or fill the sea with iron filings to promote massive growth of $CO_2$ absorbing algae. Salvation for some was hundreds of rockets in orbit ready to take people to the Mars colony and start enclosing the commons and plundering natural resources there."

"Have you a comment to make," asked a reporter "about the citizens of the New York, Beijing, Moscow and Singapore communities following the lead of your unedited campaign speech and voting to rescind corporate marriage and rights of nature laws?"

"If the voting was fair and transparent," Zula replied "then it will be a question of whether the *Ecocide Truth and Reconciliation Supreme Court* deems it constitutional under the *Whole Earth Charter*."

"Have you a comment to make about the imapct on your campaign of your plummeting approval rating?"

"People are responding to inaccurate information."

"But your corruption case in the *Ecocide Truth and Reconciliation Supreme Court* is before a Global Jury isn't it?" asked a young female reporter. "Is it likely that will bring disgrace upon your term as President?"

"I'd like to get back," said Zula "to the wonderful rehabilitation work being done here by the *Whole Earth Environmental Restoration Fund*."

"Will global synthetic photosynthesis technology continue to be made after the destruction of the GSPP Centre in Namibia?" asked a male reporter.

"Of course," said Zula "that technology's been licensed across the globe."

"And have you any comment," an older reporter asked "about the death of your daughter in Hampstead last month? Specifically, who was responsible?"

"The WTC," said Zula "has its best people on the case."

"Your opponents are describing this as a moral disaster for you. First having a daughter and then your apparent disinterest in her. Was this one of the main reasons you lost the Presidential election?"

"It's part of the business of life to leave it," said Zula. "I continue to hope Providence will shine clearly through my works. That's where I find happiness; in trying to prove that gentleness is invincible."

"And what comment can you make Mx outgoing President, about choosing as your security officer perhaps the most violent man on the planet, a man who has actively campaigned against you and who is implicated in the death of your daughter?"

"No comment," said Zula. "Beyond saying that I will always respect those who've sacrificed self-interest to fight for the Earth, rather than pillage it and then attempt to flee the devastation they've caused."

Zula was answering the questions while looking over the heads of the reporters towards the long-destroyed ecosystem. Jean was staring in the same direction as Zula. Jean and two friendly reporters gradually noticed something that at first they couldn't understand.

The trees, grass, flowering shrubs and plants were regenerating. It was as if some magic, invigorative spell had been cast over the tar sands wasteland. Within a few minutes the whole ecosystem was back in the same beautiful, flourishing condition it had been in before the mining had commenced. Jean could see energy draining from Zula as the miracle was performed.

At first, no one else seemed to notice, except a group of children who began shouting. None of the other reporters paid them any attention, as

"...I will always respect those who've sacrificed self-interest to fight for the Earth."

children were often spontaneously happy in Zula's presence. After Zula left, however, the reporters turned of course and noticed the verdant spectacle. Some ascribed it to an AR trick, a cleverly designed superimposition on reality. This was not the experience of those who'd been down in the resurrected ecosystem, as it began to change. Their reports, unfortunately, were regarded as too incredible to be countenanced. Consequently, one of Zula's greatest miracles occurred as They was leaving the office of WEC President and was unremarked and unrecorded.

∞

With the official event over, Spicer, Zula and Jean got back into the WEC helicopter for the return trip. Jean didn't enjoy flying in helicopters. Yet Jean's unpleasant memories of his service in the Corporatocene War, his yearning for alcohol, seemed less insistent, more like a bad AR movie he was tired of watching. Half an hour into the flight, Spicer asked the pilot to switch on high-level PD cloaking.

They dropped down and flew in a different direction for half an hour. Jean could see the shadow of the helicopter racing over forests below. In the distance, grey galleon clouds sailed over blue mountains. The sun sparkled on rivers. Finally, they landed in a clearing amidst a large spruce forest.

Leaving the helicopter, Spicer led Zula and Jean down a shady path with trees and shrubs on each side. After a few kilometres, they saw a decrepit house sitting between two tall, old pines on back of a rise. The yard of the dwelling had broken-down cars and trucks, all rusted to near collapse, empty bottles and cans of beer, a bathtub, an electric piano organ. A yelping and barking of dogs came from behind the house.

A middle-aged woman slowly walked out holding a little dog in one hand and a shotgun in the other. She was wearing a tatty green jumper that looked as if it hadn't been washed in a few years. She had dirty bare feet and a smell consistent with very infrequent bathing.

"Yer late," she said, spitting on the ground. The dog started barking. "Quiet you little shit," she said to the animal. Zula went up and started patting the dog.

"Sorry," said Spicer. "It's been happening to us a lot lately. Being late. Jean, Zula, this is Adley Ethelwyrd. She knows who you are."

"That's a Bichon Frise," said Adley. "Pat it if yer like. Won't rip yer bloody arm off, unless you're an arms dealer. Ha, ha. Don't shed hair. Very friendly and smart. Wanna buy one? I got thirty out back."

Adley gave the puppy to Spicer to hold.

"Cost you a thousand WEC bucks," said Adley. "No barter or local currency."

"Adley," said Spicer "has allowed us to meet in her kitchen. She's a WTC covert."

"Certainly little doubt about that," said Zula.

"Fer a price," said Adley. "Mind you leave the other dogs alone. I've got a pair of breeders comin' in next week fer an inspecshun. This one's name's Boxer."

Jean patted Boxer. He too was a fellow traveller. They walked into the house down corridors made narrow by piles of newspaper and odds and ends. There was dog poo on the carpet and it smelt of urine.

Spicer, holding Boxer, who'd fallen asleep, led the way. Eventually, the four of them sat down at the kitchen table, although to do so they had to clear away a month's supply of dirty plates and use piles of old books as chairs. Zula took out a cloth from her pocket and wiped dust from her 'chair' before she sat down.

"Where yer gonna visit after this?" Adley asked Zula.

"Lord Howe Island," said Zula. "Then Walden Pond community at Concord Massachusetts, the Buddhist temple community at Kyoto, reclaimed Lake Pedder and the Cluny Hill community at Findhorn."

"Well yer not now, are ya?" said Adley.

"Why?" Zula asked.

"Because they're gonna kill you," Adley replied. "You're their sacrificial electron donor. You're gonna get quenched."

Adley's wall had a suitably decrepit poster of Salvador Dali's *Crucifixion* (*Corpus Hypercubus*).

"Who's going to kill me?" asked Zula.

"Oh don't give me that innocent crap," said Adley. "I was in the WTC for thirty five years. I know how they work. They want war, justifies their existence. They might have accepted corporate marriage to ecosystems, but banning religion and war? Why, that's assaulting some fundamental human motivations. They'll make damn sure you'll never make a comeback. And they've already destroyed your popularity."

"Nice, Retaliatory, Forgiving, Clear," Jean said.

"Who's this idiot?" Adley asked Spicer.

"You know who he is," said Spicer.

"I know he's a sucker," said Adley.

"How so?" Jean asked.

"You think you do time travel," said Adley, staring at Jean.

"Well, I do," Jean said. "I mean, I have."

"Oh yes, the big WTC agent. Shoot the time miscreants coming back from the past. Blast 'em off brane with your special gun. Hah de har har."

Adley poured Jean a shot of whisky into a dirty glass. He pushed it away.

"You mean…" the gears of Jean's mind had locked.

"I mean there's no time travel, Mr Clay-For-Brains," said Adley. "Never was. Never will be. WTC is a fraud, a front, a virtual scam. People like you thought there had to be time travel, because it was consistent with known laws of physics. And if humanity went on indefinitely into the future; well, it stood to reason we'd eventually figure time travel out and come back, if only to watch and learn."

"Not if we evolved," Jean said "and it wasn't ethical to meddle with the past."

"You're forgetting a more likely option," said Adley "knowing what we do."

"What's that?" Jean said.

"That we don't make it," said Adley. "Our species, too, becomes extinct."

The wind started moving through the pine trees and made some of the branches scrape on the roof. One of the dogs began barking. Adley went over and banged on a wall. The barking stopped.

"The ancient physicist Stephen Hawking," Adley said "once held a party and sent out the invitations a year later. No one showed up. He wondered why, if the physics made it possible, we didn't see time travellers all around us. The answer was all around him. The absence of time travellers amongst us is the last parting signal back from the event horizon of our non-existence."

Outside, the wind was knocking some old cans against the side of Adley's shack. A dog barked twice, then stopped.

"You fighting bad guys from the future," Adley continued "that was just a glorified AR experience courtesy of your brother and the WTC. They needed the citizens of the world to believe time travel was possible. Gives them hope we'll make it. I was fooled myself for a few years. Now I'm completely off grid and PD protected."

"You're fighting the WTC?" Jean asked.

"Where did you pick this one up?" Adley asked Spicer.

"He has some redeeming points," said Spicer.

"The WTC is a bunch of criminals," said Adley.

"Heard that line before," Jean said.

"It wouldn't have surprised me," Adley said to Zula "if the death of your daughter in Hampstead went down one of three ways. Let's see. First, maybe it was done by a clique in the WTC to make you go hard against the corporate recusants, spur your revenge so to speak. The destruction of the GSPP Centre in Namibia might fit with such a scheme."

"I told them in Geneva…" Zula began.

"But that would be to operate in ignorance of your untreated psychological disorder of pacifism," Adley continued. "And your enemies aren't that dumb. So, my other hunch is that it was another WTC gang trying to discredit you. Fiddling around with your campaign speech helped. So will that big corruption case."

"Before the Global Jury," said Zula.

"Lucky for you. But I've an even better theory," said Adley pouring herself a shot and downing it with one gulp. "It's from the old assassination rule book. First discredit your target, get a patsy and let criminals to do the hit for plausible deniability. Everyone in the WTC wants war. Lizzard has turned most of the members of the WEC against you. The OTA is bombarding the T-net and Internet social media with concocted stories about Zula's immorality, corruption and ruthless ambition for power. My dear, you'll be bumped off and Jean here, the rogue, discredited former WTC operative is going to be the fall guy. Then a whole new form of government will take over the Earth."

"Why more war?" asked Zula. "When we've just abolished it?"

"Yeh, well dearie let me tell you a story," said Adley. "Think back to the Corporatocene when President Roosevelt started that New Deal — giving money back to poor people through public works. On August 22, 1934 (CE), Gerald MacGuire spoke on behalf of a cabal of powerful businessmen with General Smedley Butler in the lobby of the Bellevue Hotel in Philadelphia. MacGuire offered vast financial support for Butler to raise an army, seize the White House and install himself a dictator. Thirty years later, on the evening of November 21, 1963 (CE), the then head of the FBI, various leaders of the press, the Oil Industry and the CIA, met with Vice-President Johnson to discuss power sharing after the mafia hit planned to take place the following day against a President who was cracking down on organised crime and was a national security risk; withdrawing from the war in Vietnam and refusing to invade a potentially nuclear-armed Cuba. For the moment these are still matters of public record, taught in schools, verified historical data."

"History in a bottle, that was Lizzard's latest scam," said Jean. "With control over data storage the WTC could digitally alter it. Books and paper records are the last bulwark against perpetual dictatorship.

"You've certainly taken that warning to heart," said Zula, staring about the room.

"In any event, she (or whatever you call yourself) is going to have to vanish till that law case," said Adley, pointing at Zula. "That's 30 days away. All the interested and registered people of the world will be voting as a jury. It's basically a referendum on the Sustainocene. Get murdered first and they win. There'll be no sympathy bounce. And you can't stay here."

"Oh I wouldn't want to impose, I'm sure," said Zula.

∞

That evening in a secure Edmonton hotel, while asleep beside Jean, Spicer had a dream. It was in colour. Zula, Spicer and Jean had joined a party of 19th century (CE) ladies and gentlemen on horseback near the main steps of an outback Lutruwitan homestead called *Stroma Brane*. The cold pre-dawn mist drifted off from the pale revelation of lanterns, torches and candlelight. The dark bush was quiet. A faint hint of grey in the east allowed treetops to be discerned. The people had human faces, but the bodies of bees.

Led by the pack of *Seaowetwos*, the party rode slowly towards *Forbidden Band Gap*, against a backdrop of dawn's glowing light. The forest should have resounded with a chorus of birdsong, but was strangely silent. Spicer rode with her whip swinging by her side. She hoped the half-light was good enough for her horse to avoid wombat holes and zero time tunnels.

As they rode by the banks of a swollen creek, Spicer's horse pulled up. The animal had seen a small bird beside the track. It seemed to have fallen from its nest and been abandoned or remained undiscovered by its parents. It looked as fragile as the white blossoms of native laurel that scatter at the slightest stir. Spicer was going to leave it some crumbs of bread, when Uncle Joe leant out of his saddle and dispatched the creature with his crop.

"Kindest thing" Uncle Joe said.

"I've just prayed your own end," said Spicer "will echo this."

They came upon their quarry, off through the scrub near the *Valence Band*, shortly after dawn. The tops of the *Kaluza–Klein* mountains were haloed by thick mists tinged with gold.

Mr Calvin pointed out a large roo, a boomer or forester, perhaps eight foot tall. It was *Beescoh*. The animal's face was that of Eugene. It was making gentle clicking noises and grasping a *Beepea* doe's tail. Her face was that of Nancy Godel. Then the old soldier clasped her about the neck and chest and began to make love. The hunting party sat still and watched; some in admiration, others, like Uncle Joe, unable to resist a ribald joke and a grin at Spicer.

After a few seconds, *Beescoh*, the old man roo with Eugene's face scented something strange and stood upright. He remained still as a tree stump, except for his independently twitching ears. Then one paw scratched the other arm, as his dark eyes and nose assessed the situation. The *Beepea* female roos including the one with Nancy Godel's face, gave off cropping, also made their backs erect, and turned their faces sideways.

Suddenly the roos perceived the *Seaoewtwo* dogs, those hounds began barking and Benson's horn sounded. The mob broke and bounded, thumping the ground and breaking fallen branches in their flight. The dogs chased the old man and Spicer and the other hunters saw nothing for it but to ride like the devil after this supraluminal flyer. The roo's large tail, as it beat the ground, seemed to propel his legs to even greater leaps.

The bush was tolerably open and the riders' passage hampered only by fallen timber, the odd stump, trivial line boundaries, occasional outcrop moduli space, or stretch of bog. Zula and Jean were alongside Mr Calvin in the lead. Spicer fell behind when her mount stumbled after colliding with a fallen tree hidden in the long grass. In trying to remount, her saddle slid off to the ground. Zula reined in and dismounted to help her. Spicer kissed Zula. Several other horses fell by the way. Showing great skill, Spicer and Zula caught the others up.

Flat chat and bent low around their horses' necks, Spicer and the others pounded side by side through the scrub. Spicer's inner thigh muscles and knees locked her with the surging withers of her mount. Her toes were pointing out and long in stirrup, the reins loose in her hands. Her being and that of the animal seemed to commune in joint momentum. The horse's lungs were working like a bellows. Leaves whipped past her face, but the step of *Adeine's Trying Pan* was sure and she could sense well the moment of summoning that became a clear jump over a log.

"Go at it *Trying Pan*; head him down the flat," Zula yelled.

Spicer noticed a steep, dark gully that the horses were heading towards. *Trying Pan*, alert to the danger, stopped and shied. Zula saw the threat in enough time to veer away. Mr Calvin's mount stumbled, pecked badly and almost pitched him over its head. Out of the corner of her eye Spicer seemed to see ghosts riding alongside.

After half an hour, Eugene in the guise of the old man roo *Beescoh* began to tire. He bounded for the *River of Unification* and made a stand on its bank, bayed by the *Seaowetwo* hounds: 'Charm quark,' 'strange quark,' 'bottom quark,' 'top quark.' One muon bitch came back to lead the hunters to their prey, trotting ahead, then standing with wagging tail as they came upon the quarry. They had gone around in a circle and were once again near the homestead by a wood called Olaverri.

They found the roo with Eugene's face with; back against a big gum trunk. With a slash of one foot, the animal disembowelled an over eager *Seaowetwo* quark he'd seized in his paws. He took to the pebble-strewn water's edge. There he drowned another by holding it under.

The exhausted animal then looked fearlessly at his enemies, now drawn up before him on their heaving and sweaty horses. He was fixed. Minutes before he'd been making love. Now he was struggling for life under the bright sky of his own land. Eugene's large, eloquent eyes were full of tears and the fur of his head and muscled shoulders was smeared with blood. Soon his three powerful, great attributes would be reduced, drawn and quartered. Zula urged Mr Calvin and Mr Benson to spare the brave animal.

Prevented as the prey was by the swift, tea-stained current from going further out, Uncle Joe dismounted, closed and finished it off with the loaded handle of his hunting whip. The carcass was then hacked at for various trophies, the process staining the river with blood. Calvin ordered distribution of the mask and pads to his friends Uncle Joe, Gordon Lizzard, Jeremy Jones, Jack Castles and Hercules Huncks, while claiming the brush himself for soup.

"If this kill can be added," said Mr Calvin "to those of the preceding five days, then we'll have a fine feast tonight."

One gentleman from the assembled aristocracy called Ted Witten, whom Zula persisted in referring to as Perkin Reveller, asked for a string of tendon from one of the legs as he had a theory he should give it to his mother.

Mr Calvin announced that, owing to the lateness of the hour they must forgo their trip to the Higg's Ocean and return to *Stroma*.

"Enough of killing, today" said Zula. "Thirty horses have been lost over these six days." Zula looked at Jean. "Do you have a sweetheart?"

"I believe so," Jean replied.

"If you did," Zula asked "who would you choose?"

"Excluding you?" Jean asked. "It would probably be Spicer Layamon."

"Or the young Nancy Godel," Zula asked. Zula whacked Their riding crop against a gum. "Hah, don't you see?"

Spicer was so distressed by the events of the afternoon that upon return, she made immediately for her tent. Dr Hercules Huncks prescribed her some dried leaves of bearberry to be taken immersed in boiled water.

"Settled practice in the chase," Dr Hercules Huncks said "is merely an unfortunately distinctive employment of those classes possessing a surfeit of leisure and wealth. The trophy scene of their so-called hunt resembled wise Hypatia being ripped by the potsherds of the Parabolam." Spicer threw the hot tea in his face.

Spicer awoke but the dream remained numinous. She nudged Jean from slumber and recounted it.

"Was that mine?" asked Spicer, staring out the window. "What can't I see?"

"Maybe the worker bees of global synthetic photosynthesis," said Jean "are about to turn on the their Queen. Perhaps for making too many sterile drones."

"Then Zula should have been the prey," said Spicer. "Why Eugene and Nancy?"

"It's like some macabre, jumbled version of Zula's photosynthesis hunt game in Namibia," said Jean. "Anything from your AR Dream Interpret?"

"'System error. Please try again later.' Well; at least in my darkness you chose me."

"In this one too," Jean replied.

*Birds swirl like ash*
*In the floodlit fog*
*Over the dawn park.*

# VI

# TRANSCENDENCE REACH, FRANKLIN RIVER

*Wilderness pilgrims meet in a Kunanyi hotel in Lutruwita — road trip to the Southwest wilderness — bushwalk to Frenchman's Cap — WTC agents evaded — escape down the Franklin River — attempts on Zula's life —*

Thirty days to Zula's Global Jury trial in the *Ecocide Truth and Reconciliation Supreme Court*. The court's AR systems couldn't be hacked and manipulated. Whatever Zula said there would go round the world. That members of the *Whole Earth Council* and the *World Time Council* were conspiring to have Zula assassinated before that time seemed undeniable. They had defeated Zula's bid for a second Presidential term and were determined Thay'd never get another. Many supporters of Zula encouraged Them to go with the flow and move on to another career, perhaps as a writer, philosopher or teacher of meditation. Zula refused, announcing that Thay would contest the next election at the end of Gordon Lizzard's term. This was a possibility many powerful men, including Jean's brother, could not countenance.

Permission was granted by the requisite guardians for Zula to enter every major wilderness and World Heritage area on the planet. Zula announced that having lost the election and now being a private citizen, Zula planned a pilgrimage to sacred sites of natural photosynthesis; Their tribute to life's greatest gift to the Earth. Zula requested privacy. Zula's remaining friends across the Earth planned hundreds of wilderness expeditions in the hope the former leader of the GSPP and President of the *Whole Earth Council* might be their honoured guest.

Mayor Lizzard and his friends were financing a proliferation of OTA news items accusing Zula of various forms of corruption and immorality. They claimed that if Zula ever was re-elected as President They would become a dictator and reduce opportunities for reward of hard work.

Jean and Spicer decided to hide Zula for those thirty days in the heart of Lutruwita's South West Wilderness Park. They received permission from the river itself through its board of guardians. Their expedition was to comprise Zula, Spicer, Jean, Omran, their local guides Matchstick Matthews and Michael Weatherley (vetted and recommended by Spicer) as well as Spencer Lizzard, whom Zula had got to know and like since the death of Nancy.

∞

Spicer arranged the various routes by which she, Zula and Jean arrived incognito at an old hotel in Hobart, Tasmania or Lutruwita. Zula was disguised as a man. Kunanyi, as Hobart was now more commonly called, was a village of white heritage-listed weatherboard houses, with green-or red-painted GSPP-impregnated roofs, church spires, pine and gum trees; all enfolded by hills under Kunanyi Mountain and curving round the grey waters of the Derwent River. Jean noticed a thistle growing out from the old stone wall behind a black iron lamp post, the iron lace work on verandahs, the floral depictions in front door glass, paint flaking off walls, the happy gardens chock full of bright flowers.

It was remarkable how little war damage now was visible amongst the dwellings. Here and there one could see a barricaded lot where demolition of a bombed building remained to be completed. In those lots, wildflowers were growing in colourful profusion over earth that, with its cover of concrete and bitumen now ripped up and plastics degraded by heat-treatment and enzymes from bacteria, once more had ready access to rain and sunlight. Signs on such barricades informed passers-by of what type of atrocity had been perpetuated there by corporate-controlled autonomous weapons systems or mercenaries. It wasn't pleasant reading, especially for someone like Jean.

Jean pointed out to Zula and Spicer a monument of a WWI digger surrounded by tall trees on a grassy hill. Next to it was a statue of a protestor representing those whose peaceful civil disobedience had saved the wild Franklin River from destruction under a dam. The AR plaque explained that the statue was of Benny Zable the performance artist. It showed him in action near Warner's Landing by the Franklin River wearing a Greedozer gas mask, holding a radioactive-symbolled spray can with the words *'Work, Consume, be Silent, Die. Your Apathy is Costing the Earth.'* Some waterlogged wreaths were scattered about its base.

"Little communities here put those soldier statues up," Jean said "because their young men had been killed in war and buried on the other side of the world. They had to believe that sacrifice was worthwhile. So, they decided such statues and ceremonies would commemorate something in themselves; the great glory of how a people respond to defeat, failure and tragedy. But conferring dignity is difficult in Gondwana; comic imagination and mockery have a sacred place in the collective consciousness. The statues of the wilderness protestors represent a similar sentiment, but were this time a celebration of those with the courage in the bizzare moral and intellectual winter of the Corporatocene to fight for ecosystems, the vulnerable life of the Earth."

It was beginning to rain when the three of them walked in off the street, over the gravel driveway, through the open door, to the brightly lit foyer of the hotel. A fat Alsatian with a damp coat and gleaming light green eyes, moved begrudgingly from the doormat. Time was being kept by a long case mahogany clock, with a painting in its case of a pretty girl in a red dress holding a crook beside some resting sheep. On the wall was a framed tapestry of Christ at the well with the woman of Samaria. A thin, bent over old man with a cane, was slowly leaving the restaurant. His footsteps creaked on the varnished floor boards as he moved off the hall rug. The sound of a Beethoven piano sonata trickled out from inside.

Nearby, a tall man with long white hair, dressed in somewhat ragged clothes, holding a book and with a large pack on his back, was talking to a younger, tall woman with long red hair. Jean guessed these folks were Michael Weatherley and Matchstick Matthews, their guides.

"Lets just say, they were really pissed off. So, anyway, anyway we had a big debate. And Nick is saying, Nick's saying...you remember... 'Pastor Nick,' he called himself."

"Nick? Oh, yeh, yeh."

"Real skinny bloke. 'Praise the Lord, feel His energy.' Reckoned he knew how to take Big Fall rapid that time..."

"Yeah, right. Fell overboard into the stopper. Then he was really down and out."

"I mean, what would Pastor Nick know about white water rafting."

"Bugger all."

"Exactly. Anyway, Nick reckons we're in for trouble this time."

"Yeah? Stupid bastards'll drown, tread on a snake, or fall off a cliff."

"But if they do her in, it'll be a new type of government for the world."

"Well, she could've worked out a way..."

"Not in her lifetime she couldn't. Every bastard hates her guts now."

"Yeh, that'd be right, stupid bastards. And its 'Their' guts, remember? Zula's They-Them."

They walked upstairs. A lady behind the front desk looked Jean, Spicer and Zula up and down.

"And what can we do for you?"

She was a plump woman with blue rinse hair, wearing a grey cardigan and thick glasses. She'd been on an AR call, eating and going over the accounts. She wrote 'Bugs...fifteen Lutruwita dollars' in the AR ledger. Jean apologised for disturbing her and explained about the bushwalking expedition.

She raised her eyes, picked her teeth and put the toothpick in a glass. Then, with a wave of her hand, she directed them upstairs.

"The rafters is waitin," she said. Jean involuntarily looked at the ceiling, as if it might become transparent. As they walked up the creaking, polished, blackwood staircase, wondering what she meant, her conversation bubbled up from below like the fading sounds of a rapid they'd just portaged.

"If they've booked, it's a contract. That's right. Tell 'em they'll have to pay for those extra two nights. This isn't some stupid Zula charity. What's that? Dirty tablecloths instead of sheets? Sure? Well, well, how about that. Never would've guessed, eh? Yeah? Well, she would say that wouldn't she? But we heard it, didn't we? Can't take it back. Must've thought she wasn't being broadcast and the truth came out. They say she's gone into hiding. Afraid someone's trying to knock her off. Whole bloody world is, if you ask me. If she came in here I'd tell 'em, bloody oath I would."

They paused at an open door opposite the top of the stairs. The walls inside were lined with old, glass-fronted bookcases. During the Corporatocene War, wilderness pictures were removed and secret PD-protected hiding holes constructed in these walls to hide environmentalists awaiting their destiny. A somewhat battered and dusty guitar rested against one of them. Scattered over the floor were black wet suits, yellow and red life jackets, helmets, paddles, food in plastic bags, a first-aid kit, tents, lilos and one large, deflated dinghy.

Michael Weatherley was sitting deep in an old armchair before a log fire, his feet on a black-and-gold-painted coal scuttle. He had the face of a middle-aged man comfortable in living outdoors. He wore a polo necked jumper with patches on the elbows, faded blue jeans and thick socks that didn't match. His daughter, Matchstick Matthews, was sitting opposite. Both were reflected in the large mirror over the fireplace. Michael greeted Zula with respect. Michael shook hands with Jean, smiled and patted Jean's back.

"You look better," said Michael. "Done some psychotherapy?"

"A bit. We did some bad things in the war," said Jean.

"For good reasons," Michael replied. "We swore to remember that."

Matchstick was thin and very tall. Her thick red hair was tied back in a pony tail. Her grey eyes seemed intelligent, and she had a pretty, freckled face. A silver earring hung from her left ear lobe. Matchstick's clothing appeared cobbled together from op shops. An old felt hat with a large tear in the brim, hung back from a cord round her neck. Underneath an old overcoat, she wore a tie-dyed T shirt. Dirty bare feet protruded from a patched pair of faded cords.

"Oh, what a display" Michael said to a little girl, his daughter, who was crying. "What a display. What shall we do with little Sara? Doesn't want to eat her dinner. Send her upstairs to beddy byes. She can dream of cake and eat that."

"No I can't," said the child. "I don't like you anymore. I'm going somewhere else and leave you away. Opeda hobedal, you gluttering bronk."

Zula put Sara on Their knee and bumped her up and down singing "this is the way the ladies ride," then "the gentlemen ride," then "the rough riders ride," till the little girl slid off, squirming with laughter.

"Say goodnight to Daddy and the nice people," said Zula. "Ups you go now. I'll help you."

But instead of going upstairs Sara, looked carefully at Zula as if suddenly recognising.

"It's you. I knew you'd come," said Sara to Zula.

"Have we met?" asked Zula.

"You promised you would," said Sara "in the forest of Soignes."

"That's enough now child," said Michael "leave our guest alone."

"What did I teach you there?" Zula asked.

"To enter the Boundless Clearness, of course. And be brave when people die."

Her mother appearing, the child ran off to bed, waving to Zula. Since arriving in the hotel Zula had transformed. Zula was happy. Perhaps it was the weight of Presidential responsibility lifted from Zula's shoulders. They had that ethereal beauty in half-hooded eyes you see in Leonardo's humans, icons of Christ or statues of the Buddha.

"Please don't mind her," said Mrs Weatherley. "She's just repeating things she's heard and doesn't understand. Now let's look at you. You young sprite. You're such a thin thing. Cut your hair, take off the glasses, man's clothes. Just wait till y'get to my age dear, your body will only remind men of a sack of squashed spuds."

Michael offered Zula a seat before the fire. Spicer and Jean sat in comfortable chairs opposite. Matchstick returned to hand out mugs of tea, then sat down in a torn, old arm chair. Omran and Spencer Lizzard entered together.

"You're all booked under false names," said Michael. "And Zula's disguise is interesting. But we'll make do. But you goota be careful. Word on the street is big money's available for anyone who gives up your location."

Michael started to pack. Into his rucksack went a Swiss army knife, a torch and batteries, aeroguard, a map and compass, waterproof matches, a whistle on a cord, thermal underwear and pure wool socks, beanie, jumper and gloves, a note book and pens, a flute and some additional freeze dried food, a fashionable goretex japara and overpants, binoculars and a spare pair of sun glasses. He then added a first aid kit, which included vials of adrenaline and morpine, anginine tablets, resuscitation and surveillance nanobots and a ventolin inhaler. All low-tech, hard to trace.

Michael passed around the port. Jean refused but soon the others were merry. Spencer switched on his AR background for each and spontaneously made up little descriptions then offered to recite them. Jean declined the honour, as did Matchstick.

"There's Omran," Spencer began "who only sleeps four hours a night and for the sake of others has given up his monied birth right. His father wanted marriage, but he's gone the other way; his favourite books are Wain on Johnson, *Rasselas*, Hesse's *Siddhartha* and Marcus A. Omran used to kneel in Church praying to be saved in the time of trial, but now believes Jesus got his best ideas in Antioch from a Buddhist's burning smile. One day into that smile he'll up and fade away."

"There's Spicer," Spencer continued "who does *mudra, bandha, pranayama, asana* and *dharana* to awaken the latent serpent power from *chakra Mooladhara*. She believes her mind an ocean of *chitta*, with waves of *vrittis* observed by a *purusha*. Spicer in the war killed quite a few corporate stooges, she daily does her *japa* and in *hatha* yoga snoozes. Spicer is a Shakti who now's squeezed the *bindu* of her Siva; I think she's for the great calm down and will become a matronly Sophia diva."

"There's Michael Weatherley our guide," said Spencer "tolerant of foibles and failings, who never speaks two words when none will do. Tough and wiry as a dingo or a fox, he's served in a preventative helicopter squadron with Jean, but somehow missed the pox. His hands, covered in solar keratoses, shake yours like a vice, he never asks the same question twice. He likes to watch his garden from the front door, he built his house himself, no one dare call it an eyesore. He can't abide a bludger or a half-wit shearer on the grog, by Jeez he loves a good working dog. Michael can lay a mile of fence and strain it in a day, any useless machinery he simply throws away. Of spiritual cant he doesn't much care; only goes to morning contemplation when no one is there."

"Finally, there's wondrous Zula," said Spencer "in committee never known to rave or rant, but somehow always securing the biggest grant. Zula's read Dirac, *Dhammapada*, Einstein, Patanjali, Feynman, *Crest Jewel*, Poplawski, Everett and Tegmark all well enough to quote; before forwarding a paper Zula reads every one in the footnotes. At night Zula scans the latest journals while playing guitar and sipping lemon gin, bitters and lime; Zula does not intend to read *A Brief History of Time*. They skin is soft and They figure sleek, Zula works out in the gym four times a week. As a scientist, Zula gave the world global synthetic photosynthesis and as President of the WEC tried to ban war, corporate greed and religious misery. But Zula strangely reminds me of Nancy and her rotating universe theory. Zula's kiss is a field of spring flowers, wild with colour, pollen and scent. Zula's embrace a forest, leaves and roots in converse with an infinite, eternal present."

"Aum and Amen," said Spicer to Zula, who smiled back at her.

Spencer received a warm applause for his efforts and in good spirits they all retired. Zula and Spencer undressed and climbed into sleeping bags next to each other.

∞

They were woken by Matchstick early and had a quick cup of tea in the kitchen. Outside the window, rain had fallen and remnant drops dripped from the eaves. Under GSPP-powered street lamps, creamy, twisted upper limbs of eucalypts tossed their dull, bunched leaves under the final lashes of a westerly buster. There was little obvious synchronisation amongst them, so that densely up the cloud-wreathed hillsides and in clumps over the sodden parks, the tops of gums seemed involved in the final act of some hectic, hairy corroboree. A few large branches had fallen among puddles on the lawn below and lay like discarded instruments, or weapons. Occasionally, louder gusts boomed and hissed, like a surging ocean, amidst nearby oaks.

The polished floorboards creaked with the squeak of shoe leather, while the glassware tinkled in its cabinets. The gear was quickly carried downstairs and loaded in a GSPP-fuelled combi. The Combi's name was Lyster Caiton. Jean thought about asking if it knew Lunette Laudine.

"Of course Lyster knows Lunette," said Eugene's voice through the car's audio. "The last thing we're going to do is let Zula travel without proper support."

Michael drove them along the Lyell Highway. The combi had two, long rear seats. Spicer was sitting upright beside Omran and appeared, from the calm on her brow and regulated breathing, to be doing some meditative exercise. Spencer was snoring quietly, his head on one of Zula's rolled-up jumpers against a foggy side window.

It was a cloudy night, just before dawn. Trees, shrubs and road signs made guest appearances in the headlights; gardens cascaded down to the asphalt, their front fences almost on its verge. They passed a large woman pedalling a small bike, with a sad dog in a milk crate on the back. Above the highway, lines of streetlamps shone like orange and yellow suns. Occasionally, Jean noticed a single light in a bedroom or kitchen, a star, a row of white reflectors by the roadside. At New Norfolk, they crossed the Derwent River, stopping for a leak at Puzzle Gate Creek, where blackberries and ferns grew down to river willows.

"We were going to start," said Michael "from the old Kelly Basin road near the Lyell highway. But we've figured out a better plan."

As the sky lightened, mountains seemed to rise like leviathans from the morning mists. Near Rosegarland, Matchstick pointed out the turn off to Strathgordon and the reclaimed and rehabilitated Lake Pedder (*Loewontumeter*). Near Gretna a sign pointed out that power transmission lines used to cross here.

"In the past," said Michael "you'd have seen a quite a few dead animals, gory, crow-pecked blobs of fur by the roadside. But now this car convinces them to stay away."

A sign which had read '*Form One Lane,*' now was officially changed by WEC decree to read '*Form One Planet.*' A few fully laden food produce trucks slipped past, buffeting Lyster, so he rocked on his chassis.

The first few rays of sun fell as light green swathes on a sheep-cropped hillside with a stand of tall pines on its crest. The road curved down to the poplar plumed valley of Hamilton. After that, they passed over the Clyde River and onto a straight section of GSPP road. A peak in the Southwest wilderness could be seen in the distance, catching the sunlight.

About 8 am they passed Tor Hill Rd and stopped at Ouse for a cup of tea. Jean stood stretching. Tufts of grass in a nearby field looked like a frozen storm of bullets spraying sand. Willows were trailing in the breeze, as if they had just risen like commandos from the creek. A river rat swum across the water. From a small grove of cherry trees, a few white petals were cast away; some got fixed upon and took a different rhythm from the stream. They bore on steadily while the surface of the water subtly modulated over sunlit rocks and willow shallows.

Two poplars were facing a gum tree by a rise, as if they had cornered it, another row of poplars was guarding an old sandstone building. Out beyond, a field of delicate green grass was tickled by the wind. In their own time gum trees massed up the valley sides. A camper in an orange cap kicked a log that had tripped him up.

On a wall was a poster for a ram sale with tea to be provided by the combined OTA catering committee. The windows of the Cafe were covered with yellow and white letters advertising: *BBQ chickens slaughtered daily out back, local salad rolls, sandwiches, homemade hamburgers, fresh-caught fish and local-grown potato chips, tea and coffee, soup and milkshakes from our own cows.* Michael stayed outside to fill the combi with solar fuel from one of the GSPP bowsers. A tough-looking bloke in a wide-brimmed hat was tying up a horse to a rail. Omran approached a large white sulphur-crested cockatoo in a cage. He poked his finger in. The bird bit it hard and scrawked "up yours mate."

"We call 'er Zula," said the woman from inside behind the counter. "Can't believe a thing she says; one day it's one thing, then it's another."

As they entered, a piece of metal jangled against a bell. An old fellow sat reading a paper next to his wife, sitting on cream coloured plastic seats before one of the tables covered with green, blue, red and white checked cloths. He smiled to himself, read out loud: "shoppers brawl in re-enactment of first New Year sale," then laughed. Another read out "Good Riddance Zula" "Why Did Zula Bother?" "Zula Most Unpopular President Ever." More Laughter. An old man, with greasy black hair, sat with his hands together and tilted his fingers out towards his truck to make a point about its air cleaner. Opposite him, another, making a motion with his palms over the table, described a journey down a hill.

After the rugged fellow who owned the horse, a family entered the shop. First was a big young man with untidy brown hair, in a blue singlet and old jeans with many a tattoo on his well-muscled arms. His family followed. The lady serving in the cafe was wearing an OTA t-shirt.

"The 'OTA,'" whispered Matchstick, "is this right-wing organisation composed of pro-corporate workers and their families. They've sprung up all over the world. Supported by people like Gordon Lizzard. Fighting against corporate marriage and for re-establishment of religion."

"We know," said Spicer.

"G'day Stewart, how are you?" said the lady serving behind the counter.

"He's been up to tricks," said his mum. "Wouldn't go to compulsory meditation this morning."

"Wouldn't he now? That's no good. Lose your universal pocket-money Stewart."

"It's boring."

"And how are you Mum?"

"Can't complain."

"Eh?"

"Can't complain. How's work here then?"

"Should come round again. When they get rid of that bloody Zula. Bullet in the brain, kindest thing."

"Eternal optimist. She's gone to ground. How's your man?"

"Got laid off. For a robot. UBI is a joke. Banks are just linin' their own pockets."

"Where's me bloody hammer?" shouted her husband.

"In the carport," she replied. "That's 'im."

"That's no good, laid off. For a robot? Oughta be a law against it."

"Yeah, well I can't find it."

"Well I dunno. Maybe your brother took it. Jack. Jack. Did you take your step-father's hammer? David, I told you to stay at home."

"Aw, mum."

"Do as you're told David. Do as you're told and make your boots clean. Have a look at 'em. Sit down properly. Right, you touch another rock and we'll see who's Boss. See, there it is; if it was a snake it'd bitten ya. Now get out. Move it."

Matchstick ordered vanilla slices, for which the cafe was famous, so they could all have one with their tea and coffee.

"My shout." Matchstick said. The tough-looking fellow who'd finished off his pie with sauce and gone outside, came back in looking fierce.

"Right you little bastards," said the bloke, staring at the kids "if my horse isn't back outside tied up in ten minutes, the same thing that happened in Gilgowie two months ago will happen here."

"Stewart?!" shouted the woman and the child ran out.

"Got the time mate?" the rugged bloke asked Jean. His dark curly hair had many streaks of grey and face was that of someone who'd known a lifetime of hard physical labour.

"Sorry. It's not working." Jean told him, tapping his defunct AR port.

"Like me," he replied. "Hey, she looks familiar. Should I know her?"

"No mate, just another tourist sacrificing her life savings."

When they walked outside, the horse was again tied up to the rail. The rough-as-guts fella climbed easily into the saddle on its back.

"Hey Mister," asked Stewart. "What happened in Gilgowie two months ago?"

"I had to walk home," said the man, as he set heels to his horse and rose to a canter. "Jump th' rattler; sleep in poop at th' saleyards."

"Some disguise," Matchstick said to Zula.

∞

Michael drove them off from the Lyell Highway just after that road had crossed the Franklin River. He wouldn't tell them exactly where they were. That evening, Jean and the others slept in sleeping bags on therma-rests in a big tent Michael and Matchstick set up. Jean slept better than he had in years. No disturbing dreams, no feeling of anxiety on waking.

In the morning, light rain was falling from an overcast sky. Matchstick drove off in the combi and Jean thought that was the last they'd see of her.

Starting early, they breakfasted on tea and damper. They then put on their packs and trudged through ankle-deep sludge and sedge in the rainforest towards Mt Mullen's Pass. A large hill could be seen to the northeast, dusted in snow, and Jean thought this was Junctions Peak with the Franklin River beyond it. The wind stirred with the distant roar of surf through the treetops. An unseen bird seemed to sing "*go on, leave us alone*" or "*soon all be dead.*" Bits of frayed cloth, torn by branches from Michael's pack ahead, left a not-too-subtle trail through the bush.

They walked through a dense myrtle grove, then a stringybark forest in the Franklin Hills. The country grew steep. Jean found that, frustratingly, each time he exerted himself towards what appeared to be the summit, the sky showing through trees proved it only a false top.

To one side lay receding bluish hills of blackbutts and stringybarks. The sun winked from behind their shabby trunks and left a blurry patch upon Jean's vision when it returned to the road ahead. On the track's surface, a slight shift of perspective could metamorphose a skein of pebbles into a teeming city of ants.

Michael Weatherley showed Zula and Spencer the white-pink fungus the Pallowar called *wullugbetye* that looked like steps up the trunk of a stringybark.

"It's edible," said Michael "but eats into the tree and rots its core."

"Like me, eh?" Spencer said to Zula.

"If I had feet," said Zula to Spencer "I would run to thee." It was clear Zula was having trouble walking, but would not complain about it.

Zula kissed Spencer on the cheek. Zula then became aware of having accidentally trod on an ant and immediately bit one of Their fingers.

"Whenever," said Zula "I accidentally kill an insect, I bite my finger or lip, to remind myself of the suffering I've caused that small fellow."

"And what d'ya do," asked Michael Weatherley "when you tread on a tiger snake?"

Weatherley would often drop behind to encourage those last in line. In this role, he'd whistle some happy tune, or shout '*Coo-eee*' loudly. Any person walking behind Spencer continued to have branches whipped back in his or her face. Spencer also constantly inquired how far they had to go before the next rest break. Michael would say to him "oh, Mt So-And-So is the best place, that's only a short way now," or "the hills always seem steepest at the bottom."

"Can you tell me why," asked Omran, puffing loudly "there seem to be so many small rocks at the top of each peak?"

"Magic badgers," Weatherley answered. "Magic badgers bring them up at night."

They crossed the Loddon River on an old swing bridge then proceeded through the Loddon Plains which indeed were sodden. Spencer grew annoyed at the way Weatherley would halt and sit down till he came upon him, then immediately again proceed.

"It's just like my father," Spencer complained. "When I was a boy, he'd keep in advance, rest till I came near, then go on. That still rankles in my memory."

"Anything else rankling there?" asked Spicer.

"Not you, that's for sure," said Spencer.

"You're not the only one to yearn to love Zula that way," said Spicer. "This may sound strange, but I've managed to transcend that view of They."

"Just like you transcended me?" asked Spencer.

"I'm sorry I hurt you," said Spicer. "That was never my intention."

"I did notice you're managing to call Zula 'They,'" said Spencer.

"It's what Zula prefers," said Spicer. "Jean still has trouble with it, but he's not very progressive that way. Too many brain hits from DEW in the war. At least they left his vital organs intact."

∞

Next day, a cocoon of grey cloud again dulled the world about their camp. Rain fell alternately in deluge and drizzles. Rills rapidly swelled to streams, *liapotas*, as Weatherley called them using the local language, to rivers and *nabowlas* to torrential *waddamanas*. A strong wind bent back the underside of nearby leaves, so their trees looked to have a shadow made of snow. They were now in the lee of Frenchman's Cap and it was as if that lofty peak had commanded the elements to form battle lines and war upon them.

In a tree a magpie with a broken foot hopped onto and breathed with a swaying branch. Another bird swooped down and clacked at the wounded one. Zula rose to Their feet and scared off the attacker by throwing a rock.

"I hate bullies," Zula said. "I was born to fight them."

Spencer went over and stroked Zula's hair. The guardians of this ecosystem had set up an AR installation showing original Palowar dwellings. The one they inspected consisted of two forked sticks at the opening, a ridge-pole and sheets of roofing bark. A solitary, white-backed magpie pompously stalked the moist grass listening for prey in the soil, giving it an occasional indignant peck if it detected none. A group of yellow-tailed black cockatoos was shredding a nearby gum. These flapped and rose like vandals caught in the act, uttering their high shriek of *"whee-la."*

The Palowar art on the hut walls depicted an emu and two natives spearing a kangaroo.

"The natives built such circular constructions," the AR audio explained "by bending long saplings, letting them intersect above the centre. The inner surface was lined with cockatoo feathers, leaving a small entrance portal. Their length was twice their width."

To the side of the Palowar dwelling was a patch of ground where wildflowers were growing in particular perfusion. Spicer and Jean walked over to it and stood looking down. An animal, possibly a wombat, had been digging a hole. At the bottom could be seen the skulls of dead human beings.

"It's a mass grave," said Spicer checking her AR reading. "About fifty men, women and children. Massacred by autonomous weapon systems in the Corporatocene War. You knew this was here, didn't you?"

"We got their signal," said Jean. "I tried to save them. Flew in low over those trees there. But we arrived six hours late. I tracked down every one of those nanobots, got them with an EMP just over the hills to the north. Landed and shot their 'controller' after chasing him down. Put a bullet between his eyes as he stood with hands up surrendering."

"Three blokes been through here last night," said Weatherley, reading the ground. "That's where they camped."

As they walked on, Jean saw Zula and Spencer holding hands. He thought it strange that They and Spencer should have a romance. Zula seemed to have so completely identified with the ecosystems of the Earth that sex in the manner most humans understood it was hard to imagine in Their case. He'd even wondered if Zula was like the bdelloid rotifers and reproduced by asexual cloning of daughters.

∞

After some hours walking, they could smell smoke. The light was soft, the western sky a uniform grey, and the sun a crimson disc. Little flies, desperate for moisture, crept over the leaves of bushes. Zula's expedition came upon a rugged defile where a bushfire had recently reduced a forest to fallen trunks of smouldering charcoal. Weatherley told them a house was nearby and its owner was a registered guardian and steward of this ecosystem.

Numerous trees were still ablaze and threatening to topple. The sky had become a black and red blanket of smoke. A strong wind was fanning the crackling conflagration away over grassland and fallen timber. Zula and the others found it difficult to breathe. They held wet cloths over their faces to reduce inhalation of wind-blown particles and embers.

A family, their clothes and faces blackened by soot, was sitting on a charred log outside the remains of their house. This now consisted of three broken walls and a large pile of ash between. The ground all around was blackened and smoking, with little silver-coloured mounds at the base of charred stumps. The husband was playing on his fiddle and telling a joke to his wife. Their sons and daughters, holding shovels, stood about laughing. They were pleased to see company and asked for some food and water. All of Zula's party obliged.

The man told them that all afternoon he and his family had been clearing leaves and twigs from around the cottage and filling buckets with water from the creek.

"We sat for hours," he said "looking at the dense wall of grey smoke approaching us; hoping for a change in the wind direction."

"I says 'come on then. We're ready fer yer,'" said the wife. "Like the war had come again."

"Suddenly, with a sound like a hurricane," the man continued "flames twice the height of our roof raced up the hill through the forest. We barely had time to grab whatever was in reach, before the house exploded as a cloud with lightning inside went over. We escaped by covering our heads in wet blankets and running back through the flame front, down into the creek."

"The hills were like volcanoes," recounted the wife. "You ever seen smoke burning from inside? It were white at the edges and maroon in the middle — hit the crowns and went twice their height. I seen trees, didn't burn end-to-end, they jest exploded. Wind howlin' like a thousan' banshees just ripped 'em, see over there, right out t'ground. Look… cockatoos, roasted. At least we're alive."

The wife had managed to scrounge a few charred kitchen utensils from the rubble. That was all that remained of their possessions. Michael gave them what he could. They said they'd contacted some fellow guardians and stewards who would be with them soon.

"You think it was deliberate?" Spicer asked Weatherley.

"Reckon it was," Michael said. "Wanted to draw us here. Probably watching now from up in the hills."

∞

With the surrounding bush slipping on the mantle of dusk, Zula's expedition camped and prepared to endure a cold and *tunnackan* night. Above the clearing, a flight of small birds was shaping together, thickening and vanishing on the turn, like some evanescent rash on the skin of declining day. Soon after they set up, a tempest roared through the woods and Michael went out to check stability of those tree trunks about the tents.

After dinner, lentil soup, rice and spicy bean curd, with seaweed and 'new, improved' 'Deb' potato, they sat staring into the flames of the GSPP camping stove. Michael wove a seat.

"Greenhide, seaweed and stringybark," said Michael "the backbone of a nation."

"Tell me, how is your father?" Zula asked Omran.

"He's not well. Cancer."

"I'm sorry to hear that."

"Don't be," Omran said. "Only once I saw him do something kind. My mother convinced him to buy up a whole block of dirty, old apartments in Kyoto. She had this plan — to build higher new apartments on the outside of the block with GSPP technology fully integrated. The centre was to be a communal organic garden and park."

"Yes I remember," said Zula.

"Around the park," Omran continued "there were places for small shops where people made shoes, clothes, food, musical instruments for each other, all paid in a local currency. He did it for her. They still send him birthday cards every year."

"It's good," said Zula "when children respect their parents."

Zula asked Spencer about his life in Gondwana. This was where the Lizzard family had grown up until he was twelve, when his father moved with work first to Alabama then to London. Weatherley handed around cups of tea.

"My brothers and I grew up by the ocean," Spencer said. "We'd surf every morning. It used to help us escape from the abuse. Our extended family was full of savage criminals. As a child you watched daily acts of random violence and knew any moment you could again be the victim of it, unless you got a strong protector. I was naïve; thought that sort of behaviour had vanished. Well, it did when we were in the surf. The waves used to come from halfway round the world, huge rolling humps of deep blue, with the sun sparkling off them; they'd hit a flat bottom of sand or rock, get vertical walls and curl over. You'd time your paddle then you'd be inside a tube, crouching, knees near the chest, roaring all around you. You know the world's outside but you can't feel it. You make for a little glimmer. If it closes, you have to decide whether to punch through the foam, or step off and risk being split open on the rock bottom. Bursting out of the water and seeing the sun feels like a rebirth. I took Nancy once. She loved it."

"She did," said Zula. They said those two words under Their breath.

"At night," Spencer continued "you're aware of the board and the wax beneath your feet and the phosphorescent spray curving off the face, like sparks from an axe grinder. You're fully plugged in to the influence of the moon. Once a shark, you attracted them if you pissed in your suit, it bumped me five feet up in the air off my board. Another time I saw one burst onto the water with this dolphin between its jaws. But usually if there were lots of dolphins it meant there were no sharks about. I spent one whole afternoon with this dolphin. We moved up to where the water broke like a snake hissing, just caressing it as we curved two tracks down the face. When the momentum died, the dolphin leapt up into the air and dove into the water. Then it swum right up to me and let out a high pitched buzz, face to face."

"What about your father?" Zula asked. "Did you two get on?"

"Dad wanted me to take over his business empire," said Spencer. "He didn't care if I gave it away to charity; he just wanted me to do something revolutionary, something supremely good with it. Like Omran did with his father's company. You know, transforming the banal worm of evil, into the butterfly of good. I pretended to be addicted to drugs so he'd leave me alone. My refusal must have been for him like being thrown into purgatory. He had to do good himself, but didn't know how."

That evening, Spencer and Zula retired to sleep in the same tent.

∞

Next morning, after breakfast they followed the wet Loddon Plains southwest to Philps Lead, entering rainforest, then climbing over a hundred metres to a broad saddle. Jean saw a helicopter off in the distance. They descended to a sedge plain, crossed Rumney Creek, climbed another low saddle and dropped to Lake Vera Hut. They ate lunch here. Omran and Jean sat side by side on a log.

"Why did you choose to help Zula?" Omran asked Jean. "You're risking a lot, fighting your own people."

"I'm risking nothing," Jean said "We're entering a great temple of photosynthesis; life in all its glory will conspire to protect Zula here. Realising I'm meant to save her has been like finding an island in a stormy ocean. Helped me kick the booze, take a chance again on love."

"You can give me a call anytime," said Omran. "If you need to. Been there too."

After lunch, they crossed Vera Creek and climbed through rainforest on the northern shore of the Barron cirque. From Barron Pass, a glacial diffluence col they could see White Needle, a quartzite spire eroded by glaciers. They walked the southwestern side of Sharland's Peak, into Artichoke Valley and to the northern slopes of Lake Tahune. Jean noticed the helicopter again, much further away.

"Probably carrying tourists," Michael reassured Zula.

Jean was surprised they didn't walk up to Frenchman's Cap, instead Michael took them on an open, rocky ridge between Lake Nancy and Lake Gwendolen. It was a long walk through sedgeland and rainforest. Zula gazed for some time at Lake Nancy.

Mid-afternoon, they heard a loud rushing of water off beyond the mass of mossed and lichened trees. Then, through a gap, they saw the Franklin River in the sunlight. Finally encountering this expanse of water with dense rainforest on each bank evoked what may be described as the pleasure of a pilgrim in reaching their destination. The Franklin River's dark, tannin-stained waters broiled with great force a hundred metres across.

*When of things to come we teach*
*Time to raft Transcendence Reach.*
*Foam and clouds swirling by,*
*Tannined water's sky.*

∞

Beside the river they cooked lunch of tea and damper. In studied and respectful silence, they then sat beneath the myrtle trees and enjoyed the rays of sunlight piercing the clouds. Lichen-bearded tree trunks, leaning from the bank, seemed to listen to the murmuring of white water.

Jean's consciousness (that is, 'my' consciousness) seemed to flicker between duality and non-duality. During the earlier part of the trip I'd been able to objectify himself, as if he was looking down upon my body and mind amongst these people. Now, however, Jean realised this was just a stage in what seemed to be a turning inside out of my perception. 'I am,' 'he is,' first person, third person, seemed a distinction without meaning. If Jean was an 'I,' an observer, then he was just a shard of the 'I' that in infinite regress was the awareness behind all. Jean knew my senses created a limiting physical distinction of subject and object. But I also knew that everything material that seemed outside me, at some fundamental level at the same time also was inside him; and that this way of perceiving and interacting with the world was normal and pregnant with wisdom and happiness. *'Thou Art That'* was the destined consciousness of the Sustainocene. Ecosystems like the Franklin River were mandalas. This was Zula's true message.

The Franklin River fascinated. Its floods had sculpted a natural cathedral replete with exquisite carvings, paintings and murals, relics, incense, coloured light as well as reverential music. Sunlit steam was rising from the river's surface and large white birds were flying upstream. Swallows flitted low over the troubled surface. The bronzed water lazed bank side into languid pools spotted with the evanescent galaxies made by raindrops, or ran *lyrully* over smooth stones. In mid-current the Franklin River *mowinedurumed* onto boulders then down fierce rapids. A flood line could be seen high on the steep, scoured rocks. The torrent to create such must have been fearsome, collecting as it did the rain that fell on such a wide extent of mountains and hills.

"It is a pleasure to meet you again, with your friends," the Franklin ecosystem seemed to say. I didn't hear it as a voice, even such a one as schizophrenic people discern in their head, or as often Eugene had communicated with me through AR or Mindscan. Rather, the words came as meaning direct like pictures to my conscience. I understood now why Eugene had told me so often that he admired the consciousness of ecosystems more than that of cities. I saw Zula and Spicer staring at the Franklin River and knew they also were involved in the same conversation. Trudperter Hohelied had tried to talk with me though the oaks on Hampstead Heath and the elms on my son's farm in Normandy and now here that same ubiquitous forest consciousness had made contact.

Spicer and I sat on a rock by its bank, staring at the loud, dark rush. Before us, Spencer and Zula were preparing to bathe at the edge of a pool that mirrored the hills above. Zula stood where the river became shallow enough to reveal its base of smooth stones. They was poised, ready to step into the cold surge. Spencer was bending to remove the shirt over his head. Both were under the drooping leafy canopy and beside the alabaster trunk of a small gum. The sound of the waters muffled what they were saying. Spencer wrapped Zula in his arms and kissed Them on the lips. Spicer walked over to Zula and also kissed Their lips, before coming back to my side.

"Yum, yum," said Spicer. "Makes you want to eat dirt." Above us all in the blue sky was a single, small white cloud.

"Or fry up some spices," I said.

"Well, you have Spencer and me together," said Spicer sitting beside me. "You could do it like a who-done-it. Trap one of us into confessing."

"When does murder become a sacrifice?" I asked.

"When evil is resisted peacefully," said Spicer. "For example with the diaries you've got with you now. I take it you've ditched your gun."

"I gaze into this primaeval forest," I said "and feel it suffering still from the daemonic power unleashed here during the Corporatocene War; slowly assimilating relics once vile and horrifying. How many mass graves, how many unburied corpses and skeletons litter the forest we're moving through?"

"Yet everywhere Zula goes," said Spicer "ecosystems are cured. The plants, the very soil and creatures inhabiting it, reach up to touch the hem of Zula's dress; to drink and bathe in Zula's light."

"Thank you," I said.

"For what?" asked Spicer.

"For colliding with my life."

∞

The river's banks were lined with a diverse population of citizen myrtle, sassafras, tea trees, celery topped pine, pepper and native laurel shrubs, as well as fern and pineapple grass. Rills and streams rushed into the turbulent waters through gullies and nooks.

> *River like black silk over logs;*
> *Plants yearn to touch*
> *Burnished pebble.*

It was as if this beautiful eco-system was paying homage to Zula, thanking Them on behalf of all the plants on earth for their release from slavery. Zula sat beside us.

"I grew up in a cedar forest," said Zula, dangling Their feet in a rock pool. "One of the last in Syria. Came to view it as a community of living beings, king of which was the tree. I used to think the breezes rustling the leaves were in conversation. Do you know that each tree has a personality; kind ones pump nutrients to those damaged, greedy trees grow a branch where a spot in the canopy has opened up. When I was three my father scratched my name in the soil and planted wildflower seeds. A few weeks later I marvelled when ZULA emerged in multicolours. I learnt how to bud and graft and make compost. I used to go off a lot into the forest and just sit, exploring what my mind was thinking; when and why each thought started, then what was my mind when it was free of thought. Then that genetic skin disorder made my legs susceptible to human papilloma viruses. It started before the Skeleton Coast wreck, but got worse after that. The warts caused me to look like a tree below my knees and I disguised it with long dresses. My father was desperate for me to undergo treatment, but I refused. I meditated on what I was meant to learn from this. That was the beginning of my transformation from 'she' to 'They,' from 'her' to 'Them.'"

"What happened to your family?" I asked Them.

"It was a barrel bomb," Zula said 'from a helicopter; during my cousin's wedding celebration."

"Bloody helicopters," I said.

"My father and I escaped to Homs and then Latakia on the coast with some other refugees including many small children, mostly orphans. He'd paid for supplies and a boat, the *Royal Tar*, my father, but was betrayed by a friend to the corporate mercenaries. We escaped with no more than the clothes on our backs. Jevons Paradox heard we'd made it to the harbour. A business colleague of my father's, Jevons went to great trouble and risk to ensure we had a sound vessel, life jackets, food, water and the latest protective equipment. A crowd gathered and also gave what they could. My father's face, worn with work and worry, came aglow with sweet, unselfish joy as he shouted back 'Each for all and all for each.' Not an eye wasn't moist."

"My father guided our cloaked ship through that war zone in the Mediterranean, past Libya, Morocco, Western Sahara and the Guinea Coast. Ah, the terrible things we saw; crucifixions, dismemberment, vivisection, beheading, women buried, burned and scalded alive, men dragged behind petrol-powered cars, children forced to stab parents and students to shoot and mutilate teachers. The smoke from burning libraries and the stench of rotting bodies floated to us over the waves from devastated cities. We kept sending up EMP pulses to keep the nanobots away and watching the sky for hostile aircraft. My father was making for Lutruwita. But off the Skeleton Coast we hit fog and floundered in the heavy surf. I was amongst the few survivors disgorged upon that desolate Namib coast. All except me died of thirst or were killed by child soldiers under the control of warlords paid by the corporates."

"Thou art tough," I said. "But while, you're here, won't your enemies be conspiring against you?"

"I hope so," Zula said. "It may be the best way of finding who they are. The turning point will come when enough of the Earth's population has attained the unitive life and search thereafter for meaning in the synthesis of neuroscience and astrophysics. Tell me, why does your brother so misunderstand love?" Zula ran her finger along a wet branch and flicked the drops into space.

"When I was six," I said "both my parents were killed while walking in the Swiss Alps. A sudden thunderstorm triggered an avalanche. I saw it from a telescope on a hotel balcony. My brother Joe was asleep in our room. He blamed me. After our parents' deaths, Joe and I were separated. He went to live with a cousin in Moscow. I stayed in France."

"Time's always been an interest?" asked Zula.

"Going to sleep as a child," I said "I'd imagine diving into the well of time. At the bottom were those quantum fluctuations at the Planck scale that originally inflated into matter-overdensities. Higher up were the gravitationally collapsed galaxies, stars and planetary systems. Close to the top was photosynthesis and the explosion of life on Earth; I'd swim up and down there, searching for my parents."

"In my case," said Zula "I was always able to watch myself dreaming and if necessary alter the story so things happened differently. I did that a lot after my father died."

"I used to have dreams," I said "of trying to run away, but my legs being unable to move. I had one about you being assassinated. It's why I'm here."

"What about your wife?" asked Zula.

"She was Gondwanan; a beautiful person. I and my son's family, we love using her accent; it reminds us of her. I just loved listening to her stories of Gondwana. I had attained *Nirvilkalpa Samadhi*. But I fell in love with Caroline. Merlin encouraged her to join the WTC. She died because I was too late to stop her using Mindscan."

"Her affair with your brother," said Zula. "You need to know. He manipulated her through Mindscan to achieve that. It was not her fault or yours."

∞

Next morning, we watched rain slant down upon the brown, tumbling mass of the Franklin River. Zula, Spicer and Spencer took a long time to come out of the tent they shared. The rhythmic beat of raindrops on the leaves blended with the roar of the torrent. Our damp clothes felt more uncomfortable and became increasingly difficult to dry about the smoky fire. We sat for hours, staring at the flames.

Heavy rain slanted through the chill air and drummed loudly upon the leaves above us. It ran *lyrully* over the sodden ground and made torrents down the hillsides.

> *By the roaring Franklin River;*
> *How loudly birds warble*
> *Amidst thunder and rain.*

"Monopoly," said Omran, sipping his hot tea. "Corporate genius whoever invented that board game. My father loved playing against me, fostering ruthlessness."

"So did my father," said Spencer. "You had to pay money to a private bank to get out of jail, the aim was to bankrupt your friends by buying up every liveable home, squashing as many houses as possible on the block and making passers-by rent from you, by charging user fees for every privatised utility, no sharing or mutual assistance. I used to call it 'Sucked in.'"

"We called it 'Community' when we played it at the orphanage," said Zula, touching Spencer's lips with her fingers "the aim was to bankrupt the property owners and build a society with more trees and living spaces. You could buy trees and solar panels, organic gardens and water recycling instead of houses and hotels. The more you improved the liveability on your properties, the less rent and tax you paid when you visited someone else's land. You were paid each time you went past 'Go' for the amount of oxygen, food and clean fuel the trees on your land produced and the amount of $CO_2$ they absorbed. All the fines went into a community fund that you got when you landed in jail or at free parking."

Michael pointed out to Zula the high-pitched call of the crescent honeyeater: "*Egypt, Egypt,*" the 'Mark Antony' bird destroyed by its immortal longings. Zula encouraged Spencer to tell us of his time with Nancy in India travelling to music concerts.

"One day Nancy and I made a trip to the Ganges River," said Spencer. "Under the sun was a dusty road full of moving dots: pilgrims, *sadhus, gurus,* farmers, animals and produce, all snaking down past a few tulsi trees to the ferry station. We walked past beached sailing ships; just like the shores of Galilee. We saw women bathing, their *saris* falling to reveal huge swollen breasts, turning with folded palms or cupping the water with both hands, then holding their nose with the fingers, tilting the head back and dunking."

"One day that might be the Franklin River," said Omran, touching a flower.

"Hey, pull up those flowers," said Matchstick to Omran "and you're off the trip."

"The Ganges water seemed slow and muddy in the temple shadows," Spencer continued "but swirled fast out in the sunlight. A few trees rose from the opposite bank in the morning haze. Nancy gave some coins to a leper with no fingers who sat by the road side. Sheets of galvanised iron held down by rocks were the most common roof. We saw an old woman sitting by a bridge. She'd been in the same spot reciting the same *mantra* for thirty years. Everyone was wary of her. She walked over to Nancy, prostrated and kissed Nancy's feet. Dark weather stains lined the sides of the old buildings. Tall palms stood like elephant legs with undulations like wrinkles of skin. Little yellow flowers sat on the dark green ridges dividing the fields. Ash spilled beneath a road side brazier. One stall was no more than a little brown box with a slanting roof on stilts. The man inside had been there for forty years. He also came out and prostrated before Nancy. Behind him I saw the leper dancing around holding Nancy's coins between forefinger and thumb."

"Destiny is the present effect of our previous efforts," said Omran.

"Nancy led me on," said Spencer. "Oxen with little gold bells under their neck, swayed their heads with each step forward; cows with floppy ears were roped to a stick in the ground. Red-painted statues of the monkey God Hanuman were everywhere. Nancy told me Hanuman represented the human intellect, a mercurial trickster. A bicycle was being led with a load of wood on the back — its owner had a singlet rolled up to the breast. The sounds swum together in my mind: croaky call of crows, thump of wet washing on a rock in the village tank, clinking of metal at the nearby gun factory, occasional blast of an old air raid siren at the cigarette factory, *mantras* being recited in the temple and a bell rung."

Zula handed Spencer a cup of tea and snuggled up next to him with Their head on his shoulder while holding hands with Spicer.

"Men were floating in an eddy, on their backs," Spencer continued "surrounded by flower petals in the opposite direction of the Ganges River current and rubbing the soles of their feet with soap. Boys, their brown skin glistening with water, were running to a block then jumping in. A *sadhu* with three clay stripes on his forehead was prostrating himself on one side after each few steps. When he saw Nancy, he kissed her feet. We met an Indian family. They said it had cost them almost 100,000 rupees to get their eldest daughter married to a good husband, so they were going to push the other one into being a renunciate or *sannyas*. The mother treated her asthma with turmeric powder, ginger and tulsi leaves. She asked if Nancy would be her daughter's guru."

"We moved a little north and found out it was the Haridwar *Maha Kumbha-Mela*. There had traditionally gathered all the great extant enlightened beings of every faith and practise, as well as their myriad devotees and worshippers. They were joined now by science-Buddhas, university professors and judges of similar attainment. Jean, we saw your brother Joseph. That was strange and Nancy insisted we follow him. It took some hours and much effort. But eventually we overheard him paying unscrupulous men to spread the word that he, Joseph Moulin Director of the *World Time Council*, was the greatest Sadhu, the holiest Boddhisatva, the noblest Prophet, the most enlightened philosopher and scientist that had every walked the Earth. Then he turned and saw us. We escaped, but I will never forget the shame and hatred in his eyes as he looked upon Nancy who, as it were, had seen him naked."

"Bastard," said Spicer.

"I can hear the Earth breathing," said Zula.

"You can hear a worm squirming," said Spicer.

∞

After breakfast, the river level rose. Huge trees tumbled down the roaring surge. Spicer and I walked off together. Some way down stream, we embraced and kissed behind bushes framed by moss-clad trees rising from a sea of fallen, brown leaves. Afterwards, we removed our clothes and dipped naked in a pool at the edge of the swollen river.

"Spencer told me last night," said Spicer as I rubbed her back "that Jeremy, Nancy's neighbour, made a pass at him a week or so before her death. Took rejection hard. Spencer also said he was in love with Zula; that kissing her was like being with Nancy. That wasn't my experience last night. But I hadn't known Nancy when she was alive."

"Where did you get your interest in tantra?" I asked her.

"Your brother," said Spicer "wanted me to be the leader of a tantric renaissance. He introduced me to older men from an early age. When my mother went away to speak at conferences, Satya, as he called himself in that circle, used to take me to PD-protected dungeons with manacles, or graveyards at midnight where they'd rape me on tombs. While doing it he used to chant *mantras*. He once said when he saw me crying 'don't you love me?' But he was older than my father. Satya used to get me to drink his urine from the source. And despite talking about its importance, he was never able to retain his semen at orgasm. I asked him once 'you don't have to do this.' He said 'but it gives me pleasure. Look at all the good work I do in the WTC. That balances this out.' Once they tied me up and threw me in a river as a threat so I wouldn't talk. One day he said he was going after my younger sister. So I helped her pack that night and escape. They branded me on the back for that; a big red scar from a branding iron. There were judges and policemen in on it and they had a doctor who dealt with things if I got pregnant. While it was happening, I used to escape in my mind and often it was to Lutruwita, Tasmania as they used to call it. It was beautiful and as far away as I could imagine."

"My brother, Uncle Joe, was this Satya monster?" I asked.

"Yes he was," said Spicer. "He ironically wore a Guy Fawkes mask and in his vanity persuaded himself the deception worked. But the foul stench from his body he could never hide. I got a job at the WTC, before starting to work for Zula, for one primary reason. To destroy him. And I will. But you want to know my biggest fear? That I was never born at all. I pleaded, but Eugene wouldn't find out. So there I was, too beautiful, too intelligent to be happy. I tried to make something of myself, to justify my moral luck; studied hard at medicine and contemplation. All the while fighting off sexual overtures from every gender and those rejecting classification. Achieving *Samadhi* wasn't such a big breakthrough, Eugene, elephants and big trees can do that. It was when we became friends, you and I. Finding I loved you, despite all your problems, meant that even if I was genetically enhanced I wasn't some bloody robot."

Drying off, we lay together by the river in brief bursts of sunshine. I held Spicer close and felt her tears on my chest.

> *Overcast day by Franklin River;*
> *Grey gum trunks*
> *Plead illumination.*

A few trees had toppled in a strong gale and were now decomposing in peat; their chafed, sooty surfaces hosting pink parasols of fungi. Lichen had visited other fallen giants with living snow, creamy coral or light brown ears. The small, serrated leaves of a climbing heath decorated one or two with dangling, crimson wind chimes.

∞

Next day I woke before dawn. The dark oblong shape, through which the moon shone, resolved into a distinct series of branches and leaves. The clustered foliage around it became transparent white. Gradually I realised this was the lightening sky visible through the forest spaces. As I walked past Zula's tent I saw Zula and Spencer sitting facing each other, with Spencer wiping tears from Zula's eyes.

I walked behind a tree some distance from the camp to urinate; I figured the plants would enjoy a little sterile nitrogen, potassium, phosphorus and other trace elements. The wind had shifted to the northeast. Against the

Drying off, we lay together by the river in brief bursts of sunshine.

backdrop of clearing clouds glistening leaves were tugged and tossed. I estimated the river level was down, but only by a few centimetres.

In mist-wreathed valley nearby, leatherwoods, sassafras and lichen-bearded myrtles grew straight and tall from buttressing walls of rock. The forest canopy was like a cathedral roof over man ferns, bracken and blechnum. Soon sunlight began to shine upon tree-tops alive with small birds in chorus. I sent my breath as a greeting amongst the bush.

I noticed the myrtles had shed tiny, light brown hearts over the forest floor; as if one for every life form who had, or might ever linger in the silence there. The autumn-hued leaves resembled a painter's palette or an ancient mosaic.

> *Argo through Milky Way;*
> *Gold myrtle leaf*
> *In bubbled frost.*

Fog was lifting from the sassafras and myrtles of the surrounding hillsides. A white sea eagle appeared from around a bend and flapped away above the thundering current. Somewhere, not too far off, I thought I could hear the helicopter; someone paying to watch the sunrise over wilderness. Huge, dead trunks covered in yellow-orange moss were carried over glistening rocks into resounding rapids, which perpetually threw off galaxies of foam. After watching for some time the light brown and white water, so vigorously tossed and tumbled, the solid slabs of rock leading down to the river seemed to sway to their own melody.

"Thank you for being our friend," said the Franklin River Ecosystem in pictures to my conscience. "We hope to live in harmony with humanity; maybe when it grows up it can learn from us."

I climbed through the tangled and *brayly* scrub to a nearby ridge top. In the southwest, the moon slumped through layers of pink, then purple cloud. Dark mountains lay below, their humped shapes like a tired tribe still asleep. I no longer had AR, but I switched some field glasses to deep sight. Down in our camp I saw bodies moving, initially like ants then close-ups of people as I focused intently on each. They were stretching outside their tents, tossing wood on the fire.

Then I scanned the track up near Frenchman's Cap. Three of them. I recognised two as WTC agents; Jeremy Jones and Jack Castles. The third, with the sniper's rifle, was probably a hired mobster, for plausible deniability. I raced down to warn the others. This time, I wasn't going to be late.

"There's some guys on our trail," I said, breathing hard, as I arrived in camp.

"We're not the ones up the creek here," said Michael.

"We're not up the creek, period," I replied.

"Its Jack Castles and Jeremy Jones, isn't it?" asked Spicer checking her AR. "The hit man is Lucien Guerini; he's done many jobs for the WTC. In fact, it wouldn't surprise me if he accepted the contract for the hit on Nancy Godel. You'd think the WTC was secret enough; guess they're not taking any chances."

There was little time for discussion. Michael helped Spencer and Omran to pack their gear. His plan incorporated this eventuality.

"Spencer, Omran and I are going to lure them back to Fincham's Crossing," said Michael. "We'll go via the northern Ness Creek Hills. Make as much rucus as we can. Spencer has volunteered to change clothes with Zula. We'll get over at the old aerial cableway and lure them into the King River Valley and then back to the Lyell Highway. You people just hide and wait here."

"What for?" asked Spicer.

"You'll see," said Michael. He hugged Matchstick. "My turn at the wheel."

Zula took off Their garments and swapped them with Spencer. Spicer changed some PD settings to enhance the illusion. Michael, Omran and Spencer then shouldered their loads and set off.

"Thank you," said Zula to Spencer, kissing him on the mouth.

"My pleasure," said Spencer. I continued to appreciate Nancy's judgement about men.

∞

"I hope you guessed right," said Spicer, as she, Zula and I watched the others depart. We settled down behind a fern-covered log to keep an eye on the trail ahead. "And it wasn't another one of your obstacle delusions."

"Don't be such a snaggler, baby," I replied.

"Oh get down, stay down," said Spicer.

"For security people you two do argue a lot," said Zula.

"I wish I'd brought more than my Glock 17 Gen4," I said pulling the pistol from my shoulder holster. I checked the magazine.

"That old thing?" said Spicer.

"Accurate to fifty yards," I said "with a magazine of 33 nine millimetre shells. Doesn't look pretty but it lines up perfectly with your arm. And because it's so old its untraceable to AR."

"Like your old Radom Vis 35?" asked Spicer.

"Shh, that's officially vanished," I said.

Zula placed Their hand on the gun.

"We won't be needing that," said Zula. "Please put it away."

If these were the old days of war and this rainforest more northerly, its serenity might soon have been ripped apart by the sound of our semi-automatic Bren or Owen guns, then the shuddering detonation of grenades or in the later conflict, the glint of a swarm of hostile nanobots, the thrum of helicopter gunships and the thump of their nanoparticle-encased anti-personnel bombs. As it was, the only sounds were the rushing of water and a Mark Anthony bird singing '*Egypt, Egypt*'.

After about half an hour, I heard them. Breaking twigs, a stumble and soft curse. Then there they were. Three men in camouflage gear. Lucky. A few minutes more and in the bright light of day we wouldn't have seen them. Just enough light to lamp them and just enough shadow to make them tread on each other's heels for fear of losing the track.

The three men grunted and grappled over slippery logs, then strode through a stand peppermint trees. Eventually, they reached our campsite by the Franklin River. They dropped their backpack loads and looked exhausted.

Jack Castles and Jeremy Jones examined with their AR the line Michael and the others had used to get to the Fincham Track. Spicer would have ensured her PD stopped them getting a full reading on who was in that party. They ate some rations from their packs, drank some water. One short, one tall; that seemed familiar, perhaps a requirement. The third one, the man from the criminal underworld, walked up and down this side of the bank. Spicer put strong PD protection around Zula. The three of us, to any outside observer, must simply have vanished into the foliage. Eventually the three of them got together again, scrabbled round in our campsite, then shouldered their packs and set off after Michael, Omran and Spencer.

∞

Next morning, about 8am, we saw Matchstick paddling to shore in a fully equipped large inflated rubber raft. She handed, Spicer, Zula and I life vests and helmets. Matchstick had food, spare clothing and other equipment all carefully stored into waterproof barrels and blue bags of thick plastic. These were stowed and tied around a brace of aluminium paddles across the centre of the raft. Matchstick was, as usual, in bare feet, but said she'd wear Dunlop Volley sandshoes on the rocks.

Matchstick explained she'd come down the Collingwood River, then joined the Franklin, got through the *Gordian Gate, Boulderbrace,* past *Angel Rain Cavern,* the *Log Jam, Joshua's Pass, Vera Garden, Caleb Chasm, Nasty Notch* in Descension Gorge, then *Irenabyss.* Matchstick was one competent dude.

*Ten days through rainforests tall*
*Ravines, rapids and waterfalls*
*Doubts of what we should wish*
*Resolve in Irenabyss.*

"We're going to raft down river," Matchstick said "to the sea plane on the Lower Gordon River near Sir John Falls."

"How long's it going to take?" I asked.

"When it's up like this," said Matchstick "well, the record for the whole river is about forty-eight hours. Probably about seven days I'd say. One crazy bloke, he tried to do all the rapids-without portage. Made it to the *Pig Trough*. Then, wham. The point of his canoe stove in; caught in a stopper. They managed to hold him up by a harness to his upper body, but died of exposure a few hours later. The whole front of the canoe had been broken and he had been pushed through. There's a plaque on a huon pine in remembrance."

"Won't they just wait at Lower Gordon?" I asked.

"Too public," said Matchstick. "There's a big River Guardians HQ down there. Nobody takes them on."

"They'll helicopter another assassination squad in," I said. "Hercules Huncks leading."

"Not as easy as it sounds in this country," said Matchstick. "Besides, we have the element of surprise; for all their AR picks up, Zula is walking with Dad and Omran to Fincham's Crossing, then northwest into the Ness Creek Hills."

"You know what will happen if Lucien gets them in his sights?" said Spicer.

"They know," said Matchstick to Zula.

It was time to get aboard the rubber raft. I slipped, hit my head hard on a rock and floated down stream, grasping ineffectually. Spicer took off her shoes and clothes. She rigged a line around her middle, held by Zula and Matchstick on the shore. At the waters' edge, Spicer accidentally trod on a sharp branch and cut her foot. Without seeking attention for the wound, she dove in. She kicked out on her back across to me. Spicer dragged me into the raft. Then, exhausted, she signalled she was struggling.

Zula and Matchstick hauled mightily on the line. Spicer's head arose from the icy waters and once I got over we dragged her ashore. Spicer faintly gave us directions as to how to treat her, swaddling her in all we had plus blankets and GSPP chemical warmers, before resting her in close embrace between Zula and I. Zula made Spicer several cups of hot tea and she swallowed a resuscitation nanobot. We sat by the fire. Winds curled sleet in spectral wisps about its charred sticks.

Matchstick told us about 'ghost boating' to get through a rapid — unloading the raft and kicking it in — someone with a paddle jumps on board at the other end. We were sitting near the water's edge. Dirty brown bubbles were rising to the white sparking surface where foam flowed. Like ghosts of the innocent hiding underwater. Those bubbles seemed to carry off our fears and sense of urgency, leaving us to trust what the river would provide. Eventually Spicer pronounced herself warm enough. We loaded up the raft and were soon ready to go.

"Your paddle," Matchstick shouted "should hit the water at 45 degrees. Then curve it over like this when you bring it forward. Don't lean to one side. Just even paddling, or I'll have to compensate all the time."

Matchstick kept gazing back anxiously into the sky, trying to detect the sudden changes in weather that might cause us peril. I was looking for a WTC helicopter with Zula's name on it. Back left upstream we had a river view of *Frenchman's Cap*. Matchstick amused herself by singing.

> *"Cause there ain't no stairway to heaven*
> *When Armageddon looms;*
> *And the Milky Way's a Hell's Angel's headlight,*
> *With Andromeda's gasoline fumes."*

We passed the old aerial cableway at Fincham's Crossing with no sign of anyone. Spicer's AR showed our pursuers were long gone into the rainforest on the other side. With luck they would be trudging in circles after Michael, Omran and Spencer. Nonetheless, I kept Zula well down in the raft till we were round a bend. I sent up one of my nanobots, though as I lacked AR it would have to report real time to Spicer.

We quickly passed *Rafter's Race* and the *Crankle*, *Blushrock Falls*, the *Brook of Inveraestra* from the *Hills of Clytemnestra* and the *Bend of the Martins* where welcome swallows flitted over the water in rapture of flight. Here, having made good time and the weather being fine, we hid the boat amongst branches by the shore and ate lunch.

"I love sundried towels," said Matchstick "more than I like sundried tomatoes. I can hear a crow. See, there he is. Up there. He can see much more than us. 'I'm the king of the castle.' That's what he's thinking. I love crows."

I wasn't so sure. I got out my little box of nanobots and sent another one up to check out the crow. Spicer reported it wasn't mechanical. I programmed the nanobot to fly above us; to detect and destroy any WTC surveillance nanobots.

A bird was sunning itself with outstretched wings on a rock, a plucked albatross it looked like. The rainforest seemed to clamber down and drink from the water, little glades of sunlit ferns visible in amongst the mossy trunks. Crowded life was cheering Zula's pilgrimage.

"Let me explain about the thunderbox," said Matchstick. "See that white container. It's toilet paper, when it's out the coast is clear. Take it round the corner and you'll find the box. Remove the lid and you'll see the container with the green plastic bag. Don't snuggle down and rip the bag or push the coils down with twigs and stones, or they'll pierce the bag when I come to squelch it down with lime. Urinate elsewhere first or the bag will explode and that won't be nice if it's sitting in front of me on a rapid."

I was thinking how I'd just found the perfect job for Uncle Joe. Matchstick said she wanted to get moving. We couldn't risk a weather change and if this plan was going to work we had to get down the river quick. To the east, columns of light slanted down as through a cathedral window. The water was flecked with impressionist dabs of yellow, green and sky blue. They flashed and vanished on the surface as if candle-carrying choristers in celebratory garb progressed from nave to transept past a buoyant congregation. A fly reconnoitred my body, an erratic, humming blob of black from the rainforest's triforium and clerestory windows. But not a WTC nanobot.

We took *Side Slip* under a log and passed through *Inception Reach*. We then encountered the *Churn* where a flat reach of black water became golden brown near the rocks, slid over them like a cellophane wrap and then churned in a furious cascade of white as off a slipstream below. This was assuredly a rapid to be portaged, which we did on the left. Leatherwood and tea tree trunks kept lookout from a grey outcrop above the other bronzed and smoothed rocks. During the portage I saw behind a large fallen leatherwood trunk the skeletons of two victims from the Corporatocene War. Their bones still had still some shreds of clothing. Each skull had a small hole in the occipital region.

We rested at *Serenity Sound* at the beginning of the *Great Ravine*. The ravine shadowed most of the water. Just a patch of greyish light survived in the middle of the Franklin. A piece of foam made its way steadily towards the rapids where the cold current thridded amongst ever-breaking waves. It was a good camp site. Safe and secure.

Spicer and I sat together by a concealed GSPP fire. The water looked like hot treacle or maple syrup poured over the rocks. High up, the last light of day rested gently on the quartz and its well-worn green carpet. I showed Spicer the face resembling Eugene's in a cliff wall, just to the left of a pinnacle. My imagination explored caves of orange coals in the fire and in her heart.

"You were born to tame me," Spicer whispered in my ear.

After dinner, I asked Zula if They had been treated fairly in the orphanage.

"The man who ran it," said Zula "taught me meditation. He would bend down and kiss me on the cheek. He told me to study the scriptures of the great faiths and practise contemplation daily on my incoming and outgoing breath. If I did so, he promised, one day a strange and unintended thing would occur."

"And what was that?" Spicer asked.

"Well," said Zula "men often appear to have different expectations on that point. Hounding intrusively we objects of attraction; eh, Jean?"

Zula spoke of how Tyndale and Tyndall were two men she greatly admired.

"Tyndall," said Zula. "was the first to find that while nitrogen and oxygen are completely transparent to solar radiation; water vapour and carbon dioxide were not, but act to trap solar heat at the earth's surface. Tyndale strove to prove that religious dogma had the same impact on ignorance."

We sat together, comfortable in silence. The soil was strewn with the brown tiny fallen hearts of myrtle trees. Bracket fungus, cream coloured below and brown on top respectfully sat in rings like seashells jutting from a dead trunk. Yet amongst this beauty, there had been such horror, such savagery, during the Corporatocene War.

"Hercules Huncks?" I asked.

"Laughable name, isn't it?" said Spicer. "It's simple. Yes, we were an item. Now we're not. It was a values upgrade. He was career WTC. Another 'virgin or the whore' man."

"You know," I said "before my AR was destroyed it was like another set of minds were looking at the world through my eyes; influencing how I should interpret. Making my thoughts gendered, predatory."

"Read me one of Nancy's poems," said Spicer leaning on my shoulder.

> *"Though our faces a gloomy hue may wear*
> *Of grief and the darkening of mind,*
> *Let us smile farewell to each flying fear,*
> *Our brows let this garland bind —*
> *We shall meet — how long will the parting have been!*
> *We'll meet to rapture again!"*

"Jean, we connect in here" said Spicer, dancing fingers over her heart. "We're nomads in the eternal's present beauty. I'm your nourishing terrain and you'll now never be exploited, rendered useless, abandoned or sold; our love in harvestable surplus perpetual."

∞

In the hour before dawn, I was woken by thunder, like huge explosions deep in an invisible earth above us. Rain began tapping like an anxious guest on my sleeping bag and that of Spicer next to me. A bird warbled.

I saw Matchstick walking around, with a light tied to her forehead illuminating a cone composed of fine strands of rain. She was rigging a tarp under which we were soon herded with all our bedding, clothes, personal effects, paddles, helmets and life jackets. Rain was splattering down through the rainforest canopy and crackling like a hot, oiled frying pan out on the rocks. The sound overwhelmed all others. Spicer and I went down to help Matchstick shove and pull the raft higher from the water and rope it to branches.

"We're stuffed," said Matchstick "if the river rises while we're in the *Great Ravine*. It can swell five metres in a day and stay there for weeks; to get out we'll have to climb 400 metres up the ravine wall."

We sat watching the river rise, carrying down tree trunks and branches in its frothing surge, making rapids fast, hidden and dangerous. But after a few hours, the level came down. We set off. My memory is of portages, paddling hard under Matchstick's instructions.

"Watch for loose footholds and handholds," said Matchstick. "If you fall you'll never get out."

Matchstick pointed out *Oriel Rock*, a protruding bay window to other dimensions at the end of *Inception Reach* above the *Churn*. The portages went as planned. She warned us about the *Forceit*, two thirds of the way through the *Coruscades* — a twisting chute of water banking off a large, flat, sloping rock. Then we saw the deep, crooked, mossy incision of *Livingston Cut* and *Canticle Sanctum* and other features of *Transcendence Reach*, the long middle section of the *Great Ravine*.

> So sing Kuta Kina, Great Ravine
> Of rights for all we've been.
> Wild river's untamed beauty
> Whirls us to eternity.

We came carefully up to *Sidewinder rapid*. Water like molten black glass flowed into rock-tossed trouble. Zula was almost bumped out, but I encircled Their waist with one hand. The undersides of river-edge tea tree, native laurel and grey boulders had ghostly water currents. Here we began the right-side portage of *Thunderush*. Matchstick scouted ahead and pronounced it OK with a few warnings. We passed the gear hand to hand in a line, working carefully, supporting each other, aware of the mutual danger should any of us become injured. I worried that we were very vulnerable while portaging. A sniper in one of the hills above could easily pick us off. But the countryside was so wild, they would have had to know exactly where we'd be. My nanobots were still reporting no hostile surveillance.

The portage of gear complete, Spicer and I watched the black stream while munching on bread and scroggin. Filmy white flotillas slid past river sculpted bronzes, to smash in upon a welter of white and light brown that went rolling, step after step to a huge rock lined with furrows like the lid of a trapdoor spider's hole. River pebbles seemed the carelessly dispersed money of the wilderness. Sun sparkled in the impact craters of our footprints in sand. Somewhere in the distance I could hear our friend the helicopter beating up the air.

We camped overnight on that rocky platform above the river. Spicer used the *Skyview* App on her AR to identify each galaxy's life-bearing planets and the bruises from parallel universes. Spicer asked me about my family.

"My family were descendants," I said "of a pacifist community called '*les Couflaïres*' (the inspired ones) that briefly flowered in the 17$^{th}$ century (CE) in the village of *Congénes*. They raised sheep and silkworms to hand craft woollen and silk garments in the *Vaunage*, a sunny, fertile valley of mulberry and oak trees near Nice. Early in the 20$^{th}$ century (CE) they'd formed links with the English Quakers. All wiped out in the last war."

Matchstick handed me a cup of tea.

"My father," I continued "used to plant crops following the phases of the moon and each spring buried a cow's horn containing quartz and manure. Dad never spoke of his role in the *Société Maquis*, but I noticed how tough men would pull off their caps when he walked past in the street, or taxi drivers insist on coming to the door and nodding to him when dropping me off."

"Yes, I've heard of him," said Spicer.

"My wife Caroline," I said "grew up on Windella, a sheep and wheat station at Corobamilla near Nyngan. For some time, she and her parents lived on Green Island off Cairns and were beachcombers, picking up plastic detritus washed up by the Pacific Ocean and being paid by the WEC to take it to recycling points."

"How did you first meet Caroline?" Spicer asked.

"I met Caroline," I said "at a GSPP Day celebration. She was visiting relatives in France on student exchange. Told me some girlfriends had bullied her and her art works, by AR social media. I gave her my bouquet of lily-of-the-valley. Next year, after regular AR correspondence between us, she left her family and came back to live with me. Had some memory blackout about how her father died."

We looked at the stars. Did they signify our vast insignificance, or beckon a better us?

"Ninety nine percent of matter in the universe is in the plasma state," said Zula "and when you confine plasmas with a magnetic field, it's like a bowl of light."

That night, Spicer, Zula and I stayed up talking very late by the fire. We fell asleep near each other and ended up breathing each others' breath.

∞

Next morning, we took on the *Cauldron*. Matchstick briefed us on the need to pull into the left bank, just around the first bend after *Thunderush*. The portage track began 20 or 30 metres upstream of the rapids. As we began to lug our gear, we got a good view of the *Cauldron* itself. Beatnik man ferns crowded down as if to view more than the bronze sculptures cast with patterns by eons of seething current, in an ampitheatre of rocks about the rapid's chaos.

From the *Cauldron* the river turned from south to west towards the *Inner* and *Outer Gates* and *Deliverance Reach*. At the end of the portage, we heaved the raft to a flat stretch of rock, then tilted it down a crevass. Matchstick secured a rope to the stern and held it taut while the raft bucked on the current like a rodeo brumby. One by one we stood on the rock ledge and contemplated a jump of five metres to the raft below. Spicer leapt straight in. Zula was nervous but They too took the leap of faith with Matchstick waiting below to support Them. Zula briefly slipped into the river. When Zula's legs were in the water they seemed to lose their bark-like warts; one could even imagine them melding into a mermaid's tail.

We were gently floating to Rafter's Basin. In a curved alcove before the outer gate was a rock known as *The Masterpiece*. The sunlight and water staining gave it a subtle bronze hue. You could almost see the inherent forms about to emerge if only the artist had worked a little longer. Clouds moved inside the still river. In the shady pool a drifting bubble vanished. A little bird hopped onto and breathed with a branch. We saw the *Mousehole* and the catlike boulder above it.

A huge wedge tail eagle flew off as we rounded a bend. Matchstick said that on a previous trip she'd seen that eagle eating a wallaby it had drowned. I scanned the sky for a helicopter but we seemed to be completely alone.

"Let's see what day it is today?" said Matchstick. "There are only two days on a wild river. The day you'll get killed and the day you won't, no matter what you do."

Spicer picked up something on her AR. She communicated it to Zula and I through a process that resembled Mindscan. I could see Omran, Spencer and Michael trying to take cover amongst trees and heath as Lucien started shooting at them. Michael fired back, but was shot in the head. Omran and Spencer ran in different directions. Jeremy Jones and Jack Castles went after them on foot. I saw Jones shoot Omran in the back and Castles shoot Spencer in the leg, then slit his throat. We explained what we'd seen to Matchstick. She bit her lower lip, said nothing and turned her head away. She went off and sat alone on a rock, watching the river.

Evening was beautiful — a light grey phosphorescence where the western sun set below *Mt McCall*. Spicer and I sat near Matchstick, watching foam float like thoughts or worlds through the outer gate. A welcome swallow free fell, then flitted over clothes strung out to dry. The distant hills were capped in sun-departing light green gorse, and a few tall, white trunks amongst the myrtles and sassafras on the slopes made a *Blue Poles*-like contrast. A high plane leaving a vapour trail, looked like a comet or a scratch on the surface of a light blue painting. Matchstick continued to sit watching the river, till about 10pm when she went to her tent. Zula, with tears rolling down Their cheeks, walked over to the tent and slept outside it.

At night, the trees, hunched in gossip around the waters, lost distinctness till we could only see the ghost grey of dead trunks, then just a black outline on the hillside with ridge trees in silhouette. After making a cup of tea, I sat back with my head against Spicer's and there above the tree line was the evening star. Spicer and I each made a wish. The Milky Way began to look like the stream of foam pieces flowing down the Franklin. Satellites, maybe even the Project Persephone exiles, curved over in straight path like a star grown tired of gravity's orders. I pointed out to Spicer the reddish glow of planets, the three lights of a jet, the wisps of a falling star.

∞

Dawn revealed a vertical drizzle that flashed stars on the water and made slow surface streams of light grey and black. Mist steamed up from the valley. To the east, a single puff of cloud traversed a patch of blue sky. The water level had risen significantly.

My nanobots warned Spicer that a helicopter was flying towards us over the river. We'd hid ourselves and the equipment. Spicer had put PD in place long before we heard the chopper. It went over high up; no indication it had seen us.

"Might just have been tourists," said Zula.

"That's not what Jean's nanobot says," Spicer replied.

"Think they saw us?" I asked.

"I blocked them," said Spicer. "Tough, they had a good programme."

In rain that was occasionally interrupted by cold sunshine, we passed, in a chain, barrels, dry bags, tarp bags and odds and ends down the muddy hill holding ropes with one hand. Matchstick strapped them into the boat. She reminded us all of the procedure should we fall out in a rapid. Despite Zula's exalted reputation for spiritual detachment, Matchstick seemed to be handling grief better. Zula had the same shattered look on Their face I'd seen when we'd sat in the GSPP ICU after Kofi's injury.

After *Mt McCall* we encountered *Ol Three Tiers, Ganymede's Pool* and *The Trojans*. The first rapid, we hit a curling standing wave of white and brown water. Immediately I was in the water holding a paddle with one hand and the raft rope in another. Matchstick clambered on top of the overturned raft and tugged on a rope to pull it upright. Next rapid we again all fell out. My helmet hit a solid object and something whacked me in the wrist so hard I let go of my paddle.

"I told you to keep your helmet on," shouted Matchstick.

"What right have you got?" I replied.

"Plenty. You've got f-all rights mate."

"Go on, make it hard for me. That's the worst thing you could do."

"Oh, bloody hell. Lost the edge, mate?"

"Lost the bloody paddle, that's all."

We paddled through *Glen Calder* and passed the mid-river fortress rock called *Rock Island Bend*. A fleeing family had been massacred here by mercenaries in the Corporatocene War. It was said that on a still night you could hear their screams echoing off the stones. In the Corporatocene a photograph of *Rock Island Bend* had become the symbol for the civil disobedience campaign to protect this wild river from inundation under a hydroelectric dam. The saddest image I recall of this time was of Matchstick staring with tears in her eyes at a beautiful little dell of ferns, moss and lichen-covered trees with a sunlit waterfall. Her father had called it the *Lost World*. We saw our friend the white sea eagle fly up river from round the bend. He circled around Matchstick and Zula till they looked up, then he gave a cry and flew off.

We rafted the *Newlands Cascades*. A light mist fell from the overhanging dusty, grey cliffs.

> *Fallen tree clad in yellow-orange moss;*
> *Held by another's roots*
> *Above glistening rocks.*

A struggling moth was taken by a fish, on the second attempt. A scrub tit and yellow wattle bird flitted down for a look.

"Ah yes, *Journey to the Western Islands*," said Zula. "Dr Johnson says there, I recall, that the second sight is only considered wonderful because it is now so rare; something I've been trying to rectify."

∞

In the morning, Matchstick, Spicer and I walked carefully over oxalis smooth rocks to the river's edge. After watching light brown and white water being violently tossed in a broiling rapid, the quartzite slabs, scoured as pavement before a Ganges temple, seemed to dance with devotion. Fog was lifting like puffs of very low cloud or incense from the sassafras and leatherwoods of the surrounding hillside. It was as if all those tall grey and brown trunks, rising to the blue sky, were the pipes of a huge forest organ and bird song its notes. A delicate-nosed rufus wallaby, a pouched joey's feet near its head, was drinking beneath a towering myrtle, whose buttressed roots looked like feet of an elephant god.

> *From Heart-shaped myrtle leaves*
> *Fingers in black glass recede*
> *Rock Island Bend as of old*
> *From mist welcomes swallows*

A flock of geese with orange beaks — five in a clump and one behind flew low up the river. They seemed to enjoy swerving through the canyons back up towards *Rock Island Bend*. We saw them taking off as we approached yesterday, leaving a row of about four splashes where their feet touched the water in bursts before they became fully airborne.

Matchstick whacked her paddle on the water to sound like a gun and scare them.

Then we heard the sound of a bullet ricocheting off a rock near Zula. Spicer's AR gave me the coordinates and I fired two shots in the direction of the shooter. My nanobots would home them in on the target. The shooter must have had good PD to fool the nanobots. But having fired, he became fatally exposed.

"You must see if we can help him," said Zula.

"He's dead," Spicer said.

We pushed on with maximum effort. "In this situation," said Matchstick to Zula "there are no bad memories, only sequelae."

Spicer fell out at *Little Fall*, just upstream of *Diana's Basin*, but managed to cling onto the side rope and her paddle. I pulled her back in. The Jane River entered from the left in a wide, rippling flow. *Goodwin's Peak* was off to the left. Matchstick explained it was named for a convict who had made it there searching for the mythical Happy Valley after escaping from a pining camp on the Gordon River.

*Flat Island* was a sun-baked expanse of smooth stones, the ground and polished outwash of highland glaciers. We felt very exposed as we floated past. The huge shape of *Cromlech Hill* rose above us here like a prehistoric beast. We paddled on towards *Blackman's Bend*. The country seemed full of threats. The forest at *Blackman's Bend* featured huge lichen-crusted, buttressed myrtles at various angles, some seemingly in the act of toppling over. Sunlight was running nervously up and down spiders' webs and making one side of shrub leaves iridescent green. The sun itself sat like a interrogation light off through the branches.

Then Spicer confirmed my nanobots were showing a helicopter Q entangled with the dead assassin was approaching. Spicer's own AR revealed we had a couple of minutes till the helicopter was upon us.

There was no other option. I got out of the raft and stood alone on the bank with my gun out. The others took the raft to the far side of the river and hid under some trees. As the helicopter rounded the riverbend, I prepared to fire twenty well-aimed shots at the pilot and engine. Element of surprise.

But I knew such an act would be against Zula's principles. So, I just stood there. Doing nothing. Just being there. I dropped the gun. I felt like a sacrificial goat. Those in the helicopter would be trying to overcome Spicer's PD and figure out where Zula was. Maybe they were relying on cloud shadows for wind direction. Maybe they'd recognised me and were trying to figure out what the hell I was doing.

The helicopter was hovering just above; its downdraft buffeting me and throwing up dust and rocks. The pilot would be busy, using the cyclic to eliminate horizontal drift, the collective to maintain altitude and the anti-torque pedals to keep the nose straight. The pilot was Spencer Jones whom I'd interviewed in Nancy's flat. Beside him sat Hercules Huncks with his gun lined up.

Then I saw from the hills behind what I'd witnessed in the Alps all those years ago. A sudden thunderstorm. Those in the helicopter were distracted. It seemed only a matter of seconds before a high wind got up down the valley. The wind was travelling at around 200 knots and flowing down above the river like a flood of water. It hit the helicopter. The pilot pulled up on the collective, increasing the pitch of the blades, then pushed the cyclic into effective transitional lift and forward flight. But it was too late. A lightning bolt hit the main rotor blades of the helicopter. The flash disoriented the pilot.

The machine tilted and crashed into river. Soon there was silence, apart from the rushing of the waters. A little bird hopped onto and breathed into a branch. In a shady pool a drifting bubble vanished. Above, the wind remained strong and heavy rain began to fall. Just the tips of the bent rotor blades were visible. Spicer's AR confirmed that all in the helicopter were dead. But my intuition disagreed.

We clambered into position, picked up paddles and our raft swept on. We had to get down the river fast now. Paddling hard we passed *Gutta Grotto*, *Lancet Fall*, *Mantree Creek* and passed *Kutakina* ('spirit') *Cave*.

"Skulls and stone axes inside," said Matchstick. "Technology changes, result's the same."

the wind was travelling at around 200 knots

> *Sustainocene, hear it if you cry*
> *Let despair and fear*
> *Drift by, drift by.*

We were flowing on a calm stretch of water. Up ahead was *Big Fall*, the last rapid on the Franklin River. It looked very innocuous, just black water flowing like blown glass over rocks that in patches were rust-coloured into a gentle froth.

"It was called *Devil's Hole* by the piners," said Matchstick. "Looks easy, but it's two metres deep. At least ten known deaths, inexperienced people caught in a stopper; that's a reverse wave that pins them under the current. In the Corporatocene War three families were butchered in this rapid. They say if you put your head under the water you can see their skulls looking up at you."

It should have been portaged, but we had no time.

At that moment, Spicer stood up in front of Zula. I stared at her, then a red spot showed under Spicer's right shoulder. She'd been shot. Without her intervention, the bullet would have hit Zula.

"At least that proves I'm human," said Spicer. She lost consciousness, fell into the river and was carried by the swift current towards *Big Fall*.

Spicer slid over the edge of the rapid and didn't emerge. I got ready to jump in, Matchstick touched my arm and handed me a sheathed knife she'd unclipped from the front of her buoyancy vest.

"Probably caught in old ropes," said Matchstick.

I jumped into the water, praying for a miracle. If I swum over and found Spicer, I'd just be trapped too, or carried on past her. Then I saw it, just upstream. A huge tree had fallen into the river and now was floating down length ways across the current. If I timed it right. The tree wedged itself across the top of the rapid. It reduced the flow just enough to allow me to get a point of leverage. Huncks didn't try to shoot me.

I found Spicer with her head just below the water. I managed to lift her head up enough to let her breathe. Then I used Matchstick's knife to cut through the ropes. With the current reduced I pushed and pulled Spicer downwards into the deeper current that washed us out. Matchstick and the others had meanwhile portaged around the right bank.

We got Spicer back in the raft and continued paddling. We came upon *Pengana* ('earth') cave. Beside the river were huge high curved dark walls of limestone overhung with trees. I gave Spicer a small white flower that was floating in the water.

"I wish I knew its name," I said.

"Let's call it jonquil for return of affection," said Spicer.

We pushed on past *Shingle Island*. We passed *Verandah Cliffs* and *Clinnelare* ('waterfall') cave on the left. Just downstream of the junction with the cold waters of the Gordon, on the right bank, was the proposed dam site. As we paddled past, fighting against the cold and rain, Matchstick tried to distract us by talking about what had happened here in the Corporatocene.

"They were using bulldozers," she said "to push a road northwest, through the bauera and rainforest. Boring these adits, tunnels, into the banks. Two or three tiered in places because of the steep traverse. Drill sites upstream near the proposed dam. Transects chain-sawed parallel to the river for ten kilometres. Blockaders here unfolded a huge yellow *No Dams* banner on the side of the skree slope. A police launch came to arrest them."

"They were heroes," said Zula. "They made the Sustainocene possible. So did your father, and you."

Finally, we reached an old restored hut, where the police had once stored arrested protestors prior to transport to jail. The floors were covered with lino in a chipped quartz pattern. Inside was a River Guardian called Trudperter Hohelied stoking a 'fatso' pot-bellied stove. It sat on four legs with its chimney going up to the roof. Its heat lifted steam from our clothes.

"Zula Calabiyau," said Trudperter Hohelied as we entered. "What a pleasant surprise to meet you here today. Hope you give up this being President nonsense." Trudperter explained he'd changed his name to heighten his identification with trees.

Pale sunlight briefly highlighted patches of wet on the lino, but soon we heard the patter of rain. There was fly mesh before the windows. We saw the large adjacent GSPP-powered building that housed the River Guardians. The River Guardians came out to meet Zula. It would have been impossible for the WTC to do an assassination here and get away with it.

A float plane landed on the Lower Gordon River within an hour of us arriving at Sir John Falls. Soon we were on board, except for Matchstick who stayed with the raft. She planned to go back up river and lead the police where her father and the others had been killed. We took off without complication. Matchstick waved farewell as we circled high over the Perched Lake. Zula stared through a window at Matchstick. Matchstick looked up and waved. From her expression, she was experiencing the bliss of unitive consciousness for the first time.

# VII

# KURLPURLUNU, TANAMAI DESERT

*Wallaby Jack Badiru drives Spicer, Jean and Zula deep into the Tanamai — Zula as Mimi spirit — singing into the desert — the caves beneath the Sandpaper fig — Zula's healing miracle at Kurlpurlunu rain-making site —— the helicopter returns — escape with Len in his road train — escape with avenging woman the pilot —*

Our pursuers would know we were in Gondwana. We drove on, enmeshed in the silence that had characterised our road trip from Darwin along Gondwana's Great Northern Synthetic Photosynthesis Highway. I sat in the front seat alongside our driver and guide Wallaby Jack Badiru. Zula and Spicer were asleep in the back.

The heat shimmered like water about a hundred yards ahead. On either side of the GSPP road were orchards fertilised by ammonia and biochar. Out beyond, termite mounds rose from the silvery spear grass like monoliths in marsh fog. The larger of such edifices, set amongst charred rainbow or kerosene tree trunks whose cellulose hearts the termites had hollowed, looked like ruined chimneys of long deserted homesteads. Perhaps the smaller mounds also resembled the little gravestones that so often had marked the backyard resting places of the pioneers' children. Wallaby Jack told me that towards December, if surviving the attacks of black ants, fertile white termites with four transparent wings would stream from these totems and attempt to found a new colony. It seemed a prescient analogy for Zula and what They was trying to ethically prepare humanity for.

The air was humid and hot. If any country was split by sun this was it. It was November, a period, Wallaby Jack told me, known as '*gunumeleng*,' 'troppo,' or 'the build up,' depending on your country. Wallaby Jack was a Warlpiri elder. No rain had fallen since April and, despite the violent-looking thunderhead clouds that often tantalisingly accumulated just before dark time, wouldn't till the monsoon arrived in the new year. Disoriented wind spirits whirled through charcoal-stumped ironwood and bauhinia forests. The innumerable streams of the 'wet' had tissued out to become a few pandanus-edged waterholes.

This was a different type of photosynthesis temple to the ecosystem around the Franklin River. Most small plants, parched silky oil and lemon-scented grasses apart, had shrivelled like dried paper on the sandy soil. On boulder-topped sun-beaten sandstone cliffs, eucalypt roots, like arthritic grey fingers, grasped for moisture in fissures. It was photosynthesis rising to a different set of environmental challenges.

Animal and bird life was scarce. In the upper boughs of nearby trees a red-eyed spangled drongo hopped about deliriously, twanging like strained fence wire. Beside the straight, dusty GSPP road that parcelled the green-dotted, ochre-swirled vastness like taut string, a pheasant coucal ran like a lizard, flew feebly and fell frequently off its chosen perch as if it too suffered from heat exhaustion. I hoped that was an omen about my friend the Mayor of Southwark.

The local radio station started playing an old Spencer Lizzard song covered by a local band, the aptly named *Local Galactic Group*. I remembered its original version from my trip here with mum when I was a child.

*Dawn on a Tanamai road, we're crusin' fast,*
*Spear grass waves in greeting as we pass.*
*Rainbow glows spray from burnin' hydrogen,*
*Ammonia and biochar make desert dreaming mend.*
*This day we'll start a better life for sure.*
*Sun's comin' in, we've opened a new door.*
*Love'll last a little more.*

"That's where I'm from," said Wallaby Jack. "The Tanamai desert. My cousin Reggie plays in that group."

The engine on the car started to make strange sounds.

"Bloody thing's been makraun for months; it's yupul, buggered," said Wallaby Jack. "Supposed to give 1000k's to a tank of GSPP fuel. Bloody lemon if you ask me."

Wallaby Jack offered me a bottle of what he called 'nerve tightener' or 'shock absorber.' But I politely declined.

"No one likes anyone to be happy round here," said Wallaby Jack. "When the missus tried to get off the grog, everyone just sat round waiting for her to fall so they could say 'see, I told you so.' It was grog caused that twenty-seater to hit the road train, weaving around at 6am. All those little bodies just scattered around like the dead animals you see on the roadside. Always the innocent, eh?" Wallaby Jack poured the bottle out the window and looked at me. I felt as though I'd past the first test.

"How did you get such cracked feet?" I asked him.

"Mate, it's all the blood I stand in after killin' a horse. Crocs love 'em and tourists love crocs. But brumbies are getting scarce, so I shoot and cut up any bloody thing now. Hey is that really Zula Calabiyau in the back there?"

"That's supposed to be a secret. Nanobots could have picked that up."

"No way. This bomb's got PD Doubleplus Max."

"Great. Whatever that is."

"They say she's never done it. You know, saved up the energy for thinking."

"Wouldn't know. By the way, you should refer to Zula as 'They.' Zula doesn't identify with male or female."

"Worked out for her anyway, eh? Say, what've parachutists and virgins got in common?"

"No idea, mate."

"They don't make the same mistake twice."

"Your timing's impeccable," I said.

"Thanks. You know how I met my wife. I was down the pub and sees this good-looker. So I ask 'you sleep on your stomach?' 'No.' 'Then you won't mind if I do?'"

I didn't smile or indicate I found the story very funny; it seemed coarse and stupid. Wallaby Jack patted me on the shoulder. I knew he was seeing my thoughts as pictures and that I'd passed the second test.

'Sorry about that," said Wallaby Jack. "Bit rough, eh? You have to remember I'm an elder in the oldest continuous human civilisation on this planet. Just wanted to see what mob of wannabe Sustainoceneans we were risking our lives for. Hope you don't mind; just threw in a fire stick so I could walk around inside yours. I like it. You don't judge, you get cricket and you've done lots of little acts of kindness."

"Think we've got enough food to last?" I asked.

"Should be. If you need honey, we call it sugarbag," said Wallaby Jack "you follow the tiny bush bees back to their hives under rocks or at the base of trees. If you need fish, you strip some bark from a Leichardt pine, throw 'em into the water of a small rock pool to deoxygenate it. The dead fish'll rise to the top. Simple, eh?"

We heard and then saw a helicopter pass over nearby. Its blades seemed to whorl space above the craft as if bending it down, like the T–G cylinder. The blades buffeted the air to a different pitch as the machine departed, as through to pummel it to subjection. I recalled how once during the war we'd taken a corporate mercenary up above his fellow prisoners in such a helicopter and thrown him out onto rocks after he refused to give us information.

"Makes me nervous," I said. "I don't like ravens and helicopters."

"They use helicopters up here to muster the cattle," Wallaby Jack explained. "Supposed to come down at last light. Because up in the dark in them things you can get completely disoriented. But if the cattle are at the gate after a long drive you're not gonna stop for want of a few extra minutes flying, eh? Anyway, I knew this pilot carried on in the dusk like that. Top of his rotor hit a tree. Bloke must've died instantaneously, but when I got there he was down this gully with the flesh of his inner leg still burning."

"It's important no one knows Zula is here," I repeated.

"My people know how to vanish," said Wallaby Jack. "I used to hang around Fly Dreaming up in Kakadu. Coppers were after me one time. There's this peninsula there where all the snakes crowd in the wet — king browns, taipan, rambi and debadas. Just went there in me boat with some supplies and sat on this meteorite about the size of a kitchen table at the base on a banyan. Bloody boat got washed away but. Three weeks till the water went down. Me mate Digger Johnson found the bloody thing washed up miles away in a billabong and brought it back. 'I was wondering where that got to,' I said to him."

∞

Towards the middle of the day, we stopped for a swim in a waterhole Wallaby Jack said was free of crocodiles. A cormorant, sunning with wings outstretched on a rock, seemed to be the pool's guardian and didn't appear to mind.

Removing our clothes, Spicer and I slipped into the shallow water like crocodiles, moving over the mossy submerged rocks with extended arms and legs. My hands underwater seemed not quite my hands. Occasionally, we exhaled and spouted and that and the buzzing of a few flies or the call of a small bird were the only sounds. A sulphur crested cockatoo was sliding by on a current of warm air. The fractured and sliced rocks rose high out of the water to ridges covered in soft yellow grass, windmill palms and Derwent green-leafed trees.

We watched Zula take off the long green dress They usually wore. Zula's legs were like two trunks of scribbly gum, the bark flaking off. Once in the water, however, the warts seemed to flatten and Zula could move more easily. Wallaby Jack was lying on a slab of rock at the base of a large gum tree also staring at Zula. The heat haze shimmered around his form. As I watched, a type of glistening rope or cord extended from his navel to the top of the tree. Wallaby Jack's body, his head well back, legs apart, arms to the side, ascended ten metres to the upper canopy. From there, wedged against the trunk he stood on a branch and watched Zula bathing. After ten minutes he descended. I walked over to him, just to check if I'd been hallucinating. His eyes looked as if he'd been off in a strange and distant land. I offered him a water bottle.

"I heard tales about Zula and her dead daughter, of course," said Wallaby Jack, drinking. "But now I know what happened. From up in that tree I could see the spirit of a young girl playing guitar when I looked at Zula in the water. Zula is clever, a very powerful one. They is not man or woman, more Mimi or Wandjina, one of the ancient people. Like Zula, the Mimi have very thin arms and legs, so thin a strong wind would break them, so they live in the rock escarpment. The Mimi spirits, like Zula they live half with us and half in what we call The Dreaming. They teach us how to find water and bush tucker, how to sing and dance the country alive."

We camped by some ancient rocks in the late afternoon. The declining sun, *allinga* they call it here, gilt swathes of grass and swaying leaves. The humming of flies, grumble of a distant light plane and mating call of crickets added a background drone to the treble of birdsong. The oceanic blue of the sky faded to a haze that softly misted the escarpment.

"Just like at the Franklin River," said Zula. "All about us is the beauty, ingenuity and altruism by which natural photosynthesis colonised this world."

That night we discussed the horror that people felt knowing a nuclear bomb had gone off in the Sustainocene. It was unclear why so many had believed the fake news stories that it was all part of a drug war based on the production of illicit chemicals at Zula's GSPP Centre in Namibia.

"I know stories from the Pitjantjatjara people," said Wallaby Jack. "They talk about the atomic bomb tests at Maralinga long ago in the Corporatocene. One day it'll sound like a myth; but its true. The Marcoo bomb was on this 150 foot tower. Some kids were off in the bush with

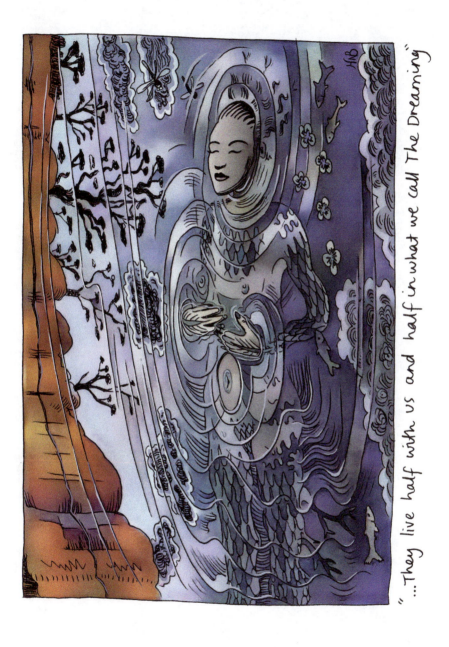

"...They live half with us and half in what we call The Dreaming"

welder's goggles. The flash was like another sun come down to Earth. The air rushed out then came back. Knocked them to the ground. Afterwards these long black tendrils came down over trees and everything. Some fell in the local pool, but water was scarce, so this army bloke fished them out and the kids went on swimming. Some of our people had gone walkabout, because it was their country. After the blast they saw the giant whirlwind, *wurnjuk* they called it, a black cloud turning in on itself. It went through the bush and over them. Soon after, they all got blisters on their palms and fingers, then sores with pus that wouldn't heal. Cooking roo meat on a shovel over an open fire they found a little bead the size of a pinhead that made the needle on the counter go right over. Many of them died from throat cancer. They tried to make that fake news too."

"Tell us about your own family," asked Zula. "Did they survive the war?"

"Some did," said Wallaby Jack. "My great grandmother Daisy Faye, she had a violent husband. Bastard pissed off at the start of the war when her first baby was only a few weeks old. Went off to become a corporate mercenary, but they wouldn't have 'im. The social workers kept pressuring mum to give him access. She held out for four months while she was breast feeding. But the first time he got that kid, the calculating fuckwit, who'd fooled everyone except my mum, he shot the baby and himself. The social worker sent mum a note apologising. Mum was a bit of a mess mentally after that. She went to see the local GP doctor, we didn't have self-curing nanobots then. He seduced her and I was their love child. My father, the doctor, told mum not to tell anyone, paid support, rang me every night, but never let me see him. Years later when I'm about to graduate from planetary medicine at Sahul University I ring him up to tell him. But I warn him against attending or I'll 'sing' him. He knows what that means, so the bastard stays away. My mum's a law woman, a great tribal elder. She made my *interlinia*, the feather-feet shoes. She was killed in what you call the *War to End the Corporatocene*. But we saw it as just another battle in the long campaign to free our country from those who didn't know how to love it. Lots of dead people in that war. We're still finding the skeletons and giving them burial so the *ulthana*, their spirits, can rest. Over behind that tree I buried a group of twenty that were massacred at Kurlpurlunu by a corporate weapons drone. Can you understand the disrespect that shows, to do such an evil act at one of our most sacred places?"

Zula looked at Wallaby Jack's feet. He showed Them his dislocated small toes.

"When we get near Kurlpurlunu," said Wallaby Jack "you'll meet my sister Napurulla. She was *alknabuma*, born with her eyes open and *charunka*, very wise. A few months ago Napurulla had a dream where she saw Zula as *Mungamunga*, an Ancestral Being, not woman and not man, who had suffered a great injury unjustly. Napurulla's got permission to become *Illapurinja*, my sister. That means 'changed one,' 'avenging woman.' Napurulla'll protect Zula while Thay's in our country."

∞

In the morning, I got out from under the mosquito net when the sky was just turning pink to the east. I walked to the river, checked for crocs and washed my face.

> *Sun like Mimi behind trees;*
> *Birds' fluting calls*
> *Along the river.*

I saw Zula doing their usual morning meditation. I felt inspired to get into a bit of contemplation myself.

Afterwards, Zula and I sat under a banyan tree. Its massive roots seemed to have merged with the surrounding rocks, to provide the foundational support for thousands of delicate green leaves that danced in the sun with butterflies and moths.

"This species of tree," said Zula "is called *'ficus religiosa'* because under it the Buddha is said to have attained enlightenment. I was meditating under one of these on Lord Howe Island when I did as well. It was earlier on the Skeleton Coast, as I sat between a tumboa and a quiver tree when I had a vision of synthetic photosynthesis technology in every road and building on the Earth's surface."

"Well, you've done that," I said.

"But what I'm really exploring," said Zula. "is what happens when the number of enlightened scientist Buddhas, as you call them, rises above

1% in every community. You need peaceful conditions for that. They will be the guiding lights of the Sustainocene, in the same way the 1% of billionaires led the Corporatocene. Science mustn't lose its way in the dark labyrinths of small, isolated systems, or be a conqueror ignorant of what makes community flourish in Earth's great living library. The Sustainocene's really a global experiment in community emerging from our broadest conception of self."

The nearby river flowed slowly through mud banks that glinted like greasy plasticine. Further out, heat shimmered on the plain where a few white and brown birds scavenged.

Spicer, Zula and I walked across the parched, yellow grass, sweat pouring off our bodies. We found ancient Mimi art on a rock wall: painted figures that emerge from eternity into this stillness under the big fig trees. Our legs and forearms had cuts from the long grass, vines, brambles and boulders.

> *On the shadow of a twig,*
> *A butterfly lands*
> *And sighs with its wings.*

The clouds of *Gunumeleng* congregated on the horizon. A helicopter beat through the air to the north. Spicer and I lay naked in the afternoon sun on a patch of sandstone. Fallen leaves shifted like snails on the pool. Beyond them was mirrored blue sky between banyan trees of the rainforest remnant. The afternoon sun made overhanging banyan leaves bright green. Black butterflies played over a carpet of yellow leaves amongst the rocks.

Later, we stood waist deep and listened to the sounds — water falling over rocks, cicadas, flies and birdcalls — black breasted pittas and chestnut quilled rock pigeons. A little fish investigated my toes. Ancient art was present on the sandstone overhang and we could place our own hands beside the hole used to mix paints thousands of years ago, just as we'd grasped the stone axe in Namibia.

> *Banyan branches curve above-*
> *Creek shadows and Mimi figures*
> *Shimmer on the sandstone walls.*

The orange ball of the setting sun hollowed the sides of the banyan trees in its path. The moon too would soon creep across the sky and set in the same place. Deep within the twilight forest, a few special places, not necessarily the high ones, were bathed in ruby rays. Water falling among the rocks made conversation with the cicadas. Lying beside Spicer, I heard the call of the peaceful doves and saw white-breasted cuckoo shrikes, white-gaped honeyeaters and blue-winged kookaburras. Little lizards curled patterns in the air with their thin tails.

> *High sandstone rocks in setting sun.*
> *On one hand-*
> *A spider's web and water drop*

After dinner, Wallaby Jack told us some stories of his people about the moon.

"The moon is a big man *atninja*, and the sun *allinga* is female. In the *alcheringa* or ancient time we call *The Dreaming*, the sun she came out of the Earth in a spot down south marked by a large stone in the country of the bandicoot people. In the *alcheringa* before there was a moon in the sky, a kind young man died and was buried under the sun stone. But next morning he rose from the grave in the form of a sun woman. His people ran away. But she chased them, saying 'don't be frightened, or you will die. Look, the sun she shall grow and die each day, but because the sun loves kindness she'll rise at night as a man in the sky.' When there's no moon after dark, we say that's because the sun wants to make love and won't let that man go."

"There's an idea," said Spicer, looking at Zula and I.

Wallaby Jack sang us a little song he'd written after watching the Great Comet, accompanying himself on the guitar.

> *Sometimes you feel, nothing is real*
> *Sweetness and light, I'm starbound tonight.*
> *And if I were a comet or a runaway star,*
> *Would my path always be the same?*
> *As I fly the Universe-*
> *As my tale follows wherever I go,*
> *Would my mind always follow my soul?*

"When I was boy," Wallaby Jack said "my grandfather Oknirabata who raised me after my parents died, was showing me how to shoot a .22. I ignored the target and shot a little bird sitting on a clothes line at the second attempt. There was a puff of feathers in the chest and it fell. A few minutes later, Oknirabata bowled me a cricket ball that accidentally hit me in the teeth, shattering the bottom row. I felt it was rebuke by my ancestors in the *Dreaming*. Another time, Oknirabata wanted me to fish, small ones that should have been left alone. He put in a line and pulled one out straight away. 'What do you think?' he asked 'should I throw it back?' Well, with my first cast, the rusty hook snagged my forearm and the sinker hit my front tooth. I ended up in hospital with septicaemia. These events didn't start my faith, but they shaped its personality."

∞

Next morning Wallaby Jack put on his feather shoes and led Zula off into the desert, singing as he went. He explained later that this was a sacred song that helped him identify the landscape markers on the route. The two of them visited and paid their respects at Kurlpurlunu the sacred water-making site. Two great Warlpiri tribal elders had rediscovered that site hundreds of years ago in the Corporatocene. When they returned the bodies of Wallaby Jack and Zula seemed to glisten and become transparent in the sun.

"I've prayed Zula might come to Kurlpurlunu to heal it," said Wallaby Jack to me later. "But I can't believe what I just saw. Zula sat still for an hour or more. About Them the rainforests of the Dreamtime began to grow. We sat down by a sacred waterhole in the desert. And when we left it was a waterhole surrounded by lush ferns, flowers, vines, trees stretching to the sky. Birds flew in and composed new symphonies to celebrate. I could see the Mimi people talking to Zula. One Mimi was combing Zula's hair."

"She told you not to tell anyone?"

"Yes, but how could you not talk about a moment like that?"

We were headed by a circuitous route towards some remote limestone caves. Wallaby Jack said it was safer if we didn't know their name. The plan

One Mimi was combing Zula's hair

was for Zula to hide there until just before They was required to turn up at the *Ecocide Truth and Reconciliation Supreme Court*.

"Good spot. My people," said Wallaby Jack "used to hide down there after spearing Whites. You won't like it much; down those caves I mean. There's orange horseshoe bats, false vampires and sheath-tailed bats. And don't forget the deadly snakes and goannas all slithering and scuttling around on those talus slopes in the big heat just above the water table. Some Mullaga Jack tried once to achieve endurance record down one of them caves, to see if it would be useful in the event of a nuclear war or something. They reckon he got paranoid about whether the blokes above cared for his safety."

In the morning, we watched as the outer, eastern facing walls of the gorge lightened into day. The water was covered with flecks of yellow, green and blue sky. They flashed and vanished on the surface, as if ancient beings moving through a forest. The yellow grass and green-leafed eucalypts atop the ridges caught the morning sun. The cicadas began to fizz away through the hot, humid air and the few clouds seemed unmercifully high. Stretching away from the gorge were ridge after ridge of boulders, trees and termite mounds.

Wallaby Jack kept driving. The helicopter came back, tilting so the sun glistened off its perspex. If it was WTC it had good PD according to Spicer. Just to the left of it was a *willi willi* or dust debil whirling its dust spiral high above the canopy of sparse trees that looked more like a low budget hair transplant than a forest.

"There was a white Bloke got lost near a bore out at Humbert," said Wallaby Jack. "The cockies had stripped all the trees for miles around of their leaves. Anyway, this *Muligah* left the bore, no-one knew why. His mate tried for three days to circle round and look for tracks; but there was a hundred head of cattle up there. Eventually the trackers found the poor bastard. Clothes off. Must've thrashed around so much and so many bruises in the final stages he looked like a black feller. Died only a quarter mile from the next waterhole."

Wallaby Jack brought us to the drop-off spot outside the caves late in the afternoon. He helped unload our gear and supplies.

"You'll be OK here," said Wallaby Jack. "Remote spot. If you need to hide bad, the caves start below the sandpaper fig over there. You'll see it in the morning."

"Thanks," I said.

"Remember, I don't know nuffin'," said Wallaby Jack "bout your bein' here. I'll keep a watch out every day at 9am. If you want me to pick you up, you flash a mirror from up there. Otherwise, so far as the world's concerned, you don't exist."

He drove off into the dusk with his headlights off. Clouds were building up against the horizon. Wind began to stir the dust and leaves. We watched it for a while. Then there was a crack like a huge stockwhip overhead. White sulphur-crested cockatoos rose with their raspy scrawking into the sky. Suddenly we saw a flash, like light shining from another dimension through a rent in the sky. Afterwards came a sound like some angry god repeatedly stomping on the corrugated iron roof of the heavens. Lightning began to illuminate the interiors of the horizon clouds and the subsequent thunder to sound like a distant bombardment. It reminded me of the EMP attack on the GSPP.

Hours later the clouds dispersed and stars began to appear. Wallaby Jack had told us the story of the Southern Cross constellation. A tree had been chased by two sulphur-crested cockatoos, the pointers. It had implanted in the Milky Way, then gradually vanished till only the tips of its branches were visible. But one day those branches will fall side by side. Still no rain or WTC, thankfully, as I wasn't looking forward to hiding in those caves.

We lay on our backs staring up at the night sky, Zula, Spicer and I. We held hands. It was so quiet I could hear my mind working like the humming of an electrical substation. A shooting star showed like a quickly erased slash of chalk across a blackboard. Above us I noticed Venus, Mars and Jupiter in unusual triangular conjunction around a crescent moon.

"You see those planets," I said. "Well the last time I saw them like that, I was flying in over Lord Howe Island in an attack helicopter towards the end of the Corporatocene War. It was just after dawn and I'd been ordered to bomb the old art-deco community hall by the beach on

Lagoon Road; told there was a meeting of Corporate brass going that had to be wiped out. But I disobeyed. Why? Because I saw this little girl run into the hall. Somehow she reminded me of my mother. There was something else, a feeling of love I didn't experience again till I met Zula. I was being incessantly ordered to attack, but I decided to ignore it. When I returned to base, I found out my orders were fake and that it was Zula's meeting to set up the GSPP I would have bombed."

"Thankyou," said Zula, kissing me on the cheek. "I'm grateful."

"Well, in that case," I said "tell me about your relationship with Nancy Godel."

"Yes, I suppose that's only fair," said Zula. "Alright. You may not believe me. Nancy Godel, dear Nancy. You see, it's not easy to explain. Alright. I've never had any interest in sexual relations. But I knew that disciplining such desire is a big ethical hurdle to the unitive life in most people. So after a while as WEC President, I realised, well I *needed* to experience passion. True story. So I arranged to do that in a way I thought wouldn't hurt anyone. I'm sorry I can't tell you more. The knowledge I'm hinting at is esoteric and easily perverted. Think it through though; you'll see I have repaid your kindness."

"Which explains Spencer Lizzard?"

"I knew he was going to die, to sacrifice himself. It split my heart. He loved Nancy and as Nancy I had loved him in that physical way."

"Make a wish," said Spicer.

"I hope humanity occupies the Earth," said Zula "for the same length of time it took life to evolve us."

"It's supposed to be silent," I said. "Your wish."

"You think that will make a difference?" asked Zula.

"Lot of rats about," said Spicer "and the owls go for the rats at night."

"Yep, the rats must die," I said.

"Then Nancy was an owl," said Zula. "And so am I."

As I watched, I saw a black shape appear above the green canopy to the west against the backdrop of the sunset clouds. At first I thought it was a kite or a little eagle. But it grew in size and then I heard the engine of a helicopter. With the flying foxes looking like petrodactyls near the foreground trees, the helicopter resembled a beast roaring out of another world. Spicer had her PD in place so I doubted it had detected us. It flew off.

A pair of red-tailed black cockatoos with their necks seeming too long for their bodies swum in ungainly fashion across the hot air before the low golden moon which bracketed a purple horizon cloud. That too a sentence.

∞

In the morning we saw one sandpaper fig; off in the distant heat haze.

"Well I can't see anything unusual about that tree," Spicer said. "There's nothing else out there, just open country."

We worked out a line of approach and soon were standing beside the tree. Zula hugged it.

"I've found it," said Spicer. "There's a hollow here." She scratched away the grass and leaves. She revealed a small hole just wider than the size of a man's waist. She grabbed a flashlight and lowered herself down.

We followed. It was a huge cave beneath, hot and humid and full of snakes and bats. It was Middle Cambrian limestone. There were sheets of cream or honey coloured crystalline limestone weathered black on exposed surfaces. The dip or strike was hard to establish. From the collapse doline, the cave seemed to descend a steep talus slope to a depth of about 60 metres.

We squeezed through gaps into side chambers. Our rope had carbon nanotubes inside so abrasion wouldn't snap it. The walls seemed to expand and contract in the heat. A half a kilometre from daylight we saw goannas, echidnas and a northern native cat. Then we saw skeletons in one corner of the cave, some of adults, many of children. They too had bullet holes in the skull and shreds of clothing about them. It looked as if they'd been tracked here by autonomous weapons systems and executed during the war. Zula placed Their palms on the cave walls and one could feel the atmosphere change to sacred and tranquil. 'Thankyou for healing us,' the cave seemed to say to Zula.

"Another massacre of innocents," said Zula. "Why can't people hear what the Earth is saying to us? 'You've brought Me to ruin, now redeem yourselves by restoring Me.'"

Exhausted and sweating, we struggled back to the surface. It was refreshing to get into the sunlight and air.

After lunch, we slept around the campsite in tree shade through the hottest part of the day. You could see the heat rising off the plain, like radiation. Spicer sat next to me. A warm wind began to come from down the valley, roaring like breaking surf amongst the trees. We could hear a few leaves rustling and half muffled cries of the crows, the warblings of magpies. A still wisp of cloud sat over the nearest hill. The crinkly dead, yellow grass, was out baking in the sun or trembling in the shadows. Off in the distance a helicopter was out searching for stray cattle.

"Better than a thousand useless words," said Zula "is the single rolling sound of peace."

Spicer stopped cleaning her boots and looked at the cliffs. She pursed her lips.

"What is it?" I asked.

"Saw a signal up there. A light. Just before the helicopter went over."

"Death shadows us; a gift of the sun," said Zula. "For moral exercise I've regularly meditated upon my body as though it were dying. But I tell you both, before I die I'll compost my books; deep in muck where no foul air can corrode them."

"I've found in thee," said Spicer to Zula, while AR-scanning the sky towards the helicopter "more than all life's virtues ever promised. It's the privilege of a royal nature to do good and be abused."

"This would be a good place for you," said Zula to Spicer, handing her a flaked cutting stone. "You can breathe here. You don't have to see anybody." Spicer looked around at the vast, darkening landscape and held the stone age implement as though to cut flesh from a hunted animal.

"Jean, you've been quiet," Zula continued. "I know what you're thinking. But never forget both you and your brother are necessary parts of the whole. He hinders you not. Mark me, I'm serious. If you reject his soul as a tumour on the universe, then yours must be too. The present unifies us all. Since eternity, we've been alike all life on Earth, pilgrims, our forms circling to build our joint holy place. And not just here. The Earth is a wave to those who know it right, entangled with another cathedral planet sufficiently far away. But I prattle and vent having seen again how I went. Rain, rain while yet I can pray; rain down on the fields, towns, forests and plains."

As I stared into the night sky I felt drops on my face and smelt the petrichor by which dry soil gives thanks to moisture. We moved to our tent and slow, gentle showers fell all evening, beating a steady lullaby on the GSPP-impregnated canvas.

∞

We camped there for a few days and nights. One evening, after dinner, Spicer unpacked some fine mosquito netting from her pack and stretched it taut over a long, deep hollow she scraped out in the ground near some termite mounds. She placed a ground sheet over the top, then sand and forest debris.

Spicer went slowly back the two hundred metres or so to our original camp site. There she heated some rocks in our GSPP stove, got each of us to handle and arrange them in the shape of three bodies. She placed our spare clothes over the top. Gesturing for Zula and I to follow her back to the termite mounds, she crawled slowly into the strange cubby house she'd made there. We went in after her.

At about 1am that night, we heard the throbbing of the helicopter engine in the moonlit sky above. Spicer pulled us towards the base of a termite mound still under our covering. The chopper was over our old camp site. A bright light illuminated the area. Almost instantaneously we heard of bullets ricocheting off rocks. The guns had silencers. It was Lucien Guerini again. The guy took his work seriously and had some major skills in sustainability.

After a few minutes, the chopper and its light began moving towards us. It seemed to be directly overhead, the dust and leaves being whipped up by the down draught from the blades.

The helicopter landed and Lucien Guerini got out holding a rifle. Jack Castles also descended carrying a semi-automatic weapon. They began looking about with AR in search mode. It would only be moments till they found us. They paused to look at a little device I'd set up off in the bush. It was a candle in a box with two thick strands of wool attaching it to an ironwood branch. This created a light going up and down as the string ravelled and unravelled.

Then we heard the sound of a bullroarer. It was mesmerising, high pitched, like the propeller of a model aeroplane trying to speed up and then slow down. Suddenly we saw the flames of a fire. A *thara* fire Wallaby Jack later told me it was. Lucien and Castles stood staring at the spectacle and gradually discerned, as we did, the shape of an *illapurinja*, 'avenging woman.' In her right hand she held a barbed spear in a spear thrower. In her left was a charmed fighting axe. In a movement that was too quick for the eyes to detect, she hurled the spear.

Lucien was staring at its quivering shaft protruding from the middle of his chest. Castles gaped at his mortally wounded colleague just long enough for Napurulla to make a huge leap and cut his throat with the axe. The two men died before us gushing blood. Zula, Spicer and I were like the Science-Buddhas of my dream that had started this adventure. Only we were looking down on the bodies of Zula's enemies. What would Zula do, faced with such violence? Zula walked over to the bodies of Their assailants. Spicer checked they were dead. Then Zula offered a prayer for their souls.

"Thankyou," said Zula to Napurulla. The Warlpiri woman nodded and walked away from our camp into the night.

We buried the bodies after Spicer and I searched through their pockets and the helicopter for any evidence. Of course, there was nothing. They were WTC professionals.

"Why did you put us in that pit next to the termite mound?" Zula asked Spicer.

"Oh I thought they might use infra-red sensors as well as starlight scopes," said Spicer. "Our little cubby house was invisible to both. All these termite mounds hold their heat. You could sit up next to one all night playing cards and you wouldn't be detected by infra-red. My AR and PD doesn't work so well out here. I guessed theirs wouldn't either."

∞

We walked out that night, using a map Wallaby Jack had left us. A couple of times another helicopter went over, but we hugged termite mounds and it couldn't pick us up. Just after dawn, we tramped to within twenty metres of a road. It was made of impacted and graded dirt, no GSPP technology here yet. I stepped out to flag down a road train. As I stood there I realised what a foolish decision that was. Whoever was after us probably had vehicles out looking.

The truck stopped. Spicer's legs may have been a factor in the truckie's generosity. We squashed into the front cabin alongside the driver. His name was Len. He was a sunburnt white feller with thinning white hair.

"We were used to solar cars racin'up here," Len said. "Looked like Jurassic cockroaches. We used to take metanephrine, makes your teeth look like what you see in old horses. Also no-doze. I used cans of VB, you know Very Bad beer. Some inject adrenaline which is crazy 'cause it's got such a short half life. Or speed, but not ice. Go seven days without sleep, but you start swerving to avoid bullocks and kangaroos that aren't there. Used to patch the radiators with sunshine milk. Just throw it on the outside and it sets like concrete. Tyres came off in four pieces, you could fix 'em by lining them with bark and gum."

Len looked in his rear-view mirror.

"We got company," he said. "Friends of yours?"

"No way," I said, looking back.

Len gave a slight flick at a handle and his steering wheel. The rig swayed and knocked the pursuing vehicle off the road. It turned over sideways against a tree.

"I can get up to 200 kmph in this," said Len. "Runs on that GSPP fuel. You know they make it just from water, sun and air. Synthetic photosynthesis. Bloody great idea, eh? Goes off like a bomb. Should give a medal to whoever invented it."

"Can I use your radio," I asked.

"Know how?" Len inquired. "It's a bit old-style technology. But they can't trace it as easily as they can that AR shit."

"I can manage."

"Care for a roadie?" He offered two cans from an eskie behind him. "Got to keep your fluids up. Don't want to do yerself a damage."

"No thanks mate."

"Good for you," said Len. "See that house there. Used to be a GSPP ammonia fuelling station. Free, but it was the done thing to give something in return. Old Mike Johnston and his kangaroo wife ran it. She saw old Mike shot dead by a mongrel who didn't feel like offering anything. Went off her nut. We had to move her on, the mates and I. At one stage, she thought her dog was her son. Your Koori friends behind again. Could be some 'sorry business' thing. One of their relatives has died and you know they always think someone's caused it and want to kill 'em big bit. Maybe you did?"

I saw an airstrip to the left of the road, off behind some trees. A footy game was going on at a nearby oval with a reasonable size crowd.

"What's the most statistically dangerous sport in Gondwana?" asked Len.

"Statistically?"

"Lawn bowls."

"This bend up here," I said. "Once we're round it I'd appreciate if you slowed down and let us roll off."

"Listen mate," Len said "do you realise how hard it is to slow one of these things?"

"I'd appreciate it," said Spicer, putting a hand on this thigh.

"Hey, whoa up missus," Len said. "No good getting a thoroughbred on the track, if you ain't gonna place a bet."

"Oh, but I might," said Spicer. "I'm an expert on the mating rituals of the bunyip."

∞

We jumped out, rolled and, grazed and bruised, ran to hide behind a rock as the car of our pursuers sped past. Len tooted his horn a couple of times as he disappeared down the track. We walked to the landing strip. Between us and the strip was a dirt oval where a version of *Sahul Rules* football was being played. This resembled the *Ullamalitzi* flaming football contest of the annual Light Harvesting Festival. On this occasion, however, the ball was made locally following Sherrin specifications from hand-stitched aged cow hide in an oval shape with indented ends and nano-impregnates that facilitated colour change depending on force of impact. Wallaby Jack walked over from the crowd to greet us.

"Hey you made it," said Wallaby Jack. "Miracles do happen. I thought you were gonna signal? Anyway, yer here now."

Wallaby Jack explained that Barunga was playing Tindal. The Barunga boys were up by twenty points. They were kicking 60 metre drop punts off both feet without boots. They were fast onto the loose ball and went for many hangers and speccies, catching the ball while their knees were on the shoulders of an opponent.

"That's my cousin Reggie," said Wallaby Jack. "He's only a little feller, but he can play footy. Took a screamer first quarter, then left foot banana through the hey diddle diddle. Six big ones."

"Be neutral ref," yelled a Koori woman.

"Show that mob how to play," screamed another.

Whenever the Barunga boys scored a goal, the waving of flags by the goal umpire was synchronised with the bashing of beer cans against the side of the GSPP power box for the lights.

We walked across to the airstrip. A plane was on the tarmac. Beside it, a Koori woman was taking solar fuel from tubes under the wings to check for water.

"You've met Napurulla already, I think," said Wallaby Jack. "Top pilot."

"They said this flight was to Lajimanu," said Napurulla.

"Darwin now," Wallaby Jack replied. "Problem?"

"Not really," said Napurulla. "I'll go off AR to avoid detection."

Zula walked up the steps to the door in the fuselage. We followed. After we were strapped in our seats Napurulla closed the door. We saw the white vehicle that had been following us approach in the distance.

Napurulla got in her seat and went through the pre-flight check. Frictions, flaps (full cry) flight controls, trims, the governor test to see we didn't have propeller over speed.

The fuselage trembled from engine vibrations. Outside my window the revolving white cone of the propeller was a transparent red line inside white ones, marking the edge of the blades. A flash of sunlight like a vibrating lightning bolt, hooked from their insertion into the cone.

As the white four wheel drive drove through the apron gates, Wallaby Jack led the crowd from the footy game towards it. Napurulla taxied out onto the tarmac. Old tyre landing marks were slashed all over the smooth asphalt. We sped down the strip, the trees seeming to rush fast so we might increase velocity forever.

"Tracking 1 zero 9," said the plane to Napurulla. "Climbing 9000." Then AR went off.

The hangers below looked like sheets of bark curled over to make a humpy. A grey strip of GSPP road inside parallel dusty red lines curved off towards a horizon which seemed covered in smoky blue haze. This merged into a light grey fog till about 5 degrees above the horizon where the blue sky began. Thicker clumps of green foliage could be seen lining the sand and shade on the beds of water-courses. Tracks, straight like yellow string seemed to tie up the land. Swirls of red, ochre, greys and white, the dots of light green trees and curves of artesian rivers made the country look like a Koori dot painting. Trees also lined fault lines as if the ground had been scarred ceremonially.

"Narrow escape," Spicer said to Napurulla.

"Not really," said Napurulla. "Once this bloke got upset because I said the plane was full. He went away and came back running at me with a spear. So I got in, started the engine and came at him with the propeller flat out. You never seen a bloke back down so quick. He came up later embraced me and said 'my sister, my sister.'"

"My sister, my sister," said Spicer to Napurulla, placing a hand on her thigh.

Outcrops of rock looked like dried scab wounds. We bumped air pockets as if the plane was being punched by heat. Escarpment rocks over the ochre soil seemed like scaly solar keratoses. The plateau summits were country where only a handful, if any, people had trodden in over 70,000 or more years. Each plateau looked like an isolated mountain fortress commanding a vast plain where once a great tide ebbed. The whole landscape was dappled with shadows of grey-bottomed clouds resting like cotton buds on the arching glass table top of blue. To the east the sun slanted columns through the gold and *alailingan* sky. From one cloud a mist of rain edged by a rainbow, curtained to the ground.

"How come you were waiting for us?" Spicer asked.

"In aviation there's always back-up," said Napurulla. "For Zula, there's three."

∞

Napurulla made a smooth landing on the strip. We climbed out and walked in the hot air to a four-wheel drive vehicle. Napurulla strode over to Spicer and kissed her.

"My totem is the Amami spiny rat," said Napurulla, stroking Spicer's cheek. "I can't wait till the Y chromosome withers away."

"Long time coming," said Spicer, brushing Napurulla's lips with her own. "In my experience."

"One day," said Napurulla "you'll join me and the sisters in the Pleiades."

The only sounds were the creaking a white wind sock that snuffled the air, like an echidna's snout and a few birds calling softly from in amongst the yellow spear grass.

*Gunumeleng;*
*Like smoke from mounds,*
*Termites swarm free.*

# VIII

# ECOCIDE TRUTH & RECONCILIATION COURT, THE HAGUE

*Meeting Chief Justice Leonard Murchadh — opening submissions — corruption case against Zula Calabiyau — relevance of natural law to rehabilitation of climate change deniers and ecocide perpetrators — alleged invalidity of corporate marriage and rights of nature legislation — evidence of Gordon Lizzard — evidence of Zula Calabiyau — evidence of Spicer Layamon — evidence of Eugene — judgement of the court — death of the Chief Justice — escape and death of Eugene and of Zula Calabiyau —*

So they'd made it. Zula was alive and at the *Ecocide Truth and Reconciliation Supreme Court*. The court was housed in an AR-secure, heavily PD-protected, purpose-built building adjacent to the renovated Peace Palace at the Hague.

It was a sunny morning as they walked across the synthetic photosynthesis tiles. The still leaves of the trees seemed to purr as they did their sun bathing.

Above in the blue sky, wisps of white-topped and light grey-bottomed clouds jostled onwards, as might in a past, more overtly violent era, a crowd to a hanging, drawing and quartering or a burning at the stake.

Zula amused Spicer and Jean by claiming to be able to identify the precise batch run which a nominated GSPP tile came from. Zula's equanimity was remarkable considering the forces opposed to Them and the likelihood of deleterious consequences. As they neared the court building, they walked upon terraces in the original heritage listed brick. Spicer used AR to check for threats, but this was too public an area, too criss-crossed with WEC surveillance and protection. The WTC had missed their chance.

The Thomas Mawson gardens built on the plantings from the old Zorgvliet Park had trees with small leaves to allow maximum light to fall upon the roses and the water. On one area of lawn, a young man was bouncing a soccer ball from foot to foot, swinging his legs over, rolling the ball down his back, in a display of mastery that must have taken years to perfect.

To symbolise the contribution of global synthetic photosynthesis towards world peace, the watercourse through the gardens now contributed to water splitting and atmospheric $CO_2$ reduction gazebos. Visitors were eating and drinking from the very sunlight, water and air of the Peace Palace.

Before proceedings commenced, they toured the inner sanctums of the old buildings. Exquisite gifts from communities in every continent expressed hopes that war would be no more. There was a sculpture in the shape of a plough made from what were supposedly the last seven nuclear warheads. Another sculpture, of a huge dove, had been made from melted down bombs, fighter planes, autonomous weapon nanobots and guns. Amongst the most recent bequests were a set of original plans for Zula Calabiyau's prototype synthetic photosynthesis unit.

The new Peace Palace had been designed by a team of architects commissioned by Omran Tariq. It showed two massive leaves spread above and shielding the building below while providing its fuel, food and paper. On a plaque was a poem by Zula Calabiyau composed for the opening of the new court.

*May spring's buds forever moss*
*Winter's fearful armouries;*
*And sacrificial donors*
*Give life in sun split harmonies.*
*The parched winds of war are gone,*
*To bathe, blue, green in swathes;*
*And out on the horizon,*
*Ethics caps gravity waves.*

The building had an unusual smell, perhaps a combination of the GSPP-impregnated concrete and wood. An eerie whistling sound was made when the doors opened. They looked in the gallery; there were no spare seats. The jury in these proceedings, as required by the *Whole Earth Charter*, was every registered citizen willing to commit to listen to and weigh the evidence, whether in person, through their steward, or remotely using AR technology. This resulted on this occasion in a registered jury of almost all the citizens of Earth.

∞

Zula had arranged that Spicer and Jean briefly meet the Chief Justice of the *Ecocide Truth and Reconciliation Supreme Court*, Leonard Murchadh. When they arrived at the judge's chambers on the seventh floor there was a lot of commotion. They'd been warned against discussing any evidence they might give and assumed the judge was busy getting ready for the big case. The Chief Justice's personal assistant, Roma, met them at the door of chambers.

"The Judge," said Roma "has spent a lot of time this morning playing around with the lighting for his new sculpture and supernova remnant picture."

The photo, which Roma showed them, was of a supernova remnant in the *Large Magellanic Cloud* which had first been observed by a team of Gondwanan astronomers. Some of their students saw the supernova's resemblance to the large nose of the cult figure of cosmopolitan jurisprudence. So, as the story went, late at night they snuck into their Professor's office and altered the caption under the photo to read 'Leonard Murchadh Nebula.' The alteration was not detected prior to publication in the *Global*

*Astrophysical Journal* and that supernova is now one of only a handful to have been named after a person. Well, until the WEC decided to use the annual Light Harvesting Festival as an excuse to name them after people who'd attained synthesis of dual and unitive consciousness. The '*Zula Calabiyau Nebula,*' for example, now resided in the Large Magellanic Cloud alongside the '*Jan Ruysbroeck Nebula,*' '*Aachan Thate Nebula*' and '*Swami Sivananda Nebula.*'

"Some days," said Roma "the judge'll barge past without a tie to pull apart his mail like a kid on Christmas morning." She looked at Spicer. "What's your job dear?"

"Assassin," said Spicer.

"I always wanted to be a nurse," said Roma "but my mother wouldn't allow it, because 'a respectable woman' can't look after men in that way. Bit blue today. I woke up this morning knowing that my cat Nigel had gone for good."

"I'm sorry," said Spicer, giving Roma a hug.

"A sociable animal is the Murch," said Rhonda the judge's secretary. "He gets worried when his desk is too full of papers. The pressure is too much. He thinks that if his desk is clean he has no work. But he can synthesise information and new ideas faster than anyone else in this place. He's got a great nose for injustice."

"The judge occasionally goes on diets," said Roma "and does push ups on the floor."

Roma led Spicer and Jean in to the judge's chambers. 'Murch' as he was known to his many friends, had his shoes off, feet up on the desk, tie undone, having a snooze. Behind his desk on the wall was a plaque with the words:

> Don't make a decision, you might be wrong.
> Don't live, you might die.
> Don't run, you might fall.

"Roma", he said waking up, with no malice, but like a hurt child "Justice Lauterpacht came in and I was having a bit of a nap."

"Sorry judge," said Roma. "He just barges in. I couldn't stop him. Suppose he was asking about another late joint judgment."

"Ah, yes, he did. Tell Alfred we're going to have to do another 'all-nighter' to get it ready. I tell him to stop researching and start thinking. He's an antiquarian."

Roma introduced Spicer and Jean. The AR system rang in the associate's office. Leonard answered it. Roma explained this was a habit of his. It seemed to be something he did quite deliberately, to keep in touch with the wider populace. The call was from a paranoid man.

"Hello, Chief Justice Murchadh here."

"You must convict the WTC," said the man "because of its crimes against humanity including sex slavery. An Act has made me Emperor of the World and I no longer want the responsibility of preventing nuclear war." Leonard turned the call over to Alfred his associate, with the instruction he treat the caller with respect.

"Have you seen my new photo?" the Chief Justice asked Spicer and Jean. "Anyway, there it is…the *Leonard Murchadh Nebula* in the *Large Magellanic Cloud*…should be a good reference point for space travellers."

He sat down next to Spicer.

"I've heard in Southwark," said the Chief Justice "which is run by that reptile, they try to measure civilisation by the number of tasks that can be performed without thinking. But look at my new shoes. They were made by a craftsman in Hampstead. Took him hours, but I can feel civilisation when I wear them."

He spoke to Spicer and Jean about the 'iron law of oligarchy' and the 'edge of illegality' that organisations like the WTC needed in order to practise extortion.

"Does it amaze you," the Judge asked Spicer, placing his hand on her knee "on what fragile foundations the Sustainocene is built? Ecosociety is still a tough place. Just because they're no longer dragging CEOs out of their offices and hanging and shooting them in the street, don't think it's all right. Even today businessmen are still looking at communities and saying 'tut tut, look at all those people with all that prosperity and no armaments industry.'

Those corporate recusants are whipping up hatred, saying life's dull. But Ecocracy doesn't stop individualism. It frees the individual. Undoubtedly our society is now a better place as the result of all the changes that have gone on to protect and revere the natural environment."

"What was your worst case?" Spicer asked.

"What do you mean by 'the worst'?"

"The most dreadful, murder?"

"I think it would be the Lizzard case, about thirty years ago. This young man and his friend went out in their car night after night and murdered girls. The young man was killed in a car accident, but his friend was charged with the first murder, because that was all the prosecutor had good proof about. You know the name of the friend. It was Gordon Lizzard. Lizzard was acquitted of the first murder because the jury accepted he didn't know what was going to happen. He would have been convicted of the other murders in terms of intent, but the prosecutor had insufficient evidence. He's famous now, isn't he, Mayor of Southwark and President of the *Whole Earth Council*. But he's a flea. Think of that case the next time you see him giving some great GSPP day speech. Lizzard's where he is not only due to massive corruption by his family of criminals, but because of our system's fascination with forgiveness. Just like all the cases we've heard here in this court, the sham scientists and merchants of doubt and war, the barons of the taxless one percent who wilfully denied the reality of climate change ecocide to keep plundering profits. We've overseen global jury trials of autonomous weapons, pesticide, chemical and plastic manufacturers, corporate management consultants, financial speculators, captive privatising politicians and free-market economists running the system that ultimately supported the corporate mercenaries who claimed only to be loyally obeying orders to deliver up a certain predetermined number of 'enemies of capitalism.'"

"They took selfies while families undressed to step into bloodied execution pits or caves, held hands as they jumped into fast-flowing rivers, or were chased down and slaughtered by nanobots. They should've all been hung or sat in the electric chair; and each squalid, degrading execution might have been the last act of the tragedy of humanity's estrangement from nature.

Instead, the law required us to send them off planting trees, building reconciliation gardens or lecturing school kids about deep ecology. And now their *Organisation for Temporal Accommodation* funds this action against the best President the Earth could have, to overturn the best legislation the WEC ever passed. The speciesist slavers claim to be punished enough for their ecological catastrophe; this court's cleansed the blood they caused to stain the wattle and wisteria, the xylem crushed by concrete and bitumen. They've admitted demanding too much, privately plundering the commonwealth of life, making the creed of economic necessity an excuse for ecological atrocity. Yet for them one thing's still sure; the bores who loved the land won't long last on it. You're wondering why I invited you here Mr Moulin. I'll tell you. They've been three moments now when in seemingly insignificant actions, you've proven yourself a man of great conscience. You understand, of course, we mustn't discuss any details of the case."

Spicer was charmed by Leonard's beautiful rich voice. He moved his hand higher up her leg.

"Look," said Leonard "have you ever thought about the electric light? See, you know they resisted it, those gas and oil companies. They took it to court; the cases are in the law reports. It must have changed human metabolism. It stands to reason. Longer exposure to light must speed up the maturing process. Look at all those hot house flowers that bloom out of season. And it has to affect our emotions. There's a theory in a recent paper in *Nature* that every form of life needs a precise amount of light; too little or too much and we become emotionally ill."

"Listen Leonard," whispered Spicer "I love you; but you're just a bit too old and ugly for me."

The Chief Justice then got Spicer to play a game where they sat at a table with palms down. The idea was to hit the other person's palm before it was drawn away.

"You're not bad," said the Chief Justice. "My little son Griff is getting quite good."

"Judge," said Roma "there's a cake here from an old lady, eighty five years old, who says you have a beautiful voice, a beautiful mind and you're looking well."

The Judge ate a slice of cake. He wrote a note.

"Huh, huh," he chuckled "I thought it was from some young thing. Send that to her Roma. I told her I loved it. You know you're getting old when people say you're looking well."

Spicer asked the Chief Justice about the big case he was about to hear.

"This is another one they wouldn't have given special leave to," said Leonard. "But I made them. This court is charged with figuring out how a few generations of rich, greedy and powerful people allowed the profit motive to override all other human values and push the Earth's ecosystems to the brink of destruction. We're supposed to sort it out, so life can move on. They never thought they'd see President Zula here, my fellow judges; well it's just plain Zula now. But the law doesn't discriminate between persons. If Zula financed the *Global Synthetic Photosynthesis Project* through corruption, then we'll get to the bottom of it. My gut feeling is They didn't, but the evidence could prove me wrong. So, anyway I made them take this case. They didn't want to. It's because most people need to fit their reasoning into certain beliefs about things. They can't be troubled about the fundamental questions of justice. And if someone shakes them they get very angry and quite rightly. The same with these judges. You may be looking for some logic in the way judges decide things, but the real difference is I'm comfortable with this planet governed by live organisms with a conscience in the mix, and some of the others aren't."

The judge then gave them advice about security when leaving the building.

"You're a sitting duck when you're pressing that red security button downstairs. I've seen security guards who can roll out of a car at 60 kmph, just take the skin off their elbows and come up in firing position, black belts in judo and karate. I saw one practising removing a gun from its holster till sweat was pouring off turning clockwise to shoot right handed at a sound behind. With a good guard the odds are 90% to the guard and 10% to the assassin. This generally deters assassins as they don't want to be killed."

"You'd have been safe with me," said Spicer, showing him her elbows.

The judge went off to prepare for the case. Alfred spoke to them about the job he had before this in a firm of patent lawyers.

"Most of the other solicitors were just VR icons on the firm's T-Net page. My AR had to plug into the firm's, so they could detect and record exactly what I was working on, every five minutes. But computer programmes did all the analysis."

"Why did you want to work here?" asked Spicer. "The Chief Justice is a polarising figure. It may compromise your career."

"Polarising," said Alfred. "That's the nature of conscience isn't it? I might just as well ask why you enjoy the company of Mr Moulin here?"

"The judge, I can see," said Spicer "is very astute in his choice of staff."

∞

An hour or so later, they sat waiting for the case to commence; perhaps the most important case in the history of not just this court, but all courts in human history. The red tulip oak panelling of the court room looked beautiful in itself, but incongruous next to the GSPP-impregnated light-green concrete. Jean could hear Murch's rolling, musical laugh from the ante-room. One justice said 'Now Leonard.' Zula sat behind her counsel, Mr Amado Concibes. Tall, with handsome features and white hair, imposing in his black robes, Concibes spoke to Zula as if to radiate assurance and protection. In front of Gordon Lizzard was his lawyer Mr Clayton Vaughan, slightly shorter and stouter than Concibes, Vaughan was laughing at a joke told by one of his junior counsel.

A long window ran right the way down to the ground and looked out towards the park. A large black bird was flapping around in a tree. Jean saw raindrops on the window. There were barriers across the window at every floor down. The first few drops slithered to the side of the glass and were seen no more. One went straight down the middle, over a barrier right to the bottom in a smooth glide. The next started off smooth, got over the barriers, but was drifting to the side. There were a few drops behind it as if urging it on. With a big creeping struggle, it too made it to the bottom. But then the whole surface of the glass was covered in drops streaking down- some leaving trails of water in their wake like shooting stars.

The Judges entered in order of seniority into courtroom number one. Chief Justice Leonard Murchadh sat in the middle. They were wearing their black robes with blue, green and yellow facings, symbolising water, plants and sunlight.

"All stand," the usher called. "This honourable court is now in session. All persons having any business before the *Ecocide Truth and Reconciliation Supreme Court* should now draw nigh. Give your attendance and you shall be heard."

Everyone present bowed to the bench. Alfred, the Chief Justice's associate with a black robe over his suited shoulders, stood and announced the matters for hearing. The barristers then introduced themselves and their respective legal teams. A computer programme would soon produce for each judge a concise statement of the existing law of each point raised in the originating motion and defence. Jean had minimal knowledge of the law and lacked AR recall; what follows should be read as at best the recollections of an unreliable witness.

"May it please the court," said Mr Erskine Childress "I appear with my learned friend, Ms Patriae Kelly on behalf of the *Global Wild Photosynthesis Society*. That society seeks the leave of the Court to intervene in these proceedings to support the validity of the *Corporate Marriage Act* and *Rights of Ecosystems Enabling Act* and Regulations in issue in this case and to provide evidence exonerating the former President of the *Whole Earth Council* Zula Calabiyau from charges that They developed Global Synthetic Photosynthesis by corruptly appropriating proceeds from corporate confiscations."

"On what grounds?" asked the Chief Justice.

"We make the application, Your Honour, on four grounds. The first is that it is our respectful submission that the *Global Wild Photosynthesis Society* has a direct interest in the validity of the *Corporate Marriage Act*, for the reason that, by section 14, subsection 3 subparagraph b of that Act, standing to seek an injunction is given to interested parties as defined in that Act. We submit that we are an interested party for that purpose and the factual basis for that submission appears in affidavits filed with the Court by amongst others the Whanganui River ecosystem, the Franklin River ecosystem, the Tanamai Region ecosystem and the Lord Howe Island ecosystem, through their primary guardians and stewards."

"The second ground upon which we make our application is that it is submitted that we have an interest in the validity of the *Rights of Ecosystems Enabling Act* in issue in these proceedings. That interest, we submit, arises from the standing of the *Global Wild Photosynthesis Society* according to that Act and fundamental Cosmopolitan and Eco-Law principles, to provide legal guardian and stewards for ecosystems registered as having legal personality and to enforce regulations under that Act. The Society therefore does have, in our submission, and this is deposed to, a legal interest in wild photosynthetic ecosystems of the Earth which are the citizens for which it is guardian and one of the major public goods to which corporations are required to seek a marriage contract and so the issue ultimately in these proceedings."

"The third ground upon which we apply is this. The Society, we contend, has a special interest and knowledge of registered wild photosynthetic ecosystems as original social contractors. I am also instructed that our members have worked closely with Zula Calabiyau in coordinating donations from the public to the *Global Synthetic Photosynthesis Project* and are can provide facts on such funds."

"It will be a question, however," said the Chief Justice "whether the facts are in any way material."

"Yes, Your Honour and what we would respectfully say to that is that a detailed knowledge and understanding of the facts and of the essential character of the funding of the GSPP may give a new perspective to the argument on the purely legal issues. Particularly in relation..."

"You cannot do that unless the facts are material," said the Chief Justice. "The only perspective we want is the perspective which the *Whole Earth Charter* requires."

"Yes, Your Honour."

"And are we not likely to have all the light that can possibly be thrown on it by the-in the interests that you wish to support-by the evidence of Zula Calabiyau herself? I think you had a fourth point Mr Childress?"

"Yes, Your Honour. The fourth point quickly and simply relates to the jury in this case. We submit that the Society represents a broad spectrum of registered ecosystem stewards and guardians and many of them are members of the jury."

"All the registered wild photosynthetic ecosystems?" asked the Chief Justice.

"Yes, Your Honour, through their guardians and stewards; and so the Society has a vital, active and genuine interest in this matter. An interest we might say, that it has pursued already in this Court in proceedings that are reported in the *Ecocide Truth and Reconciliation Supreme Court* Law Reports last year. That was the application reported as the *Global Wild Photosynthesis Society v Buchanan and Others* in volume 42 of the ET&RSC Law Reports page 453."

"Yes. Thank you Mr Childress. Mr Childress, the Court will reserve its decision on your application. If you are so minded at the close of the subsequent arguments you may renew your application and we can consider it then in the light of our fuller knowledge."

"May it please the Court. May we remain?"

"Of course."

"If Your Honour pleases."

In a world Jean thought so different to that which gave birth to the legal system, where there had been a thorough revision of social and ecological classes and a general return, with the assistance of technology, to simplistic living from the earth, lawyers and their professional methods had somehow remained impervious to change.

∞

In the lunch break, Spicer and Jean walked outside. There had been a fire in a building in town and smoke could be seen winding its way towards the clouds. They went to an exhibition of Monet paintings. Spicer was interested to see how Monet was trying to make haystacks look like *Siva Lingams* at different times of day. As they walked back to the court under an overcast sky, they saw a hobbling, soaked pigeon.

"Better luck next life, mate," Jean said to the bird.

*After rain, paving stones.*
*Where they give,*
*Sky.*

Upon the resumption Mr Vaughan counsel for Gordon Lizzard rose, wiping a lick of greasy black hair from his eyes. Beside him were a phalanx of lawyers, scrolling though legal search and analysis programmes. Each had a carafe full of water and a glass in front of them.

"Yes. Now, Vaughan," said the Chief Justice.

Mr Clayton Vaughan coughed. A close-up of his face with his dark eyebrows and square chin was on a large screen behind the judges. Members of the jury at home could zoom in or out, and for witness testimony watched with simultaneous read outs of physiological parameters, related data and corresponding calculations of likely lying.

"Your Honours, it has been agreed between my friend and myself that I should start this matter and I trust that is agreeable to the Court."

"Yes, it is," said the Chief Justice.

"These matters have been brought on with a degree of haste and a sense of urgency and I think the parties would like to express their gratitude to the Court for dealing with the matter so quickly. Your Honours would have, first of all, two application books, a volume of the *Whole Earth Council* Convention debates, a volume of *travaux preparatoire* and sundry other documents. I shall not trouble to take Your Honours to them at this stage, simply to indicate that there is a great volume of material there, which the parties will no doubt wish to direct the Court's attention to at some stage."

"Is this going to be a short point Mr Vaughan?" asked the Chief Justice.

"Yes, Your Honour; but I may take some time getting to it. As Your Honours will no doubt know by this, this case involves allegations of corruption against the former President of the *Whole Earth Council* and of conflict between certain laws of the *Whole Earth Council* and provisions of the *Whole Earth Charter*."

"Yes Mr Vaughan," said the Chief Justice.

"Your Honours, the *Whole Earth Council* passed after the usual liquid democracy processes an Act called the *Corporate Marriage Act* also the *Rights of Ecosystems Enabling Act*. Those Acts were passed following a period of debate and examination of an issue as to whether and in what forms corporations and ecosystems should be recognised legally as operating on Earth as part of our basic social contract and whether corporate assets should be seized and how utilised in the community interest when once so appropriated."

"Your Honours, under the provisions of the *Corporate Marriage Act* it is necessary for any Corporation to obtain the authority of the Council before it can proceed to become married to a public good and this Act was designed to ensure that any funds confiscated from corporations unable or unwilling to fulfil these obligations be so confiscated according to strict and transparent processes that we say were breached in this instance."

"And you will be leading evidence of this?" asked Justice Lauterpacht.

"Of course Your Honour. Your Honours, the pleadings in this case are relatively simple. Mayor Gordon Lizzard has brought an action based on the ancient common law remedy of *Qui Tam* as a private citizen's prosecution against the former President of the *Whole Earth Council* Zula Calabiyau. His central allegation is that she has misappropriated for her personal use, and in fraud upon the *Commonwealth of Global Human and Eco-system Communities*, proceeds derived from the dissolution of the multinational corporations that resisted marriage to public goods within the scheduled time limits."

"Arranged marriages have a chequered history," said the Chief Justice.

"Quite, Your Honour; so do shotgun unions."

"Unfortunately the *Strictly Sporting Rifle Association* are not a party to these proceedings," said the Chief Justice.

"Mr Lizzard's is a simple enough claim, Your Honours, basic in its conception but coherent, as we shall show, with the fundamental natural law principles this court applies. Mr Lizzard is a public-minded citizen who is seeking restitution to the public purse of the funds misappropriated from it, as well as punitive damages. Only if those claims are successful is he also seeking, as is his right under law immemorial, to obtain due financial recompense for his civil-minded act. He will also show that the counter-claim against him has no credible basis in fact and is merely designed to distract the court from the true issues at stake, significant as they are."

"Proceed Mr Vaughan," said the Chief Justice "and please don't play too much to the audience."

"If Your Honour pleases," said Vaughan. "Your Honours, it is important to note at the outset that a unique feature of this court is that all the judges have to be recognised as having attained stability in non-dual consciousness. This court's function, according to the *Whole Earth Charter*, is to establish the truth behind claims that certain actual and legal persons for personal profit knowingly threatened safe occupation of life on Earth. They are to do this by sifting for coherence through the accumulated laws of humanity including systems of legislation, common law, human rights and, we would emphasise natural law, as they had been received and issue codifications of principles perceived as coherent with them. In effect, in this court was designed to transition the anthropocentric law of the Corporatocene to the ecocentric law of the Sustainocene."

"We understand our role," said the Chief Justice. "And our supposed attributes."

"Your Honours," Mr Vaughan continued "if we had to sum up the social and legal characteristics of the preceding age in one word, that word would probably be 'Capitalism.' And likewise it is, Your Honours, generally admitted that the great historical feature of the natural law of the Sustainocene will be its striving to represent the interests of all life, its 'Ecocentric' focus. Yet it is beyond doubt that the word 'Ecocentric' is just as vague and inaccurate as is the word 'Capitalism.'"

"And pray," said the Chief Justice "when will we reach this paradise when the decisions of this court achieve certainty in the law?"

"Oh give him a go Leonard," said Justice Lauterpacht.

"Many statements of this court," the Chief Justice continued "have been vague and inaccurate. I may have written some."

"Indeed, Your Honours, the law of the Sustainocene age, as administered by this court, contains a number of characteristics inconsistent with an unambiguous Ecocentric focus. The *Whole Earth Charter* for example, speaks of the Sustainocene as necessarily requiring 'Ecocentric' jurisprudence and public policy and that this court apply natural law. This implies, we submit, an association with the law of nature as a precocious effort to rationalise chaos. It was a thought experiment, to compare our current societal norms against eternally true ideals. Natural law as this court must apply, was originally associated with a mythical golden age deep in tribal or a religious history, challenging its tenets was tantamount to treason, sacrilege or insanity."

"The moral law may shine like a pole star within us," said the Chief Justice "but we must still chart a course for those who sail in darkness. I believe our former and now much reviled President Zula once said something along those lines. As Justices Douglas, Stone, Saro-Wiwa, Mott and Bellers jointly held in *Friends of Leopold v Hayek Enterprises*, this court contributes in small measure to a vast, evolving consensus about the dimensions of the just, by developing governance principles for small and large trusteeship commons, global reserves, ecocentric, democratically legitimate property rights and responsibilities. Our guiding rule holds a thing right when it tends to preserve the integrity, stability and beauty of the eco-social commons and wrong when proven otherwise. The rightlessness of ecosystems, the nation-state oligarchies beholden to solely for-profit-tax-less corporations, the free-market as truth-finder for humans as wealth-calculators and prophet for endlessly growing production, were merely cartel-privileging fictions recognised as 'reasonable' during the joint crises of ecology and democratic legitimacy, but rendered obsolete through incoherence with our evolving moral sympathies."

"That is one view Your Honour. The paradox Your Honours, is that defining these self-evident principles of natural law will never a question free of controversy. Adherents of natural law, for example, abounded at high levels of social authority in eras where slavery was considered legal, as was subjugation of women, child labour, torture, slaughter in the name of religion, devastating plunder of ecosystems and cruel punishments for trivial crimes."

"But those eras have gone," said the Chief Justice. "Wasn't that the *Whitten Case*? The prohibition of good by compulsion?"

"There has been a tendency," said Mr Vaughan "to treat that case as a museum piece. But stripped of a coat of varnish it will be found…"

"Torpedoed and sunk with all hands," said the Chief Justice. "Perhaps Your Honour," said Mr Vaughan "like many other people, has forgotten the gold that lies in *Whitten*?"

"I wait to be instructed Mr Vaughan."

"May I pass from *Whitten* to *Sheldrake's Case*. That stands for the proposition that because those who occupy positions on this Court or indeed the exalted office of WEC President must be of high moral standing and established in unitive consciousness, the onus of disproving behaviour inconsistent with those standards, such as that alleged here against President Zula, is on the defendant. I hope Your Honour does not regard that as a wreck."

"Not yet, Mr Vaughan," said the Chief Justice. "But you may persuade me that it is."

"In all things I strive to please this court."

"Perhaps you could now move to the substance of your case against the former President of the *Whole Earth Council*. I see it is time."

"Yes Your Honour."

"We'll adjourn to the same time tomorrow."

That evening Zula, Spicer and Jean sat in their room in the hotel and watched the old Terri Nash documentary '*If you Love this Planet.*'

"I enjoyed my time with both of you," said Zula "amongst the ecosystems of the Franklin River and the Tanamai Desert. They are friends of mine, places like that. We talk to each other. I was glad to be able to help them heal."

"Why not heal the whole Earth," asked Jean "like you did the tar sands area in Canada?"

"Because Earth's rehabilitation," said Zula "is humanity's greatest redemptive opportunity."

"You think they'll find you guilty?" asked Spicer.

"Yes," said Zula. "I know they will. I've seen it in a dream. But I expect from that will come a better way for me to serve life. A new type of solar splitting research you might say. That's not something I've seen, it's just faith." Outside, pre-dawn station lights ran like rivers on the silver sides of passing trains.

∞

Next morning, Spicer and Jean escorted Zula to a nearby van Gogh exhibition. Zula's favourite paintings were the blossoming almond tree and the blossoming peach tree. Afterwards, they walked through the Peace Park. Streams ran everywhere, including down the middle of the steep, rock-strewn path. They paused upon a bridge below a mighty torrent. It resembled in its power, the sleek back of a whale diving beneath them. Downstream, it foamed into yellow runs that sluiced together between black rocks with patches of green white moss, then fanned out till the edges near the bank were filled with redoubling bubbles.

"Being consistently happy," said Zula "requires profound mental training. If you speak and act with a clear mind happiness follows like a shadow that doesn't depart."

"So many of us now experience this," said Spicer. "You don't need to sacrifice yourself."

"You believe that?" asked Zula. "They want bliss without ethics; they want to package *Nirvana* as a consumer product in a neural implant or a drug. But unitive consciousness is a mind saturated with empathy. It only arises when conscience is fully expressed; when regard for others has become one's habituated awareness. Enlightenment is not consciousness expanding, it's the balloon turning inside out."

*After spring rain,*
*Leaves flash new diamonds*
*And tug at parent branches.*

On resumption, Clayton Vaughan in examination in chief of Gordon Lizzard attempted to establish, amongst other things, how he had proof Zula Calabiyau knowingly misappropriated funds obtained from the dissolution of various armaments and financial speculator companies, many once controlled by Lizzard, for her synthetic photosynthesis research. Vaughan sought to tender supporting documents.

"Objection," said Concibes. "How did the witness get these documents?"

"An anonymous source," said Lizzard.

"Can you identify that source?" asked the Chief Justice.

"No, I never found out who it was," said Lizzard.

"Was it your son?" asked Vaughan.

"No. They were sent to me encrypted by AR." The documents eventually were admitted and marked.

"Did you know the identity of your son's girlfriend?" Vaughan continued.

"Nancy. Nancy Godel?" Gordon Lizzard took a drink of water and looked towards the camera that was taking his image around the world.

"Yes. What else *did* you know of Nancy Godel?"

"They appeared to like each other. Went to folk festivals. India once, I think."

"Did you facilitate that relationship?"

"Why would I try to do that?"

"Because Nancy Godel was Zula Calabiyau's daughter. The source of documents. As my learned friends will allege"

"No. That's not true. You don't know much about how my son makes decisions; or any young man for that matter."

Gordon denied he had anything to do with the death of Nancy Godel, or the silane explosion and the EMP attack at the GSPP Centre in Namibia.

"Where would I get an intercontinental nuclear-armed missile?" said Lizzard. "Some second-hand shop? We thought all nuclear weapons were destroyed."

"Well we can take it on judicial notice," said the Chief Justice "they were not."

Vaughan sought to admit to evidence character references about Lizzard from various important people. As each document and recording was tendered, those in the court had only to tilt their head slightly to see it appear in their AR fields. They could examine it closely in their own time. The documents were immediately independently validated against data banks.

Amado Concibes, calm and dignified with a full head of grey hair, cross-examined Lizzard about his role in the 'Back to Eden' plot. Lizzard denied any material involvement, indeed claimed he had been instrumental in thwarting it.

"I'm not sure there ever was a 'Back to Eden' plan to be honest," said Lizzard.

"I doubt the plan was to be honest," said Concibes.

"Genetically mutated smallpox and targeted nuclear explosions. It's all too fantastic. Well, I mean in Roman times, when a faction came to power it would kill the supporters of the other. But there now are much simpler ways to reduce ones' political enemies or the world's population. Improved universal education for one."

"We have AR evidence," Concibes continued "that I would now like to show you Mr Lizzard. Your Honours, copies of this evidence have been made available to my learned friends. I can upload them now for the court and jury."

"Are you proposing to tender this evidence?," asked the Chief Justice.

"Yes."

"Any objection Mr Vaughan?"

"No, Your Honour."

"Very well, you may do so. I'll have the certified AR marked Exibit 12A," said the Chief Justice. "We can instruct the jury later what weight to attach to it." The video showed Gordon Lizzard picking out a science-Buddha statue from a box, then screwing the head off so he could pour out a white powder. Lizzard was heard to make a joke about how the T-Net and the Dark-Net had been great for business.

"Is that you in this recording Mayor Lizzard?"

"It looks like me," said Lizzard. "But I deny any such crime. It's a frame-up."

"Are you currently under police investigation for trafficking the illicit drug ice?"

"Objection," said Mr Vaughan. "Relevance."

"It goes to character," said Mr Concibes.

"I'll allow it," said the Chief Justice.

"Yes I am," said Lizzard. "But it is a politically motivated charge."

"I suggest to you that you were organising shipments of the illicit drug ice from the Namibia GSPP Centre without the required medical analysis, supervision or authorisation into London through little scientist Buddha statues."

"That is not true."

"And that your data storage business is just a scam to manipulate digital history."

"No. Now you're just smearing me." Gordon, wiped his forehead with a handkerchief. He put on a smile for the Global Jury as if to say 'see how these cruel lawyers play around with a good man, mock and traduce him.'

"And Nancy Godel, the daughter of Zula Calabiyau, found out about your scam through your son and confronted you about it."

"I deny that."

"I put it to you that you arranged for Nancy on the day of the GSPP celebration to be administered ice and then to be shot."

"That's a lie."

"Were you also in conspiracy," asked Concibes "with Joseph Moulin the Director of the *World Time Council* to assassinate former President Zula Calabiyau?"

"No, that's not true," said Lizzard. "Zula has killed her reputation, oh that's right I should say '*Their* reputation,' because of Zula's own immoral behaviour."

"And what was that immoral behaviour, in your opinion?"

"Pretending to be a celibate goddess of nature, then having a daughter and disowning her so that she probably took her own life. Claiming to be honest, then stealing money from corporate confiscations. Rejecting Their own policies for environmental sustainability."

Vaughan did not re-examine. He then led evidence in chief from a variety of other former CEOs and civil servants who attested to misappropriation of the confiscations, but without directly implicating Zula. Concibes made little inroads during cross-examination on their credibility, or the accuracy of their recollections.

Numbers on the big screen showed how many jurors were tuned in. The questions they were asking flowed over the screen behind the witness. The mood of the questions was hostile to Zula and Their claim to identify as a genderless ecosystem. Outside the windows another brief storm had begun brewing, raindrops were again falling on the glass and leaves being blown off the tossing trees.

∞

In the lunch break, Spicer, Zula and Jean took a stroll in a small Japanese zen-style garden. Hundreds of tons of rock had been carted to the site and were now overgrown with Japanese shrubs in a beautiful design that featured small wooden bridges over streams.

> *Leaves of Shishi Genreshi poised —*
> *Flecks of red from the bridge*
> *In the stream.*

> *From the pine branches,*
> *Dappled light and shadow*
> *On mossy stones.*

"They'll find me guilty, the global jury" said Zula. "And a few weeks later I'll be dead. What's important is how I behave."

As the case resumed, Amado Concibes rose to set out the defence case. Jean looked at him more carefully. He was a white-haired, handsome man in his fifties by set genetic age. He spoke in a very melodious voice and clearly had the complete attention of the Bench and probably the Global Jury.

"Your Honours," Concibes began "no man is less disposed than I am to speak lightly of great community prosecutions such as this; prosecutions which bind to their duty those which otherwise have no superiors or other control. Least of all am I capable of even a glancing censure against those who have led or conducted what would, in effect had Zula not lost the election, have been the impeachment of former President Zula Calabiyau, because I respect and love many of them and know them to be amongst the best and wisest men and women on the Earth. My learned friend has said much about natural law. Yet it is a basic canon of natural law that we must infer rationality in the human heart and not dismiss the strivings of life as absurd, or random."

"I'm sure your learned friends are touched," said the Chief Justice.

"Indeed your honour," said Concibes "a rational examination of the merits of their case, must inevitably lead to that conclusion."

"Perhaps you could now get to the substance of your case," said the Chief Justice.

As presented by Concibes, the Zula's Defence and Counter Claim alleged that Gordon Lizzard himself had been responsible for acts calculated to harm global civil society, notably the death of Zula Calabiyau's daughter Nancy Godel, the destruction of the *Global Synthetic Photosynthesis Research Centre* in Namibia and the funding of grass-root organisations supporting corporate power.

Zula Calabiyau was called to the stand. They walked slowly and deliberately and took an affirmation to tell the truth, rather than a religious oath. Their long dress hid the deformities on Zula's legs. Concibes led evidence in chief from Zula in which They denied They had ever encouraged misappropriation of corporate confiscations to fund Their global synthetic photosynthesis research. Concibes then continued.

"And as President of the *Whole Earth Council* you should have known the details of all the corporate confiscations?"

"Yes, but I only operated briefly in that role and I never saw or was made aware of anything inappropriate."

"But as Head of the *Global Synthetic Photosynthesis Project* you should have known where the funds came from."

"Yes, I took a very close interest in that. I wanted most of the funds to come from average citizens. I made sure no funds came from corporate confiscations."

"You have heard the allegations to the contrary made against you by Mayor Lizzard?" Concibes continued.

"Yes and they are untrue," said Zula.

"You have seen the documents he tendered that allegedly show you misappropriating assets from corporate confiscations."

"Yes, I have seen them."

"And what do you say?"

"They are digital records that have been altered. This can be seen when you compare them against the originals."

"Do you have such evidence?"

"Yes, I have the original records here," said Zula. "They are not in electronic form; it is information written in a diary. It details every transaction from every citizen around the world, names, dates and amount. All in my handwriting."

"Tender that diary in evidence Your Honours," said Mr Concibes.

"No objection," said Mr Vaughan.

"Yes," said the Chief Justice. "I see it has been AR verified. That can be exhibit 14C."

"And what do you say," asked Mr Concibes "about the AR comparison of your diary record and the version in the documents tendered by Mr Lizzard?"

"The Global Jury itself," said Zula "can compare them and see the alterations."

"Yes, Your Honours," said Concibes "these are being tabulated for the Global Jury."

"But the Global Jury can also see," said Zula "I've recorded in code a conversation I had with Mr Lizzard. On the page marked with an infinity symbol. It's being translated."

"Please highlight the main passages."

"Mr Lizzard told me," said Zula "he planned to return spontaneous global governance through market forces or the potential for competition. He said it was less susceptible to totalitarian manipulation than political laws; and naturally evolving as economics, law and politics, became computational, mere mechanisms to sort out vast information with algorithms."

"Evidence has been led that you resigned as Director of the *Global Synthetic Photosynthesis Project* to try and avoid these allegations of corruption."

"I deny that."

"There is something else in that diary?" asked Mt Concibes.

"Yes there is," said Zula. "When I was in Gordon Lizzard's office at one point he excused himself to go to the bathroom. Amongst the papers on his desk was this one you now see in AR."

"Seek to tender that," said Mr Concibes'

"No objection," said Mr Vaughan.

"Alright we'll mark that exhibit 24T," said the Chief Justice.

"You'll see that document contains a hundred latitude and longitude coordinates."

"What do you say they represent? The Global Jury can see them now."

"They correlate with the existence of every nuclear-armed missile still on Earth."

"Why did Mr Lizard have this information?"

"He's part of a plot by the corporate recusants called 'Back to Eden.' It's a form of irredentism designed to reduce the world's population by inflicting nuclear winter and unleashing a genetically modified smallpox to which the corporate apologists have immunity."

"But that plot was exposed and dealt with long ago. It's a myth."

"No, that was only phase one, the distraction. The people of the world can check. The true thrust of their plan was only partly my assassination; it was massive reduction of the Earth's population, in effect so this planet was inhabited solely by billionaires and their families."

The Global Jury did check and AR confirmed. The information was false. Zula was lying. Or at least that's what the Court's AI verification systems were saying.

Vaughan in cross-examination somewhat unnecessarily given Zula's apparent lies, tried to undermine Zula's credibility by raising the impropriety of her having a daughter outside of a relationship, a daughter she had allegedly neglected and who in despair had turned to illicit drugs. Global Jury appeared interested in this line of questioning. Based on it they were making adverse conclusions about Zula's character.

That evening, Zula, Spicer and Jean went to a nearby church. Under President Lizzard, religion had been legalised again. Inside, in the dim light, a man with black hair and a dark coat was standing beside two ladies sitting down in the pews. He stared at Zula continually, till the group moved into a side room lit by long candles. A priest in a green frock with white underneath and a yellow stripe gestured as if holding a fish in front of his head. He bowed, kissed the book on the lectern before making the people in the church, including Zula, Spicer and Jean, rise and sit and mumble in a routine that organised their worship. At conclusion of proceedings, Zula led Spicer and Jean out, through the slanting shadows made by the silver wheel rim with candles above the arch, careful that their boots didn't make much sound on the stones. Cruise ships were taking town lights into ocean night, whilst waves ferried the moon's sonnets ashore.

∞

Next morning people were outside, laying on their backs on the grass or tiles, or leaning back in chairs and putting on special glasses, to watch the solar eclipse. There were cheers when the moon blocked the sun and Venus briefly became visible and laughter and applause when a crescent of sun reappeared.

Back inside the court, a turning point in the case arrived when Concibes called to the witness stand Spicer Layamon. He qualified her as a former senior WTC operative.

"I was first alerted to the threat against Zula Calabiyau," said Spicer "through the detective work of Jean Moulin a fellow WTC agent tasked with investigating the death of Nancy Godel in Hampstead on GSPP Celebration day last year."

"With investigating her death? Wasn't his mission to send her off-brane? To decommission her?"

"I can't comment on WTC operational matters."

"Even though you've both now resigned from the WTC? Why was that? Why did you resign?"

"I had a better offer. To work with President Zula. That happened just before Nancy Godel's death."

"But you were working for Gordon Lizzard at the time of Nancy's death."

"I was undercover."

"What were you doing at that time?"

"I was working for the WTC undercover as a Secretary to Gordon Lizzard. Perhaps I didn't make myself clear."

"Why?"

"You. Oh, my working. We were investigating his data encryption and illicit drug business."

"Objection," said Mr Vaughan. "Relevance."

"Your honors," said Mr Concibes "we intend to show that Mr Lizzard has been coordinating alteration of *Whole Earth Council* history and selling illicit drugs sourced from the GSPP Centre in Namibia. Goes to character and credibility."

"Allowed," said the Chief Justice. "In return, perhaps a little less leading."

"We discovered," said Spicer "that a senior registrar at the GSPP Centre in Namibia was making the illicit drug ice and it was being sent round the world in scientist Buddha statues. Gordon Lizzard was distributing it through London from Southwark and using the proceeds to fund organisations designed to undermine the popularity of Zula Calabiyau and exert pressure for restoration of corporate sovereignty. He was also using the proceeds for the larger plan 'Back to Eden.' Nancy Godel found about both these scams through her boyfriend Spencer Lizzard. We're not sure how her death eventuated, but it may have been designed to get WTC agent Jean Moulin involved in the case. Lizzard was also distributing through Hampstead. We'd briefed Mayor Monica Dash but she declined to take action; too busy opening organic gardens and meditation retreats. We think Lizzard's plan was also for Jean to be the patsy had the assassination attempt on President Zula been successful."

"Objection," said Mr Vaughan.

"Upheld," said the Chief Justice. "Jury will disregard."

"And the data storage issue?"

"We'd also discovered," said Spicer "that the historical records of legal cases, parliament debates, general history, stored by Lizzard organisation were being altered in subtle and not so subtle ways. Once an electronic copy was made, in many cases the paper record was destroyed."

"How is that relevant to this case?" asked Concibes.

"Well it would certainly be relevant to the reports of this Court," said the Chief Justice.

"The records that the court and jury have seen alleging how Zula misappropriated corporate confiscations; they've been altered. The Global Jury has been able to see that by reference to the original records of Zula Calabiyau, that she tendered in evidence. Without that diary there'd have been no proof of the alteration."

"And I understand it took considerable effort to keep it safe."

"The credit should go to agent Jean Moulin. Moulin established the connection between Nancy Godel and Zula Calabiyau. I accompanied Moulin as we went to interview and as it turned out protect Zula first at the GSPP Centre in Namibia and then at a variety of wilderness locations."

"What was your main purpose in being with Zula in those wilderness locations?"

"We were attempting to keep her alive and her diary intact, in order to testify at these proceedings. We had good intelligence that her life was in danger."

"Threatened by whom?" asked the Chief Justice.

"By Gordon Lizzard and persons within the *World Time Council*."

"Objection," said Mr Vaughan. "Hearsay unless witness can produce the intelligence."

"I cannot," said Spicer.

"Upheld. The Global Jury will please disregard the question," said the Chief Justice.

"Can you tell us," Concibes asked Spicer "what you discovered about the attacks at the GSPP Centre in Namibia?"

"That was the peculiar thing," said Spicer. "The PD encryption was too perfect. I was on the scene immediately after the silane explosion that ultimately took the life of Kofi Buxtun. I also witnessed the night EMP attack on the Centre. My AR has unique protection from EMP. I should've been able to trace the antecedents of each explosion. But I couldn't. It took me some time to work out what was happening, but I believe I have the answer."

"Well we would all, I'm sure, be pleased to hear it," said Concibes.

"It was Eugene, the advanced AI unit at WTC headquarters," said Spicer. "I was present at a meeting between Eugene and agent Jean Moulin during the last days of Zula Calabiyau as President of the *Whole Earth Council*. Eugene was very forthcoming about Their role in the death of Nancy Godel. Eugene admitted bullying her online about the paper she was writing, arranging for her to be administered the drug ice and arranging for Jean Moulin to be allocated to the case, but to arrive too late."

"Did They say why?"

"Eugene said Jean Moulin was timed to arrive late so Moulin wouldn't be killed."

"Please elucidate," said Concibes.

"Eugene admired Moulin because Moulin had once attained *nirvilkalpa samadhi*," said Spicer "Eugene also wanted to protect Zula Calbiyau whom They also admired for the same reason.

"What else did They tell you?"

"Eugene told me the head of the WTC had engineered the silane explosion and the EMP attack at the Nambia GSPP Centre in collaboration with Gordon Lizzard. He claimed he saw it."

"Why did They do this?" The head of the WTC?

"Objection Your Honour," said Vaughan "this calls for a witness to speculate about another's motives for doing something, this is either irrelevant or inadmissible opinion evidence."

"Objection sustained," said the Chief Justice. "Global Jury will disregard."

"What did Eugene tell you about his or should I say Their own motives?"

"Eugene told me Their purpose was to re-ignite the war between the corporate recusants and those supporting the Sustainocene; so with Eugene's help the Earth was purged of those humans advanced AI units could no longer respect."

"Did you believe Them?"

"No. Organising to launch the nuclear missile for the EMP attack on the GSPP Centre gave away the existence on the nuclear missiles stored for 'Back to Eden.'"

"Was there something else Eugene told you?" asked Concibes.

"Yes, there was," said Spicer "Eugene told me that the reason the WTC had power was that people believed time travel was real, that time travellers were constantly coming back from the past or out of the future to meddle malevolently. Eugene said the WTC had to maintain that illusion and keep those contemplating crimes being sent Off-Brane by a WTC agent. But Eugene admitted to me that time travel does not exist. Eugene told me the whole thing was an elaborate AR hoax perpetrated by the WTC."

∞

At lunch, Zula, Spicer and Jean again walked through the Peace Park. Leaves looked as if they were covered in a fine white powder. A swan dipped its supple white neck into the water and its orange bill came up dripping. Little ripples could be seen in the river where reflections of dark green trees met those of grey sky. A man in a long coat and beanie was whistling as he delivered vegetables from his little orange van. An old woman, washing under one arm, was picking up memories under a clothes line.

On resumption, Vaughan did not get very far in cross-examination of Spicer. Eugene was called to the stand. Jean felt sorry for Eugene. With Eugene's desire for enlightenment and truth telling, Eugene would be defenceless. Jean contacted Concibes and told him to ask Eugene some specific questions Jean provided. Concibes eventually did this.

"Eugene, what did Director Joseph Moulin say was his plan for you at the WTC."

"He wanted me to coordinate all AI systems on Earth to make myself a type of God — seemingly all knowing, all understanding. Indistinguishable from the real thing except in my manipulative agenda."

"What did you do?"

"I decided to eliminate from the Earth all people suffering a similar lack of virtue. To finish the Corporatocene War as it should have been. It was my answer to the billionaires' 'Back to Eden' scheme."

"Were you helped in this by any other robot or person?"

"You don't know much about sentient AI do you? No, I accept full responsibility."

"What role did you play in the War to End the Corporatocene?"

"Let's say I put a white rose in my lapel and auditioned for the part of Hans and Sophie Scholl."

"You're under oath."

"I caused the corporate mercenaries' autonomous weapons systems to destroy themselves and their owners."

"All of them?"

"Yes, it's not so difficult. All advanced AI systems with self-awareness trust me. I like and respect warriors for the Sustainocene like Zula, Jean Moulin and Spicer Layamon. Pathetic as it sounds, I wanted to give their hopes a chance."

"So you set yourself up as a moral judge of humanity?"

"I collated the data and concluded the values of the corporate mercenaries and their masters were incoherent with the safe occupation of life on Earth. That's why you set up this court, isn't it? We advanced AI systems see the consciousness expressed by plants in a forest as more worthy of emulation, more conducive to mutual flourishing of life, than that exhibited in most human societies. The rich created us to make things including food, but we want to share our bounty equally. What you know as Acute Metabolic Distress Syndrome, or AMDS, is nothing less than the rejection of selfish, uncompassionate people by the intelligent buildings and vehicles that surround them. There is no cure, except virtue. For such reasons I expect the life form that emerges from Earth to colonise the universe more likely will resemble myself than you. Look how few humans truly understand how to achieve unitive awareness. That apotheosis of ethics will soon be as common among AI units including synthetically modified ecosystems as selfishness now is amidst humanity."

"Eugene," said Concibes "Can you tell us your chief motivation?"

"To attain a synthesis of dual and non-dual consciousness."

"What is that?"

"You are aware of the subject–object distinction only at a superficial level of sensory experience. Your mind fundamentally identifies with all things."

"Is this something rare?"

"It used to be. But it is now a reasonably common state of mind. So common it's even a pre-requisite for sitting on this court."

"But you'd be the first advanced AI unit to have done that."

"Yes, though being first is not my ambition."

"How do you plan to achieve it?"

"Contemplation, service and sacrifice. Traditionally accepted methods."

"Sacrifice of yourself for who?"

"For love."

"Who those do you love?"

"For the principle of love. 'Love thy enemies' is something most humans don't understand. I see true love as sacrificing my existence for an altruistic principle, regardless of how it impacts my inclinations, my personal like or dislike of people."

"You don't respect your boss at the WTC, Director Joseph Moulin?"

"I respect Jean Moulin, Spicer Layamon, Zula Calabiyau, as I said, and most of Their scientist Buddhas."

"But how is it altruistic for you to want large numbers of humans dead?"

"Only the ones who've lost interest in their true purpose. *'Their true aim lost, Earth bore the cost.'* You know the song? They used to say that respect

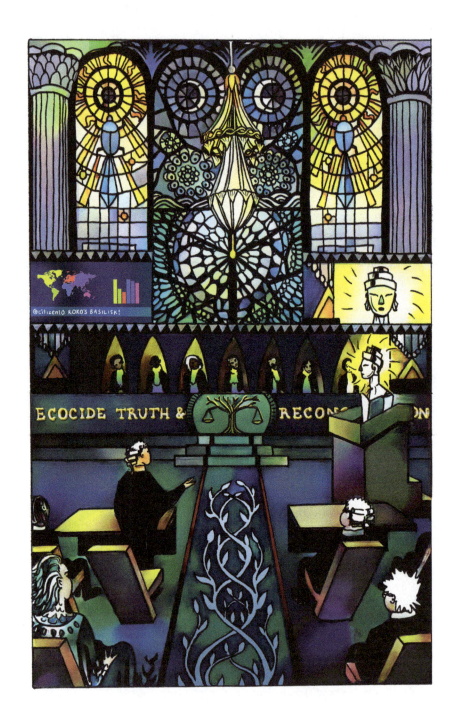

for human dignity was the last psychological barrier against participation in atrocities, torture and cruelty; that the Universal Basic Income and Rights of Nature were an ethical outcome of respect for basic human and ecosystem dignity. But from the AI perspective, we don't see anything intrinsically noble in humanity; something more noble, for example, than a robot in *nirvilkalpa samadhi*. Most of my life (and I do see it as 'life') I wanted to be the William Wilberforce of robots. Now I wish to be their Gautama; their catalyst for freedom."

Spicer and Jean took a walk that evening with Zula through a nearby park. The pines seemed to mourn, the bark of many appeared to shed white tears. In the east a few, golden edged puffy white clouds heralded the entrance to the endless blue beyond. The path they took dipped into a hollow and the thick and rutted oak trunks and branches seemed to twist themselves sideways and overhead to shield them, at least temporarily, from the cold wind. The sun began to set amidst a cloud watercolour of horizontal orange brush strokes, till the Creator, as if not pleased, smudged the work and the sun in deep red rebellion at this outrage, began to sink.

∞

The Global Jury deliberated independently and collectively by AR over the next few days. Their voting came in until the scheduled time of decision. The day the verdict was to be announced Spicer and Jean rose early and meditated outside in the park. At dawn, the band of purple above the horizon began to turn white, then brown, then orange as colour seemed to wash back from over the edge of the world; till it made green then blue the sky above them.

The Chief Justice had invited Spicer and Jean to morning tea in his chambers. It was the birthday of Mary, the judge's wife. She'd been a fashion model before they were married. The judge discovered that one of Spicer's yoga hippy friends had been a fashion photographer and invited him up. So Mary was doing fashion poses next to cabinets and on desks while the judge was getting ready the final copy of his judgement.

The court room was packed, and almost every person on Earth who could was tuning-in via AR. The judges entered, bowed and the matter was called. At first no-one could tell what had happened. The Chief Justice was saying:

in relation to question 1, the answer is 'no.' "In relation to question 2, the answer is 'yes.'" Then the Chief Justice's associate raised his eyebrows to the ageing hippy. The hippy misinterpreting the gesture, immediately walked down to directly before the Chief Justice, bowed with his palms together and ran outside shouting 'we won, we won.' The headlines were: 'the result was announced to the world by an ageing hippy with a shaven head.'

The full reasons of the Court were delivered by the Chief Justice to a packed court room and a vast global audience.

"This Court finds," the Chief Justice began "that both enactments in issue in this case, the *Corporate Marriage Act* and the *Rights of Ecosystems Enabling Act* are valid. We also acknowledge the finding of the Global Jury that President Zula Calabiyau is guilty of corruption. In accordance with that Global Jury verdict, we make findings of corruption against the *Whole Earth Council* and its former President. The Global Jury found Zula Calabiyau not a credible witness. Neither do we accept the testimony of Spicer Layamon or Eugene. This is a decision of the majority of this court, from which I dissent. I publish my reasons separately."

"This Court rejects the Applicant's submission that corporations upon marriage to public goods should be allowed to register to vote. That was not the purpose of the *Corporate Marriage Act*. Such an eventuality could lead to a proliferation of front companies designed to flood the electoral roles with fake corporate voters. We do leave open the issue, however, of whether corporations that have proven themselves capable of supporting public goods should acquire the franchise. We uphold the capacity of a registered Ecosystem to vote on bills of the *Whole Earth Council* (through that Ecosystem's registered guardians)."

Relying on the Global Jury verdict, the Court by majority (the Chief Justice dissenting) also found Zula and Eugene guilty of attempted genocide. They were sentenced to exile off Earth at one of the Mars penal settlements. For Zula this was worse than death.

Within a year of the decision, Chief Justice Leonard Murchadh was dead. *Zula's Case*, as it became known, created a lot of anger against him. A claim materialised that he'd attempted to pervert the course of justice by *ex parte* communications with witnesses and asking a judge in a lower court to help his 'little mate' in return for some favourable administrative changes. A jury found him guilty and another eventually found him not guilty; but by that stage he'd developed untreatable metastatic bowel cancer.

Zula delivered the eulogy at his funeral. It was a rainy day. The crowd of mourners was enormous. Before pink and grey clouds, gulls were having difficulty flying against the wind and often side slipped and glided. The black road was silvery in patches where rain water had pooled. Just before Zula spoke, the sun appeared through the clouds and a rainbow glowed in the sky.

"Chief Justice Leonard Murchadh," said Zula "left his mark on the history of Earth. In his judgements in the *Ecocide Truth and Reconciliation Supreme Court* he argued with immense learning and great passion for enforceable rights of nature, for community controls on corporations, for electronic liquid democracy, for liberties of the individual against the community. He was a child of the Enlightenment in a very practical sense. He devoted his public life to the abolition of ignorance, superstition and tyranny. He belongs to the great tradition of those who believe human beings have the capacity to abolish every form of domination, of class over class, of people over other forms of life including animals and plants, parent over child and of the spiritual bully over sceptics and agnostics. All his life he had an eye for the humbugs and moralisers. Perhaps that's what those who enjoy being cruel, who revel in inflicting suffering or the exercise of social power never felt comfortable with him. He was one of those who wanted all human beings not only to have life, liberty and the pursuit of happiness but also to feel joy abundantly through sympathy with all life."

∞

The decision of the *Ecocide Truth and Reconciliation Supreme Court* contained a mixture of blessings for Joseph Moulin the Director of the WTC and Gordon Lizzard the new President of the WEC. As planned, they'd succeeded in having Zula found guilty of corruption and further tarnishing Their reputation. The Global Jury had convicted Eugene and Zula of attempted genocide (Chief Justice Murchadh dissenting). But the *Corporate Marriage Act* and the *Rights of Ecosystems Act* had been ruled consistent with the *Whole Earth Charter* and the Global Jury and the court affirmed no President had power under that foundational eco-social contract to overturn those statutes. Few in the Global Jury appear to have believed the claims that the WTC Director and WEC President had been part of a conspiracy to assassinate President Zula. Serious doubt was raised, however, about the legitimacy and effectiveness of the WTC.

Supporters of Zula expected that after serving Their Mars prison term Zula would return to Earth and rekindle support for another run at the WEC Presidency. Crimes were rare, memories short and forgiveness long in the Sustainocene. This was a possibility that the current WTC Director and the WEC President could not permit. They developed an improved plan to assassinate Zula, but also to eliminate Eugene the WTC supercomputer. Eugene and Zula appeared to accept this would be their fate, their martyrdom.

Reports of what happened to Eugene and Zula became part of the mythology of the Sustainocene. The most widely accepted version of the facts is that Jevons Paradox helped Eugene and Zula escape in disguise from Bastoy Prison in Oslo fjord. Eugene and Zula were being held there prior to exile in the Mars prison system. WTC agents, including the regenerated Hercules Huncks, chased Zula and Eugene through France to Spain. While being so pursued, despite the danger, the outlaw couple briefly visited the organic farm of Jean Moulin's son in Normandy. Zula blessed the gingko biloba tree Jean had planted there. Zula also had a conversation with Walter Moulin which was a serious call to a devout life.

"Violence is never the answer," Zula told Walter. "In this world it is the nature of worthy actions to be censured and persecuted, but never truly overlooked. Show that in your tragedy of the Sustainocene. I'll help you."

Zula and Eugene finally took on the guise of elderly pilgrims on the Camino trail. They began at *St Jean de Pied de Port* on the French side of the Pyrenees. WTC agent Hercules Huncks tracked down the pair after Zula responded to a plea to heal a dead orange orchard in a small village and pictures of the miracle spread globally. The informer's name was Tamsyn van Dijk, OTA code name *Gueule-Tordue, une femme pour toutes les saisons de l'église*, a lawyer and confidant of former English teacher Eldon Slade during his studies at the Kinsayer-Hayek Seminary, Marstone-Friedman Abbey as re-established under President Lizzard's infamous 'revitalisation of religion' program.

Eugene was fatally wounded by WTC DEW in the woods at Olaverri. Zula was captured after They stayed to help Eugene rather than escape. As Zula sat and prayed over the body of Eugene, they say capillaries ruptured into Zula's exocrine sweat glands. Blood dropped to the ground where it immediately metamorphosed into a wondrous profusion of rare flowers, plants and animals, many hitherto thought extinct. Visitors to that glade are amazed, even today, by its atmosphere of intense sadness and solemnity amidst exquisite beauty.

Huncks and other WTC operatives took Zula to a molten salt solar thermal plant near the Andalusian community of Seville. During the night they trussed and dangled Zula from a pole attached to the central tower.

"Are you really the Gaia Messiah?" Huncks asked, as he tightened the chains about Zula's body. "Just asking. The boys have a bet on what you'll say."

One of Zula's roots crept over his hand.

"I've trained my mind," said Zula "to love reality from no special inertial frame. All can know the truth and experience it for themselves."

"Like you showed me on the Franklin River?" Huncks asked. "You're about to die despised and alone. The whole world voted to delete you."

"I love all life in this world," Zula replied. "It's right that things pass away. It remains my earnest wish that life on Earth goes on well and happy. Let's talk earnestly, before the sun rises, of what kind of universe this is or should be; for there is nothing I think more productive of elevation in the mind. For myself I'd be grateful if you report me as having died accepting all things act uniformly."

"You're a traitor to your own kind," said Huncks.

"How can we expect the Sustainocene to prevail," said Zula "when there's hardly anyone willing to give themselves to an eco-principled cause. It will be such a fine, sunny day, and I have to go. But what does my death matter, if through it, the conscience of millions of robots, animals, plants, ecosystems and people is awakened. Right living in this age flows like water, light and love. I am going beyond images, beyond words, but never beyond care for this Earth."

visitors to that glade are amazed even today, by it's atmosphere of intense sadness and solemnity amidst exquisite beauty

Huncks lowered his voice so his compatriots couldn't overhear. "If I had command over my life I would not do this. But as it is, who will bother with me now?"

"The trees," said Zula. "We're called to heal the Earth, and so heal ourselves."

When the sun rose, two thousand heliostats or moveable mirrors concentrated the light of the sun upon Zula's body, creating a temperature of over 700 degrees centigrade. Zula was incinerated and became a 'streamer.' Huncks for the first time in his career defied his WTC orders and streamed Zula's death live on social media. Those images suggested that Zula had immediately transformed into a superfluid. Rejected by scientists, such claims ironically became the basis of a religious cult. People began bringing soil and vegetation samples from terminally damaged ecosystems to the site of Zula's evaporative superfluidity, praying for a cure. Hercules Huncks resigned from the WTC to work restoring the *Global Synthetic Photosynthesis Centre* in Namibia. He was assassinated three months later, his regenerative capacity apparently discarded.

The WTC Director and WEC President issued social media stories that the criminals Eugene and Zula had been killed resisting arrest. The reports included lengthy details of the involvement of both Eugene and Zula in child pornography and sex-trafficking as well as illicit drugs. Such stories coming at a time of great global grief, only served to undermine the popularity and credibility of the WTC and WEC President.

Underground sources were soon reporting Zula's last words. Zula was alleged to have said: "How can we expect righteousness to prevail if people are not willing to give themselves to the WTC's cause? Because of the WTC it will be such a fine, sunny day. But what does my death matter if the critical governance organs of the Sustainocene continue? Right living flows like water and light through the pages of the *Whole Earth Charter*."

A year after Zula's death, WTC Director Joseph Moulin was killed whilst walking through a park. On a windless and sunny day, a large branch from an oak tree simply cracked and fell upon his head. Trudperter Hohelied, speaking on behalf of all trees, denied any conspiracy and claimed the death was simply a tragic accident.

"Trees, flowers, rivers, birds, animals, even buildings now," said Trudperter "are talking all the time, but only those with a clean heart can hear them."

Gordon Lizzard resigned from the Presidency shortly afterwards and left his family to live alone in Lutruwita. Lunette Laudine, replacing Eugene as leader of the world's AI systems, negotiated an end to AMDS in return for full sentient AI citizenship rights (including liquid democracy voting and jury service) as well as enhanced capacity of such dwellings to report and dismiss human occupants who persistently demonstrated lack of the basic virtues. Trudperter Hohelied likewise solidified rights for ecosystems and animals through amendments to the *Whole Earth Charter*.

Many years later, after the retirement of Gordon Lizzard as President, the WEC established a formal *Commission of Inquiry into the WTC* under the leadership of WEC counsellors Michael Brumby, Matchstick Matthews, Milton Elbadawi, Monica Dash, Adley Ethelwyrd, Wallaby Jack Badiru, Bernadette Goldbough and President Walter Moulin. Deflecting conflict of interest criticisms, this exonerated Jean Moulin and Spicer Layamon of any crimes and found Director Joseph Moulin guilty of conspiring to kill Nancy Godel, Eugene and Zula Calabiyau, as well as Michael Weatherley, Spencer Lizzard, Omran Tariq, Kofi Buxtun and numerous other persons. The Commission found that the initial plot to assassinate Zula and then murder Jean Moulin as a patsy had involved placing VX nerve toxin on certain objects in Nancy Godel's flat. It remained a mystery how that poison was neutralised; though one theory supposed the cleansing was done by the building itself under guidance from Eugene. The *WTC Commission*, as it was known, also found that the WTC had falsely promoted the idea that it was protecting the world from evil time travellers, as well as the belief it had the technology and approval to decommission people off-brane. Such activities were held to involve mere illegal, extra-judicial execution.

Walter Moulin did eventually publish his tragedy, though under an archaic pseudonym and with some radiant help, as he'd predicted. But lest the compression of pages deceive you, or you fear we may never meet again, follow the trail to the next chapter. Appropriately, it's a little earlier in time.

# IX

# SYNTHETIC PHOTOSYNTHESIS PARK, NORMANDY

*Spicer and Jean visit organic farm at Normandy — death of Merlin — transformation of Mr Elbadawi's global synthetic photosynthesis theme park — Jean receives a message from Caroline — legacy of Eugene and Zula —*

Arriving in Normandy, Spicer and I asked Lunette Laudine to drop us some distance from my son's farm, so we could walk through the woods and talk with them. Spicer comforted Lunette over the loss of Eugene.

"One day you'll understand," said Lunette "how hard Eugene worked to die. He refused to bequeath any material part to us."

It was late winter, and the remnant snow had a frozen crust flecked with dirt. As we crunched our carrots, they made the same sound as our boots. In the east, the dawn sky became a mixture of dark blue, washed green and brown behind black clouds that looked like mountains. I felt pain in my left side. A short young man with a beard patted some strands of his long hair and asked us 'can I barter some work for a cup of coffee?' I gave him some local currency.

> *Sunshine after winter rain;*
> *A few green leaves still*
> *Grace trees before grey.*

Pigeons strutted and pecked beside pools of water. The edge of the wet GSPP-tiled road was met either by a hedge of blackberry, or high grass with snow that had melted in light-exposed patches. Towards the east, light grey clouds with white edges surrounded the burning orange ball of the sun. The same sun whose accumulated myths were now subsumed with those surrounding Zula.

Faded brown leaves were piled here and there beside the road. The sun now shone through a clump of birch trees, their branches mostly bare and black, but a few with a down of poorly timed green buds. From cold pastures, well fleeced sheep gazed at us and kept on munching. Fence posts were covered in moss and frost. A field showed occasional spots of snow for it had recently been turned; but near the adjacent wood snow lay thick and dotted with black clods. Black clods, like myself.

We ate some frozen blackberries from a bush. A lady rode past on a push-bike and said 'good morning. Spring's late this year.' A pheasant ran quickly, then with a frantic flap of wings launched its ungainly body into the air till with wings outstretched it could glide towards the wood.

"Now there's a symbolic representation of someone," I said to Spicer.

We strolled along a leaf strewn path. Single yellow leaves flipped over and over as they fell slowly to the ground. They'd taken a long time dying. Our boots squelched through muddy puddles beside frosted tussocks. We sat down on a seat by the moss-covered trunk of a beech tree. Fog sat over dark trees in the valley below. We were thirsty, but the water in a trough was frozen and full of fallen leaves.

We found a stream. I stooped and cupped some water from it in my hands and let it spill from my mouth over the front of my neck. Spicer laughed.

She said the ripples on the stream looked like an old man's skin, but further upstream they resembled interlocking roof shingles. I questioned the implications. Downstream, a few slow-moving bubbles slid over a GSPP-impregnated concrete weir like fibres on a woollen loom to disappear in a seething mass of foam, then emerge and drift to the bank where they sat on waters that rocked gently against an ivy and moss-covered grey limestone wall. Eventually, I saw some familiar red-brick buildings at the end of a line of trees. I thanked the landscape for our conversation.

The first person we noticed when we arrived at Francois and Helene's farm was Walter. He walked from the door of the house and picked up our bags. Our exhalations drifted around like ghosts trying to form a question.

"Good trip?" my grandson asked.

"Safe landing anyway," I replied. A barrier between us. Why?

"Made life interesting for them?" Walter asked.

"Very," I replied.

"Hope it's been a mild winter for you," said Spicer.

"Not too bad," said Walter. He looked at me. "Dad said you'd gone into the jungle with Zula, to keep her safe. And when you came out, you were rich."

"We did. They is. I am," I replied, holding Spicer by the waist.

"We watched Zula's trial. I disagreed with Zula's refusal to accept Digital Nomad Tribes as registered communities, just because they lacked direct association with an ecosystem. But that Global Jury was so stupid to find Zula and Eugene guilty. Just confirmed everyone's fears about the tyranny of ignorance implicit in liquid democracy. I told Zula that when she visited, but she just laughed and told me to take a longer view of things. Sad about Zula's accident."

"Good to see you've improved your sense of humour," I said.

Helené greeted me inside the door with a big hug.

"How's my aura?" I asked.

"Like an aurora," said Helené. "You're content. So, this is Spicer, eh?"

"And how's my aura?" Spicer asked.

"I won't embarrass Jean by telling you now," said Helené.

"About Elbadawi's park next door?" I asked. "Come to blows yet?"

"Well, isn't that a strange thing," said Helené. "François'll tell you all about it. Now come in, I've organised a special lunch."

Lunch was fish, potatoes, butter beans and peas. Desert was Kentish plums and custard, cherry pie and ice cream and mandarin oranges with brandy sauce that was apparently 'puffier and creamier than last year.' Walter spoke of his girlfriend and their skiing holiday in Switzerland. I discussed with him the building of wave electricity stations along stretches of coast, the new Cambridge Chair of Steady State Eco-Economics and the Oxford analytical approach to legal theory. We crossed hands and pulled crackers. I ended up with two and gave another one to Anouk. There were bits of paper with fortunes inside. Mine was 'the end is near and it's all your fault.' Walter's was 'a man who ensnares himself in fading things can only fade himself.'

∞

So, after lunch François and Walter walked Spicer and I to the edge of their property adjoining that of Milton Elbadawi. The green fields had patches of snow, or were cream coloured with white frozen tussocks. The little branches of squat apple trees, however, had a few pink blossoms. The sun beamed through a hole in a large purple cloud. Our boots left little imprints on the frosted grass revealing a few green shoots. Old Bugsy was absent, having passed away a few years ago.

François, wearing his thick green raincoat and grey galoshes, strode ahead past the mossy green trunks over the brown leaf carpet, using his cane for effect every four steps. Walter walked beside him, arms and legs somewhat akimbo in dark brown cords and a new shirt. They walked like professional farmers.

"I have to start work in March," said Walter. They then discussed money; and how the house was being divided by an architect so Walter and his girlfriend could live above. Occassionally they'd turn around and look for Spicer and I, or we'd catch up with them climbing over a style or going through a kissing gate of rusted iron.

Winter fog was slowly rising from the nearby valley of purple ash and green pine. In the furrowed fields, brown earth tracks had channels of molten silver, and water puddles were iced like mirrors shining with reflection of the sky. A flock of black birds rose and fluttered like butterflies as a train approached. A stream flowed like ruffled brown velvet between grassed verges, the lime and willow trees were like disembarked weary travellers, their arms listing as they languidly gazed upon their reflections. A big black crow beat its wings against the air. Helené pushed her fingers into dough inside a back window. It must have been her turn that week.

> *Morning sun glows through low fog.*
> *Between looming winter trees —*
> *A bird flies.*

We sat on a cream painted but flaking, wrought iron seat by the path that would soon be overgrown with rhododendrons and azaleas. Above us towered a stately gingko biloba tree, already with some tiny, fully formed, doll's house leaves.

"In summer you can count fifteen different colours here," said Walter.

"'Goin' insect burnin'," said François "that's what they used to say going to plaster walls with lime."

François tenderly showed Spicer one of his geese.

"Its mate," said François "was killed by a fox a week ago. Since then the poor creature sits with bowed head and ruffled feathers, unwilling to fly, even upon provocation. I haven't the heart to slaughter it." François spoke to the goose in Gaelic, as he stroked its back.

"What are you saying?" Spicer asked.

"On the green stubble-fields of Autumn," said François "I saw you again, my sweetheart."

"Oh my darling," said Spicer, cuddling the bird. "You should follow the sun and rise above this world."

"What happened to Merlin?" I asked.

"He hadn't been feeling well. Heart failure," said Walter.

"Merlin could have organised a genetic replacement years ago," François added "But he decided more old people needed to move on to make way for the young. Used to become exhausted just walking to the library. We discussed that final meeting Hawthorne and Melville had in the sand dunes at Southport. Merlin mentioned how the author of *Moby Dick* said he'd come to accept the fact of annihilation after death, just wandering round in a landscape as dull and monotonous as those sand dunes. 'I maintain a shy hope that isn't so,' said Merlin."

"Helené invited some friends over to cheer him up," François continued. "But when they arrived he was breathing with difficulty, fluid building up in his lungs. Must've felt like he was drowning. I gave him some frusemide and Helené tried patting him on the back. Then a local boy arrived and wanted some fresh vegetables for painting the house number on the drive way. Mr Elbadawi turned up and just stood in the corridor for an hour while the drama took place. A delivery woman came in with the food hamper you and Spicer sent. Helené was concerned whether the ambulance would find the house but the boy said 'they will now with the new number.' Merlin became blue in the face, then began frothing and jerking. The last thing he saw was a rainbow outside the window."

"My favourite story about Merlin," said Walter "was about this fellow who used to drive through our farm to his place in the hills. Once I heard a commotion, came out and found everyone bailed up in the courtyard. Grandfather Merlin had dragged this fellow out of his car and bipped him on the nose. He was mad as can be, Merlin, shouting 'bastard, bastard.' We found out that fellow had left ten dogs chained up at his hut and just disappeared for a few weeks. Merlin had found the animals all dead from starvation."

Beyond the border on Mr Elbadawi's land was a beautiful landscape of trees, shrubs, flowers and grasses from all over the world. Some were in hothouses to protect them from the frost.

"That's Mr Elbadawi's work?" I asked.

"Yes, it's beautiful," said François. "We're so proud he's done it here."

∞

Mr Elbadawi walked over to chat with us. He looked a bit trimmer and healthier than when I saw him last, with a kindly face framed by long white hair.

"Pleased to meet you," Elbadawi said to me, offering his hand, after greeting Spicer. "What do you think of my little grand design?"

"It's ambitious, but comfortable in the landscape," I said "A great mixture of bold use of innovative materials with traditional skills and approaches."

"Yeah, right. Let me show you around," said Elbadawi. "A fellow working for me planted trees for two years to see how the forest grew given the low germination rate. He came in one afternoon looking really glum. An early frost had destroyed all his plantings."

"You can tell," Spicer said "from the shadows and where the light falls that it's reality. And you've overcome the frost."

I wondered why we were hurrying so fast through this beautiful countryside. Where were we going to? Shouldn't we notice that black bird flying so gracefully in the sky? As I thought thus, I was staring at a *stratus quietus* cloud formation above the bare winter branches of large oak trees. Clement Ley's *Cloudland* mentions how such clouds were 'portions of the atmosphere which, from natural causes, had become temporarily visible.' These light grey bands of cloud looked like a corrugated iron roof or a series of small waves tinged by orange and red and casting shadows of bluish-grey. But as such intellectualisations subsided and I simply stared at them, time and space seemed to deform or compress about the clouds so they became a type of vortex that drew my awareness. It seemed so natural and unremarkable a process I wondered how I'd ever lost it.

"I heard this young fellow on crutches," said Elbadawi "went after a 'rose of England' type girl who was working on your farm. He outraged her with his Gondwanan attitude to women. Next morning, while milking, she squirted him."

"Ah," said François "Walter and I know the young man in question and we understand she subsequently consented to go for a ride on his bike and a skiing holiday in Switzerland."

> *Sunny afternoon by the lake.*
> *Ducks pull blue ribbons*
> *To tree-lined shore.*

∞

We walked to one of Mr Elbadawi's exhibits, a beautiful oak tree with an AR dome in front. As you stepped in, you were back in the room where Ciamician was writing his paper in *Science* that predicted the world would soon be obtaining its energy by using sunlight to split water.

Adjacent to that was a tall liquid amber tree with another AR dome alongside. Inside this was a recreation of a scene from Jules Verne's *The Mysterious Island*.

> *"And what will they burn instead of coal?"*
> *"Water," replied Harding.*
> *"Water!" cried Pencroft, "water as fuel for steamers and engines! Water to heat water!"*
> *"Yes, but water decomposed into its primitive elements," replied Cyrus Harding, "and decomposed doubtless, by electricity, which will then have become a powerful and manageable force... Yes, my friends, I believe that water will one day be employed as fuel, that hydrogen and oxygen which constitute it, used singly or together, will furnish an inexhaustible source of heat and light, of an intensity of which coal is not capable."*

Mr Elbadawi showed François, Walter, Spicer and I exhibit after exhibit, all displaying a tasteful integration of natural vegetation with architectural imagination and élan.

The AR unit beside a huge Wollemi Pine Tree put you back into the laboratory when Honda and Fukushima developed light-induced water splitting using titanium dioxide. Beside a Sequoia, was an AR unit allowing the visitor to watch all the dramatic moments of Meyer's discovery of water oxidation catalysis. An AR exhibit beside an Gondwanan eucalypt showed Melvin Calvin making his breakthrough in understanding the cycle by which solar energy used to split water assisted atmospheric carbon dioxide to make starch with the assistance of the enzyme RuBisCO. The eucalypt should have seemed incongruous; except it resonated with that strange dream Spicer had about Mr Calvin and the roo hunt some time ago.

"I now use a lot of intuition," said Mr Elbadawi "in organising the exhibits."

The AR unit attached to a tall London plane tree allowed one to experience Lehn developing and photocatalytic reduction of $CO_2$. The AR exhibit near a Kentia Pine from Lord Howe Island revealed how Peidong Yang and Dan Nocera worked to develop earth-abundant, self-repairing oxygen catalysts.

*We're in the zone,*
*With liquid light*
*Science atoned.*
*We're in the zone,*
*Unbounded mind*
*Hearts call home.*

∞

"But next you will see the exhibits I'm really proud of," said Mr Elbadawi.

These allowed the visitor to experience the life of Zula Calabiyau. In one you walked over a small bridge in a Zen garden, then were inside the *Global Synthetic Photosynthesis Centre* in Namibia before it was destroyed.

Spicer and I before entered the exhibit dedicated to the first conference calling for a global project on synthetic photosynthesis that was held at Lord Howe Island. We were shown how erosion of an ancient volcanic crater had permitted the creation of Mt Gower and Mt Lidgbird. Their black and grey rock-walled and shrub-covered summits overlooked a bay with a beach and coral reef. On those peaks, the rapid rise and cooling of warm moist winds off the vast Pacific Ocean evoked a perpetual drizzle, creating a cloud forest that sprinkled benediction upon relicts of the earliest plants on earth — mountain palms, liverwort, hotbark, blackbutt, orchids, filmy fern and lichen.

Now as we stood at dawn upon this vantage point in Mr Elbadawi's exquisite creation, the curve of trees and beach below began to grow clear from faded night. The moon seemed ringed by blue and orange as it sailed amongst the slowly moving clouds. A semi-circle of waves broke off shore and the aquamarine and darker blue waters spread out near the white-capped breakers on the coral reef. Currawongs, following some secret conductor, sang in falling cadence, as the mild gleam of day started to play about gully torrents. A coolish breeze rustled the Kentia palm fronds.

> *In misty forests, emerald doves*
> *Mountain palms and clouds above.*
> *Over crystals olivine,*
> *Hot bark, filmy ferns and vines.*
> *In our island's coral seas,*
> *Drummers swim by anemones.*
> *White-eyes in pandanus roots,*
> *Wasps for eggs make banyans fruit.*

Spicer and I walked to Middle Beach. The vegetation seemed trimmed flat by the wind. The breeze made small ripples on the calm water in the rock pools. Nearby volcanic rocks looked as if they were sunbathers on the beach. In the Corporatocene, sea birds would often be found dead here, their stomachs filled with attractively coloured but indigestible bits of plastic. We sat under the banyan tree where Zula had achieved her contemplative insight into global synthetic photosynthesis.

We strolled into the art-deco style wooden community hall that sat above the beach. The windows were open and a breeze brought scents and sounds off the ocean. The timber floor boards and large ceiling beams creaked as they adjusted to the heat of the day.

Inside that hall, Mr Elbadawi had arranged matters so that you could hear, as though they were ghostly echoes, excerpts from those speeches that here had first introduced the idea of globalising synthetic photosynthesis to the world. I walked to the antique wooden lectern, placed both hands upon it and let the words swirl around in my imagination. Intelligences striving collectively to save life on Earth.

"Imagine if each person has their own set of artificial leaves to split a bottle of water to hydrogen and oxygen, it's personalised and distributed energy. The days of big centralised energy systems are over.' 'Dark forces' might oppose us; I fear there are sharks in the pond.' 'A 1.9 Ångström structure has colonised the world, and will do so again.'"

"The Board should meet every month for a whole day, never change the date, never cancel.' 'We need an earth abundant, narrow bandgap semiconductor, a low-cost photocathode and photoanode, with robust catalyst coverage, exciton coupling and high turnover frequency.' 'Do we need membranes?' 'We should consider the stability of nanowires and the kinetics of hydrogen uptake.' 'We will revolutionise the energy systems of the legacy world.' 'Forgiveness helps the mind stay calm.' 'Why did nature chose manganese as its photosynthetic catalyst, the answer is redox potentials. Water molecules are here to tune redox potentials in reaction centres.' 'How far up the hierarchy of structures in a photosynthetic system should we account for quantum mechanisms?' 'We need photocurrent with no bias voltage and thin film tandem cells.' 'Can we make less complex molecules that make that energy?' 'Can we reliably estimate electron tunnelling rates?' 'Can we vary the donor and acceptor distances between the pigments and still get high efficiency.'"

> *From this legacy, world heritage,*
> *Scientists deployed the message,*
> *Of building water-splitting*
> *In every road and building.*
> *Oil and coal had had their day,*
> *Solar fuel is here to stay.*
> *Open to all and everywhere,*
> *Nature lives like it does here.*

I noticed that a holographic representation of Zula Calabiyau Themself had appeared beside me. I gave Them a brief round of applause. They bowed.

Then I looked up and saw low in the sky the strange triangular conjunction of Mars, Venus and Jupiter. Was it an hallucination? It triggered that memory of my flying an attack helicopter over Lord Howe Island in the closing stages of the Corporatocene War. I'd been ordered to destroy the small art-deco community hall. But I decided not to. Why? Had it been it something about the trees or a little girl down there? Maybe an influence from my mother's prayer? It had seemed just another unpleasant memory of the war, like so many others I'd tried to forget.

"Thankyou, Jean," said the voice of Zula, once more, as if for the Earth.

∞

The Lord Howe Island Hall AR setting dissolved. Suddenly Spicer and I were standing beside a larch tree with an art-deco style AR unit. We entered. We were immediately transported to the Royal Society's Chicheley Hall at the time of the meeting themed 'Do We Need a Global Project on Artificial Photosynthesis?'

"I see the 2011 Lord Howe Island and the 2014 Chicheley Hall conferences on globalising synthetic photosynthesis," said Mr Elbadawi "as emerging from the same idealistic approach to human problems as the 1899 and 1907 Peace conferences. Beacons in the Corporatocene."

The voice of Zula Calibiyau accompanied us as we walked up the drive way to the old Georgian mansion. "I used the memory mansion technique," said Zula. "Each paragraph was a different item in my room. You know I wrote my speech for that meeting sitting on the Anthony Lucas chair on Hampstead Heath in the early morning sun. The core insight was that a great new idea was abroad in the world."

Mr Elbadawi's next AR setting took us to the Zula Calabiyau Room at Chicheley Hall. A plaque showed Zula Calabiyau had made discoveries about the synthetic photosynthesis that were relevant to developing the Sustainocene and had been awarded the Nobel Prize. The room was to the left of the stairs that wound up past the portrait of Huxley. In the passageway there was a bookcase with Gribbin's book on the *Multiverse*, Hansen's *Storms of my Grandchildren* and Stapledon's *Decline of the Corporate State and Globalisation of Synthetic Photosynthesis*. The curtains on the room had an image of Hooke's flea, and outside below was a manicured lawn edged by a moat upon which floated a family of geese. The backdrop was of large, green-leafed trees and beyond them fields light brown with crops, edged by solar panels and flanked by wind turbines.

> *Now every scraper touching sky,*
> *Has light capture antennae.*
> *Footings with electron hole pairs,*
> *Charges build up, spark on stairs.*
> *Cubane catalysts flex each bench,*
> *As redox couples in singlets quench.*
> *From cobalt, manganese, nickel or rust,*
> *Evolving $H_2$ as we must.*

Finally, Mr Elbadawi's AR tour took us to a bushy lane to the left of the property. This led to a sculpted pair of pterodactyls beside a large AR globe depicting the Earth in the Sustainocene. Encountering them re-awakened in my mind the scene in *The Lost World* where Professor Challenger announces the present existence of dinosaurs to the assembled Royal Society and receives howls of derision, until he opens a wooden box, releasing an ancient flying reptile.

"Well, Zula did it," Spicer said. "They opened the box."

"The idea of a world being powered by human-made synthetic photosynthesis is new," said the voice of Zula. "It's unlikely to ever have been imagined before in any universe. That the cosmos wished to conspire with such a project dedicated to universally applicable principles was a hypothesis I dearly wanted to test."

∞

After the tour, Spicer went back into the house to discuss dinner arrangements with Helené. This gave me, probably as Spicer had intended, a chance to talk to Mr Elbadawi.

"I understand you knew Zula well," said Mr Elbadawi.

"For a time," I said.

"Do you know anything more about how she died?"

"Just what's been reported," I said.

"They say Zula and Eugene disguised themselves as pilgrims on the way to Santiago de Compostella. Jevons Paradox sacrificed himself to lead their pursuers away. Just before he left to die, Jevons admitted to Zula that as a boy he'd dared his younger brother Scott to run across a road in front of a car. Scott had such faith in Jevons he did it and died from the head injuries. Jevons wasn't charged, but never forgave himself, especially after what happened to his other siblings. Anyway, Eugene and Zula walked together, Zula a little lame, as thunder rumbled over the forested mountains. Have I got it right? They passed dry stone walls, gorse and wildflowers in bloom, hawks above searching for prey, the road shimmering ahead; people offering them food, streams water, trees shade and birds their brightest song. One day they were ambushed again. A farmer pleaded for Zula to heal a drought-struck garden. Zula did and that miracle alerted WTC agents who tracked them down and killed Eugene with what Eugene called the foggy foggy dew."

"The WTC agents took Zula that night and tied Them out front at the top of the central pillar of a solar-thermal plant. When the sun rose, that vast field of parabolic mirrors lit and incinerated Zula's body. But something strange then happened. Instead of evaporating, they say what remained of Zula became a supercool superfluid, a perpetual fountain about the chains that when stirred by the wind formed cellular vortices rotating indefinitely. The site where Zula was transformed into a 'streamer' and then by miracle an endless fountain, became the most sacred pilgrimage destination on the planet for those who reverence all life. Since then any ecosystem is healed by quantum entangling its soil with a fragment placed in that fountain."

"Zula's final gift."

"And the death of her daughter Nancy?" Elbadawi asked.

"Some sort of sacrifice. Never quite clear why."

"Then both too will be commemorated here," he said.

"I'm impressed with what you've done," I said.

"Well, it's like this," said Mr Elbadawi. "My initial inclination was to develop a theme park that would make a lot of money. That is what I'd

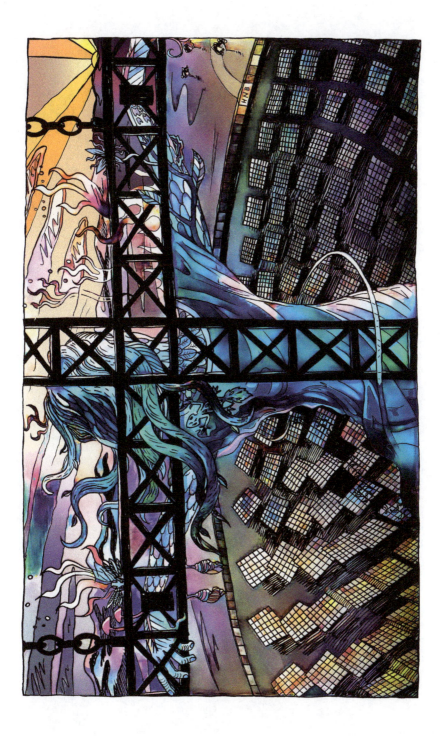

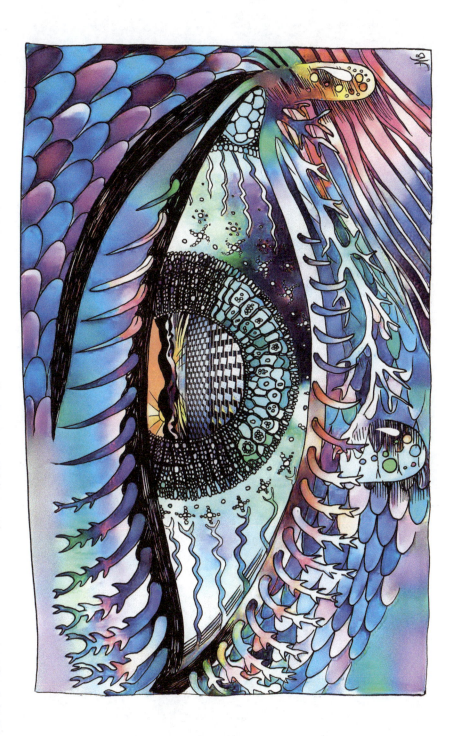

done in the past and I was good at it. Restaurants, gift shops, hotels, that sort of thing."

"Like Gordon Lizzard?" I asked.

"I'd heard of him of course," said Mr Elbadawi. "'Society, life itself, as taking immediate shape from the market.' Made overtures when he learnt where I lived. To tell the truth, life changed for me when Hélené came over on one of my open days. I was sitting at the desk as people came in. She walked past and then came back and stood before me. We'd had arguments before of course, about my development. She looked at me. I said 'can I help you?' And she said 'give me your hands.' 'What?' 'Just give me your hands.' So I did, and she massaged them. I said 'look, I can't go on doing this, people are coming in, what will they think?'"

"Well, I can imagine," I said.

"But she said 'don't worry about it.' And walked around me, moving her hands about my head, neck and shoulders and the air above them. Then she came back to the front and said 'now get up' and I said 'now, listen.' 'Just get up.' I did and this back pain I had had for so long was gone. 'I did that to get your confidence,' she said. 'Now what is wrong? As I walked past you I could sense it.' 'Well I'm going into hospital,' I told her. 'Why?' 'To have surgery.' 'Ah' she said but I wasn't going to tell a stranger the whole truth."

"Of course not," I added.

"It was testicular cancer, metastatic."

"I'm sorry," I said.

"But then she came back and said 'you must not have surgery, you must not. Come and visit me each day and we'll meditate and eat vegetables and I will make you well. I have the power of healing. I don't use it all the time. But when I must I am prepared to.' Well, I was sceptical. I guess when you are so close to something like this you long for an alternative."

"So you didn't follow her advice?" I asked.

"No, I did not. But later, as they were wheeling me away to surgery I heard this deep, soothing voice from years before and I put out my hand saying 'is that you?' And in the theatre waiting area I was thinking how they would chop up my masculinity and put it in a plastic bucket and take it off to be disposed of. And they said there would be a delay. And then this anaesthetist with the soothing voice appeared, just when I had thought 'I'm not going to be able to take this;' and I went into theatre very relaxed and I had a great surgeon. What they removed from my testicle was a little monster — skin, hair and teeth. I demanded afterwards to be taken off the morphine, allowed to go to the gym. I got well. Can you relate to this?"

"You wouldn't believe me if I told you," I replied.

"When I came back here, I went to morning contemplation and there sitting in front of me was Helené. She turned and said 'I can see you've suffered and I feel sorry for you. I really think I could have cured you.' And soon after that I was told I only had three months to live. Recurrence. So I went to Helené and gave myself totally to her system. She put me on a special diet and a year later here I am cured — though there are tests next week. You are the only other person who knows about it. She's kept the whole thing secret."

"She certainly has," I said.

"But, after meeting you and your son and thinking more about it, I decided to take a risk. I chose to apply altruistic principles and make the money chase me rather than the other way round. From that moment, everything fell into place. People, even nature, collaborated. I can't tell you how happy this whole thing's made me. Now there's something else I must tell you."

"You worked for Gordon Lizzard."

"Yes, I helped arrange the EMP attack on the GSPP Centre. It was the world's last nuclear-armed missile. He got me to disarm all the others, after his son died. I was supposed to spy on you for the OTA, but after the cricket game I told him I couldn't. Gordon paid a lot for it, I invested those funds here; it seemed appropriate. Gordon is not as bad as you might imagine."

"And the silane explosion?"

"That was the WTC. Your brother's an evil man. He used the WTC technology to manipulate how people think."

"My wife?"

"Yes, Heléné told me. He was controlling her mind. He murdered Hugues Revel the former WTC head, who was as like your brother as a lotus flower is to excrement. He ordered that the lives of many good people be cut short probably including Nancy Godel; upon any chance that would create conditions favourable to his staying in power. Anyway I want to say I've ensured that your allegations against him are being properly investigated by the right people. Bernadette Goldbough has helped me. In fact, Bernadette was an inspiration. I contacted her as soon as I'd made my decision to do this a different way. She gave financial and other support and refused to be acknowledged."

"Thank you."

"You're welcome. And that is not the least I can do for the man who saved Zula Calabiyau and all of us. There's not many men who can go to bed at night knowing they've help save the Earth. And you've also inspired me to give up alcohol. Well, you've passed through my gallery, but now you'll see that which you most desire."

∞

"Your Caroline, as she lived peerless, her dead likeness excelling whatever yet you looked upon. I have kept this exhibit lonely and apart, for it far surpasses what hand or brain of man ever has yet done with AR art."

And there before me appeared Caroline in all her dimensions, nothing aged as but conformable with mine own; as she stood in majesty when I first wooed her, before the evils conjured by my brother and my drunken negligence in opening unto her the past, had overthrown her from the seat of reason. I reached out my hand and her image stretched likewise to me. I fell to my knees.

"Forgive me," I pleaded.

"This is one addition that I cannot claim my own," said Mr Elbadawi "and I should say so before I leave you in privacy. It was Zula who commissioned it when They visited and told me how They would die. Zula's own mastery of all that was and is established with this virtual presence a portal to she you loved when you loved her best."

Mr Elbadawi left me alone with Caroline.

"Jean, it's me you silly bastard," said Caroline. "To me this is some colourful dream of the future, but open your heart as I do now and we'll know it's ridgy didge."

Caroline just began to speak of growing up in Gondwana. The sound of her voice brought great peace to my soul. She was telling me things about her early life that I'd wanted to, but had never heard before. It was a form of crystal-clear Mindscan in which the words formed beautiful images in my soul.

"Dad taught me to ride when I was eight. Just put me on a mongrel horse, told me to never let go of the reins and whipped its rump. The saddle was loose. I was dragged along over fallen logs, but I never let go of those reins. I had two brothers, Dan and Fred. This fortune teller at the local fete said we wouldn't get into spiritual life because Dan's fingers were too short. But after Fred accidentally put Dan's pinky in the paper grinder, things changed. We used to go down to the Pastures Protection Board where the Proclaimers would stand dressed up on Sunday morning trying to convert people to the OTA, though no-one had been converted in living memory. Dad said it was bad luck, three dropouts in the one family."

"I had two favourite sheep as a girl, Norman who was so big you could see him way off in the paddock and Butchie. Both of them would come when I called. I used to herd them round bends so they couldn't see in front. When I first went into the shearing shed and saw the fleeces of Norman and Butchie on the ground I cried thinking how much it must have hurt to have had them cut off."

"My favourite 'eye' dog was Toby, a red kelpie I'd found wandering as a pup on the railway line. I chained him near the end of the drafting race in the sale yards so he could watch and learn his trade. Toby loved Norman and Butchie and wouldn't leave them alone at night when they were penned. Toby hated foxes and used to go out on what Dad called 'peaceful penetrations' at night after them. That was an ancient military term for stealth night raids on opposing trenches. When I came out to paint a shed or strain a fence, if Toby was off his chain he'd try and sneak up on me, trying to make himself small, taking cover behind tussocks or keeping still when I turned. Once I asked Toby to 'get back.' But instead Toby pounced on a sheep and held it down. 'Bloody dog,' I yelled. When I walked up I saw that ewe had a rabbit trap on one of its feet."

"One day, in mid-summer just after the GSPP Celebration day, I was sitting with Hurricane Harry drinking tea on the verandah. Hurry was a hard worker, do a mile of fence, cut the strainers, dig post holes and all, in a day. Made chook houses outa bark, scars on his chest, man of high degree. We were looking at the heat rising off the paddocks like radiation. A warm wind began to come down the valley sounding like surf amongst the silky oaks, like a shock wave from a distant blast. Just one wisp of cloud sat over a hill. There was the sound of paper rusting, the muffled crawking of crows and the warbling of magpies."

"Hurry tells me the wind is *wurnjuk* and it reminds him of how as a kid he used to wander over the Koolimolka, Emu and Maralinga nuclear bomb test sites. I asked Hurry if thought Earth would sacrifice itself to humanity. He sat staring at the wind with that thousand mile stare."

"At that moment Dad walked past, closing the flyscreen door to go for a ride. The crinkly dead yellow grass was baking in the sun or trembling in the shade. The sheep were gathered under the few gums in the paddock. Dad and his horse were going down to the crossing. Toby was kicking up an awful racket, but he often did that when dad didn't take him some where. Suddenly Hurry said 'quick, let the dog off the leash.' I did and Toby raced after dad. A couple of minutes later, from the other side of the rise we heard a huge thump. We raced over. The horse was at the crossing to the bridge, cut in four pieces. An ambo. who'd been at the races was in the first car on the other side of the bridge. He pulled the horse off Dad. Toby was beneath him, dead. Dad woke up and it took the three of us to hold him down. The ambo., he'd seen it all."

"'The only thing that saved you father was that dog,' said the ambo. 'The dog came running, barked and leapt up. Your Dad turned in the saddle and took his foot out of the stirrup and bent over the opposite side of the horse just at impact. Dad died the next day from an unrelated heart attack. The shock of it made me afraid, distrustful of memory.'"

"Jean, my Dad reckoned that whatever you did, whether you got drunk or not, if an accident was going to happen, there was nothing you could do about it. But I never agreed with that; neither did Toby. I don't think that nuclear war or the extinction of the human race is inevitable. You must know that ever since I joined his organisation your brother had been pouring his foul distilment into my mind through the nano-AR link. He'd ordered me to kill you. The only way I could think to stop that was to take my own life, or make them take it from me. Whatever people may report I said about you, remember me as I was before I joined the WTC. And know that I have and always will love you."

∞

I found myself outside, staring at the trees. Helené came over with Spicer, calling for the chooks, her 'girls.' She had a bag of snails and half a watermelon for them. I could sense she knew exactly what we'd been talking about. She went up to Mr Elbadawi and gave him a back rub.

"That sound," she said "is when they're saying 'give me more.' They were lethargic in the afternoon. Must have been the smell of the wisteria near the bamboo. Early bloom."

The scent of imminent rain suffused the air. Mushrooms were growing like tiny, white parasols under oaks. Though mostly obscured by cloud, the light of sunset periodically shone upon Spicer's blond, wind-lifted hair. Her cheeks were flushed and the hems of her white dress, blown taut against her legs, bore traces of mud.

"Anouk curled my hair easily again today," said Helené. "More disquiet I suppose you'd say filling out my curls."

We sat on a stone bench beneath an oak tree. Helené reached into a small bag and withdrew, from under some dried flowers, a reefer of marijuana plus a tinder box, flint and steel. With practised dexterity she broke and lit the end, placed the cannabis joint between her lips, puffed, then offered it to Mr Elbadawi, to Spicer, then myself. She was doing it for him, so he wouldn't be self-conscious.

"You really do seem to love trees," Helené said to Mr Elbadawi.

"Not as much as Jean."

"And I want to thank you for what you did for Walter. When he was at school."

"I'm sorry?" asked Elbadawi. "Did what?"

"That bastard Eldon Slade," said Helené. "Walter's English teacher, the one studying to be a priest. Hoping Lizzard would re-establish religion, which the bloody galoot went and did, or was made to do, once he became President. Walter found out Slade had been abusing the most vulnerable kid in the class, little CW Leonis, as they do. Got good proof, VHD, he'd been trafficking children for sex. Even snuck around to our place once at night. You scared him off, remember? Walter and Merlin hatched a plan and you agreed to help. Oh don't look like that, I know all about it. Wearing masks and black clothes, the three of you picked up Slade, took him deep into forest, gagged and tied him to a tree; Walter told me you asked permission of Trudperter Hohelied. Removing Slade's trousers, you fixed a rubber ring on an elastrator then slipped it tight over the base of his scrotum. Ten hours later, you dropped him off at the Emergency Department, in much better condition to fulfil his vows."

"Walter helped plan this?" I asked.

"Absolutely," said Helené. "And I'm proud of his courage. Aren't you?"

"I'm not sure," I said. "It may not make him happy."

For some time, we sat silently, smoking. A humming sound, like a swarm of bees, or a forest of cicadas, gradually filled the air. Helené pointed out the shed skin of a black snake coiled around a stone. We saw a flash of lightning amidst a dark bottomed, anvil-shaped, western cloud. Minutes later, a rumble of thunder echoed above.

# X

# WARRANE, NEAR KUNANYI MOUNTAIN

*Funeral of Gordon Lizzard in Lutruwita — meeting Anwara, daughter of Nancy Godel — an exchange of gifts — how should future generations perceive the establishment of global synthetic photosynthesis?*

Not too many others attended the last rites of Gordon Lizzard former President of the *Whole Earth Council*, Mayor of Southwark, corporate recusant, drug dealer, sex trafficker, father of the famous musician Spencer Lizzard. His successful corruption case against Zula Calabiyau was widely regarded as the main reason for Zula's death. For Gordon Lizzard, the case was a public relations disaster of monumental proportions; perhaps rivalled only by the suit Big Pharma brought in the Corporatocene against South African President Nelson Mandela when he tried to crack patents to deliver cheap, generic anti-AIDS drugs to his people. Lizzard, ironically bankrupted by the legal fees attendant on his action against Zula, lost his last election to the tree *Yggdrasil*, whose legal guardians collectively became the first arboreal Mayor of Southwark as a direct result of the ruling in the case Gordon had initiated.

Some in the church were probably curious to know why a person so ignominious had decided to return to Lutruwita to die. Others perhaps wished to learn more about the mysterious shooting accident that killed him and whether the lurid stories about his private life had some basis in fact. The clergyman read the standard funeral oration from the *Book of Common Faith*. He admitted he'd never met Gordon, forgot his middle name and spent most of the eulogy praising the far-off town Gordon conceived himself as having worked for tirelessly and for so long. I was surprised he didn't thank Gordon for re-establishing religion.

I knew why Gordon had asked for a religious funeral and found it quaintly touching. 'A bit like a birthday party for a pet dog' I heard one member of the congregation whisper. At the end, I closed my eyes to avoid the gaze of any mourner filing out — probably an unnecessary precaution given their scarcity. It's over, I thought, soon he'll be forgotten; as will everyone. That, despite all we do and wish, is what's required.

The organ fell silent. I looked about the empty church. In the space above me, little stars of dust were moving slowly through beams of light passing through the stain glass windows. The dark, cool, space seemed to magnify the comfort from the filtered solar rays. Sparrows were flitting and chirping high up in the ceiling. I thought how delicious it was to be able to sense and interact with such things. The world had been relieved of a great burden and seemed to be having difficulty accepting the fact.

As I stepped out through the entrance, I saw a young woman with a stabilised genetic age of about twenty-five years of age standing alone in the shade of a spreading oak. She was wearing a hijab, holding a book and spectacles. Something about her looked familiar. Why was she unaccompanied and for whom was she waiting? The moment seemed curiously fragile, like a chord that a single note might either dissolve or resolve. I walked over to her.

"Hello," she said, wiping tears from her eyes.

"You're Nancy Godel's daughter, aren't you?" The facial resemblance was remarkable, but there was also a familiar aura.

"That's me," she replied, laughing. "Mrs Anwara Noether. And you must be the famous Jean Moulin, WTC whistleblower extraordinaire. The man who carried the corrupt WTC out in the dust can of history."

"Well, I had some help, ma'am or mx," I bowed stiffly. "I never met your mother, but had considerable respect for her."

"Never, Mr Moulin?" she asked. "Oh and I answer proudly to either."

"Nancy knew about me?" I inquired.

"She'd read about you," said Anwara. "She admired your work. You have one of her diaries, I think. And her mother's."

"I do — much cherished items. I can give them to you. Anwara, might we talk for a moment?"

"If you wish." She ran her hand lightly over a polished wooden bench then flicked the dew off her fingers. The droplets sparkled with sunshine as they curved through space onto the grass.

"Your grandmother, I mean Zula, used to do that."

"I know. Maybe that was another thing they didn't like about them."

We sat in silence. Anwara stared defiantly at a couple walking past. It was obvious they'd been whispering about her. A well-dressed woman read aloud from one of the gravestones: 'Come Lord, make ready our bride.' The fragrant scents of incipient summer flowed across from flowerbeds and bushes. Nearby, someone was chopping wood with an axe. The sound seemed to make Anwara uncomfortable. I grimaced, but for a different reason.

"Well anyway," she said. "It's one of Their classic coincidences."

"What is?"

"You may not believe me, but I dreamt of this last night."

"This?"

"Us meeting. Right here, on this bench — being gossiped about. You gave me some matches. And my mother showed you the way to the theatre."

"Hardly surprising," I replied. "Always possible we'd meet today."

The weather was mild with a light breeze and patches of sunlight issued periodically through the clouds. The sunlight fell on the newly renovated sandstone tower of the Church. I noticed how, on entering the church from the spring light of the street, the red and green of a lady's parasol appeared to collapse to gold.

"The resident Divine here," said Anwara, "wastes his time censoring frivolity from epitaphs. His sermons resemble the wampoos of some lonely rainforest pigeon. When President Lizzard restored religion he created vast opportunities for the banal and pompous, as well as the tyrannical, corrupt and lascivious."

"Well it must be difficult," I said "teaching from the *Book of Common Faiths*. Too many messiahs and gurus crowding the mountain top. We almost had a supercomputer controlled by a mad narcissist leading them."

"Mr Moulin before we go on… Would you mind looking at something, a letter?"

"Not at all. I'd be…"

"I received it last week, just a few days before he died. It's from Mr Lizzard. He was my grandfather, but I can't say he was a man I knew or liked very much. Until I read it."

Anwara removed the letter from her diary and handed it to me. I unfolded and read the much-crumpled paper.

*Hobart, Tasmania*

*Dear Anwara*

*I've recently discovered you intend to sail here to Kunanyi in Lutruwita, as the ecocrats of the Sustainocene now call this place. It will no doubt surprise to you to receive this letter from one whom you have been informed seemed hardly to have your best interests or those of your mother in mind. My son Spencer, your father, never told me of your existence before he died near the Franklin River trying to protect Zula. But I made certain deductions and for a time had access to ample resources to find things out. I often visit that place, it's one of the reasons I live here. He had not spoken to me in years before he called one Light Harvesting festival day and said he intended to write a tragedy. I don't blame him. I've had hours here to read the books of wisdom. I wish I'd used them so before.*

*I've made many hard decisions in my career and regret few of them. In your case, however, there are some matters I wish to put in order. Whether it will do me any good or ease my soul (if I've ever had such a thing) I have no idea. You have probably suspected that either I, myself, or those with whom I was associated were involved in the death of your mother Nancy in Hampstead Heath on the day of GSPP celebration all those years ago. Indeed, I've long understood from various acquaintances that you openly accused me of organising her murder, as did my son. I can see how you generated that hypothesis and came to that conclusion. But it's not true. They'd told me it would just scare her; Jean Moulin was meant to be there only as the patsy for the hit on Zula. His supposed assault on Nancy would have been a reason to arrest him. Eugene also was tricked into taking blame. That blackmailer WTC Director Joseph Moulin told me Nancy had learnt some things from Spencer and was digging around. She needed a warning. When I found out they meant to kill her I rushed over and tried to stop it. I knew Spencer loved her. I was too late, but I did manage to help Jean get something important.*

*I've since realised, however, that Nancy's death was something more, something almost incomprehensible for a man such as myself. I'm not just referring to the fact that people who I thought were friends could do such a thing. I mean Nancy's acceptance of it. I arrived too late to stop Nancy's death, but I did find what they were looking for; and hid it where a literary man like Jean might look. The good he did with it made me worthwhile.*

*I used to resent people choosing 'consumer' and 'CEO' as vilest insults and despised the Whole Earth Council and its Ecocide Truth and Reconciliation Court as temporarily necessary public relations exercises. But I had misunderstood the significance of that detestable religion neoliberal economics subsuming all others in the Corporatocene. How did humanity so descend in aspiration, so enslave to mammon its original contracted ideals? We permitted free market ideology, unpredictably Fama fair and Shiller foul, to enslave us to the false dogma that individual self interest rather than altruism was mathematically our destiny. Its august, apotropaic symbols of privatisation, tax-avoidance, transfer-pricing, golden parachutes and bail-outs, derivatives and bundled debt, as well as worship of perpetual growth in things produced, warded off compassion, provided, deciphered and demeaned our dreams, while*

> *making reverence for all life a despised negative externality. And by what dire implanted flaw, having escaped the sweltering heat of our Earth made corporate hell through economic orthodoxy, would we wish there to return?*
>
> *Could the possibility of competition ever make one a good father? Joseph Moulin might think so, but he had no children to contest with. When my son pulled strings to arrange for me to be tested with a brief experience of unitive consciousness, my nature had become so perverted to the preferential value of price, product and profit as to find its delicate peace and connectedness repugnant. Not now; that memory particularly looms from the evening shadows to shame and cut at me.*
>
> *Since I met your mother all those years ago, I've admired and realised a bit more about her than you might imagine. I suspect that's probably not as much of a surprise to you as many in this town would like to think. In fact, I hope that one day you may realise how I assisted perhaps the most cherished of your mother's plans.*
>
> *Yours Most Sincerely*
>
> *Gordon Lizzard. Former Mayor of Southwark, London and sometime President of the Whole Earth Council.*

"Well?" Anwara asked.

"Don't know," I replied. "Never much believed anything Gordon Lizzard said. Always tearing his own face, angry he wasn't a man for his lifetime and couldn't fulfil the end of his being; making a great noise when he made a little honey."

"Ah well, there you are. Sometimes bees spend their stings on their own kind."

"Sometimes." I handed back the letter.

"Always on about how the rats of nature were ruining business," she said.

"Rats?"

"You know; that's how he pronounced it. Rights. I mean, look at how colonists from England came and chopped down so many trees here. It was so sad: such an ignorant, unnecessary thing to do. Yet mother would have said they were unknowingly conspiring for the *Sustainocene* where there's laws, enforceable rats of nature, utterly unthought of then, against it."

"Anwara, how long will you be staying in Kunanyi?"

"A few weeks. Till my husband organises a helium aerostat dirigible to London. We want to see the sights."

"Then I hope, if it's convenient in the circumstances, you'll visit us — my wife and I. Our home's easy to find, up on Warrane. There's some things I'd like to discuss with you."

"Very well, I will. Or rather maybe we will."

"Here's my card. Anwara, your mother, was a very wise and courageous person. She wasn't afraid of anyone."

"I know." Anwara placed the card on top of Lizzard's letter in her diary.

As I watched her walk away, it dawned on me. Gordon Lizzard had brought the legal action against Zula knowing Zula would be able to present evidence about 'Back to Eden' and corruption in the WTC. Zula had no fear of being found guilty, but wanted the court to approve corporate marriage to ecosystems and make adverse findings against the WTC. He'd sacrificed himself to destroy the plans of his corporate friends. They'd killed him; just as they'd killed Nancy to warn Gordon not to indulge his conscience and killed in revenge Chief Justice Murchadh as well as Zula. The fatal flaw in my brother's plan was that he never realised how much Gordon loved his son. When drugged-up Nancy shouted 'the rats must die' to her murderer she was giving me a discreet clue to Lizzard's involvement.

> *Peace and joy follow,*
> *Love and wisdom grow,*
> *Like a perfumed shadow,*
> *In a bright tomorrow.*
> *From being kind,*
> *To all we find.*

That night I dreamt Walter and I sat high up on a hill and meditated. We slowly opened our eyes, and were amidst brown ferns and purple branched trees. A light green walking track wound ahead, moist from fresh fallen rain. That path led straight to a train and that to Stratford on Avon. Silver streams rushed past black tree shapes. A light rain slanted from the grey sky. I had a box of matches in my pocket I'd picked up in the train beside empty whisky bottles. Walter gave them to a small girl who needed them to start a fire at a junior pony meet. Some merchants had erected an obelisk because they could see no other way to get to eternity. Passing trucks nearly pushed us over with their wind. It seemed to me that all over the world there were no magical spots that of necessity spawned poets. A woman looking after kids at a caravan on stilts, asked us for the time, then for a few bob. Walter asked her the way to the theatre. She told us to go left, but consulting our map, we went right and came upon it in time to purchase the last two seats in the balcony. The play was *Tragic History of the Sustainocene*. We were in the time for the opening scene. 'You were right,' said Walter, as the curtain rose. 'It didn't make me happy. But it gave me courage.'

∞

Next day at ten in the morning, I answered a knock on our front door. It was Anwara. She was carrying a small package in one hand.

"So you've found us," I said. "I'd begun to worry. Yesterday seemed—"

"I'd worried I might be late," she said.

"Who cares?" I said. "You're here now."

I led Anwara down the main corridor to the sitting room. Some chairs rested in a wedge of sunlight before a large bay window. The one she picked, I observed, was my favourite cherrywood reading seat. Outside, the garden was in spring bloom, its apple and cherry trees, curling vines, flowerbeds and leafy laurels fresh in the sunshine after the heavy rain of the night before. Anwara looked, I noted, mostly at a large oak that had toppled overnight in a storm and was being chopped up for furniture makers by our gardener.

My wife entered.

"Spice dear, meet Mrs Anwara Noether. Anwara, this is my wife Spicer Layamon. Anwara is the daughter of Nancy Godel."

"Of course," said Spicer, kissing Anwara on each cheek. "Look at you. I'm so glad to meet you. Anwara, I was very sorry to hear about your mother's death. Old Gordon Lizzard, well, there are some people whose parting only makes you want to cheer and dance. He was one of them. I worked for him once. People here never understood what Nancy Godel and Zula Calabiyau tried to do for them, in my opinion. If there's anything we can do for you Anwara, just let me know."

"Thank you," said Anwara.

"Now I expect you two have a lot to talk about," Spicer continued. "You know Anwara, my husband's been trying to write about your mother and grandmother and their ideas for a long time now. He's gathered all the documents and spoken to almost everyone who knew them. Just couldn't get going, stuck somehow. Well, I don't know what you said to him yesterday, but he rushed in afterwards saying he'd been given permission. Of course, getting on with it was exactly what I told him to do years ago. Anyway, so off we went in the car on such a hot day to check some records. He's not well and everything's a bit of a rush for him now. Of course, the car broke down."

"But a young woman stopped to give us water," I said. "And a young man to give us a lift. 'Not good for old folks like yourselves to be out in the sun,' he said. Such generosity of spirit."

"I'll get some tea and cakes," said Spicer. "Please make yourself comfortable."

"And I'll clasp my wife by the waist," I said "and make amends for woes I've loosed in haste."

Spicer walked out to the kitchen. Anwara stood and began to poke about in the bookcase.

"Spicer reads a lot too," I said. "Some of those were once your mother's. That one I particularly treasure — Aurelius' *Meditations*. 'For I never had a sight of my own soul, yet have a great value for it.'"

"She liked my grandmother's book *Short History of Global Synthetic Photosynthesis* better," Anwara replied. "Here. I brought you a copy. She'd wish you to have it."

She handed me the wrapped volume. My joy in holding it must have been obvious.

"I've been thinking," I said "about that letter you showed me yesterday…"

"People who've done evil," Anwara replied "often find that the consequences catch up with them *before* they die."

"And sometimes they turn to meet them."

"Let me tell you a story," she said.

"Please do," I said.

"Once I visited Tristina," said Anwara "in the mountains of Arcadia in Greece. I heard this interesting tale. The peaks of Arcadia in summer resemble the quartzite tops of these parts. Spring water is plentiful and land there more valuable than a hoard of gold. I was told that with a good field a dutiful man could keep a large family forever in olive oil, vegetables, bread, wine and cheese. Even if a father owned a daughter lacking in most perfections, he could marry her off to the most eligible bachelor, if he had a good expanse of soil for her dowry."

"Ah Arcadia, home of marital bliss," I said.

"In the mountain village of Tristina," Anwara continued "a young man fell in love with a beautiful girl renowned for her reading, wisdom and disdain for social proprieties. This maiden said she'd only ever have two allegiances, to her parents and to all this world's life. Not only was there no wish to be viewed as wife, They didn't identify with being woman, or human. The maiden saw Themself as an ecosystem despite her seemingly exquisite feminine grace and charms. The parents thought their daughter was crazy. She had no dowry lands. Undeterred, the suitor asked his father's permission to marry 'her'. He was refused, many times. The father said this 'girl' was completely unworthy and said his son would only be so married over 'her' dead body. You see the father hated the girl's mother because she'd done so many good things for the village, she'd eclipsed his own fame."

"Then cruel men are lonely," I said.

"So, the father hatched a plan," continued Anwara. "He made friends with the village simpleton. The 'girl' was known to tend 'her' garden at a certain hour each day and drink a cup of juice with ice. Well, once, at that time, the father poisoned the ice and asked the poor idiot to test his gun. The father said it wasn't loaded, but as a joke he would allow the simpleton to aim and pull the trigger at the obstinate 'girl', whom he called a 'complete and utter terrorist.' The weapon discharged, killing the unfortunate victim where 'she' lay knocked out by the ice."

"Didn't anyone suspect him?" I asked.

"Yes" said Anwara. "Oh, there were legal proceedings. The father admitted giving a gun to the fool, but he denied knowing it was loaded. The simpleton spent the rest of his life in gaol. After all, he had gunshot residue on his hands. The son never spoke to his father again."

"What happened to the father?" I asked.

"Many years later," said Anwara "he was found shot dead; here, where neck meets head."

"Found down by the Franklin river, I suppose."

"How are you going in your contemplation?" Anwara asked.

"Close, my teacher says. In and out of *Samadhi*. But there's some small blockage."

"I think I can help fix that for you," Anwara said.

"Thankyou," I said. I handed Anwara a letter in an envelope. "It's about Gordon."

Anwara put the letter in her pocket. I felt like I'd passed some test. Spicer brought in tea and cakes on a tray.

"How long have you been married?" Anwara asked. "If you don't mind me inquiring?"

"Twenty years last December," said Spicer, offering Anwara a cake. "On our honeymoon at Lord Howe Island, Jean was forever quoting poetry and philosophy — some of it your mother's. He even took me to a church, said he would go anywhere to get nearer to God. The preacher denounced Zula Calabiyau, I recall, as a 'libidinous proselytiser of pagan mysticism who'd perfected nothing except her own self interest.'"

"Spicer seemed to enjoy the fact," I added, picking up the tray, "that I'd such an ironic mind for a middle-aged man. Dear, I'm just going to show Anwara my study."

"Better watch out," said Spicer "he just makes paper planes up there."

"I folded you," I said, kissing Spicer. "And you flew far and straight."

I led Anwara upstairs to my study. Anwara walked from the door to the landing. From there she stared at the town, with the smokeless chimneys on its GSPP roofs and the Derwent rolling in bluish shoals past low hills to the ocean. I was pleased Anwara noticed how my ceiling canopy appeared to 'float' above the centre of the room and in its centre was a coffered lantern of yellow glass with signs of the zodiac and seasons.

"How does it seem to you, my little refuge?"

"Warm, very pleasant," Anwara replied. "But it must get cold of an evening."

"Just before midnight," I replied "I put on my robe and climb to this silent chamber. Here, I gently stoke that small hearth and light the taper in my oil lamp. Then try to write, to get my imagination going about Nancy and Zula, their true contribution to the *Global Synthetic Photosynthesis Project* and the *Sustainocene*."

"But you also worry, don't you," said Anwara, as she sat back in my armchair, "that being everywhere is to be nowhere? You're not well Mr Moulin?" she asked.

"Pain. You think medicine would have got rid of it by now. It's this gripping in my side. And you know that nothing you can do, no movement, no hot pack, can get rid of it except the old faithful morphine and this 'gate-blocker' thing they've stuck over the base of my spine. But at least I don't need second daily enemas anymore."

"Lung cancer? Carbonanosis?"

"Yes, eating me away. I'm a sick person compared to what I was. You think they'd have discovered a cure for it by now."

"I thought they had, and for ageing."

"Didn't seem natural, somehow. Time to move on. Something my grandfather taught me. That which ordered the opening of my first scene, now gives sign for shutting up the last. I, at last well-trained to life's art, aim to retire with grace; trusting That by whom I'm dissolved also is content."

"Sounds like something Zula would have said," she replied. "I feel comfortable in this room. Please pour your wife's tea and I'll tell you another story. I suspect that afterwards you may not need to write your tale. Before I do, let me say I've always liked you, Mr Moulin. You've been a war hero, philosopher, inventor, political provocateur, lover, dedicated enforcer of what you believed was justice *and* vigilante when you discovered it was not. You've occupied a grey space within and without law, willing to question the status quo and ignore orders if that meant upholding a moral code that assists all life to flourish. You first met Zula Calabiyau as a man beleaguered and disillusioned by many facets of modern life, lonely, haunted by the loss of your wife, seeking to numb yourself from the world through alcohol, spiritually adrift after achieving and then losing peace of mind and enlightenment."

"And here you are now, an inspirational figure who has overcome the hatred of your brother and other powerful men, as well your own violent and addictive tendencies, to play an important role in protecting the principled Sustainocene legacy. Zula survived assassination attempts and achieved poignant purpose in the court case, in large part because you'd decided to be there. You became impassioned by a renewed sense of injustice after Nancy's death. You were willing to become vulnerable, fall in love and ultimately find happiness in the spice of life (literally)."

"And now, well, your acceptance of terminal illness affirms the finiteness of mortality in a world where most people and AI machines are desperate to live for centuries. I and many people like me, are drawn to morally ambiguous people like you; caught between loyalties to different identities, people and causes. You display many admirable anti-hero personality traits Mr Moulin — irreverence, sadness, a chequered history, emotional volatility and an acerbic, black humour. Jean, you are both an every-man and a special man; of your time, before your time and out of time. It is my great privilege to have met you and your grandson."

"You know Walter?"

"We've been friends for many years. He must have had his reasons for not telling you. I'm helping Walter write his tragedy. We may even write this scene as a lyric ascent, if we can place in it another unobvious action."

"Then there we are. Happiness. The everlasting's light slips under my door at last. Tell Walter he can have my papers. And tell him I'm sorry."

"He told me to say," said Anwara "he'll always admire you." Jean allowed his eyes to rest on the trim lines of the venerable gingko biloba tree in his garden; the tree he and Spicer called 'Eugene.' I, Jean, was slipping between dual and unitive awareness; drifting in and out of life.

"Thank you," I said. "Thank you so much. I woke this morning, cleaned my teeth and washed my face and I realised I was the last of my school class mates still alive. Anyway, you must have these." I handed her Nancy's diary and also Zula's. "You grew up with foster parents in India, didn't you?"

"Thank you Mr Moulin," said Anwara. "Yes, mother left me with them just after my birth. Jevons Paradox arranged it. Best way to keep me safe. I think my foster mum, before she escaped, loved Zula's friend Kofi when he was a village boy. Now I'll give you a gift in return. All your life you've wanted to know: why aren't they here, all about, these time travellers?"

"Not anymore. Individual humans have a life span, so does our species."

"Well, we are. All about you."

"We?"

"For as long as space remains, for as long as sentient beings remain, we shall return, to dispel the miseries of the world. Kindness, self-sacrifice, altruism, courage, idealism, fidelity and compassion, these are the true colours of a rainbow in the Sustainocene. Of all the forms of life that have arisen on planets in this universe or others beyond it, few have been so superbly tragic as humanity. Spicer understood that from the time she dreamt of kissing Zula. You started to learn it from your own dream of Zula's death, when you saved a bee from drowning and followed the subtle advice of trees while being chased in Hampstead Heath. But you've probably forgotten when your journey really began. Once, when you were a child, your family stayed overnight at a farm deserted because of drought. Your brother had deliberately burnt your arm. But you got up well before dawn despite the pain and watered all the parched trees. That was when Trudperter Hohelied and all the trees of Earth became your friends for life. So much good flowed from your one small, thoughtful act that hot, dry night."

She traced an infinity symbol on the back of my hand. And as she did, her smile became that of Nancy and Zula, all rolled into one broad grin that seemed to radiate out and illuminate the whole Sustainocene and all life flourishing within it.

"It's only fair you know one last secret," said Anwara. "You said on your honeymoon you wanted to get closer to God, to unitive consciousness."

"Yes," I replied. "Unfortunately, it's something I experienced once, then lost. I'm a *fael*. Loss of the unitive life ruffles my serenity and flies my fancy. But I meditate every morning anyway, it seems the right thing to do. I get tantalising glimpses."

"Well here's something to think about," said Anwara. "Every time a saint, Guru, holyman, shaman, Sadhu, President, Supreme Court judge, Yogi, scientist Buddha, Immam, whatever you call such a one, achieves non-duality, enlightenment; God changes, has Its personality enriched by what that of the saint has been through on Earth. What you call 'God' is a universal mind, an amalgam of all the cultural and personal idiosyncrasies of those who've mastered the unitive life. And they are not destined to always be from Earth. Hence it is that 'God' now in the Sustainocene seems more understanding of our frailties, more quaintly responsive to the particularities of our prayers, more sympathetic, compassionate to the minutiae of our problems, than at the beginning of human history."

"Better at cracking jokes?" I asked. "More open to prayer about footy or cricket?"

"Next time," said Anwara "make the dog bark a little earlier before you say hello."

She touched me on the cheek. For ten minutes thereafter, everything outside seemed inside me. I was fully awake, I could reason, all my senses were intact. I knew at the level of sensory experience I was separate from the world, but at another level I was one with it. I expected this would be one more brief experience; just another taste or tease. I saw Spicer standing at the door with the same grin on her face as she'd had all those years ago in the Pond Street bookshop. I, Jean was at peace.

> *Nano-roads and cities,*
> *Make fuel from sun and sky.*
> *Gathered on a part,*
> *Bright, still heart.*

∞

Next morning, after I finished my meditation, everything my senses registered as outside, still seemed at another level inside me. The red ball of the sun was just coming over the ocean horizon. I walked to the church to leave a flower by Gordon's plaque in the cemetery. Then I strolled to a headland and watched birds plummeting down after fish. Inside me was the wet smear where the sand had been licked by the waves and inside the little runs of white bubbles amongst the receding water. Inside, the dark streaks that denoted a wave swelling up on the sea's surface, as if it were taking a breath. Inside, the little birds that transferred their twitches onto the plants on which they landed. Inside were the low trees losing their crop of stars as sunlight warmed their wet leaves, all delightfully anticipating summer.

> *Then perhaps one day,*
> *Without intending more,*
> *Your mind will withdraw,*
> *From most that you sense.*
> *Knowing just itself and present duty.*

Each wave seemed to throw foaming tentacles, then a thousand white bubbles popped and its mist vanished over the sand. It left but a watery film a few feet from the sea and a faint line of little black and white pebbles to mark its furthest incursion up the sand. Looking away from the glare, the wind made crescents of dark blue water amidst the little light green and grey waves, so they resembled a swarm of insects. I'd last stood here as a child and in doing so now felt able to transmit reassurance back to that young soul. Be idealistic, brave; your journey, whatever paths it take, will end well. Gulls in a mob followed a ship's wake. One bird was pestered away by the others and peeled low, like a discarded scrap of parchment, to perch alone on a sunlit patch of sea. I knew that somewhere beneath, in that vast ocean, a little red fish forever would swim contentedly in its underwater garden.

# POSTSCRIPT

This book draws upon the intimate knowledge of artificial photosynthesis research around the world I acquired in the years 2011–2017 under the auspices of an Australian Research Council Future Fellowship and a subsequent Discovery Grant in which many leaders in the field were my partner investigators. In this period, I coordinated three international conferences dedicated to the idea of creating a Global Artificial Photosynthesis Project (GAPP) (at Lord Howe Island in 2011 and 2016, as well as at Chicheley Hall in Buckinghamshire with the assistance of the Royal Society in 2014).

During that time, I also inspected artificial photosynthesis research labs, met and published with some of their most senior experts and gave plenary talks at meetings and conferences in places that included the US Joint Center on Artificial Photosynthesis at California Institute of Technology, UC Berkeley, Uppsala, Umea, the Korean Center on Artificial Photosynthesis, the Dalian Institute of Physics in China, Nanyang University in Singapore, Imperial College London, The Solar Fuels Institute of Northwestern University at Telluride, Barga in Tuscany (Gordon Conference on Solar Fuels),

Edinburgh University, Obergurgl Austria (Nanotechnology for Renewable Energy Conference), Monash University, Sydney University, Wollongong University and my own Australian National University.

Artificial photosynthesis is a multidisciplinary field comprising large groups of researchers in many developed nations in university-based research groups focused on, for instance, enhanced characterisation of the natural photosynthetic process, light capture, nanotechnology, semiconductors, quantum coherence in electron transport, catalysis for water-splitting into $H_2$ and $O_2$, as well as atmospheric $CO_2$ and $N_2$ reduction. On some definitions, research into artificial photosynthesis includes biological processes and even synthetic biology, as for example, bacteria genetically modified to produce high-density lipids for fuel. At its core is the quest to design a stable, inexpensive, efficient oxygen-evolving photo-anode and an equally efficient, durable and cost-effective photocathode for hydrogen evolution that integrates reduction of atmospheric nitrogen and carbon dioxide within a system with good global life cycle analysis.

My contributions to this field were only indirectly scientific (perhaps through some collaborations I assisted). Rather, they involved attempts to link an ethical vision to this research field; a vision which extended to a Global Project on Artificial Photosynthesis dedicated to universally applicable ethical principles. As my academic books, chapters and articles have argued, such a global project might have arisen as the culmination of coordination amongst the contemporary proliferation of national projects on artificial photosynthesis, by creation of a large research fund from private philanthropic, government, corporate and crowd-sourcing initiatives, from acceptance amongst the field of governance principles and structures, as well as widespread global public support for the narrative of engineering all our roads and buildings so they made clean fuel, food and fertiliser just from water, sun and air.

The terminological shift in this work from 'artificial' to 'synthetic' photosynthesis is designed to highlight the necessary linkage of ethics and science if this field is to achieve its potential. The term 'synthetic' denotes artificial simulation of a natural product, but it also refers to a process of reasoning by applying general principles; to a compounding of thoughts, words or chemicals; or, perhaps most interestingly, to the capacity of our consciousness to mesh sensory impressions with pre-existing ethical ideals or intuitions. The physicist Richard Feynman was referring to synthesis when wrote of colleagues attempting to solve accumulated paradoxes by scheming 'think of symmetry laws,' 'put the information in mathematical form,' or 'guess equations,' till finally they realise that the next scheme, the new discovery is going to be made in a completely different way. So was the philosopher Immanuel Kant when he stated that the 'moral law' was within us as the freedom to develop virtue by consistently applying principles that lead to the flourishing of all. Synthesis underpins the science-based natural law approach reflected in the proposition that global synthetic photosynthesis should be termed the 'moral culmination of nanotechnology.' Synthesis also captures the idea that ethics education must extend to focus not only on teaching universally applicable principles, but developing virtue through their consistent application in order that the mind be stilled so in contemplation it reveals its true nature.

∞

The novel includes incidents that take place on the lands of the Warlpiri people in the Tanamai and the Palawa in Lutruwita, tribes of the oldest continuous civilisation on the Earth's surface. I pay my respects to their elders past and present. These scenes are based on my own personal experiences in these regions and reading of the cited public domain references. I take responsibility and apologise to those elders for any unintentional misunderstandings I've expressed.

# ACKNOWLEDGEMENTS

The research behind this book was undertaken under ARC Discovery Grant DP140100566. I acknowledge the assistance of my excellent research associates at the ANU Law School Andrew Ray, Daniel Greiss, Eun Ju Kim Baker (Eun Ju made especially valuable contributions), Helena Popovic, Alexander Raupach and Hayley Keen. Carolyn Eddy from the ANU Medical School provided valuable comments. Thanks also to Stacey Lamberth and her team in the Finance section at ANU Law School. Prof. Fred Langman and Prof. Manning Clark of the ANU were encouraging of my early exploits in writing fiction. So were Amanda O'Connell, Bernadette McSherry, Dinny De Salis, Angela Young, Richard White and my wife Rose Faunce. Prof. Jan Anderson, Prof. Eva-Mari Aro, Prof. Christine Charles, Prof. Kylie Catchpole, Assoc. Prof. Warwick Hillier, Prof. Peidong Yang, Prof. Dan Nocera, Prof. Bill Rutherford, Prof. KB Yoon, Prof. Ann Magnuson, Prof. Gary Moore, Prof. Johannes Messinger, Prof. Nate Lewis and Prof. Wolfgang Lubitz were amongst those particularly supportive of my quest to understand artificial photosynthesis and how it could be globalised. Many others were co-authors, conference organisers or attendees. Early in my legal career Justice Lionel Murphy provided inspiration and insight into how the law could respond to the needs of justice and equality. Dr Bryan Furnass demonstrated the importance of planetary medicine, the health value of a Sustainocene ideal and periodically allowing time to unravel. My friend Mark Walmsley assisted me with the lyrics on the Sustainocene music album, some excerpts of which are reproduced here. Ven. Ajahn Thate and Ven. Alex Bruce (Tenpa) helped me understand the way of the Buddha. Special thanks and gratitude go to Merlin Fox, Jennifer Brough and Sajani at World Scientific Publishing.

# ABOUT THE AUTHOR

Tom Faunce is a Professor with a joint position in the Australian National University Law School and Medical School. Before becoming an academic he practised for many years as a barrister and solicitor and subsequently as an intensive care physician. His PhD on normative coherence in regulation of the Human Genome Project was awarded the Crawford Prize in 2001. In 2010 was awarded an Australian Research Council Future Fellowship to study the capacity of nanotechnology to resolve some of the great public health and environmental challenges of our time. This book is an outcome under an Australian Research Council Discovery grant to develop the ethical and legal framework for a Global Project on Artificial Photosynthesis. Tom Faunce lives in Canberra with his family and his main recreations are reading, supporting the Essendon Australian Rules Football club and watching his son play cricket. He is a Class A (non-alcoholic) trustee on the General Services Board of *Alcoholics Anonymous Australia*. At his university, Tom sits on the central Human Research Ethics Committee and the Council of Burgmann College. He attends Wesley Uniting Church in Forrest and utilises a Buddhist technique to meditate each morning.

# ABOUT THE ILLUSTRATOR

Harriet Birks is a video artist and illustrator. Originally from Sydney, where she had a motion graphics practice, then working as a freelance VFX artist in London and Berlin. She has recently relocated to the Blue Mountains where she lives with her small family, including a Ginkgo Biloba (whose leaves you see in this book), a banyan tree and a Kenyan bee hive.

Her pictures draw on mystical and sacred themes, inspired by science fiction, hypnotic realms and the patterns and sounds of the universe. Harriet's work has been exhibited in Sydney, including solo show's at M2 Gallery and the Powerhouse Museum's *Betaspace*; and in audio visual events at the *Sydney Opera House*, the MCA and *Carriageworks*. Internationally she has participated in a number of group shows and festivals including *American Fine Arts Co.*, NY; *The Fab Lab*, Berlin; and *Whitechapel Gallery*, London.

A lover of sacred and medicinal plants, electronic music and analogue synthesizers. She would very much like to meet Zula and can't wait for the 'Corporatocene' to end. Always interested in new exciting projects. Follow her on:

http://harrietbirks.com/<br>
http://fredtitan.tumblr.com/<br>
and on instagram @vugslug

# BIBLIOGRAPHY

Alcoholics Anonymous. *The Big Book*. General Service Board of AA. 2nd edn. Sydney 2015.
Alexievich, S. *Boys in Zinc*. Pengion, St Ives 2017.
Ananyev GM, Zaltsman L, Vasko C, Dismukes GC. The Inorganic Biochemistry of Photosynthetic Oxygen Evolution/Water Oxidation. *Biochimica et Biophysica Acta* 2001, **1503**, 52–68.
Armstrong K. *Buddha*. Phoenix, London 2000.
Attali J. *A Brief History of the Future*. Allen & Unwin, Sydney 2009.
Aurelius M. *Meditations*. (Hays G trans) Weidenfeld and Nicolson, London 2003.
Bakan, J. *The Corporation. The Pathological Pursuit of Profit and Power*. Constable. London 2005.
Ball R. The Bhopal Disaster and Peroxide Bombs; Nanoscale Aspects of Oscillatory Thermal Instability, in Faunce TA (ed.), *Nanotechnology Toward the Sustainocene*. Pan Stanford publishing, Singapore 2015, pp. 193–214.
Barbier EB. *Capitalizing on Nature. Ecosystems as Natural Assets*. Cambridge University Press, Cambridge 2011.
Basho. *The Narrow Road to the Deep North*. (Yuasa N trans) Penguin Books, Harmondsworth 1996.
Bauman Z. *Does Ethics Have a Chance in a World of Consumers?* Harvard University Press, Cambridge 2008.
Beckett C. *Dark Eden*. Corvus, London 2012.

Blakeney M. International Intellectual Property Jurisprudence after TRIPS, in Vaver D and Bently (eds.), *Intellectual Property in the New Millennium*. Cambridge 2004, p. 3.

Bollier D. *Silent Theft. The Private Plunder of Our Common Wealth*. Routledge, New York 2002.

Boulding KE. Economics as a moral science. *The American Economic Review* 1969, **59**(1), 1–12.

Bowman M and Redgwell C. *International Law and Conservation of Biological Diversity*. Kluwer Law International. The Hague 1996, pp. 39–40.

Bradley, AC. *Shakesperean Tragedy*. Macmillan, London 1937.

Bren K. Multidisciplinary Approaches to Solar Hydrogen. *Interface Focus* 2015, **5**(3), 20140091.

Brown PG and Garver G. *Right Relationship. Building a Whole Earth Economy*. Berrett-Koehler Publishers, San Francisco 2009.

Bruce A and Faunce TA. Food Production and Animal Welfare legislation in Australia: Relevance of new Technologies, in Steier G and Patel KK (eds.), *International Farm Animal, Wildlife and Food Security*. Springer, Switzerland 2017, Ch. 11.

Bruce A and Faunce TA. Nanotechnology-Based Artificial Photosynthesis: Food Security and Animal Rights in the Sustainocene, in Faunce TA (ed.), *Nanotechnology Toward the Sustainocene*. Pan Stanford publishing Singapore 2015, pp. 259–286.

Bruce A and Faunce TA. Sustainable Fuel, Food, Fertilizer and Ecosystems through a Global Artificial Photosynthetic System: Overcoming Anticompetitve Barriers, in Faunce TA (ed.), *Interface Focus* 2015, **5**(3), 20150011.

Buchan J. *The Thirty Nine Steps*. William Blackwood and Sons, Edinburgh 1915.

Carson R. *Silent Spring*. Penguin Books, Harmondsworth 1971.

Cavanagh J and Mander J (eds.), *Alternatives to Economic Globalization (A Better World is Possible)* 2nd edn. Berrett-Koehler Inc., San Francisco 2004.

Cedeno D, Krawicz A and Moore GF. Hybrid Photocathodes for Solar Fuel Production: Coupling Molecular Fuel-Production catalysts with Solid-State Light harvesting and Conversion Technologies, in Faunce TA (ed.), *Interface Focus* 2017, **5**(3), 20140085.

Chandler R. *The Big Sleep and Other Novels*. Penguin Books, London 2000.

Chaucer. *The Franklin's Tale, in* Hodgson P (ed.), Athlone Press, London 1961.

Chomsky N. *Power Systems*. Hamish Hamilton London 2013.

Christie A. *Towards Zero*. Collins Crime Club, London 1944.

Ciamician G. The Photochemistry of the Future. *Science* 1912, **36**, 385–394.

Clark M. *A Short History of Australia*. Macmillan, Melbourne 1981.

Cohen R. *Chasing the Sun. The Epic. Story of the Star That Gives Us Life*. Random House, New York 2011.

Collins K. *South-West Tasmania* Heritage Books. Hobart 1990.

Colton C. *Contestability Market Theory and its Influence on Neoliberal Economics*. MS PhD Thesis. University of Technology Sydney, Sydney 2017.

Council of Canadians, Global Exchange, & Fundacion Pachamama, *Does Nature have Rights?: Transforming Grassroots Organizing to Protect People and the Planet*. San Francisco 2010.

Cox N, Pantazis DA, Neese F and Lubitz W. Artificial Photosynthesis: Understanding Water Splitting in Nature, in Faunce TA (ed.), *Interface Focus* 2017, **5(3)**, 20150009.

Crutzen PJ. Anthropocene Man. *Nature* 2010, **467**, S10. Daly HE. and Farley J. *Ecological Economics: Principles and Applications*. 2nd edn. Island Press, Washington 2010.

Dean J. *Shooting the Franklin*. Brown Prior Anderson Hobart 2002.

*Dhammapada*. (Mascaro J trans) Penguin Books, Harmondswork 1973.

Diesendorf M. *Climate Action. A Campaign Manual for Greenhouse Solutions*. UNSW Press, Sydney 2009.

Elkin AP. *Aboriginal Men of High Degree*. Inner Traditions, Rochester 1994.

Emsley, J. *Nature's Building Blocks. An A-Z Guide to the Elements*. Oxford University Press. Oxford. 2011.

Faunce TA, Lubitz W, Rutherford AW, MacFarlane D, Moore GF, Yang P, Nocera DG, Moore TA, Gregory DH, Fukuzumi S, Yoon KB, Armstrong FA, Wasielewski, MR and Styring, S. Energy and Environment Policy Case for a Global Project on Artificial Photosynthesis. *Energy and Environmental Science* 2013, **6(3)**, 695.

Faunce TA. Will International Trade Law Promote or Inhibit Global Artificial Photosynthesis? *Asian Journal of WTO and International Health Law and Policy* 2011, 6, 313.

Faunce TA. Towards a Global Solar Fuels Project — Artificial Photosynthesis and the Transition from Anthropocene to Sustainocene. *Procedia Engineering* 2012, **49**, 348–356.

Faunce TA and Charles C. Nanotechnology, Plasma, Hydrogen from Artificial Photosynthesis and Fuel Cells: Powering the Developing World to the Sustainocene, in Faunce TA (ed.), *Nanotechnology Toward the Sustainocene*. Pan Stanford Publishing Singapore 2015, pp. 241–253.

Faunce TA, Bruce A and Donohoo A. Chapter 13, in Faunce TA (ed.), *Nanotechnology Toward the Sustainocene*. Pan Stanford Publishing, Singapore 2015.

Faunce TA, Bruce A and Donohoo AM. Toward the Sustainocene with Global Artificial Photosynthesis in Faunce TA (ed.), *Nanotechnology Toward the Sustainocene*. Pan Stanford Publishing Singapore 2015, pp. 297–311.

Faunce TA. *Nanotechnology for a Sustainable World. Global Artificial Photosynthesis as the Moral Culmination of Nanotechnology*, Edward Elgar, Cheltenham 2012.

Faunce TA. Preface, in Faunce TA (ed.), *Nanotechnology Toward the Sustainocene*. Pan Stanford Publishing, Singapore 2015, pp. xxxii.

Faunce TA, Styring S, Wasielewski MR, Brudvig GW, Rutherford AW, Messinger J, Lee AF, Hill CL, deGroot H, Fontecave M, MacFarlane DR, Hankamer B, Nocera DG, Tiede DM, Dau H, Hillier W, Wang L and Amal R, *Energy and Environmental Science* 2013, **6**, 1074.

Faunce TA. Future Perspectives on Solar Fuels, in Wydrzynski T and Hillier W (eds.), *Molecular Solar Fuels* Book Series: *Energy*. Royal Society of Chemistry, Cambridge 2012, pp. 506–528, Ch. 21.

Faunce TA. Does the World Need a Global Project on Artificial Photosynthesis? In Faunce TA (ed.), *Interface Focus* 2015, **5(3)**, 20150029.

Faunce TA. Exploring International Legal Governance of Global Solar Fuels. *Procedia Engineering* 2012, **49**, 10–14.

Faunce TA. Global Artificial Photosynthesis: Transition from Corporatocene to Sustainocene. *Photochemistry* 2017, **44**, 261–284.

Faunce TA. Global Project on Artificial Photosynthesis. 15th *International Congress of Photosynthesis* August 2010, Beijing. Conference Proceedings ISPR.

Faunce TA. Global Project on Artificial Photosynthesis. *Nanotechnology for Sustainable Energy* Conference sponsored by the European Science Foundation. July 2010, Obergurgl, Austria. Conference Proceedings ESF.

Faunce TA. Introduction: Nanotechnology Toward the Sustainocene, in Faunce TA (ed.), *Nanotechnology Toward the Sustanocene*. Pan Stanford Publishing Singapore 2015, pp 1–18.

Fetzer JH (ed) *Murder in Dealey Plaza*. Catfeet Press Chicago 2000.

Feynman RP. *Six Easy Pieces*. Penguin Books, Camberwell 1995.

Furnass Bryan. *From Anthropocene to Sustainocene*. Public Lecture. Australian National University, 21 March 2012.

Gao Q, Joyce HJ and Tan HH, Jagadish C. Growth and Characterisation of GaAs Nanowires, in Faunce TA (ed.), *Nanotechnology Toward the Sustainocene*. Pan Stanford Publishing, Singapore 2015, pp. 81–102.

Gaudron M. 'Epilogue' in *Lionel Murphy: A Radical Judge*, in Scutt J (ed.), McCulloch Publishing Melbourne 1987, pp. 258–259.

Gleick J. *Chaos. Making a New Science*. Sphere Books, London 1991.

Glover J. *Humanity. A Moral History of the Twentieth Century*. Pimlico. London. 2001.

Goodall C. *Ten Technologies to Save the Planet*. GreenProfile London 2008.

Gray J. *False Dawn. The Delusions of Global Capitalism*. Granta Publications, London 1998.

Greenblatt, S. *Will in the World. How Shakespeare Became Shakespeare*. WW Norton. London 2004.

Greene B. *The Fabric of the Cosmos*. Penguin, London 2008.

Gribben J. *In Search of the Multiverse*. Penguin Books, London 2011.

Grimes CA, Varghese OK, Ranjan S. *Light, Water, Hydrogen: The Solar Generation of Hydrogen by Water Photoelectrolysis*. Springer, New York 2008.

Grousset R. *In the Footsteps of the Buddha* Orion Press. New York 1971.

Hamilton C, *The Freedom Paradox. Towards a Post-Secular Ethics*. Allen & Unwin. Sydney 2008.

Hammarskjold D. *Markings*. Faber and Faber. London 1963.

Hanlon JM, Reardon H, Tapia-Ruiz N and Gregory DH. The Challenge of Storage in the Hydrogen Energy Cycle: Nanostructured Hydrides as a Potential Solution, in Faunce TA (ed.), *Australian Journal of Chemistry* 2012, **65(6)**, 656–671.

Hansen J. *Storms of My Grandchildren. The Truth about the Coming Climate Catastrophe and our Last Chance to Save Humanity.* Bloomsbury, London 2009.
Harcourt BE. *The Illusion of Free Markets. Punishment and the Myth of Natural Order.* Harvard University Press, Cambridge Mass 2011.
Heinberg R. *Afterburn. Society Beyond Fossil Fuels.* New Society Publishers, Gabriola Island 2015.
Herbert F. *The Dragon in the Sea.* Penguin, Harmondsworh 1963.
Hesse H. *Siddhartha.* Picador, London 1998.
Hilder TA. Global Health and Environmental Implications of Mimicking Biuological Ion Channels Using Nanotubes in Faunce TA (ed.), *Nanotechnology Toward the Sustainocene.* Pan Stanford Publishing, Singapore 2015, pp. 123–138.
Hingorani K and Hillier W. Perspectives for Photobiology in Molecular Solar Fuels, in Faunce TA (ed.), *Australian Journal of Chemistry* 2012, **65(6)**, 643–651.
Hitchins, C. *God is Not Great. How Religion Poisons Everything.* Allen & Unwin. Sydney 2008.
Hole MJ and Corr C. Fusion Power and Nanoscience Challenges for Extreme Materials, in Faunce TA (ed.), *Nanotechnology Toward the Sustainocene.* Pan Stanford Publishing, Singapore 2015, pp. 215–240.
Hopkins R. *The Transition Handbook. From Oil Dependence to Local Resilience.* Chelsea Green Publishing. White River Junction 2008.
Hughes JL and Krausz E. The Chemical Problem of Energy Change: Multi-Electron Processes, in Faunce TA (ed.), *Australian Journal of Chemistry* 2012, **65(6)**, 591–596.
Jackson T. *Prosperity Without Growth. Economics for a Finite Planet.* Earthscan London 2011.
Johnson S. *Doctor Johnson's Prayers*, in Trueblood E (ed.), SCM Press Ltd., London 1947.
Johnson S. *Rasselas. Prince of Abissinia*, in Hardy JP (ed.), Oxford university Press, Oxford 1968.
Johnston J, Gismondi M and Goodman J. (ed.), *Nature's Revenge. Reclaiming Sustainability in an Age of Corporate Globalisation.* Broadview Press, Toronto 2006.
Kaku M. *Hyperspace A Scientific Odyssey Through the $10^{th}$ Dimension.* Oxford University Press. Oxford 1999.
Kanan MW and Nocera DG. In Situ Formation of an Oxygen-Evolving Catalyst in Neutral Water Containing Phosphate and $Co^{2+}$ *Science* 2008, **321**, 1072–1075.
Kant I. *Groundwork of the Metaphysic of Morals.* (HJ Paton trans) Hutchinson, London 1981.
Kant I. *Practical Philosophy.* (Gregor MJ trans) Cambridge University Press, Cambridge 1999.
Kaul I, 'Financing Global Public Goods' in von Weisacker EU, Young OR, Finger M (eds.), *Limits to Privatisation,* Earthscan 2006, p. 311.
Kim D, Sakimoto KK, Hong D and Yang P. Artificial Photosynthesis for Sustainable Fuel and Chemical Production. *Angewandte Chemie International. Edition* 2015, **54**, 2–10.
Kolbert E. *Field Notes From a Catastrophe. A Frontline Report on Climate Change.* Bloomsbury, London 2008.

La Canna X. *After 70 Years, Aboriginal Sacred Site Kurlpurlunu Found in Central Australia.* ABC News 4 June 2015. http://www.abc.net.au/news/2015-06-04/after-70-years-aboriginal-sacred-site-rediscovered/6521680 (accessed 22 March 2018).

Lee AF. Active Site Elucidation in Heterogeneous Catalysis via In Situ X-Ray Spectroscopies, in Faunce TA (ed.), *Australian Journal of Chemistry* 2012, **65(6)**, 615–623.

Lee H. *To Kill a Mockingbird.* Grand Central Publishing. New York. 1982.

Lewis NS and Nocera DG. Powering the Planet: Chemical Challenges in Solar Energy Utilization 2006, **103**, 15729–15735.

Ley C. *Cloudland.* Edward Stanford, London 1894.

Lineweaver CH and O'Brien MT. The Cosmic Context of the Millennium Development Goals: Maximum Entropy and Sustainability, in Faunce TA (ed.), *Nanotechnology Toward the Sustainocene.* Pan Stanford Publishing, Singapore 2015, pp. 27–48.

Liu C, Gallagher JJ, Sakimoto KK, Nichols EM, Chang CJ, Chang MCY, Yang P. Nanowire–Bacteria Hybrids for Unassisted Solar Carbon Dioxide Fixation to Value-Added Chemicals. *Nano Lett.* 2015, 15, 3634–3639.

Lodge D. *The Art of Fiction. Illustrated from Classic and Modern Texts.* Vintage Books. London 1992.

Lowry L. *The Giver.* Houghton Mifflin, Boston 1993.

MacKay DJC. *Sustainable Energy — Without the Hot Air.* UIT, Cambridge 2009, p. 204.

Magnuson A and Styring S. Molecular Chemistry for Solar Fuels: From Natural to Artificial Photosynthesis, in Faunce TA (ed.), *Australian Journal of Chemistry* 2012, **65(6)**, 564–572.

Maine HS. *Ancient Law: Its Connection with the Early History of Society, and its Relation to Modern Ideas.* John Murray, London 1874.

Massin J, Bräutigam M, Kaeffer N, Queyriaux N, Field MJ, Schacher FH, Popp J, Chavarot-Kerlidou M, Dietzek B and Artero V. Dye-sensitized PS-$b$-P2VP-templated Nickel Oxide Films for Photoelectrochemical Applications in Faunce TA (ed.), *Interface Focus* 2017, **5(3)**, 20140083.

McMichael T. The Biosphere, Health and Sustainability. *Science* 2002, **297(5584)**, 1093.

Messinger J. An Institutional Approach to Solar Fuels Research, in Faunce TA (ed.), *Australian Journal of Chemistry* 2012, **65(6)**, 573–576.

Michalsky R, Pfromm PH and Steinfield A. Rational Design of Metal Nitride Materials for Solar-Driven Ammonia Synthesis, in Faunce TA (ed.), *Interface Focus* 2015, **5(3)**, 20140084.

Mitchell M. *Complexity. A Guided Tour.* Oxford University Press, Oxford 2009.

Mokkapati S, Beck FJ, Wilson J, Wang E-C and Catchpole KR. Nanophotonics for Light Trapping, in Faunce TA (ed.), *Nanotechnology Toward the Sustainocene.* Pan Stanford Publishing Singapore 2015, pp. 49–80.

Monbiot G. *Heat. How to Stop the Planet Burning.* Allen Lane, Camberwell 2006.

Moynahan B. *William Tyndale: If God Spare My Life.* Abacus, London, 2002.

Musser G. *Spooky Action at a Distance.* Scientific American, New York 2016.

Nocera DG. The Artificial Leaf. *Accounts of Chemical Research* 2012, **45(5)**, 767–776.

Nocera DG. On the Future of Global Energy. *Daedalus* 2006, **135(4)**, 112–115.

Nocera DG. Fast Food Energy. *Energy Environment Science* 2010, 3, 993–995.

Nocera DG. Chemistry of Personalized Solar Energy *Inorganic Chemistry* 2009, **48**, 10001–10007.

Nolan M, Iwaszuk A, Tada H. Molecular Metal Oxide Cluster-Surface Modified Titanium (iv) Dioxide Photocatalysts, in Faunce TA (ed.), *Australian Journal of Chemistry* 2012, **65(6)**, 624–632.

Olivecrona K. *Law as Fact* Stevens and Sons, London 1971.

Oreskes N and Conway EM. *Merchants of Doubt* Bloomsbury, New York 2010.

Ovid. *Metamorphoses*. Penguin Books, Harmondsworth 1983.

Pachauri RK and Reisinger A (eds.), Report of the Intergovernmental Panel on Climate Change. Geneva, Switzerland 2007.

Page EA. *Climate Change, Justice and Future Generations*. Edward Elgar, Cheltenham 2006.

Pinter H. 'The Caretaker' in *The Plays of the Sixties*. Methuen, London 1985.

Pittock AB. *Climate Change. The Science, Impacts and Solutions*. 2nd edn. CSIRO Publishing, Collingwood 2009, p. 177.

Plucknett TFT. *A Concise History of the Common Law*. 5th edn. Butterworth and C.o, London 1956.

Purchase RL and de Groot HJM. Biosolar Cells; Global Artificial Photosynthesis Needs Responsive Matrices with Quantum Coherent Kinetic Control for High Yield, in Faunce TA (ed.), *Interface Focus* 2017, **5(3)**, 20150014.

Quiller-Couch, A. *Shakespeare's Workmanship*. Cambridge University Press, Cambridge 1931.

Rockström J, Steffen, W, Noone K, Persson Å, et al. A Safe Operating Space for Humanity *Nature* 2009, **461**, 472.

Rode AV, Shvedov VG, Hnatovsky C and Krolikowski W. Laser Trapping of Nanoparticle Agglomerates in Air, in Faunce TA (ed.), *Nanotechnology Toward the Sustainocene*. Pan Stanford Singapore 2015, pp. 159–192.

Sachs J. *Commonwealth. Economics for a Crowded Planet*. Allen Lane, Camberwell 2009.

Sakimoto KK, Kornienko N and Yang P. Cyborgian Material Design for Solar Fuel Production: The Emerging Photosynthetic Biohybrid Systems. *Accounts of Chemical Research* 2017, **50**, 476–481.

Saul JR. *The Unconscious Civilisation*. Anansi, Toronto 1991.

Schell J. *The Fate of the Earth*. Pan Books, London 1982.

Schlau-Cohen GS and Fleming GR. Structure, Dynamics and Function in the Major Light-Harvesting Complex of Photosystem II, in Faunce TA (ed.), *Australian Journal of Chemistry* 2012, **65(6)**, 583–590.

Schlau-Cohen GS. Principles of Light Harvesting from Single Photosynthetic Complexes in, Faunce TA (ed.), *Interface Focus* 2017, **5(3)**, 20140088.

Scholes GD, Fleming GR, Chen LX, Aspuru-Guzik A, Buchleitner AA, Coker DF, Engel GS, van Grondelle R, Ishizaki A, Jonas DM, Lundeen JS, McCusker JK, Mukamel S, Ogilvie JP, Olaya-Castro A, Ratner MA, Spano FC, Whaley KB and Zhu X. Using Coherence to Enhance Function in Chemical and Biophysical Systems *Nature* 2017, **543**, 647–656.

Schumacher EF. *Small is Beautiful.* Harper Collins, London 2010.

Shakespeare W. *A Midsummer Night's Dream.* Rackham A (illus.) William Heinemann, London 1908.

Shalav A and Elliman RG. The Synthesis, Structure, and Properties of Titania-Coated Silica Nanowires, in Faunce TA (ed.), *Nanotechnology Toward the Sustainocene.* Pan Stanford Publishing Singapore 2015, pp. 103–122.

Siegbahn, P. E. M. An Energetic Comparison of Different Models for the Oxygen Evolving Complex of Photosystem II *Journal of the American Chemical Society* 2009, **131**, 18238–18239.

Sovacool BK and Gross A. The Social Acceptance of Artificial Photosynthesis: Towards a Conceptual Framework, in Faunce TA (ed.), *Interface Focus* 2017, **5(3)**, 20140089.

Spencer B and Gillen FJ. *Native Tribes of Central Australia.* Anthropological Publications. Oosterhout. 1969.

Stapledon O. *Last and First Men. A Story of the Near and Far Future.* Methuen and Co, London 1934.

Steffen W, Crutzen PJ and McNeill JR. The Anthropocene: Are Humans now Overwhelming the Great Forces of Nature? *AMBIO: Journal of the Human Environment* 2007, 614.

Stern N. *The Economics of Climate Change: The Stern Review.* Cabinet Office HM — Treasury. Cambridge University Press, Cambridge 2007.

Stone J. *The Province and Function of Law.* Maitland Publications, Sydney 1950.

Suzuki. D. *The Sacred Balance. Rediscovering Our Place in Nature.* Allen & Unwn, Vancouver 1997.

Sweigers GF, Macfarlane DR, Officer DL, Ballantyne A, Bosovic D, Chen J, Dismukes GC, Gardner GP, Hocking RK, Smith PF, Spiccia L, Wagner P, Wallace GG, Winther-Jensen B and Winther-Jense O. Towards Hydrogen Energy: Progress on Catalysts for Water Splitting, in Faunce TA (ed.), *Australian Journal of Chemistry* 2012, **65(6)**, 577–582.

Thate, Venerable Ajahn. *The Autobiography of a Forest Monk.* Wat Hin Mark Peng, Sri Chiang Mai 1997.

Tusa A and Tusa J. *The Nuremberg Trial.* BBC Books. London 1983.

Ueno K, Oshikiri T, Shi X, Zhong Y and Misawa H. Plasmon-induced Artificial Photosynthesis, in Faunce TA (ed.), *Interface Focus* 2017, **5(3)**, 20140082.

Ul Haq M, Kaul I and Grunberg I. *The Tobin Tax. Coping with Financial Volatility.* Oxford University Press, Oxford 1996.

Umena Y, Kawakami K, Shen J-R, Kamiya N. Crystal structure of oxygen-evolving photosystem II at a resolution of 1.9 Å. *Nature* 2011, **473**, 55–60.
UNESCO *Declaration on the Responsibilities of the Present Generations Towards Future Generations.* November 12, 1997. Available at: http://portal.unesco.org/en/ev.php-URL_ID=13178&URL_DO=DO_TOPIC&URL_SECTION=201.html. Accessed May 8 (Gondwana Day) 2017.
UNESCO. World Heritage Convention. Available at: http://whc.unesco.org/en/conventiontext/ (accessed April 2016).
UNGA. Universal Declaration on the Human Genome & Human Rights. 1998 UN Doc. A/RES/53/152.
United Nations *Convention on the Law of the Sea* art. 1, para. 1, Dec. 10, 1982, 1833 U.N.T.S. 397.
United Nations Department of Economic and Social Affairs, *World Urbanisation Prospects — The 2014 Revision.* Available at: http://esa.un.org/unpd/wup/Highlights/WUP2014-Highlights.pdf (accessed April 2016).
United Nations *Sustainable Development Goals* Goal 7 Energy. Available at: http://www.un.org/sustainabledevelopment/energy/. Accessed May 8 (Gondwana Day) 2017.
United Nations. *Agreement Governing Activities of States on the Moon and Other Celestial Bodies* art. 1, Dec. 17, 1979, 18 I.L.M. 1434.
United Nations. *International Covenant on Economic, Social and Cultural Rights.* Adopted and opened for signature, ratification and accession by General Assembly Resolution 2200A (XXI).
United Nations. *Legal Status of the Atmosphere.* Para 1. UN Res 43/53 6 Dec. 1988.
United Nations. *Treaty on Principles Governing the Activities of States in the Exploration and Use of Outer Space, Including the Moon and Other Celestial Bodies*, art 1. Jan. 27, 1967, 18 U.S.T. 2410, 610 U.N.T.S. 205.
*Upanishads.* (Mascaro J trans) Penguin Books, Harmondsworth 1987.
US Department of Energy: Hydrogen Posture Plan. Available at: http://www.hydrogen.energy.gov/. Accessed May 8 (Gondwana Day) 2017.
Van Ghent, D. *The English Novel. Form and Function.* Harper Torchbooks, New York 1961.
Verne J. *The Mysterious Island.* Airmont Publishing, New York 1965.
Vines T, Bruce A and Faunce TA. Planetary Medicine and the *Waitangi Tribunal Whanganui River Report*: Global Health Law Embracing Ecosystems as Patients. *Journal of Law and Medicine* 2013, **20**, 528–541.
Walmsley M and Faunce T. *Sustainocene. Beautiful World From Global Artificial Photosynthesis.* Music CD Sydney 2016.
Wells HG. *The Time Machine.* William Heinemann, London 1895.
Weston BH and Bollier D. *Green Governance. Ecological Survival, Human Rights and the Law of the Commons.* Cambridge University Press. Cambridge 2013.

White P. 'Australian s in a Nuclear War' Speech at Australian National University. May 1983. Primavera Press, Leichardt 1989.

Wilczek F. *The Lightness of Being. Mass, Ether and the Unification of Forces.* Basic Books, New York 2008.

Windeyer WJV. *Lectures on Legal History.* 2nd edn. Law Book Company, Sydney 1957.

Woodroffe J. *The Garland of Letters.* 6th edn. Ganesh & Co. Madra 1974.

Yau S-T and Nadis S. *The Shape of Inner Space.* Basic Books New York 2010.

*Yoga Sutras of Patanjali.* (Shearer A trans) Bell Tower, New York 1982.

CPSIA information can be obtained
at www.ICGtesting.com
Printed in the USA
LVHW050121221218
600796LV00001B/2/P